Brokering a Race War

Brokering a Race War

Japanese Americans in the Pacific War and the Occupation of Japan

EIICHIRO AZUMA

OXFORD
UNIVERSITY PRESS

OXFORD
UNIVERSITY PRESS

Oxford University Press is a department of the University of Oxford. It furthers the University's objective of excellence in research, scholarship, and education by publishing worldwide. Oxford is a registered trade mark of Oxford University Press in the UK and in certain other countries.

Published in the United States of America by Oxford University Press
198 Madison Avenue, New York, NY 10016, United States of America.

Library of Congress Cataloging-in-Publication Data
Names: Azuma, Eiichiro author
Title: Brokering a race war : Japanese Americans in the Pacific War and the occupation of Japan / Eiichiro Azuma.
Description: New York, NY : Oxford University Press, [2026] | Includes bibliographical references.
Identifiers: LCCN 2025049523 (print) | LCCN 2025049524 (ebook) |
ISBN 9780197781401 paperback | ISBN 9780197781395 hardback | ISBN 9780197781425 epub
Subjects: LCSH: World War, 1939–1945—Participation, Japanese American | Japanese American soldiers—Japan—History—20th century | Japanese Americans—Social conditions | Japan—History—Allied occupation, 1945–1952 | United States—Foreign relations—Japan | Japan—Foreign relations—United States
Classification: LCC D769.8.A6 A98 2026 (print) | LCC D769.8.A6 (ebook) |
DDC 940.53089/956073—dc23/eng/20260211
LC record available at https://lccn.loc.gov/2025049523
LC ebook record available at https://lccn.loc.gov/2025049524

DOI: 10.1093/9780197781432.001.0001

Printed by Integrated Books International, United States of America

MIX
Paper
FSC FSC® C183721

The manufacturer's authorized representative in the EU for product safety is Oxford University Press España S.A. of Parque Empresarial San Fernando de Henares, Avenida de Castilla, 2 – 28830 Madrid (www.oup.es/en or product.safety@oup.com). OUP España S.A. also acts as importer into Spain of products made by the manufacturer.

Parts of the Introduction, Chapter 1, and Chapter 4 were published as "Toward a Transnational History of Wartime Japanese Americans: Nisei and Imperial Japan's Race Propaganda" (2023) and "The Lure of Military Imperialism: Race, Martial Citizenship, and Minority American Transnationalism during the Cold War" (2017) in the Journal of American Ethnic History (University of Illinois Press), and as "Brokering Race, Culture and Citizenship: Japanese Americans in Occupied Japan and Postwar National Inclusion" (2009) in the Journal of American-East Asian Relations (Brill).

Preface and Acknowledgments

I started research for this book shortly after I completed my first monograph, *Between Two Empires: Race, History, and Transnationalism in Japanese America* (Oxford University Press, 2005). Chronologically and thematically, *Brokering a Race War* can be considered a sequel to *Between Two Empires*, which focused on the experience of first-generation Japanese immigrants stuck between the two Pacific empires: their original homeland and their adopted land. With a focus on their Nisei children in the Pacific War and the subsequent military occupation of the defeated ancestral land, this book examines the continuities and ruptures between the prewar immigrant era and the wartime and postwar years of Japanese America in a transimperial military context.

Whereas my first book narrated the contentious yet inseparable connections between prewar Japanese America and imperial Japan, *Brokering a Race War* looks specifically at varied manifestations of negotiations, conflicts, and collusions between Nisei soldiers and defeated Japanese nationals in the semi-colonial context of military occupation, and between Nisei soldiers and their white American commanders. Having caught up in the entanglements of US and Japanese imperialisms and their racisms, the diverse groups of Nisei navigated the shifting ground of US wartime nationalism in order to claim a full-fledged American identity and colorblind national citizenship that shored it up; yet, while brokering between the white American conquerors and vanquished foreign Japanese, they also had to grapple with Japanese racism and nationalism, which still sought to claim them on basis of blood ties. Thus, in many ways, *Brokering a Race War* is a logical extension of *Between Two Empires*, and it is fitting to see the book now being published by the same publisher, Oxford University Press, and under the aegis of the same acquisition editor, Susan Ferber.

In the span of almost twenty years, myriad people have assisted me in a variety of ways. The support of knowledgeable staffs at archives and libraries is indispensable. I was a frequent visitor to and received much help from archivists at: the National Archives and Record Administration in College Park, Maryland and Washington, DC; the United States Army Heritage and

Education Center in Carlisle, Pennsylvania; the Hoover Institution Library & Archives at Stanford; the Charles E. Young Research Library Special Collections at the University of California Los Angeles; the Bancroft Library at the University of California, Berkeley; the Archives and Manuscripts Department, Hamilton Library at the University of Hawai'i at Manoa; the University of Pennsylvania Libraries; the Special Collections at the University of Washington; the Japanese Studies Collection, C. V. Starr East Asian Library at Columbia University; the John Embree Papers in the Division of Rare and Manuscript Collections at Cornell University; and the John Maki Papers in the Special Collections and University Archives at the University of Massachusetts at Amherst. In Japan, my preferred stomping ground for research included: the National Diet Library, especially its Modern Japanese History Materials Room; the Diplomatic Archives of the Ministry of Foreign Affairs; Tokyo Metropolitan Government Archives; and the National Archives of Japan. I thank all the professional archivists and librarians I met during my research for their invaluable assistance and guidance.

I presented some portions of my book research at various venues, including academic conferences, symposiums, and workshops, between 2006 and 2025. Among them, the Translation and Ethnic Studies Symposium organized by Mae Ngai at the University of Chicago in February 2006 gave me the opportunity to start thinking seriously about the concept of "cultural brokers." During invited lectures and workshops at Portland State University, Pennsylvania State University, Kyushu University (Japan), and University of Hawai'i, organizers and participants provided me with the intellectual motivation to think through many of the conceptual issues that my book ended up addressing due to their insightful comments and pointed questions. The annual conferences of the Association for Asian American Studies, American Studies Association, Association for Asian Studies, Organization of American Historians, and American Historical Association served as a forum for me to share my research findings and test my ideas in the formative period of this book project. Audiences, panelists, and discussants all contributed to it.

During my many years of international research endeavors, I have benefited from financial support from several institutions. At Penn, I was honored with the term endowed chair named after my former colleague, Alan Charles Kors, between 2009 and 2019. This provided me with steady, annual funding for my research trips. Since 2020, the Hoover Institution has hosted me as a visiting fellow and provided generous research subventions, enabling me to consult its valuable collection of personal papers relating to the inner workings of the US military government in occupied Japan. I thank Eric Wakin and Kaoru Kay Ueda for facilitating my research at the Hoover Institution Library & Archives. In 2008–9, the Donald D. Harrington Visiting Faculty Fellowship, which I received from the University of Texas at Austin, allowed me to conduct research and begin an initial writing process, one that led to a referred journal article in 2009.

Parts of the Introduction, Chapter 1, and Chapter 4 were published as "Toward a Transnational History of Wartime Japanese Americans: Nisei and Imperial Japan's Race Propaganda" (2023) and "The Lure of Military Imperialism: Race, Martial Citizenship, and Minority American Transnationalism during the Cold War" (2017) in the *Journal of American Ethnic History* (University of Illinois Press), and as "Brokering Race, Culture and Citizenship: Japanese Americans in Occupied Japan and Postwar National Inclusion" (2009) in the *Journal of American-East Asian Relations* (Brill). I thank these journals for the courtesy permissions to allow me to incorporate portions of the articles into this book. My gratitude also goes to: Asahi Shinbun, Densho: Japanese American Legacy Project, Hoover Institution Library & Archives, and Japanese American National Museum, for permissions to use photographic images for this book.

When I was engaged in research for and the writing of *Brokering a Race War*, colleagues in Asian American history and US history have inspired me by their scholarships, comments, advice, insightful conversations, and their kindness to share sources and expert knowledge with me. Though I cannot possibly name them all, I would like to mention these colleagues, friends, and mentors—some have unfortunately left us—with gratitude: Sucheng Chan, David Aiona Chang, Gordon H. Chang, Catherine Ceniza Choy, Augusto Espiritu, Sayuri Guthrie-Shimizu, Brian Masaru Hayashi, Jim Hirabayashi, Lane Hirabayashi, Evelyn Hu-DeHart, Madeline Y. Hsu, Yuji Ichioka, Loyd Inui, Michael R. Jin, David Johnson, Moon-Ho Jung, Daniel Y. Kim, Monica Kim, Richard S. Kim, Ben Kobashigawa, Paul A. Kramer, Lon Kurashige, Scott Kurashige, Erika Lee, Simeon Man, Valerie J. Matsumoto, Hiromi Monobe, Don Nakanishi, Mae Ngai, Brian Niiya, Franklin Odo, Gary Y. Okihiro, Michael Omi, Greg Robinson, Christen Sasaki, Naoko Shibusawa, Amy Sueyoshi, Yasuko I. Takezawa, K. Scott Wong, David K. Yoo, and Henry Yu. Chris Suh offered me valuable feedback on Introduction.

In Japanese, East Asian, and global history, the following scholars gave me intellectual support and shared their insights with me when I was working on this book project: David Ambaras, Matthew R. Augustine, Tokiko Bazzell, Adam Clulow, Martin Dusinberre, Takashi Fujitani, Mariko Iijima, Hiroshi Kitamura, Mire Koikari, Akira Iriye, Mike Shichi Lan, Mark Metzler, Fred Notehelfer, Kenneth Ruoff, Jordan Sand, Toru Shinoda, Miriam Silverberg, John J. Stephan, Kayoko Takeda, Yuma Totani, Jun Uchida, Samuel Yamashita, Christine R. Yano, and Lisa Yoneyama. Emily Anderson went over an entire draft of the earlier manuscript, providing me with a native check, editorial suggestions, and invaluable overall assistance.

Many colleagues and graduate students at University of Pennsylvania offered me morale and intellectual support as well as friendship to keep me going with this book project despite all sorts of difficulties along the way. They are: in History and East Asian Studies, Oscar Aguirre-Mandujano, Kathleen M. Brown, Hardeep Dhillon, Frederick R. Dickinson, Conor Donnan, Siyen Fei, Antonio Feros, Ann Farnsworth-Alvear, Adam Goodman, Steve Hahn, Robert Hegwood, Bailey Hoy, Michael Katz, Suyoung Kim, Walter Licht, Greg Loh, Sidney Xu Lu, Amy C. Offner, Anthony Pratcher II, Kathy Peiss, Roberto Saba, Barbara Savage, Camille Suarez, Thomas Sugrue, Julian Tash, Eve Troutt-Powell, Beth S. Wenger, Shang K. Yasuda, and Peter Zhaoyuan Yu. In Asian American Studies, I benefited from intellectual collegiality and political commitment of David L. Eng, Grace Kao, Fariha Khan, Bakirathi Mani, Rupa Pillai, Rosane Rocher, and Josephine Park, as well as Dana Nakano.

At Oxford University Press, my editor Susan Ferber has been supportive since when I first discussed my half-baked ideas about what would become this project back in 2005. Seventeen years later, she still showed a strong interest in my book manuscript despite the long interval of time, subsequently putting it out for external reviews. Her selection of anonymous readers was perfect, because both provided me with detailed and extremely helpful comments and suggestions that contributed to the sharpening of my arguments. I thank Susan and these anonymous readers for their invaluable inputs. Thomas Deva (Straive production manager) and Zara Cannon-Mohammed (Oxford University Press project editor) assisted me in navigating the complicated production process. Thomas's team produced beautiful illustrations, and Robert Swanson compiled a detailed index. I am grateful to Timothy Beck for making my narrative more readable with his superb copyediting skill and close attention. Thanks also to Ben Pease, who created wonderful maps for this book.

Last but not least, I would like to express my gratitude for the unfailing support of my family. This book is dedicated to them, and to my teachers, who gave me education and knowledge necessary for not only academic endeavors but also for living and working with a social conscience.

Contents

Glossary of Terms for the Subgroups of Japanese Americans

Issei First-generation immigrants without US citizenship due to their status as aliens ineligible for naturalization until 1952.

Kibei US-born second-generation citizens who were educated and acculturated in Japan before returning to the United States.

Nisei US-born second-generation citizens who were educated and acculturated in the prewar United States.

Renunciants Nisei who renounced US citizenship after failing the loyalty test in the wartime US incarceration camps.

Repatriates Issei leaders and Nisei renunciants who were deported from the United States to Japan during and after the war.

Strandees Nisei who resided in Japan during the Pacific War. Many lost US citizenship due to their work to support Japan's war efforts against their birth country.

Note on Translation and Japanese and Japanese American Names

Translations of Japanese sources are all mine unless otherwise noted.

Names of Japanese nationals and those of Japanese Americans are provided according to the following rules: for Japanese nationals, including former US immigrant residents, the family name comes first, and then the given name. Names of American-born Japanese (Nisei and Kibei) are indicated in the Anglo-American manner, with given name and family name in that order. This latter rule also applies to wartime "strandees" and postwar "renunciants" in Japan, even though most of them lost their US citizenship and hence became legally Japanese nationals.

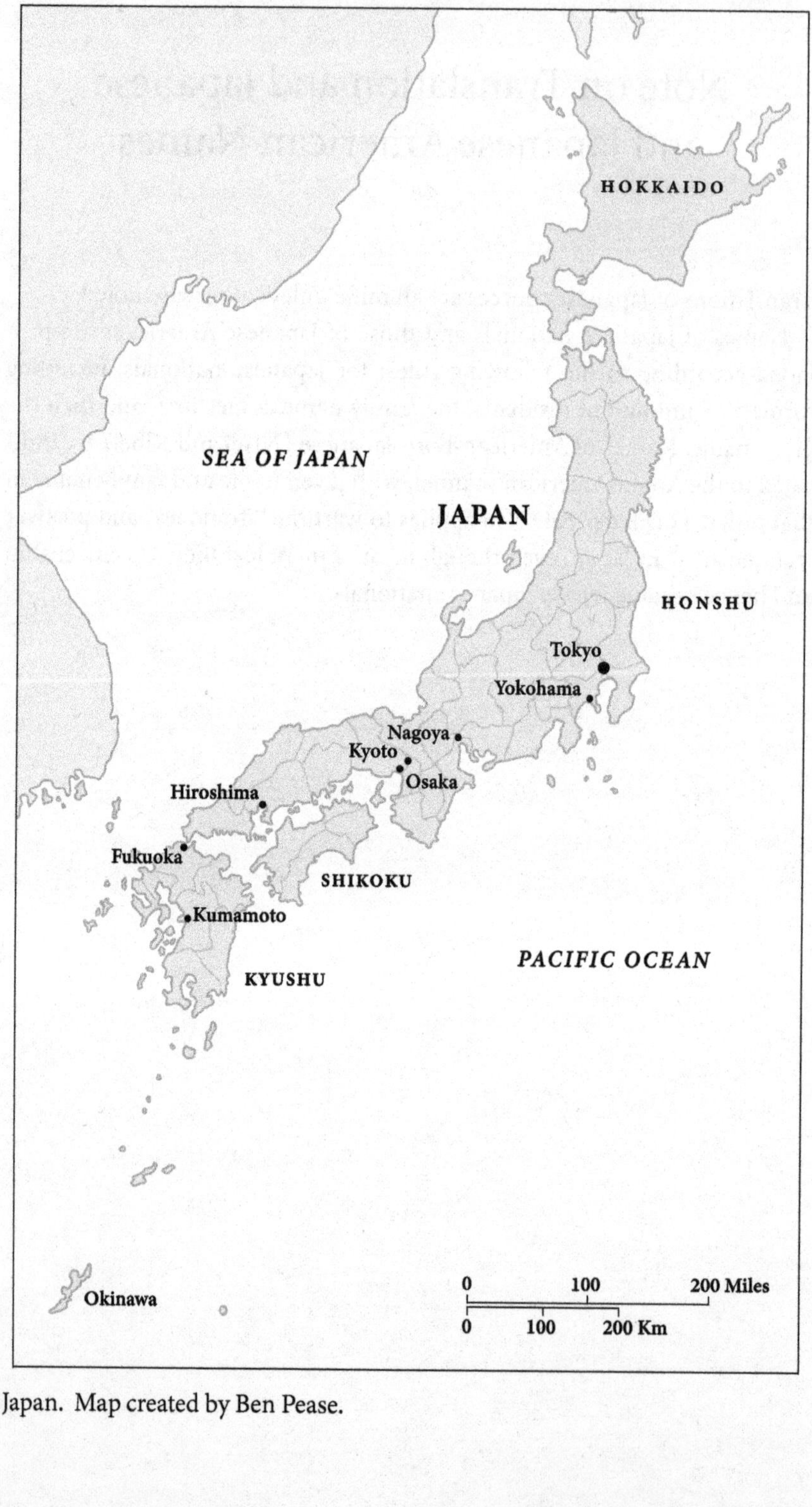

Japan. Map created by Ben Pease.

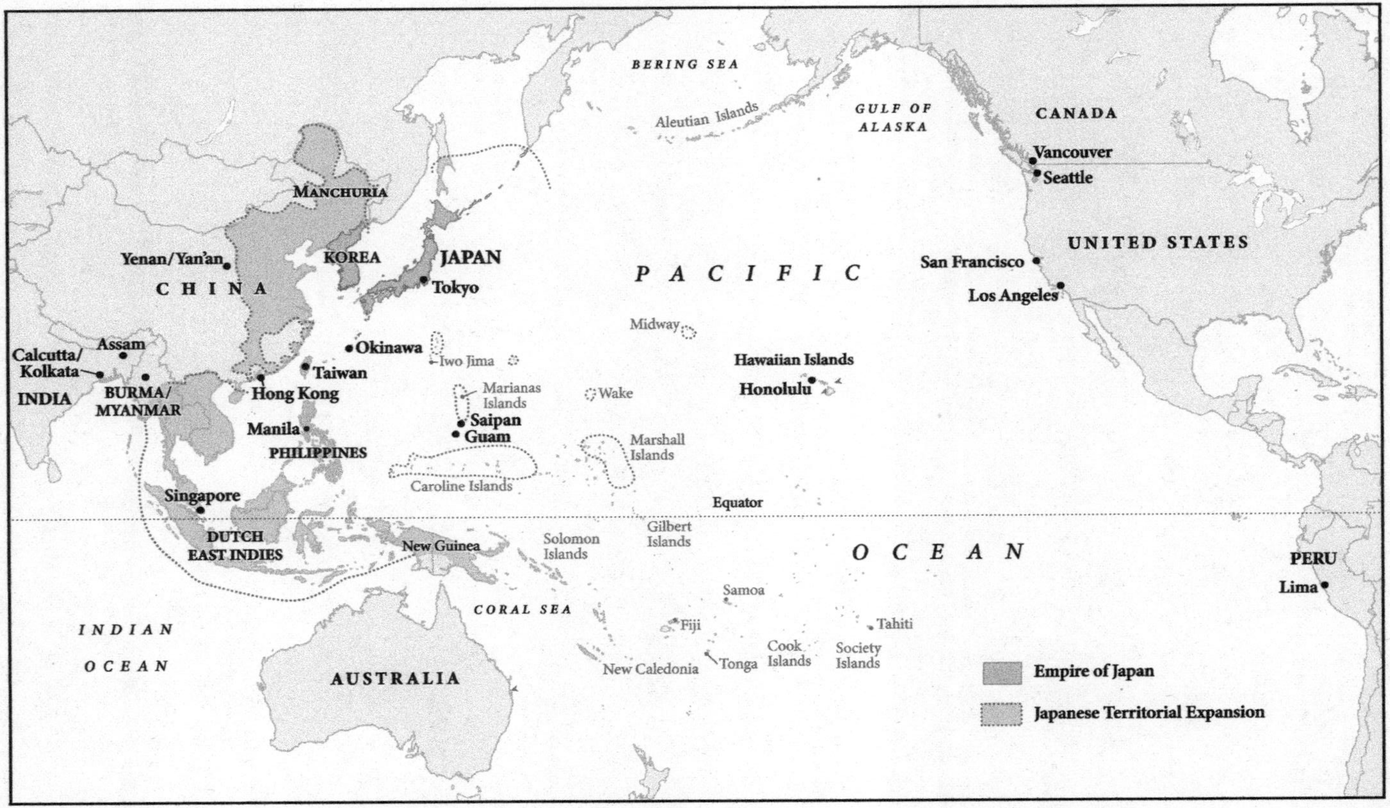

Wartime Pacific Rim. Map created by Ben Pease.

Introduction

Minority Soldiering, Imperial Citizenship, and Cultural Brokers

Submitted to President Harry Truman two months prior to the defeat of Japan and the beginning of military occupation, a high-level army report offered a recommendation about a preferred US approach to the vanquished nation with a specific reference to the fundamentally racial nature of governing the "Oriental" enemy and the utility of the second-generation Japanese Americans (Nisei) in uniform in that US endeavor. The June 1945 report contended:

> American justice and fair play toward Oriental people is reflected in the honor, loyalty and courage of American soldiers of Japanese extraction, and in the friendly attitude of Japanese civilians once they realize we are not the barbarians their militarists claim we are. The accomplishments of the Nisei and American reaction to their achievements prove that Occidentals and Orientals do cooperate to the mutual advantage of both.[1]

Predicated upon this approach, the report outlined guidelines for American psychological warfare in the final weeks of the hostilities, which mandated that propaganda leaflets and radio programs against the Japanese had to incorporate a celebratory narrative of Japanese Americans. It also spelled out that "American justice and fair play toward Oriental people" specifically meant the United States was colorblind enough to embrace the Nisei on the basis of their "accomplishments" in the war against the ideologies of the Axis Powers.

This narrative had been in effect since late 1943, several months after US domestic race propaganda had redefined Americanism as "a matter of the mind and heart, not…a matter of race or ancestry" to justify the induction of loyal Nisei men into the US armed forces from the race-based incarceration camps and Hawai'i's martial-law regime.[2] Widely publicized as the most decorated army unit of its size, the saga of the all-Japanese 442nd Regimental Combat Team (RCT) constituted a major part of that propaganda narrative and the anti-racist US nationalism that foregrounded it. That narrative illuminated not only the Nisei's undying love of their birth country and their military heroism ("accomplishments") but also white Americans' ability to embrace people of an enemy race on account of their dedication to citizenship and universal democracy ("reaction to their achievements"). Moreover, as the June 1945 guideline revealed, the wartime propaganda narrative, and the new top-down definition of Americanism that shored it up, already foretold how the victorious United States would deal with vanquished Japanese. Indeed, even before the end of the hostilities, Nisei US soldiers were expected to serve to demonstrate "American justice and fair play"—that is, the military occupation and democratization of the "Oriental" enemy under benevolent white Americans.

Despite the divorce of "race and ancestry" from the official dictum of Americanism, the parallel mentions of "Nisei" and "American" in the guideline implicitly denote the way in which this subset of US citizens was constantly singled out for certain prescribed roles and tasks that were imagined as existing between the ruptured worlds of "Occidentals" and "Orientals" during the Pacific War and subsequently under the US control of defeated Japan. This tacit form of othering placed Nisei at the interstices of "Americans" and "Japanese," thereby rendering their work of brokering something so essentially and literally embodied in them that it could not be performed by anyone else. During the war years (December 1941–August 1945) and occupation period (September 1945–April 1952), more than ten thousand Nisei soldiers and civilian workers were enlisted as Japanese-language experts in the US armed forces and their campaigns in combat theaters and occupied enemy land in the Asia-Pacific. Often known as "strandees," several thousand more Nisei lived and worked on Japan's side. Underneath these Nisei's work as militarized brokers lay the complex interplay of race, culture, and citizenship, which anticipated the distorted manner in which Japanese Americans became involved in the destruction and subjugation of the consanguineous enemy race and subsequent management of defeated foreign Japanese.[3] *Brokering a Race War* employs a transimperial perspective to situate enlisted Nisei linguists, occupation troops, and civilian workers in the militarized entanglements of the United States and Japan between December 1941 and April 1952.

Toward a Transimperial History of Japanese American Military Service

Proclaimed in early 1943 by President Franklin D. Roosevelt, the anti-racist rendition of Americanism ("a matter of the mind and heart") revealed the wartime political exigencies of government officials and white racial liberals in the US military. Yet, a purely instrumentalist analysis would obscure more fundamental changes and contradictions regarding the meaning of US citizenship, one that became less racially exclusive but still functioned to co-opt Nisei and other minority American soldiers as enforcers of the military power of the multiracial US empire against non-western foreigners. Under the post-1943 ascent of anti-racism in US national(ist) discourse, the Nisei's multifaceted experience of wartime propaganda—both as the contrived images in it and as its knowledge producers—set a crucial stage for their roles and practices as militarized cultural brokers. Such attributes continued to define their ambiguous positions relative to the shifting meanings of ancestry and legal belonging under the volatile relations between the two empires and races from military campaigns through Allied occupation.

President Roosevelt's valorization of colorblind Americanism and US citizenship was inseparable from two seemingly polarized aspects of the US national identity and its wartime history: an enforcer of racist policy that had indiscriminately locked up Nisei citizens and their parents in the incarceration camps, and a champion of universal democracy that was eager to accept domestic racial minorities, like Japanese Americans, and to uplift foreigners, even including treacherous Japanese enemy. Packaged together, these contradictory episodes reveal a theme of America's unceasing progress—exceptional democracy that purportedly has the capacity to right the wrong to become continuously better.[4]

Implemented under the policies of the same president, the saga of the mass incarceration points to America's "blood-will-tell" racism of a bygone era, and the legend of the Nisei soldiers epitomizes the subsequent rise of anti-racist nationalism that embraces even those of damned ancestry as long as they proved themselves to be loyal to the American creed of democracy, as well as its capitalist system, especially during the Cold War. Indeed, this anti-racist progressivist narrative has been reified by enchanting stories of the 442nd RCT heroes and other minority American patriots, like the Tuskegee airmen and Navaho code-talkers.[5] The same narrative was reinforced when, in 1946, President Truman commended Nisei combat troops returning from the European theater: "You fought not only the enemy [abroad] but... [race] prejudice [at home]—and you have won." Almost seventy years later, President Obama again celebrated the iconic Nisei soldiers in his re-articulation of anti-racist Americanism and colorblind democracy by declaring "what makes us American is not a question of what we look like... [but] is our fidelity to a set of ideals that all of us are created equal."[6]

There are a number of studies—many congratulatory, some more critical—that narrate the experience of the 442nd RCT Nisei in the European theater in the context of changing domestic race politics.[7] Due to the security-classified nature of their activities, Nisei US servicemen in the Asia-Pacific theater did not receive much publicity until the 1990s, since they mostly served as Japanese-language and cultural specialists for the Military Intelligence Service (MIS) and other entities of clandestine psychological warfare operations. Furthermore, many Nisei members of the MIS and other US propaganda agencies came from a subgroup of Japanese Americans called "Kibei," literally those who had returned to America (from Japan). Due to their education and acculturation in their ancestral land, they were generally vilified as so-called disloyal elements among US-born Nisei to the extent that a white naval intelligence officer insisted in 1942 that they should be deemed "guilty (of anti-Americanism) until proven innocent."[8] Kibei have been thus marginalized in narratives of Japanese American history and ethnic community affairs, making it unlikely that they receive public and scholarly recognition.[9] Compared to the 442nd RCT Nisei on the European front that served in combat, fewer works exist that address these Japanese American linguists, who were involved in the war against imperial Japan and the post-defeat military occupation of their ancestral land.[10] Even less information is available about several thousand Nisei residents across the Pacific. These so-called strandees were hired as propagandists and military linguists based on their bilingual skills by Tokyo's militarist regime before finding work as locally hired civilian translators and interpreters for the US occupation government following Japan's defeat.[11]

In a transnational context where Nisei linguists shared common racial and cultural ancestry with the Oriental enemy, the celebratory remarks made by the US presidents about the 442nd RCT war heroes look far more complex than they appear. They beg a careful analysis of the meanings of race and citizenship as well as America's seemingly one-directional progress from racism to anti-racism, not to mention the ominous presence of a military-backed colonial power structure and violence throughout the Asia-Pacific and beyond after 1945. Put another way, what do these tidy and triumphalist narratives conceal about the demands placed on these Nisei to embody the resolution to these contradictions to save the progressive narrative of American history and its global future? And how did these Nisei perceive in this narrative room to carve out their own space by taking advantage of these expectations, even at the expense of their consanguineous former enemies? It was under such overbearing constraints and contradictory forces that Nisei inmates from America's incarceration camps managed to refashion themselves as patriotic US citizen soldiers and democratizers. They took advantage of their hitherto-detested cultural traits to purportedly help America overcome domestic racism and turn the former "enemies into friends" in occupied Japan.[12]

Nothing can be more simplistic than this teleological narrative, which has become particularly noticeable in public discourse since the US conquest of Afghanistan and Iraq and its subsequent failed efforts at democratization there.[13] As these recent episodes of failure and its counter-example of success in occupied Japan underscore, the stories of US attempts to reform enemies under military occupation or through armed interventions should not be simple-mindedly understood as examples of democratization. With a focus on the role of Nisei military linguists in the Pacific War and US occupation of Japan, this book is intended to change the terms of interpretation from a narrative of democratization to that of domination and imperialization through the agency of minority soldiers, and the liberal anti-racist discourse that allow for their involvement in the rehabilitation (if not Americanization) of the non-western enemy in the first place.[14]

Brokering a Race War therefore aims to expose the intricate workings of American imperialization that relied not only on manipulating racial difference/sameness and the meaning of birthright citizenship but also on the complicity of minority US citizens. They had their own reasons to embrace and act on the official dictum of Americanism and its professed anti-racism and vailed imperialism. The idea of democratizing minority solders as a central aspect of US global imperialization requires extending the story of the Nisei's military heroism beyond the confines of domestic US race politics. Their US patriotism was as much a story of national inclusion as it was that of self-induced differentiation from alien Japanese of common ancestry—the symbol of a rival imperialism in a geopolitical context.

Looking at the war-torn Pacific and a conquered enemy land through a perspective of shifting US race relations and Janus-faced imperialism, this book rescues the analysis of the Nisei's roles and experiences from an exceptionalist national narrative of US military as a democratizing force.

With a transimperial perspective, *Brokering a Race War* unveils how the self-styled anti-racist regime of the United States operated in accord with its counterpart of imperial Japan when they both took advantage of the labors and representations of American-born Japanese in their respective war aims. In relation to the operation and demonstration of the state governing authorities and legitimacies, this work also examines the historical agency of minoritized subjects stuck between the conflicting demands of being acceptable national members in the imperial Pacific. These themes—that is, the technologies of wartime state control and subject formation, and the Nisei's attempts at navigating them in and between the two empires—form the central theoretical underpinnings of this book.[15]

The technologies of state control and subject formation stemmed from the racisms and nationalisms of the United States and imperial Japan that rendered the parameters of the Nisei's acceptable roles and positions extremely narrow and regimented in both societies at war. A transimperial perspective illuminates the mutually reinforcing relationship of bilateral wartime state control in shaping the Nisei's complex experience across the militarized Asia-Pacific. Here, historian Simeon Man's observation is particularly valuable: war situations "did not simply form the backdrop for racial minorities to assert their claims to national belonging; rather, those wars were the very ground upon which racial liberalism emerged as a dominant force in US politics."[16] The imperialist war between the United States and Japan, and the subsequent military occupation of the latter by the former, presented such ground where minoritized US-born Japanese variously engaged America's inclusive racism and Japan's pan-Asianist racism within a transpacific field in search of their national belonging, survival, and prosperity.

To elucidate how the process of US-engineered imperialization involved not only militarized Nisei but also imperial Japan and its subjects it is necessary to juxtapose these minoritized US soldiers with the actions and responses of their co-racial foreign enemies. Japanese Americans, who served in the Asia-Pacific from the early 1940s through the early 1950s, included military and civilian interpreters and translators, propaganda workers, and intelligent agents, as well as entrepreneurial businessmen and intellectuals. In Japan, resident Nisei—most lost American citizenship during the war—were also involved in similar lines of work, although their lack of legal status put them in different life circumstances than their US-based compatriots after Japan's defeat. Still, by birthright US citizenship and/or US acculturation, these young men and women of Japanese ancestry generally considered themselves to be American. By blood ties and heritage culture, however, Nisei tended to be identified—and some self-reflexively associated themselves—with their ancestral land of Japan. With their own essentialist presumptions drawing from state nationalisms and racisms of the respective empires, white America and imperial Japan not only complicated the Nisei's conflicting positions and self-awareness but also greatly exploited them. Therefore, underneath the flimsy narratives of their contributions as loyal US soldiers (or outstanding imperial subjects) lay the complex entanglements and clashing visions of Japanese Americans, white Americans, and Japanese nationals. Adopting the Nisei's experience in the contentious triangular relations as a central lens, this book uncovers the contingent meanings and relational formations of race, culture, and citizenship, as well as the interplay of various historical agents, including the US and Japanese empires.

Navigating the Shifting Terrains of Race, Culture, and Citizenship in the Militarized Pacific

Before the outbreak of World War II, Japanese Americans—unnaturalizable immigrants and native-born citizens alike—were generally excluded from mainstream America. Still, they enjoyed a degree of flexibility in putting their own spin on the definitions of race, culture, and citizenship that were fundamental to group relations and the social order of the United States (and Japan). Many prewar Nisei embraced an idealized role for themselves as "a bridge of the Pacific," one that relied on bicultural and international ideals that promised to resolve the tension they experienced between their Asian racial heritage and the US-bred sense of who they were. It was not uncommon for adult Nisei and adolescents to self-impose this lofty internationalist role by learning Japanese language and culture, migrating to Japan for education and employment, and even engaging in publicity campaigns for bilateral friendship when Japan's invasion of China caused the deterioration of US-Japan relations during the 1930s.

American racism also made the bridge concept and deep engagement with their ancestral land more attractive to many Nisei. Their understanding of Japanese language and customs enabled them to pursue career and life opportunities in their ancestral land that had not been available to them in their own birth country during the same decade.[17] These transnational Nisei immigrants, many of whom highly educated, became strandees after December 8, 1941.

Japan's attack on Pearl Harbor indeed put a decisive end to such an optimistic idea about their intermediary role, since the outbreak of war had completely burned down bilateral links. The subsequent mass incarceration of West Coast Japanese compelled every Nisei to grapple with the more regimented meanings of race, culture, and citizenship, given that both the United States and imperial Japan saw no possibilities of relations other than mutual opposition. Having been forced into the incarceration camps by their own government, Nisei US citizens had no choice but to acknowledge that the publicly accepted parameters of national identity offered little room for them to remain normal rights-bearing Americans for the time being. On the other side of the war-torn Pacific, Nisei strandees found that their ambiguous status as US-born Japanese brought them enormous difficulties in their everyday lives.

One of the main themes of this book entails Nisei's negotiations with these bounded and yet shifting categories of race, culture, and citizenship, and the actions of the two warring empires that reified these categories during the hostilities and ensuing military occupation. Even though the United States and Japan viewed one another as totally opposite and incongruent throughout this period, their racisms and nationalisms worked in a remarkably similar—sometimes complementary—way.[18] For this reason, the comparable positions of Nisei in the two racial-imperialist regimes led to similar challenges and responses, which included rejection, violence, and imprisonment, on the one hand, and a desperate pursuit of national acceptance through military service and other forms of patriotic contributions, on the other. Racially segregated from white Americans and legally separated from the people of their ancestral land, the Nisei occupied precarious positions. Public understandings of their cultural characteristics tended to stay on the side of their racial identity, hence the demonization of Kibei.

Even though both warring regimes initially shared a similar attitude by privileging the Nisei's blood ancestry as the most decisive marker of their allegiance (or the absence thereof), the United States made a blatant about-turn in early 1943, with President Roosevelt's proclamation on color-blind Americanism. That shift radically reconfigured the relations—but not the fundamental definitions—of race and citizenship, thereby paving the way to new terms of national belonging that empowered certifiably loyal Nisei. Still, despite America's reversal, various forms of loyalty tests on both sides exemplified how each war regime continued to use the prescribed categories of race and citizenship to compel Nisei to either adopt a legally constituted identity of native-born US citizen or a blood-based notion of Japanese subject—with grave consequences of ostracism, (continuous) detention, and possible deportation if they failed. These were the simultaneous transpacific processes in which the Nisei's individual choices, albeit made under enormous constraints, led to the emergence of militarized national subjects who were subsequently celebrated as national heroes. On both sides of the Pacific, they overcompensated their stigmatized identities with hyper-identification and exaggerated expressions of national allegiance, including honorable deaths as patriotic soldiers.

Contrary to race and citizenship whose definitions were cemented by the languages of science and law, culture was more in flux, and its unsettled meanings gave Nisei leeway and sometimes even an advantage to prove their Americanness or Japaneseness. As ethnic Americans, Nisei's cultural heritage always marked them as fundamentally and irrevocably separate from the Anglo-centric norms that defined belonging in the United States, and the war made it a symbol of their unavoidable bonds to the enemy. At the same time, the US armed forces needed to utilize the Nisei's command of Japanese and their knowledge of the inscrutable enemy, given the paucity of white experts on Japan in wartime America. In imperial Japan, too, the Nisei's grasp of English and American society created the basis for strong public suspicion; yet, these could also be assets for Japan's propaganda and military intelligence needs. The ambiguous meaning of culture explains the decisions of wartime United States and Japan to recruit experts of Japanese or English language out of the Nisei for the respective national armed forces and propaganda machines while categorically disowning them as a part of the enemy. By distancing themselves from negative public ideas about their background, Nisei endeavored to turn these positive renditions of them into a special kind of cultural capital that other Americans or imperial Japanese could not offer in the context of the respective national war efforts, especially the propaganda wars and enemy mind control. In the militarized Pacific, this cultural pigeonholing formed an integral part of their national inclusion, specifically the rehabilitation of their status as native-born US citizens or consanguine imperial subjects.

Through the war years and subsequent US military occupation, Japanese Americans on both sides navigated the complex entanglements of the assumptions and expectations associated with their racial, cultural, and citizenship status. What lay at the heart of all these developments was their varied and changing engagement with state militarisms and military institutions, including the apparatuses of psychological warfare and intelligence. This book attempts to unveil the contestation of state actions and Nisei's agency—the transimperial processes that encompassed stories of tacit resistance, complicity, acquiescence, and at times a brazen about-face for self-preservation at the cost of others' well-being.

Military Service as Migration and the Problems of Anti-racism and Martial Citizenship

Brokering a Race War also examines Nisei military service as a form of migration and an important aspect of their distorted transnationalism. Historians have rarely related the concept of soldiering to that of migration or transnationalism, or vice versa.[19] For most minority Americans of the 1940s and 1950s, including Nisei, military service provided the first, and perhaps only, opportunity to migrate to a place outside the United States to develop a different understanding of what it meant to be racialized American citizens. Under the 1940 Selective Training and Service Act, the US armed forces became the first major branch of the federal government that eliminated race-based exclusion of minority American citizens, although white supremacy still ran deep to maintain the systems of white officer control and racial segregation or compartmentalization within military institutions.[20] Yet, under war conditions, the shifting terrains of race and citizenship also made the consequences of the militarized migration of minority US soldiers comparable to the privileged mobility of white colonial masters. They could stay above the laws of the vanquished foreigners over whom they reigned as citizen-members of the conquering army. It is not hard to imagine how significant a ramification such a colonial experience must have had on minority soldiers' view on and struggle for equal civil rights, as many African American servicemen demonstrated in their embrace of US imperial projects.[21] During and after the Second World War, the Nisei's deployment as intelligence workers, combat soldiers, and occupation troops gave them an equally distorted transnational experience. It allowed these historical subjects to materially inhabit the two completely different environments inside and outside the military apparatuses on foreign soil and develop complex ideas about being American vis-à-vis overpowered foreigners, including the people of their ancestral land.

This new perspective on the nexus between military service and minority mobility offers an important intervention into the normative understanding of migration in US history, as well as the country's settler colonialist identity as a "nation of immigrants." Under that national myth, the United States is seldom viewed as a sender of native-born emigrants to foreign places.[22] Whether on the battlefields or in occupied lands, however, the minority military experience outside of US sovereign territories constitutes a variation of "American immigration history," where a group of native-born Americans lived the life of immigrants in a foreign place instead of foreigners immigrating to the United States.[23] But this transnational experience was extremely skewed, because it was colonial in nature. Instead of being forced to adapt to local conditions as alien newcomers, these militarized immigrants were in the position to force local people to conform to their ways, to cater to their wishes and expectations, and to endure their fitful violence and abuses, if not whimsical shows of compassion. A precondition for their enlistment, their birthright US citizenship was the source of such power for these militarized American immigrants in the Asia-Pacific.

This migration was also a form of labor mobility. Colored soldiers, including Japanese Americans, came from ethnic enclaves where they had been confined to the peripheries of the US capitalist system. Even if they had college educations, for example, prewar Nisei generally worked within the ethnic economy, replicating the preexisting occupational patterns of the immigrant generation. Most Japanese American servicemen were of working-class background and suffered from a materially deprived status as wartime camp inmates, which made their military stint even more attractive from a financial standpoint. They received steady pay in US dollars, free meals, and subsidized accommodations in a war-devastated land where everything was dirt cheap. This working-class dimension of minority soldiering is key to understanding why it had such a profound impact on the masses of Japanese Americans.[24]

Furthermore, minority military service, and the massive migration of working-class armed Americans that resulted from it, helped connect US domestic race politics of inclusion to the country's rise as an imperial hegemon that was able to dress itself in an anti-racist garb. Beneath this oxymoronic development lay the state-sanctioned concepts of colorblind citizenship and democracy as articulated by President Roosevelt. The ascent of what historians have variously called "racial liberalism," "polite racism," and "inclusionary racism" in 1940s–1950s America could not be divorced from the dramatic and contradictory historical developments surrounding Japanese Americans: their race-based mass imprisonment in 1942, the enlistment of Nisei inmates who passed the loyalty test in 1943, and the mythologizing of the salvaged citizen-soldiers to signal a national disavowal of blood-based racism and the country's progress as the world's best democracy. This process was integral to the remaking of the United States as a multiracial nation that began to stride towards the civil rights movement era as much as it was to the country's Cold War rise as the global power touting colorblind definitions of democracy and freedom backed by the destructive military forces.

As this book will reveal, minority inclusion still entailed the processes of being perceived as different and fitting in a racial hierarchy within the purportedly non-racist nation, and hence was not an antithesis of racism per se. Thus, some historians adopt the typology of "polite racism" vs. "vulgar racism," or "inclusionary racism" vs. "exclusionary racism," to illuminate the codependence of the ostensibly opposite forms of racial formation, which functioned to maintain the conditions of white supremacy with the appearance/practice of colorblind inclusive democracy.[25] The history of US imperialism in the world is crucial for understanding these complex functions of US race ideologies and relations in the domestic sphere, and vice versa. The minoritized racial groups within the inclusive US armed forces played an integral role in enhancing US geopolitical and colonial interests during and after the Pacific War when blatantly racist and predatory actions ceased to be viewed as a norm in domestic politics and international relations.

By looking at minority military service as a transnational articulation of US race politics and imperial formation, *Brokering a Race War* builds on the theoretical insights about the mutually reinforcing nature of American minority inclusion and exclusion as well as its relationship to US foreign domination. Yet, this book purposefully employs the concept of "anti-racism" to narrate such oxymoronic phenomena. Here, it does not mean the opposite of racism; instead, anti-racism refers to the representation and effect of state-backed racial liberalism as such in the context of rhetorical battles between the white-dominated regime and its minoritized subjects. Dominant iterations of anti-racism constituted a new and more insidious form of racism—similar to polite and inclusionary racism.[26] This study aims to underscore what public impression and politico-ideological effect the racist regime wished to generate under the official disavowal of racism, or its "anti-racism." At the same time, such public discourse of ostensible anti-racism empowered minority national subjects when they grappled with the articulations and consequences of actual polite racism. They could weaponize the state-certified anti-racist language for their own interest—whether to reap benefits of official racial liberalism or to reject harmful effects of polite racism in pursuit of more genuine racial equality and hence their own version of anti-racism.

Minority military service constituted a site of such complex negotiations, where the dominant renditions of racially conditioned inclusion became entangled with real anti-racist counteractions employed by minority soldiers. Equally importantly, it paved the way to the paradoxical processes by which their national inclusion and anti-racist struggle helped buoy a new phase of American imperialism that thrived on the active participation of minority US soldiers as frontline enforcers of its violent power throughout the Asia-Pacific and beyond.[27] Inevitably, as these processes enabled the US empire to obfuscate its domineering power under the façade of anti-racist benevolence and colorblind democracy, minority American servicemen were rendered complicit in US military domination of foreign others, especially non-western (colored) nations despite their struggle for equality and democracy. It is then necessary to investigate the asymmetric relations that these non-white soldiers had with foreigners—enemies and vanquished—during their overseas deployment while critically examining the skewed trajectories of their inclusion into US armed forces. These contexts are indispensable for the reassessment of the multilayered and shifting meanings of US citizenship for minority soldiers and civilian armed-forces employees, not to mention a more nuanced understanding of how Cold War US imperialism worked. The notion of soldiering as a transnational migration experience makes it possible to consider why their new sense of being full-fledged Americans became colored with colonial meanings in the context of overseas military deployment. Bluntly put, after the mid-1940s, the definition of what it meant to be an American was, for many minoritized male citizens, synonymous with participating in the American imperial project abroad.

During the Cold War, US-occupied areas became key locations for such distorted minority transnationalism. That experience led Nisei and other non-white soldiers to embrace inclusive "martial citizenship." Popularized by feminist scholars and activists, the original concept of martial citizenship illuminates the deeply gendered nature of being a national citizen whose rights are entwined with the male-centered privilege of serving in the military and demonstrating/monopolizing patriotism and national legitimacy. While some feminist scholars regard women's access to military service as a means of obtaining full citizenship, and hence political and economic equality, other scholars of martial citizenship espouse an anti-militarism/anti-military position by criticizing the armed forces as a fundamentally masculine and violent institution.[28] Both perspectives are useful. On the one hand, hundreds of Nisei women did participate in the Women's Army Corps (WAC) even while being excluded from normal combat duties. That auxiliary service enabled many female Nisei to move to occupied Japan to serve as War Department civilian linguists alongside their Nisei male MIS counterparts.[29] Although they were not equal to enlisted men in such extra-military positions, these Nisei women—equipped with the same cultural capital—still attained a degree of martial citizenship as they worked under the military occupation. On the other hand, a critical perspective calls attention to the problematic nature of inclusionary military service, which cannot be divorced from the rise of anti-racist US imperialism and its colonial power even for these and other Nisei women on the US-occupied foreign lands.

Aside from gendered citizenship rights, *Brokering a Race War* focuses on racially prescribed aspects of martial citizenship and scrutinizes the ramifications of minority integration in the US armed forces as well as their militarized overseas mobility. Within US society and military institutions, Japanese and other minority soldiers were deemed subordinate to their white counterparts even after the official end of racial discrimination in 1948. Yet, outside of the racially restrictive United States and inequitable military ranks, minority US soldiers encountered different dynamics of race and citizenship, where the latter identity took precedence over the former in defining power relations. In this militarized transnational context, inclusive colorblind citizenship often turned into "minority imperial citizenship"—the embodiment of colonial power and privilege vis-à-vis unarmed/disarmed foreigners. Skin color did not mean much in such a relationship.

In their daily interactions with local foreigners, usually vanquished enemies, minority US soldiers were compelled to reevaluate the meaning of their American nationality. They came to the battlefields and occupied areas as virtual colonial overlords in terms of their status and power despite their subordinate standing relative to white comrades and officers within military ranks. Outside the institutional confines of the armed forces, then, being Black or Asian ceased to matter insofar as they possessed birthright US citizenship and wore military gear, which allowed them to carry guns and use them against foreigners when they felt it necessary, with minimal consequences. In the Jim Crow South, Black Americans had little recourse against white violence. Yet, in US occupied areas, uniformed Black soldiers from Mississippi represented uncontested American power, and they lived above local laws because of their legal standing as US citizen soldiers.

The skewed transnational experience that military service generated led many minority Americans, including Nisei, to recognize the real value of birthright citizenship for the first time. It had previously held only limited significance because of their racially inferior status but came to symbolize privilege, domineering power, and the possibility of violence against foreign others, including those who might share identical racial heritage. Minority imperial citizenship was, and still is, a specific condition that can materialize as a result of militarized migration and subsequent encounters with non-citizens. Insofar as military service enabled racial minorities to claim access to national membership and coveted civil rights, it provided many Americans with a rare opportunity to fight against minority "rightlessness"—a mechanism that rendered them external to the bounds of its protection of legal, civil, and human rights despite inclusionary national discourse and even policies.[30] Thus, in the context of their continuous struggle for racial equality and justice, the soldiers' embrace of US citizenship and all the privileges it afforded resulted in their generally uncritical stance towards America's military actions, as well as its militarized domination of the wider world.

To fully understand the trajectory of minority imperial citizenship in Nisei's transnational military experience, it is important to look closely into the three-way entanglement that involved Japanese American soldiers as well as their white American overlords and the Japanese enemy in wartime and occupation contexts. In this entanglement, Nisei soldiers pursued national acceptance by enacting imperial citizenship against foreign Japanese in the battleground and occupied Japan. White Americans took advantage of Nisei's imperial citizenship by brandishing a new language of inclusive polite racism to maintain the structures of racial and military domination. Foreign Japanese countered their enemy's anti-racist racism and Nisei's imperial US citizenship by turning to their racist ideas and imperialistic beliefs. Between 1941 and 1952, the Asia-Pacific theater was a paramount site of these hitherto neglected historical developments and multilateral contestation.

Practicing Minority Imperial Citizenship in Occupied Japan

The relational formation of race and citizenship in the experience of minority US soldiers was most striking in the wartime Pacific and occupied Japan, where the foreigners were also colored and deemed undemocratic and anti-American.[31] With a focus on Nisei soldiers and civilian personnel, *Brokering a Race War* looks closely at the complex, asymmetric, and yet contingent relationships that they developed with the vanquished from the perspective of their performance—conscious or unconscious—of Americanness, which often entailed imperialistic practices and characters. Their relationships defy a simple characterization of race-based sympathy or citizenship-based hostility toward the foreign enemy. The articulation of minority imperial citizenship coexisted with the rise of postwar anti-racism that officially rendered US nationality free from race-based discrimination and hence could uphold special sensitivity to the oppressed. By calling it performance, this book is deliberately highlighting the agency of Nisei (and other) minority soldiers vis-à-vis structural constraints and forces in the overall process of becoming colored colonial masters under a banner of colorblind American democracy. Minoritized soldiers were often compelled to harmonize their conduct with acceptable norms of behavior as national citizens prescribed by the white-controlled power structure. That performance was always an integral part of their everyday practice in occupied Japan.

Titled *An American Dream*, the memoir of Clarence Adams, an African American soldier, succinctly captures the performance of minority American behavior in the semi-colonial conditions of US military occupation. When he was in occupied Japan in 1949, Adams was assigned to guard duty on the docks in Kobe with another Black soldier nicknamed "Aggie."

Adams describes what his partner one day decided to do to a Japanese passerby on the spur of the moment.

> We were on Pier One when along comes this old Japanese man.... Aggie decided he wanted to beat him up, so he walked over and hit him in the stomach. The old man doubled over, and Aggie looked back at me and said, "See how hard I can hit."[32]

Adams continues:

> I yelled at him, "What in the hell are you doing?" He mumbled something about "slant-eyed Japanese," and he hit him again. I told him, "Hey stop that! Would you want somebody to do you like that?" I was thinking of what happened so often to blacks back home. "That's the way we've been treated."[33]

Aggie gets upset at Adams's intervention, and later tells other Black soldiers, "Hey, Adams stuck up for a Jap."

It is tempting for the liberal-minded to glamorize Adams's expression of interracial empathy as a case of transnational Afro-Asian solidarity by assuming that it represented what most minority soldiers must have thought and done when dealing with the oppressed and powerless. Yet, the flipside of liberal fascination with Adams's kind of anti-racist/anti-colonialist transnationalism is a tendency to downplay, if not neglect, Aggie's embrace of uncontested power as a triumphant American citizen against a vanquished Japanese national. This accounted for what minority imperial citizenship embodied and what it offered to these soldiers in occupied overseas areas. As crucial as it is to analyze instances of interracial alliances in practice or thinking, this book argues that it is important to try to make sense of why Aggie acted in the way he did for a fuller understanding of how minority imperial citizenship worked in a complementary fashion with its seeming opposite of colorblind inclusionary citizenship. Together, Aggie and Adams provide an intriguing glimpse into the duality of Cold War US racial liberalism and the troublesome role that minority Americans sometimes played in reifying US military imperialism overseas.

The entanglements of the dialectical expressions of postwar US citizenship started with a statement by President Roosevelt in early 1943 that formalized a top-down process of minority national integration through military service. The process, which showcased the enlistment of much-despised Japanese Americans from the incarceration camps, paved the way for a government-sanctioned narrative of Nisei's patriotism. Framed in the language of compensation for their exemplary allegiance to colorblind democracy, this official disavowal of blood racism, and the inclusive national discourse that stemmed from it, also hailed military service and martial citizenship as expressions of the minority soldiers' self-consciousness as full-fledged Americans. While this contrived narrative urged racist white America to acknowledge Nisei's cultivated Americanness and accept them back from race-based national exile, the militarized consciousness of Japanese Americans in turn buoyed their quest for equality and fuller integration. The embrace and practice of citizenship's imperial power by them would be a logical product of that newly constituted ethnic consciousness as minority Americans in a transwar context and after.

It was not surprising, then, that many Nisei in occupied Japan frequently felt it necessary to play a role as executors of US military oppression, like Aggie, in their attempt to safeguard their hard-earned national membership as patriotic American citizens. Yet, contrary to African American and other minority soldiers who could have also "stuck up for a Jap" without serious repercussion, Japanese American occupation troops found themselves compelled to engage in a constant act of differentiation due to their shared racial and cultural ancestry with the "slant-eyed Japanese." As many local Japanese bitterly recalled after the end of occupation censorship, stories of Nisei's abuses of Japanese nationals were not hard to find in US military and local vernacular sources. Those examples can be read as ironic consequences of their embracing a de-racialized national identity—a calculated and visible performance of national allegiance according to their American "mind and heart" rather than their "race or ancestry," as the President put it. Indeed, while Aggie decided to indulge in the power of militarized US citizenship on the spur of the moment by punching a random Japanese passerby in Kobe, a Nisei military linguist bragged about having routinely "kick[ed]" around Japanese workers when he was on duty supervising them in the same city. Calling his victims "dumb and lazy," this Japanese American private showed no remorse to his white interrogators, and he proudly maintained that it was necessary not to "spare the rod" as a victorious American.[34] For most Nisei occupiers, a public display of intra-racial solidarity with their consanguineous foes would look utterly antithetical to the idea of colorblind Americanism, for Japanese nationals were by definition undemocratic and anti-American in the occupation context.

During the Pacific War and after, Japanese Americans needed to grapple with the contradictions of race and citizenship more than any other group of minority Americans—especially when they were saddled with the role of supervising and disciplining the vanquished enemy of their own ancestry in occupied Japan. The last thing these Nisei linguists would want to be associated with was the idea that they "stuck up for a Jap," as Aggie criticized Adams of doing due to a simple display of sympathy. What was at stake was whether they were seen as loyal to their blood relations or to their citizenship—the very question that the United States had foisted on them after Japan's attack on Pearl Harbor. As US military linguists and civilian occupation workers, young Nisei men and women, ten thousand strong, made their choices in defining the terms of their relationships to local Japanese depending on what their white bosses and colleagues might feel. This is the basic mechanism by which the self-styled democracy of the US military empire managed to dominate the postcolonial "colored" world through the active participation of minority Americans without getting white hands dirty. The self-reflexive acts of non-white US soldiers, like Nisei occupation troops, are key to the control of foreign others in the Cold War Asia-Pacific and beyond.[35] This explains the inner workings of minority imperial citizenship that allowed them to claim a piece of an American identity.

Between the clashing forces of the two warring empires, the Nisei's equivocal cultural identities solidified their imperial citizenship. Compared to the bounded categories of race and citizenship, the idea of culture relative to Japanese Americans offered more room for ambiguities, and hence negotiations, by Nisei occupation troops and civilian linguists. Indeed, the very role assigned to them derived from such ambiguities: white Americans expected Japanese Americans to act as cultural brokers between what were deemed completely different systems of languages, traditions, and mentalities.[36] Seen from a purely theoretical standpoint, the concept of cultural broker is deeply flawed, because it assumes essentialist distinctions and incompatibilities between cultural traditions, practices, and ways of thinking in Japan and the United States. But insofar as white Americans (and Japanese nationals) believed firmly in the Orientalist proposition that "East is East, and West is West, and never the twain shall meet," the category of cultural broker looked real and indispensable in the contexts of war propaganda and intelligence and of the post-defeat management of the enemy. The new intermediary position of Nisei, including longtime Japan residents, between the two warring races and empires was therefore inseparable from the dichotomized and essentialized ideas of Japanese culture and American culture. There, the act of "brokering" for clueless white conquerors was required of Nisei according to presumptions about their Japanese cultural literacy. The resultant social standing of these Japanese Americans in occupied Japan resembled that of colonial middlemen who inhabited and crisscrossed the rigidly divided worlds of colonizers and colonized. The Nisei's flexible performance of intra-racial difference was a logical result of their expected role as middleman cultural brokers, and that status made it imperative for them to embrace an imperial dimension of their citizenship of their own volition.

It is important to note that defeated Japanese could still shore up their sense of racial and national superiority by repudiating Nisei's practice of imperial citizenship. Instead of intra-racial differentiation, many Japanese continued to claim their likeness to Nisei servicemen according to their own essentialist thinking. In occupied Japan, US military censorship and propaganda presented Japanese Americans as proof that colored people could be as democratic as whites if properly guided. According to this narrative, the vanquished regarded Nisei soldiers and occupation personnel to be evidence toward the innate capacity of the Japanese to absorb democracy despite, or because of, US tutelary governance, thereby enabling them to continue to imagine the superior characteristics of their nation, culture, and race. The sustenance, if not resurgence, of imperial racism in post-defeat Japan was intertwined with the Nisei's work as cultural brokers and ideological icons as much as it mirrored Japanese indignation at their display of US citizenship's power against their racial cousins.

Brokering a Race War interrogates the contested but entangled categories of race, culture, and citizenship that cut across the boundaries of the United States and imperial Japan—with Nisei linguists as a focal point. The overlapping forces of inclusive colorblind citizenship and minority imperial citizenship dictated the life experiences of Japanese American soldiers and civilians, who worked for America's war and propaganda machines between 1941 and 1945 and then for the US military regime in occupied Japan. In the triangular relations of power, their interactions with white Americans and Japanese nationals were more strained, contentious, and violent than friendly, humane, or peaceful, as existing narratives often portray them.

This book examines the shifting places and roles that second-generation Japanese Americans held in the labyrinth of meanings and power relations associated with the three key identity constructs in the transimperial and transwar Asia-Pacific.

Nisei Cultural Brokers in the Propaganda War and Military Occupation

Thematically and chronologically organized, *Brokering a Race War* is divided into three parts. The first war-year chapters look at the entangled transpacific processes by which the propaganda machines of the two warring regimes co-opted Japanese Americans and turned them into epitomes of anti-racism that both sides claimed as their own. America's Nisei war heroes and propagandists and their counterparts in Japan made their choices to weather the difficult conditions that offered limited possibilities of safety and acceptance. The role of militarized cultural broker was among the few options they found that afforded them refuge from societal persecution and state detention, not to mention economic means of survival in light of their sudden displacement, on both sides of the war-torn Pacific.

With their ambiguous traits as racially Japanese, legally American, and yet culturally both, Nisei fit the bill as the bilateral broker. Many eagerly took on that essentialist identity, since it gave them a chance to serve as US army linguists, who were also farmed out to other propaganda agencies, like the Office of War Information. In wartime Japan, US-born residents were similarly roped into the role of experts on the enemy in accordance with public presumptions about the special cultural capital they possessed due to their American upbringing. Yet, they needed to renounce birthright US citizenship and/or restore *jus sanguinis* Japanese citizenship in order to demonstrate the primacy of blood ties to the ancestral homeland. Chapters 1 and 2 narrate the intertwined processes of the Nisei's wartime mobilization and their propaganda activities in imperial Japan and the United States, respectively. The former regime took the initiative in the utilization of Nisei as propagandists in the state war machine, catalyzing the latter's response by which to replicate a similar anti-racist practice despite the wholesale incarceration of all West Coast Japanese. Hence, this book starts with the story of the Japanese American experience in wartime Japan, followed by that of Nisei MIS members who were recruited for US counter-psychological warfare.

In the middle chapters, *Brokering a Race War* focuses on the relations between US Nisei occupation linguists and vanquished Japanese as well as between the former and white occupiers in defeated Japan. These chapters examine how Japanese Americans navigated the complex social, political, and cultural milieus of US-controlled Japan. The Nisei's ancestral land was an extension of US domestic society in terms of how racial hierarchy re-articulated and reproduced itself within the military government apparatuses of the General Headquarters (GHQ) under Douglas MacArthur. Yet, outside these confines, occupied Japan was a virtual colony that consisted of rightless foreigners dominated by soldiers in US and Allied military uniform regardless of skin color. Thus, whereas they were placed under white supervision and surveillance within the occupation forces, Nisei troops and civilian GHQ staffers simultaneously lived above local laws, enjoyed the privileges of virtual colonial overlords, and yielded enormous power over people of their ancestral land because of their birthright citizenship. In their everyday work as linguists, Japanese Americans presided directly over native Japanese workers as supervisors—the middleman status that often propelled them to perform intra-racial difference by enacting the violent power of their US citizenship. That status also explains the prevalence of Japanese American agents in GHQ's counter-intelligence divisions, which often engaged in extra-legal actions, including the abduction and inhumane treatment of suspected Japanese communists and subversives. Chapter 3 examines the positions and works of Nisei linguists as semi-native cultural brokers within complex apparatuses of the US military government and occupation forces after the summer of 1945.

Shifting focus onto Nisei's experience outside the military structure in occupied Japan, Chapter 4 investigates the terms of their relations to defeated Japanese that were highly contingent, albeit always asymmetrical. Due to their role as military translators and interpreters, Nisei occupation troops and GHQ staffers had to keep close contact with local Japanese, making them preoccupied with how their white bosses and comrades thought of their interaction with consanguineous enemy nationals. Because white Americans held the ultimate power to determine whether Nisei were acceptable Americans—that is, whether their loyalty stayed with their enemy blood or their birth citizenship, Japanese Americans in occupied Japan were often compelled to treat Japanese nationals harshly. It often accounted for their calculated act of demonstrating which side they were on so that they could rehabilitate their American identity denied during incarceration. At the same time, even though Japanese nationals were legally powerless, they could and did still strike back with remnants of their imperial racism in a passive-aggressive way, making the Nisei-Japanese relationship very tumultuous. This book offers the first substantive account of such entanglements between the two groups of Japanese on the opposite end of the spectrum: victorious Americans and defeated foreigners under tutelary US democratization.

The fourth chapter also documents the economic and social opportunities that Nisei cultural brokers could monopolize in occupied Japan. These opportunities subsequently rendered many Japanese Americans important players in the postwar Japanese economy and US-Japan trade relations. Some Nisei linguists took advantage of their cultural capital and connections to Japanese nationals, especially elite Japanese for whom they had translated; other occupation troops sometimes engaged in illegal and unethical acts to maximize their personal gains and exploit local women for their pleasure. Combined with their performance of intra-racial difference, such behaviors led to various forms of the vilification of Nisei in Japan's public discourse, although the information was largely muzzled under occupation censorship until it erupted in the liberated print press after April 1952. What can be characterized as the criminalization of Japanese Americans entailed the pejorative images of Nisei as foreign bandits, thieves, pimps, swindlers, and, above all, traitors to their blood compatriots. These ideas nonetheless coexisted with a positive notion of Nisei servicemen as a model for democratic citizens/soldiers of a new Japan, especially when the agenda of rearming that country drew public attention. Here, too, the clash between minority US imperial citizenship and remnants of Japanese imperial racism forms an important theme. Combined, the middle chapters elucidate the entanglements of gradated power relations defined by race, culture, and citizenship. These multilayered contestations unfolded in the form of white vs. Japanese; American vs. Japanese; Nisei US citizens vs. foreign Japanese; and members of the conquering military vs. those conquered by it.

Chapters 5 and 6 concentrate on the critical years of 1948–1951. During this later period of the occupation, the struggles between Japanese Americans and vanquished Japanese were locked into the geopolitical developments that reversed the course of US occupation aims to turn Japan into its junior military ally in Cold War East Asia. Under the occupation censorship regime, Nisei did more than the work of linguistic interpreters and translators; they also produced new meanings and signifiers suitable for the democratization of a non-white/non-European people. One such signifier revolved around a trope of Nisei 442nd RCT soldiers as exemplary defenders and promoters of democracy. In the context of US-backed (re) militarization of Japan, it served as a crucial politico-cultural symbol that some Japanese American occupation troops took the initiative in transplanting from US anti-racist discourse into the ideological terrain of their ancestral land, which was craving for a point of pride after its devastating defeat.

Around 1948–1950, the mythologizing of Nisei war heroes became particularly important to US military policymakers and Japanese officials when postwar Japan faced the pressure to rearm itself in conjunction with the rise of Communist China and the Korean War. The US-originated celebration of Nisei's military heroism was viewed suitable for the upending of the Japanese mindset about the state armed forces and soldierhood on which the American occupation propaganda had earlier cast an extremely negative light. As GHQ began to allow the myth of Nisei war heroes to enter the public discourse of post-1948 Japan, individual Japanese American servicemen took it upon themselves to propagate this contrived story across the Pacific. They also collaborated with their co-ethnics back home in their ongoing pursuit of a common group agenda: to solidify their identity as exemplary American citizens through a transnational story of their exceptional valor, patriotism, and dedication to democracy.

No sooner had the censored media started to publish this story in Japan than local Japanese elites attempted to hijack the Nisei military trope under the general blessing of the Pentagon and local US military brass. Both sides agreed that the legend of the exemplary democratic soldiers of Japanese blood would enhance the goal of disarming the negative attitudes of Japanese people toward the new Cold War agenda of reestablishing the pro-US Japanese armed forces. The ideological trope of Nisei war heroes had the effect of overturning a post-defeat rendition of Japanese soldierhood as unequivocally evil and barbaric. In this development, as Chapters 5 and 6 narrate, Japan's popular culture managed to claim the heroism of Nisei 442nd RCT soldiers as their own achievement in accordance with their essentialist rhetoric, which attributed the reason for Japanese Americans' success to their racial/cultural background. The way the vanquished managed to co-opt the Nisei's war heroism was to stress the innate superiority of their blood and ancestral martial traditions in the same way imperial Japan had celebrated the valor of its own soldiers as modern-day *samurai*. The excess of Japanization worried some at GHQ, and attempts were made to reinforce the boundaries between the victors and the defeated along the citizenship divide by importing a Hollywood-made film on the 442nd RCT rather than allowing a Japanese film production to materialize.

Yet, by the end of the military occupation, the trope of Nisei war heroes became substantively Japanized in Japan's domestic discourse, thus paving the way to strange coexistence of blood-will-tell Japanese racism and multiculturalist US minority militarism in the transpacific trope of Japanese American soldiers. Removed from US race politics, Nisei war heroes in occupied Japan became "Japanese" soldiers defined by blood and culture, no longer "American" by citizenship. This rhetorical appropriation reformulated the tale of Nisei's military accomplishment as a historical crystal ball—a teleological example that citizens of a free Japan were likewise destined to become exceptional soldiers of the democratic world, just like their US-born compatriots of the mid-1940s. While they acted self-reflexively as storytellers, moving cultural icons, and living ideological symbols of the model democratic soldiers, Nisei occupation troops played no subsidiary role in the co-optation of their own ethnic story by the geopolitical and nationalist agenda of rearming Japan after 1948. The last two chapters detail these complex processes and entanglements inside and outside occupied Japan.

Brokering a Race War concludes with a brief history of what happened after the Nisei's involvement in the Pacific War and the occupation of Japan. It traces the afterlife of Nisei war heroes and occupation linguists in the United States and postwar Japan, examining how minority imperial citizenship was normalized and celebrated without creating conflict with another aspect of Cold War US citizenship—a legal and rhetorical basis of domestic civil rights progress and minority acceptance since the 1950s.[37] With a transimperial perspective, this book's epilogue complements the well-documented story of the Nisei's civil rights struggle and their rise as the first Asian model minority stateside with a lesser-known account of their continuous dedication to US military and its violent power in the postwar years, especially during the redress and reparations movement of the 1980s. Because the constitutive contexts for minority imperial citizenship were transnational US military domination and the soldiering of minority

Americans under the resultant colonial conditions, their pursuit of equal citizenship rights and justice in a domestic context did not simply lead to something so transparently positive on a global scale. Ultimately, this book provides a new perspective on what it means to be right-bearing Americans in the militarist empire that continues to unabashedly tout and believe in anti-racism, multiculturalism, and "liberty and justice for all."

Brokering a Race War: Japanese Americans in the Pacific War and the Occupation of Japan. Eiichiro Azuma, Oxford University Press. © Eiichiro Azuma 2026. DOI: 10.1093/9780197781432.003.0001

PART I

PROPADANGA WAR AND THE TRANSPACIFIC GENEALOGIES OF NISEI CULTURAL BROKERS

1
Nisei as Model Imperial Subjects and Japan's Race War Propaganda

The story of Nisei's involvement in the Pacific War commenced in imperial Japan, dating back to before the US War Department began to deploy a select few hundred Nisei military linguists and decided to form the all-Japanese 442nd Regimental Combat Team (RCT) in early 1943. Since long before the outbreak of the war, Japan had its own population of American-born Japanese, who were considered presumedly loyal to the cause of their ancestral empire because of their blood ties. Preceding the US campaign to incorporate a story of Nisei soldiers' embrace of democratic ideals into its own anti-racist propaganda, imperial Japan had already capitalized on the resident Nisei's lived experiences of racial victimization in the land of their birth, especially the mass incarceration of those living on the West Coast solely because of their ancestry. Few studies have looked at the interrelated nature of the racial propaganda of these two warring empires, and the integral role Nisei played for each as brokers of competing knowledge and imagery centered on the selected, skewed presentations of their group experiences.[1]

During the Pacific War, the official anti-racist propaganda of each imperialist regime exploited aspects of Nisei's historical experiences and struggles, creating a homogenized image that served to vilify the enemy as racist and inhumane and simultaneously vaunt itself as the polar opposite. In these bilateral exchanges, the disavowal of national racism through the contrasting representations of Nisei's life experiences—especially their mass imprisonment in the United States—articulated dueling "trans-pacific racisms" that contested the meanings of race, culture, and citizenship.[2] Thus, the Nisei's work in US psychological warfare and military combat can be only properly understood in the context of America's response to Japan's race propaganda.

As Tokyo took the initiative in the war of words and images centering around Japanese American experience, its utilization of Nisei (and their parent generation of Issei) served as an important and necessary development that established their value as brokers in the inter-imperial contestation. In the early phase of this propaganda war, the United States remained on the defensive, responding only ineffectively to the terms of engagement set by Japan that vilified the former's acts and history of racism through Nisei's lived experience as an American minority. While Japan's initial focus on the victimization of Japanese immigrants did not ruffle many feathers because they were "enemy aliens," its growing emphasis on white racism against Japanese American US citizens caught the wary eye and ear of American propagandists. The United States was not able to distance itself so easily from biology-based "vulgar racism" due to its ongoing policy to incarcerate its own citizens on account of their standing as belonging to an enemy race. Yet, what imperial Japan had said and done in its racial propaganda about Japanese American citizens ironically solidified the US belief in the utility of Nisei in its counter-psychological warfare, albeit in a reactive way.

This chapter delves into these developments inside wartime Japan, which started to mobilize US-born Japanese residents living in their ancestral land for propagandist roles soon after the attack on Pearl Harbor. An analysis of Nisei's role and work in their ancestral land speaks to their varied identities in the imperial Pacific—the positions that rendered them not only otherized racial subjects in America's white empire but also diasporic subjects of Japan's blood empire. Such an analysis underscores Nisei's utilitarian importance to US psychological warfare and its subsequent management of vanquished Japanese. In order to establish that crucial historical context in which the United States made cultural brokers out of forsaken Nisei citizens after their mass incarceration, this chapter unveils a neglected history of Nisei as Japan's propagandists and soldiers, providing a glimpse into the parallel and yet intertwining processes of minority military service in the two empires at war.

Japan Takes the Initiative: White American Racism and Japanese American Incarceration

Imperial Japan began the war with the upper hand in projecting itself as the defender of the rights of non-whites against racist white regimes, the United States included. In its constant effort to paint itself in a favorable light, the

Japanese propaganda machine heavily relied on the voices of Japanese Americans, resident Nisei who were stranded in their parent's homeland because of the war. Drawing on the firsthand accounts of these Nisei who bitterly and angrily recalled their mistreatment in the country of their birth, this propaganda was hard to discount. The US government's immediate detention of thousands of Japanese immigrants with the outbreak of war and the complete incarceration of all people of Japanese ancestry living along the American West Coast soon after only seemed to prove their point.

Back in the early 1930s, Japanese diplomats had already recognized the value of Nisei's US-bred cultural capital, particularly their language abilities and understanding of the American national psyche. In the context of their public diplomacy, American-born Japanese leaders were induced to work together with immigrant leaders to engage in pro-Japan publicity campaigns as English editorial writers and public speakers. The structure of this "campaign of education" (*keihatsu undō*) in prewar Japanese America was three-tiered. On the West Coast and Hawai'i, local Japanese diplomats oversaw and dictated the overall operation of pro-Japan propaganda in accordance with Tokyo's policy mandate; immigrant leaders put together the grassroots apparatus and executed actual publicity campaigns within and without the ethnic community; and senior Nisei cooperated with the first generation in preparing English-language materials, publishing them in English-language outlets, and presenting them to English-speaking audiences in the western United States.[3] Once the Pacific War started in December 1941, imperial Japan proceeded to recreate this three-tier system of propaganda staffed by immigrant returnees and Nisei residents in Tokyo. Even though prewar Issei and Nisei had very different agendas for self-preservation than the diplomats' geopolitical goals, they became a cog in the state-backed transpacific apparatus of propaganda knowledge production without ever thinking that their cooperation might register as an anti-American act in the distrustful eyes of the US authorities.[4]

Towards the late 1930s, in conjunction with the organization of the US-based pro-Japan publicity campaign, the prewar Japanese government was also busy finding ways to train and use US-born Nisei for anti-American race propaganda in the Asia-Pacific. With the global rise of negative publicity about its military aggression, Japan's state officials and diplomats organized a special boarding school in Tokyo to produce bilingual Nisei propagandists and intelligence workers. At the same time, seasoned Nisei journalists from the West Coast and Hawai'i were recruited for the state-run Dōmei

News Agency and Radio Tokyo, as well as English-language propaganda outlets in Singapore and Shanghai.[5] In addition to their linguistic command, what one foreign-ministry official referred to as "race problems" bolstered Japan's reliance on Nisei cultural brokers. While calling for the need to combine the new theme of America's "race problems" with the "ongoing exposé of so-called Yankee imperialism," this official identified US Nisei as key players in propagandizing "race problems" for a new "anti-American campaign" on a global scale.[6] Hence, even before the outbreak of the Pacific War, Tokyo had already begun to formulate a race-based propaganda plan that capitalized on the powerful theme of racial oppression with Nisei American citizens as the mouthpiece. Once the US army-led "relocation" of 120,000 Japanese commenced in the American West in the spring of 1942, the Japanese government was quick to exploit this to shore up its self-proclaimed identity as the savior of all colored peoples in Asia and beyond.

From the outset, Japan was on the offensive in racial propaganda that featured the mass incarceration of Japanese American citizens, often compounded by better-known examples of racial atrocities against Black citizens and Native Americans. For the roles of story-makers and storytellers, Tokyo enlisted the service of Issei and Nisei residents in Japan soon after the attack on Pearl Harbor. As in the prewar case of the publicity campaign, the former—particularly US-educated immigrant returnees—initially stood at the forefront of this effort, dictating the pattern of wartime Japan's propaganda formation. For example, in May 1942, when the forced removal of Japanese residents from the West Coast was still underway, a recent immigrant returnee contributed a propaganda piece to a Radio Tokyo shortwave broadcast. In his commentary, this former Issei juxtaposed the acts of two American presidents to illuminate the "hypocrisy" of the current US administration: one had paved the way to the emancipation of Black slaves, and the other was allegedly instigating the enslavement of Japanese American citizens. After repeating the entire Gettysburg address, the radio commentary argued, Abraham Lincoln "would be shocked to death to see that his country is now [a] boiling pot of minority races instead of a melting pot of all races" under the "uncivilized" policy of Franklin D. Roosevelt. To epitomize such a travesty, according to the broadcast, Japanese Americans "have been driven into what Washington officials call a resettlement project which is another term for a concentration camp in American official language."[7]

This broadcast might have been the brainchild of Dodo Masao, who helped set the basic frame and tone of anti-American discourse in the initial phase of Japan's propaganda campaign. Formerly a revered Issei leader of Southern California who had been instrumental in the execution of the local "campaign of education" back in the early 1930s, Dodo was a prolific writer whose background as a staff writer for the *Rafu Shimpo* (*Los Angeles Japanese Daily*) allowed him to continue to work as a newspaperman in wartime Japan. At the same time, Dodo had a weekly commentary feature on Radio Tokyo called the "Truth behind the News," where he critically explicated contemporary socio-political developments in the United States. Based on his expertise in American politics and history, the former immigrant intellectual was also instrumental in transforming the incarceration story into a coherent propaganda narrative of American "hypocrisy" and "beastliness." Dodo's signature rhetoric was to compare a long tradition of white atrocities against Black and indigenous Americans with the ongoing imprisonment of Japanese Americans—especially citizens—as they all purportedly derived from the same source: imperialistic Anglo-Saxon supremacy that had conquered much of the Pacific until Japan finally confronted it.[8]

Whereas prewar returnees like Dodo crafted a basic context and frame of racial propaganda, some Issei wartime repatriates—armed with actual experiences of imprisonment—assumed the role of producing specific knowledge about the Japanese American incarceration after the two civilian exchange ships arrived in the summer of 1942 and the fall of 1943. No sooner had Japan's domestic print media begun to report on the "innate barbarism" of white Americans for a domestic audience than its foreign-language press and radio propaganda took advantage of the personalized tales of racial suffering incurred by recent repatriates from America.[9] After the first civilian exchange ship delivered many Issei repatriates, Radio Tokyo aired eye-witness accounts of "cruel treatment exercised by the US government toward Japanese internees" after Pearl Harbor Day.[10] Multilingual shortwave programs of September 1942, for example, featured an elite immigrant woman, Sakanishi Shiho, who had previously worked as the chief Japanese librarian at the US Library of Congress. "The close confinement of the ordinary detention house or an army camp for six months," she related, "taught us that the steel wall [and] iron bars, to say nothing about the electrified barbed wire fences and machine guns, do make prison and even the noblest of spirit does at times find difficulty in soaring out beyond them."[11] According to Sakanishi, the US government "seems to vent its spite against the poor victims of circumstances," even though the war was not of Japanese Americans' making. "When an elderly Japanese, loaded with luggage over a several-mile stretch, lagged," she lamented, "your army officers hurried them at the point of bayonets." Nisei citizens fared no better, because they were "stripped of their legal rights and thrown into concentration camps."[12] Yet, as architects of Japan's propaganda saw it, Sakanishi's last point—already a core of Japan's anti-racist message—would logically be most effectively related by resident Nisei themselves.

Narratives of lived experiences and eyewitness accounts of detention, including exaggerated and even fabricated stories, constituted a powerful verbal and representational weapon that Japan enjoyed capitalizing on in the initial phase of its war propaganda. Increasingly, severe criticism of the US imprisonment of West Coast Japanese Americans, especially Nisei US citizens, filled Japan's propaganda air waves and print materials when their mass removal was still in progress during the months of March through September 1942.[13] It was not coincidental that some US government officials, especially those connected to its psychological warfare divisions, became concerned about the negative consequences of race-based mass imprisonment during the same critical months. It was during those months that they started to deliberate on the utility of "loyal" Japanese American soldiers as a public-relations ploy to advertise colorblind democracy and freedom for which the United States was purportedly fighting during World War II. Assistant Secretary of War John J. McCloy first entertained the idea of a US Nisei combat unit in May 1942. It was followed by similar plans and proposals by Colonel Oscar N. Solbert, head of the Psychological Warfare Branch of the War Department, as well as the Office of War Information brass, including Director Elmer Davis and Associate Director Milton S. Eisenhower by October 1942.[14]

It is fair to argue, then, that the early phase of Japan's propaganda against America's race-based incarceration—the "barbaric" treatment of its own citizens in particular—catalyzed the US response, that is, its counter-propaganda that likewise centered on Japanese American citizens after early 1943. Each side generated messages of anti-racism by accusing its opponent of racism, and at the locus of contention stood the Nisei—with the contested meanings of their citizenship, racial lineage, and cultural dispositions forming a focal point of this transpacific discursive battle. Yet, as far as the first year of the Pacific War was concerned, Japan continued to monopolize the propaganda use of Japanese Americans, especially the contrived stories of their mass imprisonment in the racist United States that were initially narrated by immigrant repatriates and increasingly by US-reared Nisei residents in Japan.

Various factors foregrounded this generational shift in Japan's voice of anti-racist messages. First, Nisei's linguistic skill as native English speakers enabled them to make Issei's scripted narrative of American hypocrisy and beastliness legible to non-Japanese speakers and effectively disseminate such information to foreign targets on the air or in writing. Nisei's real-life narratives of racial victimhood by their own birth country also held high value as propaganda knowledge towards both domestic and overseas audiences. Combined with the shift from Issei pundits to Nisei storytellers in Japan's early propaganda narrative, its growing emphasis on the legal status of incarcerated Japanese rendered Japan's general condemnation of American racism inseparable from a scathing attack on the fallacy of color-blind birthright citizenship guaranteed by the Fourteenth Amendment to the US Constitution (and reinforced by the US Supreme Court in the *US v. Wong Kim Ark* in 1898).[15]

Japanese authorities seemed to have felt less weary, if not more trustful, about the pro-Japan stance of resident Nisei, especially those who responded positively to the call for being mobilized into the state-sponsored Nisei Association of Nippon (NAN). On the contrary, Issei repatriates were subjected to close scrutiny due to the official suspicion of their long-term residence in the enemy country and their exposure to its harmful cultural mores. After all, those who returned on exchange ships had not opted to come home to support Japan's war effort until after being repatriated by the enemy. Many resident Nisei, especially NAN leaders and its senior members, had been in the bosom of their blood home and supported it since Japan had begun military campaigns against China in the 1930s. For this reason, the utterances of Issei repatriates were well regulated and tightly scripted in accordance with state guidelines.[16]

Indeed, as soon as they landed at Yokohama, the repatriates were all ordered to enroll in a "reorientation" program for "re-Japanization." While the Japanese military police examined their political backgrounds and ideological tendencies, they spent their first two weeks in virtual confinement at a fully guarded special boarding school. From morning to evening, government officials briefed the former US residents on Japan's war doctrine, proper behavior in their homeland, and the moral code authorized by the current militarist regime, with which many overseas residents were not familiar. They also had to "cleanse" themselves of Euro-American influences while deepening their appreciations of Japan's national spirit. They were told not to discuss in public anything they had heard and read in the United States before their return, because the authorities feared such knowledge was likely be tainted with pro-American tendencies. No talk of America's economic might was permitted, either, since it would undermine the public morale. Tokyo officials sternly warned against leaking any unauthorized information about their US experience other than the prescribed stories of racial oppression. Hence, their writings and public talks were all subject to prior censorship.[17]

Therefore, in the machinations of Japan's racial propaganda, Nisei residents played no less significant a role than former immigrant pundits or other Japanese. The key outlets of Japan's English-language propaganda—most notably Radio Tokyo and the *Japan Times* (renamed *Nippon Times* in 1943)—were staffed mostly by resident Nisei in wartime Japan. Although they were placed under the nominal supervision of native Japanese bosses, many of these Nisei took charge of actual content design and planning. A US World War I veteran and long-term resident of Japan since the mid-1920s, San Francisco-born Kiyoshi George Togasaki was at the helm of Radio Tokyo's international programing during much of the war years. The *Japan Times* operated under the editorship of Los Angeles native Goro Murata, a veteran Nisei journalist who had edited the English section of the *Kashū Mainichi* (*California Japanese Daily News*) before joining the English press in his ancestral land in 1935. Both Togasaki and Murata commanded a team of Nisei employees, who also translated and edited Issei's Japanese-language writings to suit the cultural sensitivities of Anglo-American audiences.[18] In broadcast propaganda, Nisei announcers verbally transmitted Japanese American-generated propaganda in their native tongue without foreign/Japanese accent—a task very few could do in wartime Japan. They represented only a small portion of the greater and more ubiquitous Nisei involvement in the anti-American publicity apparatuses of imperial Japan. In this sense, Japan's propaganda machine could not have functioned without resident Nisei, who served as translators and announcers, editors and program planners, and content producers. While Issei returnees like Dodo and Sakanishi initially tended to make up the face of anti-racist Japan in the war of words and representations, a wide array of resident Nisei youths continued to work behind the scenes as brokers of anti-American knowledge and message.

Nisei Association of Nippon and the Mobilization of US-Born Japanese in Wartime Japan

In wartime Japan, the government-backed Nisei Association of Nippon (Zai'nichi Nisei Rengōkai, hereafter NAN) played a central role in steering resident Nisei into Japan's state military apparatuses—both its propaganda machine and armed forces.[19] Not only did it single-handedly represent the interests of those deemed as Nisei in imperial Japan, or US-born/reared individuals tainted by enemy influences, but the NAN also generated specific ideas of the Nisei dispositions that were considered valuable to imperial Japan. Declared at a general assembly to commemorate its one-year anniversary, the NAN's November 1942 resolution defined who these Nisei were in racial-nationalist terms:

> [W]e Nisei in Japan, who have been brought up under special circumstances, must, as possessors of Japanese heritage (blood/lineage), live up to the honor of our ancestors, who are the pioneers of overseas development, by displaying our special ability (culture), and push ahead with the construction of the Common Prosperity Sphere of Greater East Asia.... [T]he majority of us are separated from our parents and brothers.... We in our parents' land and they in the enemy's country, this is the supreme test given by Heaven, and only by pushing through this hardship, can we claim ourselves worthy of the blood we have inherited.[20]

Such concepts as blood ties and "special ability," emphasized in this resolution, elucidated how Nisei managed to weather social persecution and other challenges in wartime Japan. Invoking the primacy of their intrinsic biological linkage to imperial Japan and utilizing their cultural capital as US-reared Japanese constituted crucial aspects of many Nisei's social strategy for survival when they found themselves mired in public hatred for everything American. This strategy marked a sharp contrast to the manner in which their co-ethnic compatriots in the United States—in response to allegations of being loyal to their ancestral home and possibilities of mass imprisonment as domestic threats—valorized the value of their birthright citizenship and the national allegiance based on it.

According to a reliable 1942 estimate, as many as five thousand individuals were identified as "Nisei" in wartime Japan due to their American cultural attributes and recent migration history, although ten times more US-born individuals were said to have resided throughout Japan. The vast majority of resident Nisei were nativized enough to pass as ordinary Japanese; typically, they had gone to rural Japan with their immigrant parents or had been sent to live with relatives as young children in order to be educated. The Americanized Nisei, on the other hand, were mostly well-educated and ambitious youths who had migrated to Japan during the 1930s and usually resided in the urban regions of Tokyo-Yokohama and Kobe-Osaka-Kyoto for work and higher education.[21] In the eyes of the Japanese authorities, this group of several thousand US-reared/educated Nisei looked foreign and potentially treacherous, not only for their cultural traits but also their American citizenship status (dual nationality included).

Notwithstanding frequent police repression, their blood ties to the ancestral land still gave them recognition as consanguineous immigrants to be rehabilitated for the war effort, separating them from white American expatriates who were summarily interned.[22] Established on the eve of the attack on Pearl Harbor, the NAN was expected to control these Americanized Nisei according to state mandates and military needs, which included the enlistment of its members for anti-US propaganda. As the only state-authorized Nisei organization in wartime Japan, the NAN had a relationship to the government, and its functions were not dissimilar to the roles of the Japanese American Citizens League (JACL) that spearheaded the consolidation of US Nisei residents around the identical theme of uncompromised national loyalty and hyper-identification with the warring regime and its militarism.[23]

Formally supported by the foreign ministry, NAN's stronghold was Japan's capital region, and its Nisei brass were in direct contact with central government bureaucrats.[24] The NAN leadership consisted of the Tokyoites who had already established themselves in ordinary Japanese workplaces, especially the print press, international trade, and higher education. In addition to its board members Kiyoshi George Togasaki and Goro Murata, NAN's acting president Takizo Frank Matsumoto was a professor at a major private university in Tokyo. These Nisei elders had cultivated close relations with Japan's influential statesmen, military officers, and top bureaucrats, thereby making it possible for NAN to continue to operate despite public scrutiny. Other directors of NAN's Nisei board included journalists, like Tamotsu Murayama and Welly Tatsuo Shibata; the former had been one of the first Nisei to be recruited by the state-run Dōmei News Agency, and the latter had served as the English news editor of the *Osaka Mainichi* since the mid-1930s. Usually with Japanese spouses and local-born children, these adult Nisei Tokyoites had established deep roots in prewar Japanese society, and they dominated the leadership of NAN as self-styled spokespersons for the rest of the American-born in Japan, such as younger students and bachelors as well as those living outside the capital region. NAN's general secretary/director, as well as some board members, were Issei returnees and former US-stationed diplomats, who oversaw NAN's daily operations just as they had in the pro-Japan publicity apparatuses of prewar Japanese America.[25]

In wartime Japan, NAN's Nisei leadership attempted to construct a consanguineous "ethnic" identity for its members, whose "problems [we]re one"

Fig. 1.1 Portrait of Tamotsu Murayama visiting Honolulu as an English staff writer of Japan's state-owned Dōmei News Agency in November 1938. Courtesy of *Nippu Jiji* Photo Archives, *Hawaii Times* Photo Archives Foundation and Hoover Institution Library & Archives, J1248.001.

and "status [wa]s one" as Acting President Matsumoto declared, in spite of being an integral part of imperial Japanese citizenry.[26] The making of this unique identity had to unfold in such a way as to avoid contradictions with their public persona as loyal and trustworthy despite, or because of their US cultural upbringing (but not citizenship). In this sense, the NAN engaged in the double ethnicization of resident Nisei. First, it strove to present Nisei as foreign-born constituents of Japan's expanding empire and its global racial diaspora, thereby challenging the monolith of imperial citizenry. Intra-racial differentiation was predicated on gradations of relations of race and cultural upbringing that became core elements of what it meant to be US-born Nisei in wartime Japan. As articulated in its 1942 public resolution, the NAN positioned its members first and foremost "as possessors of Japanese heritage" and being "worthy of the blood [they] have inherited," although they had also "been brought up under special circumstances" outside the racial home.[27] Insofar as Nisei in Japan were represented as inseparable from their blood brothers and sisters of the ancestral empire, the meaning of being Japan's Nisei residents had less to do with being Americans of Japanese ancestry than with being minoritized/ethnicized Japanese nationals.[28] The former definition had been a conventional identity that many Nisei leaders had advocated for their compatriots in the prewar years to distinguish themselves from the rest of people in Japan. Yet, the exigencies of the war compelled them to reverse their stance—the shift that explains why the NAN emerged as the chief facilitator of Nisei's de-Americanization even though it still managed to present their US-bred cultural capital in a positive light, albeit only to serve the interests of their blood home at war with their birth country.[29]

Simultaneously, the NAN aimed to dismantle the undifferentiated public notion in Japan of second-generation Japanese Americans—another form of ethnicization—by driving a wedge between its members "worthy of the blood [they] have inherited" from the ancestral land and their US citizen counterparts who did not declare an allegiance to Japan. These representational strategies helped create the sub-categories of imperial Japanese and Japanese Americans, respectively, thereby allowing Nisei in Japan to preserve a delicate balance between the ostensibly contradictory identities, albeit at the cost of privileging blood relations over birthright citizenship, and ancestral culture over the culture of their upbringing. Put differently, Japanized Nisei could be impeccable imperial subjects fully dedicated to the victory of their homeland while avoiding completely casting off their past life experience and acculturation rooted in enemy land.

Even though resident Nisei insisted on nuanced distinctions between themselves and their native-born compatriots of their ancestral land and their fellow Japanese Americans across the Pacific, the NAN still needed to operate under the watchful eyes of the totalitarian Japanese state.[30] To offset official and public hostilities, it solicited the patronage of social and political elites beyond diplomatic circles. These patrons included many prominent figures of the militarist regime, including former army minister General Araki Sadao. Fundamentally, they viewed resident Nisei as no different than the rest of imperial Japanese, hence their call for equal treatment.[31] Representing NAN's Japanese advisory board, one patron extolled Nisei, arguing they "have shown proof to the Japanese people here that [they] have actually possessed the pure Japanese blood of the old Samurai... as a subject to shoulder the burden of this war... to bring forth victory." Their war involvement was tantamount to the process of their imperialization—the opportunity to "mould [them] into a perfect Japanese."[32]

Penned by another Japanese supporter, a feature article in a major Tokyo daily discussed the extent to which the once-despised Nisei were being glamourized in Japan's domestic public discourse under state approval. Titled "Fighting Nisei of Our Military Regime: Boiling Blood of the Fifty Thousand," the January 1943 report presented the stories of individual Nisei men and women, "who [had] restored [Japanese] nationality and [had] been struggling hard all over Greater East Asia, because their innate love for fatherland [could] not but spring up." According to the newspaper, some Nisei men had already sacrificed their lives as ordinary combat soldiers on various warfronts, while others were "putting their command of English and expertise of the American mindset to good use" by serving as members of the special military intelligence and army press bureau. Female Nisei were doing their part, too, as many were eager to volunteer as military nurses after medical training. In line with the doctrine of blood-based national belonging, the Japanese daily quoted the young Nisei women saying in unison: "Even though we happen to be born in America, we all share the splendid Yamato spirit that is burning inside our hearts."[33]

Likewise, the NAN's annual report lauded the Nisei's embrace of the racial homeland and their rebirth as wartime Japanese:

戰ふ軍國の二世

沸る五萬人の血潮

南に北に轟く"み民われ"の進軍

必然的に湧き上つた祖國愛・日本在住五万の二世たちが敢然祖國を回復して如何に大東亞戰を敢闘してゐるかこれは赤坂の在日二世聯合會事務所に屬された戰ふ軍國二世の報告書である

戰ふ二世達（上）龜田君（円内右上）和田君（同下）中田君（下左）福永君

「たとひ産湯をあげた屋根の下がアメリカでも、僕たち、私たちは立派な大和魂に燃えてゐる日本人です」大東亞戰勃発と同時に、その態度を注目されてゐた二世たちが、彼等の肉体に根深く潜在してゐたアメリカ意識を決然捨て去り放つた最初の言葉はかうであつた、野村前駐米大使もその報告に私はこの片方の眼で彼等の日本人として生きる悲壯な奮闘ぶりをはつきり見て來たと强調してゐる、支那事變の初めにはハワイ生れの黒川秀雄君が二世出身の兵士として立派に呉淞攻略の華と散つた、そして今次大東亞戰には黒川君の後に續く"軍國二世"たちが

南…の戰線へ雄々しく出陣、かくて在日男女五万の二世たちが全部祖國のために起ち上る決意をした

カナダ生れの○○○君が遞信省の地方航空機乘員養成所操縦生の試験に合格して皇軍としての第一歩を踏み出し、福永幸雄君（ハワイ）竹下高雄君（カリフォルニヤ）等○○名が一人の落伍者もなく全部幹部候補生の試験に合格して目覺しい二世の意氣を見せた、このころシンガポール陷落の歴史的ニュースを第一番に全世界の耳に打込んだ東京放送局員小林進君は敵後絡者の調務から遂にマイクに殉じ、國際放送戰の華と散つたのである

日…本人に更生した濱田兄弟勇士の一人、同胞ヘンリー兵長は壯烈南の海に散り、在米二十八年の竹村秀雄氏の三兄讓治、透、龍利の三君はマレー戰線に活躍、また彼等の巧な英語とアメリカ民情に對する豊かな知識が今次戰爭に大いに役立ち、軍屬として志願した元明大野球部主將龜田雄（ハワイ）同野球部選手和田隆太郎（ハワイ）中田寅（ハリファックス大學）の三君が波荒き大東亞海に闘てた殊勲は聯合艦隊を感激させてゐるほどだ、ミッドウエー作戰に、或は遠くアリューシャンに、南方に、彼等の活躍振りは實に勇ましいものがあり

女…子二世では聖路加病院内の看護婦養成所や女子醫專在學中の者など、いづれも白衣の天使として第一線に立つ日を待機してゐるなど、係員を感激させてゐる

Fig. 1.2 “Tatakau gunkoku no Nisei: Tagiru goman-nin no chishio” (“Fighting Nisei of Our Military Regime: Boiling Blood of the Fifty Thousand”), *Asahi Shinbun*, January 15, 1943. Courtesy of the *Asahi Shinbun*.

> With Japan prosecuting the Greater East Asia War by mobilizing all her resources, there are many Nisei aiding the nation to carry out her tremendous task. Many are in the fighting services, many are in the Southern Regions setting their shoulders to the great construction work, many are also in the home front giving their best. Nisei who are on the front lines fighting against enemy propaganda are found working with the Domei News Agency and the Broadcast Corporation of Japan [Radio Tokyo].[34]

These narratives of the Nisei's exceptional war support constituted a mainstay of emergent official discourse, which under tight state censorship publicized the American-born as impeccable Japanese patriots.[35] It also characterized a militarized form of ethnic formation that facilitated the integration of US-born Japanese into Japan's war machine. The NAN was chiefly responsible for that process, where the definition of being Nisei in Japan was meshed with that of being exemplary soldiers and home-front patriots. The public representations of the Nisei's war contributions obscured the everyday experiences of many individuals, like students, housewives, and non-defense workers, who did not fit the descriptions of militarized national subjects. Still, the fruits of NAN's public-relations endeavors became suddenly eye-catching in imperial Japan from late 1942 onward, embellishing the censored news and propaganda publications and compounding the simplistic public understanding of what Nisei were. Such imagery and public understanding merged into the knowledge that had been generated by Issei and Nisei pundits since the spring of 1942 for the audiences inside and outside Japan: the incarceration of American-born Japanese as the epitome of American white supremacy and racial oppression.

Couched in the language of exceptional nationalism, the militarized ethnic formation of American-born Japanese subjects resulted from the NAN's ongoing programs of imperializing ordinary Nisei residents, and hence engaging its membership of nearly two thousand in the battle against their birth country. First, because it professed as its primary goal the promotion of Nisei's interests and welfare in Japan, the NAN was compelled to take the lead in the indoctrination of its members. It launched an education program about the Japanese (Yamato) spirit, the national language, and Japan's war aims in response to the urging of Japanese supporters, who subsequently served as instructors.[36] Second, in addition to fostering Nisei's allegiance through the educational program, the NAN organized a campaign to restore their Japanese citizenship. In this regard, NAN leaders offered

Fig. 1.3 "Nisei on the Home Front." An illustration of Nisei's varied roles and contributions to Imperial Japan. Taken from *Reimei* 1, nos. 1–2 (1943), p. 34 (English section). Author's collection.

legal consultation and logistical assistance to its members and non-members alike, so that Japanese American residents could "retain their position (jobs) and to maintain their livelihood" in wartime Japan. During the first three-quarters of 1942, the organization distributed "written (bilingual) instructions explaining how to file an application for citizenship restoration and its

AID OFFERED TO NISEI

With new developments in East Asia, many openings have been created for Nisei residents in Japan. To make these channels available to them, the Nisei Association of Japan offers the facilities of its organization to all Nisei in need of counsel. Those wishing to obtain information are advised to communicate with the undersigned.

SOYEN YAMASHITA, general secretary
Nisei Kyokai.
No. 48, 1-chome Aoyama Minami-cho,
Akasaka-ku.

Fig. 1.4 "Aid Offered to Nisei." A Nisei Association of Nippon (Zainichi Nisei Kyōkai)'s announcement for job referral service. *Japan Times*, January 23, 1942. Courtesy of the *Japan Times*.

importance."[37] Its audience included over 1,500 American-born residents all over the Japanese archipelago. About three hundred Nisei in the Tokyo metropolitan region had the opportunity to consult directly with volunteers from the NAN leadership to process their citizenship applications.[38] This program of legal imperialization made the American-born youths subject to military service and other forms of patriotic works and contributions to their ancestral land.

NAN's leaders knew all too well that their endeavors deepened the Nisei's involvement in the war against the United States, where they still maintained deep psychological and family connections. Yet, given the difficult circumstances surrounding them in Japan, resident Nisei leaders felt that the organization "render[ed] a service of at least assisting in the choice of two evils," that is, the choice of collaborating with Japan's war effort or that of being further ostracized as enemy citizens.[39] Nisei war complicity and legal Japanization accounted for the simultaneous workings of societal coercion and self-propelled action, where the former served to narrow down the possibilities of the latter to "the choice of two evils" for the pivotal goal of individual and group survival as despised American-born/reared individuals. The historical experience of Japan's Nisei residents, like that of their US counterparts, defies a simplistic narrative of the treacherous turncoat or that of the helpless victim of circumstance. Yet, what NAN leadership deemed the lesser of "two evils" had devastating implications for the long-term interests of American-born residents.[40]

Nisei as Japanese Propagandists and Brokers of Racial Knowledge in the War-Torn Pacific

The militarized ethnic formation of American-born immigrants in imperial Japan was contingent on another important factor. What the NAN constantly boasted as the Nisei's "special ability" derived from having been "brought up under special circumstances" in the United States. Frequent references to the Nisei's role in "fighting against enemy propaganda" and "military intelligence" work foregrounded the NAN's central contention about the importance of their US-bred cultural capital. Without it, Nisei residents could not have converted the meaning of being the American-born from treacherous to patriotic in wartime Japan, because, as the leaders declared, "the Nisei's capabilities, adaptabilities and possibilities" enabled them to "further...the interest of the land of their parents" during the military struggle against America.[41] This assertion corroborated the dominant view in the elite circles of imperial Japan, Nisei's detractors and sympathizers alike. At a special lecture sponsored by the NAN, for example, General Araki urged the American-born youths to "make use of their special talent in addition to their knowledge of Japanese (language) and things Japanese to become worthy subjects of the Empire."[42] As Araki's statement elucidates, the success of Nisei's self-ethnicization in wartime Japan was preconditioned by how useful they could make their US-bred cultural capital for their ancestral home.

The desirable capabilities of resident Nisei meant not only their linguistic and cultural abilities to understand and manipulate enemy minds but also the propaganda knowledge they could generate from their past experience as minority American citizens. All these comprised the extremely rare qualities that few other people could offer in the local context for Japan's war propaganda. At the same time, outside the prescribed roles that drew on their US cultural attributes and life histories in the enemy land, American-born youths were not permitted to deviate from the undifferentiated masses of imperial Japanese. When everything American was deemed reprehensible and dangerous, it was in the work of "fighting against enemy propaganda" that the Nisei's foreignized upbringing stood out as beneficial and acceptable. For this reason, Nisei dominated the everyday operations of Japan's propaganda apparatus as linguo-cultural brokers and producers of anti-American knowledge, albeit under the dictates of native Japanese supervisors.[43] Paradoxically, the value of the Nisei's "special talent" lay in their generally abhorred American background, and in this context, NAN members, especially its highly educated and articulate leaders, embodied the living expertise in Japan's anti-American propaganda.[44]

Radio Tokyo's propaganda broadcasts, for example, featured many self-proclaimed Nisei with insider knowledge, who played the role of English announcers, scriptwriters, and program managers. California-educated Iva Toguri, the infamous "Tokyo Rose" convicted after the war for treason, was but one of these North America-educated English-speaking Nisei radio announcers; an NAN board member worked more prominently as one of the "Tokyo Roses."[45] At the Tokyo headquarters of the state-run Dōmei News, twenty-eight Nisei were engaged in its English-language reporting and editorial writing.[46] Likewise, all other English-language print media of Japan's foreign propaganda had many NAN members and leaders as editors and staff writers.[47] Their published editorials and reports were incorporated into Japan's broadcast and leaflet propaganda. When few other people of imperial Japan could grasp colloquial English speech or interpret obscure cultural mores of enemy society, the NAN inadvertently offered a pool of irreplaceable talent for the tasks that required those valuable qualities and skills.

Aided by their monopoly on US-bred cultural capital, resident Nisei simultaneously worked as chief producers of propaganda knowledge for not only foreign audiences but also the Japanese public. This role was as important as their service as linguistic specialists, including announcers and translators who primarily targeted the outside world. Drawing from personalized narratives, these Nisei characterized their racial experience in prewar America as the precursor to the atrocious US program of the mass incarceration of Japanese Americans, as well as a microcosm of American/Anglo-Saxon imperialism and the global white supremacy against which Japan was purportedly fighting. Such a narrative was expected to be effective from both psychological and ideological standpoints, because the Nisei's firsthand accounts of victimization as Japanese persons would have a direct emotional appeal to the domestic audience in particular.

NAN's acting president Takizo Frank Matsumoto took the lead as a producer of propaganda knowledge for both foreigners and Japanese.

Educated at Meiji University and Harvard University, this Fresno-bred college professor was one of a few resident Japanese Americans who was completely bilingual in speaking and writing. Even though he was not a US-born citizen as he was brought from Hiroshima to California in his infancy, Matsumoto had been widely recognized as an elder leader of Japanese American residents in Japan since the early 1930s. While working as a professor of his alma mater in Tokyo, Matsumoto nurtured close connections to government officials and social elites.[48] Identifying himself as a "Nisei" leader during the war, Matsumoto self-consciously stood "on the front lines fighting against enemy propaganda." Not only did he publish numerous print materials in Japanese and English and participate in shortwave radio programs as a bilingual commentator and editorialist, but he also held a series of large-scale public lectures about the evils of the enemy country in which he had spent his formative years.[49] His adoption of a Nisei identity reveals the centrality of US citizenship in Japan's war propaganda that elucidated its failure and hypocrisy under white oppression.

Combined with his background as a (masqueraded) Nisei growing up in racist California, Matsumoto's status as a respected intellectual made him stand out among Japan's propagandists, especially vis-à-vis domestic targets. The wartime incarceration of Nisei by the US government was among the topics he frequently discussed in his Japanese-language writings and lectures. He alleged that the "violation of Nisei's citizenship and their exclusion from military service... has brought about a great racial awakening" in the Japanese American incarceration camps. By citing the words of his Nisei "friend who just returned from Los Angeles," Matsumoto explained what that awakening meant to him and his fellow Nisei in Japan and elsewhere: "having undergone the mass imprisonment, we are now determined not to be defeated in this war. We would like to be the ones to spearhead the invasion of our enemy, America."[50] Tied to the theme of the preponderance of race, Nisei-generated narratives served to illuminate the racist betrayal of US citizenship and all the "American" ideals that came with it, like democracy, equality, and liberty.

Matsumoto's public lecture of July 3, 1942, which was published as a booklet one year later, explicated these twin themes in a highly personalized manner that was designed to stir up anti-American racial hatred and empathy toward Nisei, the latter being NAN's most important goal.[51] In this sense, Matsumoto's propaganda rhetoric still mirrored a covert but ongoing struggle for Nisei's ethnic survival in wartime Japan, although it no doubt pulled his US-born compatriots further apart from their birth country. Held in central Tokyo, Matsumoto's lecture opened with the declaration, "I was born in Fresno," to legitimize his credibility despite being actually born in Hiroshima. A recounting of "extremely unpleasant experiences" as a Nisei child in rural California paved the way for a discussion of the fundamental "contradiction" that American citizens of Japanese ancestry had "never [been] treated equally" because of their race. Matsumoto organized this storytelling around his Issei mother's lesson: that Nisei "must live strong"—a motto that all Japanese in America had purportedly abided by in weathering white oppression. He then explained how he had devoted himself to sports and always managed to compete on par with white men, an experience that had convinced him to believe in the ability of Japanese people to take on Americans and "never lose on the same footing." This is how he also excelled in schoolwork, leading to his admission into the Massachusetts Institute of Technology and later his graduation from the Harvard Business School. Like his personal triumphs against racist Californians, Matsumoto underscored that imperial Japan was also on its way to its final victory over the United States in the contemporary geopolitical manifestations of racial struggle. As narrated by the self-styled Nisei intellectual before a Japanese audience, the past tribulations and triumphs of Japanese Americans did not look dissimilar to the current historical path their ancestral empire had been treading since December 1941.[52]

Whereas Matsumoto's race propaganda was mostly devoid of direct references to actual war stories, many Nisei members of Dōmei News and the imperial army's press bureau experienced actual battle, witnessing Japan's victories against Anglo-American armed forces.[53] Having worked for Dōmei in Singapore from 1939, for example, John Tatsuki Fujii spent the turbulent few months after December 8, 1941, there. He was imprisoned by the British authorities and liberated by Japanese troops—a story of high propaganda value this Japanese American would be telling the world. Fujii was brought up from infancy in California and hence was identified as Nisei, even though he did not hold birthright citizenship. After graduating from Pomona College and working as a US-based correspondent for a Japanese newspaper, Fujii was recruited to edit a Japan-funded English daily in the British colony. His reportage from the battleground of Singapore was published in both English and Japanese in 1943.[54]

The English and Japanese versions of Fujii's book share common storylines, as the latter was a translation of the former, with one significant exception. The main nine chapters trace the history of British colonization in Singapore, Anglo-Saxon oppression of colonized Asians there, internment and violent treatment of Japanese by the British authorities after the outbreak of the war, and their release and return to post-"liberation" Singapore following Japanese invasion. However, although the English book introduction simply sets up the usual themes of Japan's global propaganda focused on white colonial oppression and its defeat at the hands of the "righteous" imperial forces, its Japanese-language counterpart stresses the Nisei's racial experience and its relevance to Japan's war effort. The respective versions of Epilogue differ in much the same way. The Japanese iteration of Fujii's book is also dedicated to "the Nisei who have sacrificed their lives for the fatherland on various warfronts of the Great East Asian Theater," thereby impressing their impeccable patriotism on Japanese readers.[55]

Titled "the creation of Shōnan" (the new name for Japanese-controlled Singapore), Fujii's translated reportage employed a narrative scheme identical to Matsumoto's public lecture by featuring the trajectory of his personal struggle against white racism in California. What distinguished Fujii was his ability to interweave the Nisei life story into the pivotal war narrative of Anglo-Saxon atrocities against local Asians, including himself, and Japan's military "liberation of white-control Singapore." The "creation of Shōnan" thus represented the multiple forms of cultural capital that Nisei battleground propaganda workers could claim: a monopoly on firsthand knowledge of US anti-Asian racism, of Anglo-Saxon colonial domination, and of Japan's messianic military victories. Presented to Japanese readers as highly personalized accounts, the entangled stories of the local and geopolitical unfolding all over the Pacific basin elicited emotional support for what both American-born Japanese and their ancestral land were supposedly fighting for. Indeed, as Dōmei's top official commented in the postscript to the Japanese version of Fujii's reportage, the military success of Japan was meant to reflect the parallel "transformation [of Fujii and other Japanese Americans] into full-fledged Japanese after shedding the [US-bred] characteristic of Nisei."[56]

Imperial Japan found the Nisei's experience in Hawai'i relevant to its war effort as well, since the militarist regime regarded the mid-Pacific islands as an important base of its eastward expansion in the establishment of the Greater East Asia Co-Prosperity Sphere. Some Nisei residents were called upon to narrate Japan's rightful ownership of Hawai'i in terms of the pivotal theme of race over citizenship. In the early 1940s, more than one-third of

Hawai'i's population was of Japanese ancestry, and the vast majority were native-born Nisei US citizens. Thus, Japan's war propaganda theme—especially in its early phase—entailed the representation of Hawai'i as an integral part of Japan's transpacific racial empire despite it being mostly populated by American citizens. In 1942 and 1943, two Hawai'i-born Nisei published Japanese-language books under the tight state censorship of wartime Japan. As the foreign minister noted in the preface to one volume, their accounts were deemed far more credible and authoritative than any scholarly expositions in terms of their intimate firsthand understanding of enemy society.[57] These Nisei, Noboru "Fred" Miike and Itsuko Kito, were hitherto unknown and significantly younger than NAN leaders. Yet, their sudden appearance as book authors underscored the utility of all Nisei men and women for Japan's propaganda machine, since those who had experienced racial victimhood were not limited to older educated leaders and professional journalists, like Matsumoto and Fujii.[58] Every Nisei in Japan held the "special talent" to tell the firsthand stories of suffering at the hands of brutal white overlords.

Assisted by a Japanese journalist, twenty-six-year-old Miike put together a "personal memoir" of his life in Hawai'i for a Japanese audience. Published in 1942, Miike's book, *Hawai'i, My Birthplace*, focused on the structural oppression that Japanese Americans had endured due to the asymmetrical race relations of prewar Hawai'i, as well as its culture and mores, under Anglo-Saxon (Hawaiian *haole*) dominance. Characterizing the islands as a "paradise," the Nisei author still expressed profound affection and acute nostalgia for his birthplace.[59] At the same time, as the publisher's advertisement dubbed it "a record of a young Nisei's bitter tears," the book principally offers a colloquial account of white-dominated Hawai'i, especially its sugar industry and the US military's brutalization of Japanese residents. Accompanying Miike's emotion-filled memoir were not only sensationalized episodes of military-led mass detention—deliberately mixed up with the West Coast Japanese incarceration—but also the fabricated reports of the US authorities' "determination to arrest all suspicious Japanese and execute them by shooting."[60] In reality, no such incidents happened in Hawai'i; even though the mid-Pacific islands represented the starting point of the war and a US congressional investigation initially alleged the collaboration of Nisei agents with enemy, the local military authorities decided not to carry out wholesale imprisonment. In this "autobiographical" account, the Nisei's lived experience of prewar white-dominated Hawai'i was fused with the projected racial conditions of wartime Hawai'i, thereby creating a coherent propaganda narrative based on the combination of truth and fabrication.

Idyllic stories of Miike's beloved Hawai'i and its Japanese community were thus juxtaposed with the atrocious history of white Americans' violence against Nisei citizens and their Issei parents that would logically seek their total annihilation under the condition of a race war according to Japan's standard propaganda line. Yet, in the end, Miike did not neglect to tell Japanese readers that he was "counting down the days till [he] finally returns to [his] beloved Hawai'i." That message signaled the fast-approaching conclusion of America's "rule by violence" under the ascendancy of imperial Japan's "righteousness."[61] The predicted liberation of Hawai'i—another pivotal storyline of Japan's official propaganda—must have looked more than credible. Average Japanese readers of Miike's book had no concrete knowledge of what had actually transpired in wartime Hawai'i. Moreover, his forecast for Japan's triumph dovetailed neatly with a prewar story of local Japanese anti-racist struggles. It is not difficult to imagine that Miike's book had significant impact on the rise of anti-American sentiment among ordinary Japanese because it became "one of the best-selling books," according to the NAN's annual bulletin in early 1943.[62]

The case of a Hawai'i-born Nisei woman named Itsuko Kito is an important reminder that non-masculine perspectives were also instrumental in shaping Nisei's martial citizenship, that is, women's involvement in Japan's war effort. In her Japanese-language treatise titled the *Stories of Hawai'i's History*, Kito recounted a concise history of her native islands from ancient times to the present, as well as an introduction to local culture and customs. Despite its pretence as an objective exposition, Kito's book was full of ideological implications. As the Japanese foreign minister noted in the preface to her book, its goal was to make known to the public the importance of Hawai'i that "has close relations to our country in many ways" when Japan was trying to rid the Asia-Pacific region of Anglo-Saxon colonialism and their racial supremacy.[63] This point was apparent in the sudden change in Kito's storytelling from the semi-scholarly explanation of Hawai'i's premodern past to the emotionally charged narration of racial oppression and Japanese resistance under US rule.

When Kito went on to conclude the "stories of Hawai'i's history" in the last section of her book, another shift took place in the narrative from the third person to the first person. This sudden move made Kito's rendition of

Hawai'i wholly personal, which, as the foreign minister pointed out, further augmented its ideological value. The Nisei woman wrote: "Hawai'i is where our ancestors have cultivated the wilderness with blood and sweat. My (Issei) parents, too, have dedicated half their life to the development of Hawai'i, and I was born in that Hawai'i." Predicated on this very fact, Kito then contended that the mid-Pacific islands should not remain under the clutches of white men. "Hawai'i in the hands of Americans" must be replaced by "Hawai'i in the hands of Asiatics," since the majority of island residents were Japanese and other Asians. According to the Nisei author, "when the Philippines, Thailand, and Burma are all making a giant step forward towards the construction of the Greater East Asian Co-Prosperity Sphere under the glorious imperial guidance...we must strive to bring our Hawai'i into the hands of the Asiatics."[64] Mired in anecdotal references to Hawai'i's Japanese past, this teleological discourse, like Miike's, predicted the final triumphs of local Japanese society and imperial Japan in the languages of pan-Asianism and anti-white struggle—the basic grammar of Japan's psychological warfare. Yet, often couched in a gendered form of Japanese writing, Kito's book added a less militant flavor to Japan's war rhetoric, demonstrating the varied importance of resident Nisei's role that transcended gender lines, albeit under the fundamentally masculine war talk.

American-Born Nisei as Japan's War Heroes

The Nisei teleological narrative was not complete without a glorified account of their direct contributions to actual military operations against the Anglo-American powers as self-motivated combatants of Japan's armed forces. Whether narrated by Nisei storytellers themselves or rendered by their Japanese supporters, the tales of their military service and sacrifices were indispensable for a contrived image of the patriotic imperial subjects of American background, who allegedly placed the imperatives of their blood homeland and its anti-racist struggle above their own lives. Published in the *Nippon Times*, this report—authored undoubtedly by its Nisei staff—reiterated a standard narrative that had been prevalent in Japan since 1942. It exemplifies how the empires' print media propagandized the contrived image of the American-born war heroes within and without the Japanese archipelago:

Nisei in Imperial Forces Increase; Many Apply for Positions in Front

Were Formerly Looked Upon With Suspicion—War Gives Them Chance to Show Their True Color

Nisei, or people with Japanese parentage, whose devotion to Japan's cause was often looked on with suspicious eyes, are in reality as faithful subjects of Japan as any of the regular Japanese, it is being attested now as the War of Greater East Asia progresses on and on.

There are at present about 1,100 Niseis in the Tokyo-Yokohama area. From this number these stout and high-spirited sons of Japanese parentage are enlisting as servicemen at the war front. They are taking up arms to advance the cause of their mother country which is fighting a total war. Many who have not joined the fighting forces of Japan are volunteering for positions, as interpreters, in the Army or Navy.

The result is that the number of the Nisei is daily increasing at the front. With this increased number in the Army and Navy, reports of their meritorious services at the front are trickling in.

Soen Yamashita, managing director of the Nisei Association of Japan, was met Thursday by a Nichi Nichi reporter and sang praises of the Nisei.

"I have often heard unfavorable words about Niseis," Mr. Yamashita said. "They have often been described as Americans with only facial resemblance to Japanese. This remark, I thought, was unavoidable considering the ways in which the Niseis were brought up outside of Japan, for instance in the American way.

"The case became quite different with the Manchurian Incident focussing attention on the Niseis. Those Niseis have all turned remarkably patriotic to their parents' country, though they were scantily favored with chances to express their devotion in an open manner.

"A growing number of Nisei have flung aside their citizenship in their decision to live in Japan. They thought they would be able to find here some work to help increase Japan's prestige and power. These returning Niseis' number attained the height just before the outbreak of the current War of Greater East Asia. Almost all returned to Japan burning with the desire to fight for Japan.

"I know a young Nisei graduate of an American university, who may be cited as a model example. He is now in service of a research institute. Some time ago he called on me with his face glowing with uncontrollable joy. He said he had just passed his conscription examination as an A-1 candidate for the Imperial Army.

"I would like to join in a Japanese landing force on the American coast," he said with full intention.

"This attitude is shared among all Niseis now. When I think that I had some apprehension about the genuineness of the Nisei's loyalty to Nippon, I feel much ashamed."

Fig. 1.5 "Nisei in Imperial Forces Increase." Press celebration of Nisei's military service. *Nippon Times*, September 11, 1942. Courtesy of the *Japan Times*.

> Nisei, or people with Japanese parentage, whose devotion to Japan's cause was often looked on with suspicious eyes, are in reality as faithful subjects of Japan as any of the regular Japanese.... [T]hese stout and high-spirited sons of Japanese parentage are enlisting as servicemen at the war front...taking up arms to advance the cause of their mother country.... Many who have not joined the fighting forces of Japan are volunteering for positions, as interpreters, in the Army or Navy.[65]

Citing a leader of the Nisei Association of Nippon, an unnamed *Nippon Times* reporter went on to explain that "[a]lmost all [had] returned to Japan burning with the desire to fight for Japan" while having "flung aside their [American] citizenship." A story of an US-educated Nisei who rejoiced at his conscription into the imperial army was presented as "a model example" of "the genuineness of the Nisei's loyalty to Nippon." This young man is cited as saying: "I would like to join in a Japanese landing force on the American coast."[66] This attitude, which the *Nippon Times* described as "shared among all Nisei [in Japan]," allegedly derived from their "parentage"—the Japanese blood that had been passed onto them by their ancestors.[67]

With an emphasis on the primacy of immutable racial bonds over contingent legal belonging that these Nisei had purportedly "flung aside" so casually, Japan's propaganda machine preceded its US counterpart in exploiting the trope of Nisei war heroes. That is, although the United States systematically appropriated the theme of Japanese American fighting men in its counter-propaganda after late 1943 in order to disavow the notion of race's precedence over citizenship, imperial Japan had already propagandized Nisei's military service for the opposite purpose. It is important to place that theme in the context of inter-imperial entanglement and contestation, because doing so makes it possible to clarify both the conflicting and the overlapping terms in which the parallel stories of minority military heroism helped reify and reinforce the wartime nationalisms and mobilizations of marginalized populations by the respective regimes. By juxtaposing what evolved around the idea of the American-born patriot in imperial Japan with the comparable development that ensued in the United States, it becomes apparent that Japan's dogged belief in blood ties foreshadowed and then collided head-on with America's post-1943 valorization of Japanese Americans' citizenship and military service. Moreover, this comparative perspective allows for an analysis of the mutually reinforcing processes in the production of the heroic Nisei soldiers in the two warring empires.

The notion of US-born patriots had initially taken hold around October 1937 in Japan's national discourse. In the early months of the Sino-Japanese War, a Hawai'i-born sub-lieutenant of the imperial army was hailed as a Nisei war hero after he was killed in action during the Japanese invasion of Shanghai.[68] Once the Pacific War began, this story frequently functioned as a rhetorical ploy to illuminate the persistence of the national allegiance that American-born Japanese had supposedly held towards their ancestral land. According to news reports and official explanations, what kept American-born Japanese and their ancestral empire together was the irresistible power of blood bonds that always managed to resurrect a national/racial spirit in Nisei despite their cultural immersion in Americanism. Reprinted in the *Nippon Times* and other English-language propaganda outlets, a Dōmei News dispatch noted: "the current war has undoubtedly given the Nisei an opportunity of awakening to the glorious honor of their blood being tied firmly with that of their brothers and sisters at home, and also of realizing the sense of responsibility of rising up as a member of the Japanese race." Indeed, as the official propaganda line had it, this metamorphosis explained the making of "brave and heroic Nisei boys" who "have either sacrificed their lives for the country or are making best possible efforts toward the cause of the State."[69]

A Japanese news story about their unparalleled martial virtue and military contributions reveals how the interrelated themes of racial blood and national spirit served to illuminate the Nisei's Japaneseness in spite of their foreign birth and (former) citizenship status. Penned by NAN leadership and published in the domestic print media, this reportage began with this statement: "Even though we uttered our first cry in America, we are Japanese with the blazing Yamato spirit inside." With that spirit, it continued, "Hawai'i-born Hideo Kurokawa sacrificed his life as a Nisei officer at the outset of the China incident (in October 1937). And in this great East Asian war, many Nisei patriots have followed in the footsteps of the late Mr. Kurokawa to fight courageously in the southern front line. Now all Nisei in Japan—men and women of 50,000 strong—are determined to rise up for the sake of the homeland." The story then offered examples of a "mixed-blood" Nisei who "became fully Japanized" as an imperial soldier before his heroic death in the battlefield; three Chicago-born brothers who served on the Malay theater "with their excellent command of English and understanding of American social ethos that prove[d] to be extremely useful"; and female Nisei who were anxiously "awaiting their chance to be in the frontline as the 'angels in white gowns' (military nurses)."[70]

In keeping with the central thesis of racial reprisal, frequent news reports had Nisei imperial soldiers express their earnest wish to redeem their experience of having been racially discriminated against in the United States by taking up arms against white Americans. Cited in his March 1943 interview, one San Francisco-born conscript bitterly recalled how he had suffered oppression at the hands of racist white neighbors and classmates. The exuberant Nisei rejoiced at the idea that his tormentors must have been in deep shock after witnessing the real might of the imperial forces, pledging himself to crush American "arrogance" and their "supremacy" once and for all.[71] The overflowing desire for "swapping the school uniform" with military gear was allegedly shared by many other Nisei students in Japan for the same reason. One adolescent was said to have "filed a petition written in his own blood at five different occasions" to be able to serve in a special army detachment.[72]

Aided by the highly personal theme, theatrical descriptions of Nisei's super-patriotism also filled domestic newspapers. In the summer of 1943, for example, reports on the mass enlistment of more than seventy Nisei for the air fighter units of the imperial forces were accompanied by similar stories of personal victimization and revenge. A California-born college freshman purportedly "joined forces with his younger brother who already [had been] in the army air youth squadron" to take vengeance on a white classmate named "George." When the Nisei brothers were grammar school pupils in Pasadena, "George" made fun of the younger brother and attacked him with a knife, prompting the older Nisei to beat the assailant up in self-defense. Although the fault was clearly with the white classmate, their Issei mother had to rush over to the neighbor's house, bowed down to the white boy and his parents, and begged for their forgiveness. The Nisei brothers had never forgotten the words of their crying mother, who had lamented: "Japanese in America cannot do business if we displease (white) Americans." An old scar on his brother's arm was not only a permanent reminder of racial humiliation that he and his parents had long endured in the white men's country but also struck them as a call to arms against their personal nemeses once Japan entered the war. This Nisei was extremely eager to meet "George" again somewhere over the Pacific after his pilot training. This time he would deal his childhood foe and Japan's enemy a crushing blow.[73]

As in the case of propaganda knowledge producers like Matsumoto, Fujii, Miike, and Kito, it is possible to detect in Japan's celebration of Nisei war heroes a clear causal nexus between their lived experience under white American oppression and their overflowing patriotism towards the blood homeland. As the theme of Japanese American incarceration formed a significant part of wartime Japan's discourse against US racism, the trope of Nisei war heroes incorporated that theme, too, thereby conflating the familiar tales of prewar indignation with the ongoing saga of massive racial victimization by the enemy's hands. Thus, while celebrating their "Yamato spirit that permeated the blood," another news report on Nisei military service ascribed their decisions to enlist to the deep-seated desire to avenge their parents' ongoing incarceration across the Pacific. Embellished with mischaracterizations and exaggerations, these stories typically explained that the soldiers' families were coercively banished to "sterile deserts and deep mountains," subjected to "forced labor," and "harshly treated under the domination of the brutes."[74] Originally propagated by Issei returnees, this side story became a necessary ingredient in the making of the extremely dedicated Nisei war heroes in imperial Japan's public discourse and external propaganda. There were no better narrators of this story than resident Nisei themselves.

Between mid-September and mid-November of 1943, the public displays of Nisei's martial spirit climaxed with the send-off ceremonies of new US-born conscripts—drawn from universities and colleges—as well as Shintō memorial services for fallen Nisei patriots.[75] The NAN sponsored these highly-publicized events with the aim of giving these national heroes a proper farewell. The first mass send-off was held in mid-September before a contingent of thirty-seven Nisei college students left for air pilot training. About two months later, the second ceremony attracted more than three hundred participants to see off dozens of additional Nisei conscripts. Hundreds of NAN members and government dignitaries attended these ceremonies, where the new conscripts typically declared their desire for a victory in the two battles they were supposed to fight: "for the fatherland and the honor of Nisei students" in Japan.[76] As minoritized soldiers, they had an additional burden to bear in the practice of their blood patriotism. The special memorials that the NAN periodically held were meant to requite the double sacrifices of those heroes. At the November 12 Shintō service, for example, over four hundred people gathered to pay tribute to all such valorous Nisei who had sacrificed themselves for their ancestral land and other US-born imperial subjects through their heroic deaths.[77] Japan's valorization of blood bonds allowed Nisei youths to claim membership in Japan's racial empire, but it demanded their superfluous willingness for the shedding of that very blood for their own demise. Across the Pacific, their compatriots were about to be compelled to do in the same way, albeit not for their racial home, but for their birthland of citizenship and the so-called colorblind democracy it stood for.

In wartime Japan, where every individual was molded into a narrowly circumscribed ideal of imperial subjecthood under enormous societal pressure, it was still possible to live as American-born Nisei while being Japanese subjects. While the notion of shared blood called for hyper-identification and exaggerated conformity with the ancestral land and its policies, their identity as a sub-group of imperial subjects drew from the types of unique cultural attributes, rooted in their American background, which the militarist regime viewed as useful. In addition to their language skills and cultural insider knowledge, these attributes included their own experiences of having been racially discriminated against in the past and of being currently separated from their loved ones trapped in enemy imprisonment. Their being Nisei was no longer predicated upon the possession of legally prescribed bonds to their birth country as American citizens, since their racial ties to the ancestral land precluded the option of being anything other than the legal subject of their blood-based empire. Such a complex mixture of race, citizenship, and culture formed the organizing rubric that produced self-reflexive Nisei super-patriots and cultural brokers in wartime Japan.

Brokering a Race War: Japanese Americans in the Pacific War and the Occupation of Japan. Eiichiro Azuma, Oxford University Press. © Eiichiro Azuma 2026. DOI: 10.1093/9780197781432.003.0002

2

America Speaks Back through Nisei Soldiers

On January 30, 1943, the *New York Times* published a commentary titled "Japanese-American 'Yanks.'" Like other US print media and American society in general, this newspaper had enthusiastically supported not only the incarceration of 120,000 West Coast Japanese Americans but also the race-based exclusion of native-born Nisei from the right of serving in the US armed forces. That was a privilege and responsibility embedded in birthright citizenship that had been extended to all male citizens regardless of race or ancestry, including African Americans, under the 1940 Selective Training and Service Act. Only one year after its support for mass incarceration, the *Times* suddenly called for these otherized Nisei to be legitimized as US soldiers. The nation's premier daily newspaper even predicted that "Japanese-American Yanks" would "ameliorate their rather lonesome lot (racially segregated status) in this country" as well as "help to interpret America to a chastened and sobered Nippon" after its defeat.[1] Put another way, Japanese American citizens in the US armed forces were expected to be a driving force for America's fight against domestic racism, on the one hand, and serve as a cultural broker to effect a positive change in the enemy that shared the same racial strains, on the other. In this way, Nisei soldiers suddenly emerged in US public discourse as a key trope for an anti-racist America and a democratized Japan. That trope was intended to facilitate both the remaking of US domestic society and then of the defeated enemy, in accordance with America's war aim to defend and spread the universal (colorblind) ideals of liberty and democracy.[2] The Nisei's intermediary positions and roles served to blur the boundaries of domestic and foreign in wartime US race politics and beyond.

Under these anti-racist campaigns, Japanese American citizens were prompted to serve in similar capacities as their counterparts in imperial Japan—as propaganda symbols and knowledge producers. Whereas Japan utilized US-born individuals of Japanese ancestry based on its belief in the immutability of blood ties from the beginning, the United States struggled to devise a consistent rationale and method by which to recruit Nisei for its psychological warfare under the shadow of the race-based mass incarceration. The principal rhetoric that eventually enabled and sustained the incorporation of selected Nisei into its propaganda machine and military apparatus was predicated on the de-racialized notion of birthright citizenship, which subverted the contrary rhetoric of total exclusion. The anti-racist idea of equal birthright citizenship rendered even those with enemy heritage acceptable insofar as they were loyal to what colorblind America supposedly stood for. Yet, this idea was hard to sell to the domestic populace. Most Americans still held onto the dogged belief in the indivisibility of race and loyalty as far as the war in the Asia-Pacific was concerned. Like its Japanese counterpart, the US psychological warfare needed to put as much, if not more, emphasis on the domestic audience when it dispatched contrived anti-racist messages.

Indeed, as the *New York Times* commentary revealed its flipflopping, this new rhetoric derived from an abrupt policy change on the part of the US government. In January 1943, the War Department opted to upgrade the enlistment status of Japanese American citizens from "enemy alien" to "eligible for service." A part of the broader US response to Japan's war propaganda reliant on the story of mass incarceration, this change had a profound impact on Japanese Americans in particular, and wartime US race relations in general, because it overturned the relative importance of race and citizenship in the government definitions of American nationalism and identity. It did so in an artificial top-down manner by striking a wedge into the hitherto monolithic public view of the Japanese as an enemy race. Deemed "good Japanese," Nisei citizen "Yanks" were offered a chance to redeem themselves as Americans by distinguishing themselves from "enemy (bad) Japanese" by practicing and demonstrating their uncompromised loyalty. Just as their compatriots had in Japan, these US Nisei started to engage in their version of militarized ethnic formation following their induction in the spring of 1943.

The elevation of citizenship over race in official US rhetoric took hold in accordance with a series of dramatic changes in the history of the Japanese American incarceration between December 1942 and March 1943. Thereafter, America's reliance on loyal Nisei in its racial propaganda unfolded in the context of counter-assaults against Japan's renditions of US white supremacy. Revolving particularly around the themes of mass detentions and patriotic contributions, this war of words and images was fought in the Asia-Pacific largely through the cultural labor of second-generation Japanese Americans. The crux of the matter was this: whether Nisei's national belonging should be articulated and practiced in terms of their allegiance to racial ancestry or legal citizenship.

Building on the preceding discussion of Japan's use of Nisei propagandists and military heroes, Chapter 2 traces the parallel historical process in which a colorblind notion of Japanese American citizenship took shape in the context of Washington's reactive policy formulations during the first year and a half of the Pacific War. Paving the way to the enlistment of loyal Nisei men as combat soldiers and military propagandists, the course of events between late 1942 and early 1943 provided a pivotal context for Washington's decision to reverse its stance as well as Nisei's hyper-identification with a new definition of Americanism that gave birth to a previously oxymoronic idea like "Japanese-American Yanks." The chapter then narrates Nisei's participation and crucial roles in US anti-Japanese leaflet campaigns—examples that led the white military brass to entertain an idea of utilizing Japanese Americans as co-racial brokers of democratic rehabilitation among defeated enemies.

Japanese American Incarceration and the Making of Wartime US Anti-racism

During the first year of the Pacific War, the architects and operators of US propaganda were defensive vis-à-vis the question of national racism. Above all, they regarded the ongoing program of Japanese incarceration to be a public relations nightmare because it utterly contradicted the image they wished to present of the wartime United States: America as an anti-racist liberator fighting against the Axis Powers. Since early 1942, Tokyo's propaganda machine had been busy crafting its narratives of American atrocity and hypocrisy by illuminating the nexus between longstanding anti-Asian racism and wartime oppression often described by Nisei and Issei victims. US propaganda chiefs thus felt that the first problem to tackle was the government policy of forced Japanese removal from the West Coast. For example, on October 2, 1942, Elmer Davis, the head of the Office of War Information (OWI), voiced his opposition to the treatment of incarcerated Nisei citizens as enemies on racial grounds. "Japanese propaganda to the

Philippines, Burma, and elsewhere insists that this is a race war," Davis argued in his letter to President Roosevelt. According to the OWI director, the United States would be able to wage effective counter-propaganda "only if our deeds permit us to tell the truth."[3] To the chagrin of Davis and other propaganda planners, it took several more months before such counter-propaganda was actually possible, and the subject of Japanese Americans remained absent in America's propaganda—with the exception of an OWI film that justified the military-necessity rationale for Japanese "relocation" in November 1942.

US propagandists did not sit idly by in the face of Japan's representational attacks, however. By May 1942, the OWI and the Military Intelligence Service (MIS) of the War Department (US Army) had already shared an anti-racist propaganda blueprint created by Colonel Oscar N. Solbert, chief of the army's Psychological Warfare Branch. Entitled the "Japan Plan," it urged the United States to "make conspicuous use of the native-born American citizens of Japanese race" for the purpose of "demonstrat[ing] that the Japanese are disunited"—counterevidence to "the myth of Japanese solidarity" and "the race war against White supremacy."[4] Despite the rise of racial hysteria, these architects of US psychological warfare fully recognized the potential value of Japanese Americans in their counter-propaganda. Given the widespread popular support for the forced removal and imprisonment of Japanese Americans, and the "blood-will-tell" racism that supported it, they felt it necessary to engage in "propaganda directed toward people in this country [the United States] to lessen the strong racial prejudice."[5] Conducted mainly by the OWI and the War Relocation Authority (WRA), such domestic publicity campaigns were the prerequisite for the incorporation of the Japanese American theme into the US overseas counter-propaganda charged by the OWI and Office of Strategic Services (OSS) with the logistical assistance of the MIS. Ironically, or perhaps logically, this early stage of US race propaganda surrounding Japanese Americans followed a remarkably similar trajectory to how wartime Japan's anti-American campaigns had to focus on the domestic populace, as Takizo Frank Matsumoto and Itsuko Kito did through their Japanese-language lectures and publications.

In order to convince the American public to give up its embrace of biological racist thinking, the OWI and WRA first attempted to portray the Japanese "relocation" not as a summary action against an enemy race but as an expression of America's tolerance and benevolence while maintaining the principal rationale for military necessity. That is, merciful Uncle Sam intended (1) to protect defenseless enemy aliens and their young children from threats of misguided violence and (2) to provide even this unpopular minority with not only shelter and food but also the opportunities to build a "pioneer community" in a wilderness. Produced in November 1942, an OWI film called the "Japanese Relocation" suggests that Japanese Americans moved from the "potential combat zone" of the West Coast to "points in the American Interior" almost of their own volition. According to the narrator Milton S. Eisenhower, OWI associate director who was the former WRA director, Japanese Americans "cooperated wholeheartedly" in the process of the "mass migration," and "many loyal among them felt this was the sacrifice they could make in behalf of America's war effort." The authorities, too, "determined to do the job as democracy should, with real consideration for the people involved." At both "assembly centers" and "relocation centers," the US Army and WRA took good care of the "evacuees" to make their "life nearly as normal as possible," with "plenty of healthful nourishing food for all." Although time was not yet ripe for taking these contrived characterizations outside of the United States, Eisenhower concluded his portrayal of Japanese incarceration in direct opposition to Japan's ongoing propaganda lines: "We are setting the standard for the rest of the world in the treatment of the people who may have loyalty to the enemy nation. We are protecting ourselves without violating the principle of Christian decency."[6] Yet, the reference to the thorny problem of Nisei's citizenship rights, which the policy of the mass imprisonment violated indiscriminately without due process, was still nowhere to be found because the domestic political reality did not allow discussions of it yet. Not until June 1943 did the US Supreme Court finally tackle the constitutionality of some of the military orders in the Yasui and Hirabayashi cases.[7]

In addition to presenting most Nisei internees as loyal and self-sacrificing, albeit without invoking the question of their citizenship rights, the OWI endeavored to suppress contrary discourses and representations in the domestic sphere. In July 1942, when Twentieth-Century Fox released the incendiary and racially charged *Little Tokyo USA*, the agency condemned the film as an "invitation to the Witch Hunt." In order to homogenize a public understanding that benefited its psychological warfare agenda, the OWI hastily instituted a censorship program against anti-Nisei bigotry in the Hollywood movie industry.[8] Despite, or perhaps because of these proactive official interventions to "lessen the strong racial prejudice," many ordinary Americans, especially those on the West Coast, were growing incensed by the "cuddling of Japs" by the US government. Their racist frustrations climaxed when a series of "disturbances" transpired in WRA incarceration camps.[9] The belief that "Japs are Japs" was firmly rooted in the public mind, and cursory rhetoric or censorship did not subvert it. Some fundamental change had to take place with regards to the government policy toward Nisei internees. A catalyst for that change came unexpectedly in late 1942.

From the standpoint of US counter-propaganda, the so-called Manzanar riot of December 5–6 looked like a blessing in disguise. The initial incident stemmed from longstanding conflicts among Japanese internees, especially between Nisei members of the pro-government Japanese American Citizens League (JACL) and disgruntled internees, including many "Kibei," a subgroup of Nisei who had spent often significant periods of their childhoods in Japan. This intra-ethnic conflict in the Manzanar incarceration camp resulted in the arrest of some people of the latter group who allegedly assaulted a JACL leader. In response, a few thousand internees, including many ordinary Issei and Nisei, came out of their barracks to voice their discontent about the incarceration while demanding the release of the arrested by the camp administration.[10] On the second night of the protest, several hundred gathered around, but the camp administration brought in the military police, which used tear gas to create mayhem and then fired into the crowd, killing two Nisei youths.

In the eyes of US propagandists, the ramifications of this incident were extremely troublesome. Understandably, the story of the riot blew up in the American domestic press and it was reported using stereotypical narratives of Japanese Americans as sinister and untrustworthy characters. To the dismay of OWI and WRA officials in Washington, DC, US domestic newspapers portrayed Issei and Nisei protestors as enemy subversives, whom the army brass had deemed a national security risk to be removed from normal society. Even in their incarceration, as the fearmongering press reported, these Japanese remained so loyal to their emperor that they dared to commemorate the first anniversary of Japan's surprise attack in the form of a mass uprising. Both the *Los Angeles Times* and *New York Times* cited the words of the white camp director, declaring: "This ["mob riot"] started to be a celebration of Pearl Harbor by the pro-Axis group of Japanese." The California newspaper succinctly summed up the incident as yet another case of enemy attack with a sensational title: "Troops Called to End Riots at Manzanar: Violence Flares When Pro-Axis Japs Celebrate Bombing of Pearl

Harbor."[11] Even though some reports of "loyal" Nisei's counter acts appeared, the incident seemed detrimental to what US propagandists had come to deem a new mandate of anti-racist publicity efforts.[12]

In addition to its adverse impact on domestic racial discourse, the government brass had another cause for concern. The Manzanar situation could give Tokyo more ammunition for its anti-US racial propaganda, given that it involved the use of deadly force by white soldiers against unarmed Japanese civilians in confinement. This turn of events seemed to substantiate the alleged US "determination to arrest all suspicious Japanese and execute them by shooting," as Japan's Hawai'i-born Nisei propagandist predicted in his 1942 book.[13] On a global stage, however, this possibility did not materialize. For some unknown reason, Japan's propaganda machine remained virtually silent about the Manzanar incident until almost a year later. By November 1943, when the *Nippon Times* finally broke the story for an overseas audience, the subject had already lost much of its propaganda value.[14] In the months following the Manzanar incident, the official fear was nonetheless strong enough to hasten US administrative action to end the indiscriminate confinement of Japanese American citizens.[15]

Equally important, the incident also made it possible for US propagandists to give a positive spin to mass incarceration, which fed a contrived notion of the Nisei as a symbol of America's anti-racism and universal democracy. WRA officials interpreted the "riot" as instigated by a small but influential group of "pro-Japan" agitators—especially Japan-educated Kibei and some Issei—in the Manzanar camp. As officials saw it, these "most disillusioned and maladjusted members of the whole evacuee population" had been fighting with "the most ardent advocates of cooperation with the American Government," with "the bulk of the residents somewhere in the middle" who were considered neutral or at least passively loyal to the United States.[16] These people were nonetheless placed under the constant influence of strong-arm disloyal internees who allegedly resorted to intimidation and even physical violence against those who did not see things their way.

It was a common perception that the situation in Manzanar was not unique. Should disloyal elements be left untouched in other camps, it was believed, they would sooner or later corrupt the entire camp population, therefore ushering in the outbreak of more riots elsewhere. Based on this line of thinking, for which JACL Nisei leaders gave their unqualified affirmation, the WRA was compelled to separate the "disillusioned and maladjusted" elements from the loyal internees once and for all. Not only would the segregation free the good Japanese from the influence of the bad, but it would also make loyal internees eligible for "leave clearance" from confinement.[17] This procedure would require a camp-wide test of internees' national allegiance, dubbed "loyalty registration," which was carried out in the early months of 1943 under the joint effort of the WRA and the War Department. The former was primarily interested in starting the process of phasing out the race-based mass incarceration through the segregation of the disloyal and the release of the loyal. The military, on the other hand, intended to use the registration as a means to enlist loyal Nisei men in the US armed forces for propaganda purposes, as envisioned by Assistant Secretary of War John J. McCloy and Colonel Oscar N. Solbert.[18]

The new course of government actions benefited the cause of US psychological warfare in two ways. First, the program of controlled Japanese release would help substantiate the official reasoning of the mass removal as military exigency impelled by national security concerns, thereby allowing the US authorities to disavow the notion they had implemented a racist policy. It also enabled the federal government to effectively address the pending constitutional challenges against the legality of its policy to imprison US citizens without due process. Since 1942, the US Army had emphasized the need to round up all the West Coast Japanese as a preventive measure, because there was supposedly no ready means to identify disloyal elements among Issei and Nisei in a timely manner when additional Japanese attacks looked imminent after the destruction of Pearl Harbor.[19] Not only would the loyalty registration legitimize the government claim that the mass imprisonment was not racially motivated but done out of genuine military necessity, but it would also promote the impression that the United States cared about the individual liberties of Nisei citizens guaranteed by the US Constitution as long as they were proven loyal to it. The WRA and other civilian government authorities were particularly concerned about this matter.

Second, the loyalty test would pave the way for the large-scale enlistment of certifiably loyal Nisei for the purpose of anti-racist US propaganda and MIS-related work as well as combat duty, resulting in the formation of the all-Japanese 442nd Regimental Combat Team and the training of Nisei military linguists. The War Department had long considered the latter an actual military necessity from a strategic standpoint, given that war planners and propagandists had become troubled by the dearth of American citizens able to understand the language, cultural mores, and mindset of the "inscrutable" Japanese enemy.[20] Because of its racially exclusive enlistment policy against and lack of access to Nisei under the army-controlled evacuation program, the US Navy and Marine Corps had not entertained the idea of recruiting Japanese American citizens for the position of military linguists. Instead, the navy utilized a select group of Issei and Nisei instructors—many hired from outside the West Coast—to offer white naval linguists (about 1,200) intensive training at a naval language school at Boulder, Colorado, between 1942 and 1945.[21] The US Army, on the other hand, had under its control a large pool of Nisei citizens who could serve as semi-native language specialists should their loyalty be verified. Encompassing the overlapping military goals of propaganda and intelligence, the loyalty registration began inside the ten Japanese incarceration camps between February and March 1942.

These historical developments entailed another government action that would upend the official meaning of Americanism. This ideological project sought to effect a top-down change in national identity in the form of the proclamation by President Roosevelt that conveniently de-racialized the definition of national belonging in the context of the war. In order to justify the controversial policy of reinstituting the draft eligibility of despised Nisei, albeit without even naming them in his proclamation, the President formally declared in early February of 1943:

> No loyal citizen of the United States should be denied the democratic right to exercise the responsibilities of his citizenship, regardless of his ancestry. The principle on which this country was founded and by which it has always been governed is that Americanism is a matter of the mind and heart; Americanism is not, and never was, a matter of race or ancestry.[22]

Heavily edited by OWI chief Elmer Davis, this radical redefinition of Americanism signaled the rise of wartime American nationalism. It rejected the tradition of racial exclusion while embracing anti-racism as the national creed and character of the American republic.[23] Under OWI press censorship, the *New York Times* already started to propagate this new motto, interlacing it with the ongoing story of the incarceration saga. According to the newspaper, the mass incarceration had to happen, because not only did Nisei "still look Japanese" but the War Department had also not been able to "tell whether or not they still thought Japanese" until "individual inquiry" (the loyalty test) was conducted. In the January 30, 1943, issue, the *Times*

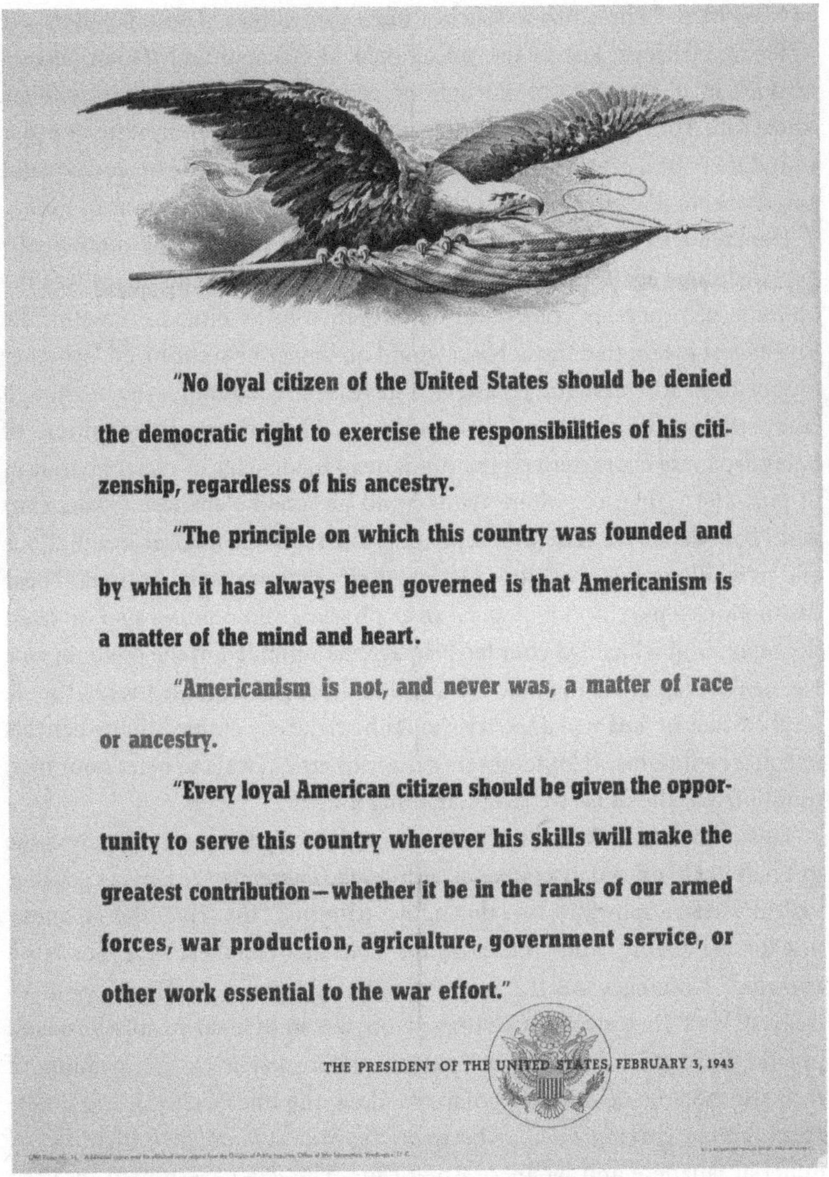

Fig. 2.1 Statement of Americanism by President Franklin D. Roosevelt, February 3, 1943. United States Government.

editorialized: "The episode touches one's sympathies. These Japanese are American citizens, just as the young men of German and Italian descent who are loyal members of our fighting services. Their education has been American. They would not be at home in Japan, nor even in time of peace would there be a place for them there."[24] Thus, they must be treated equally, and those eligible for enlistment should become "Japanese-American Yanks."

Deploying this new line of justification, the US government unabashedly declared once again that the incarceration of Japanese Americans was the epitome of America's colorblind benevolence to its citizens. Passing the loyalty test meant that those Nisei would no longer be scrutinized "whether or not they still thought Japanese"—at least procedurally—even though "they still look[ed] Japanese" by appearance. These divergent definitions of being Japanese characterized the fundamental language of racial liberalism of post-1943 America, where there could be "good" Japanese (American) and "bad" Japanese (enemy) depending on their ideological orientations and psychological dispositions, despite their common racial features. These distinctions—psychic/ideological over physical/biological—also dictated the manner in which US counter-propaganda unfolded in the ongoing race war against Japan. As the new OWI/WRA propaganda guidelines outlined, loyal citizens of Japanese ancestry should be rightfully entitled to the benefits of equal civil rights. "Not to observe these liberties [wa]s to betray our own tradition and the cause we [we]re fighting for."[25]

Thus, the monolithic characterizations of the Japanese race largely came to a halt in US official discourse in early 1943. Thereafter, America's psychological warfare split into two distinctive patterns: "the 'Hate the Japanese' line for the enemy" and "the 'Love the Relocated Japanese' line" for Nisei citizens.[26] No longer was the meaning of being Japanese static or essentialized, at least rhetorically. Contingent on the individual expressions and practices of national allegiance (passing the loyalty test), the meaning of race also became definitively polarized along the line of citizenship difference, thereby driving a wedge between the hitherto conflated identities of imperial Japanese and Japanese Americans. This US government-induced shift paralleled what had taken place in Japan: militarized ethnic formation of resident Nisei as patriotic foreign-born imperial subjects. Thereafter, the transpacific propaganda war formed a battleground for the contested renditions of race and citizenship over the symbolisms of Nisei's military actions.

In order to spearhead the new anti-racist mandate relative to state-certified loyal Nisei, the US propaganda agencies took the lead in the fair treatment of their own Japanese members and collaborators and engaged in the education of white staff workers who, like most other Americans, had a hard time casting aside old racist attitudes and suddenly having to embrace those of enemy heritage. Persuading the racist public to accept the top-down redefinition of Americanism required white staffers of the propaganda machine to come on board before everyone else—a task that proved to be daunting due to the tenacity of deep-rooted exclusionist sentiments. As late as February 1945, OWI regional officials and staff workers in the China-Burma-India (CBI) theater were still compelled to hold an emergency general meeting for the purpose of stamping out race-based discrimination against and resultant internal friction with Nisei members. One high-ranking official admonished his subordinates, "point[ing] out that careful behavior on the part of OWI personnel was essential" and "remind[ing] the group that now and henceforth all OWI men must work together as a team without prejudices regarding race or creed."[27] Given the long tradition of blood-will-tell racism, such changes did not come easily even within the propaganda agencies that hoisted a new flag of colorblind democracy.

As the stigma of biological racism was being strategically purged from the Japanese incarceration program after the early months of 1943, Japan's treatment of the internment theme became more retrogressive, redundant, and hence less effective in the context of the global propaganda war. Issei returnees and resident Nisei offered eyewitness accounts of the race-based mass incarceration, but their narratives tended to concentrate on the pre-1943 phase of the saga.[28] Indeed, when Japan's propaganda outlets did discuss the nexus of American racism and the mass incarceration in a post-Manzanar context, they generally dwelled on the harsh treatment of disloyal internees, who were segregated in the Tule Lake camp after the loyalty registration.[29] Little was said about loyal Nisei and Issei in and out of the other WRA camps. Japan's condemnations of the US violation of Nisei's citizenship rights also became less and less frequent. According to an US army internal memorandum of August 1944, "the Japanese Imperial Government had at no time made any official protest against the use of Japanese-Americans in the military service nor had there been any propaganda by radio or otherwise concerning these Niseis in the Army."[30]

From the summer of 1943 on, the US propaganda machine took the offensive against Japan's exploitation of the Japanese American theme. Instead of simply thrusting the opposite interpretations of the mass incarceration in a reactive manner, this phase of American counter-propaganda attempted to de-racialize the theme entirely and detached the discussion of America's war aims from specific discursive parameters set by Japan's racial propaganda. The basic storylines, and the chief protagonists in them, were predicated on shoring up the US claims for championing colorblind democracy and universal equality through the war against the Axis Powers. Dubbed the "Japan plan," a 1942 blueprint for US psychological warfare explicitly spelled out how such a narrative should be crafted around the subject of Japanese Americans' individual actions, not their biological/group attributes, by the "telling of [their] accomplishments." This blueprint set the basic discourse used by OWI and MIS in the ensuing years: "publicity could be given to valuable work being done by Americans of Japanese ancestry," and "this policy... might be followed throughout the implementation of" all other propaganda objectives against Japan.[31] Indeed, the post-1943 development of American propaganda specifically entailed the use of the Nisei as a major ideological trope, cranking out slanted representations of "good Japanese" who supposedly embodied (new) Americanism.

The instrumentalist anti-racism that formed the core of liberal white thinking of post-1943 America foreshadowed the precarious position of Nisei for the rest of the war years and beyond. Ironically, America's disavowal of indiscriminate biological racism offered the US authorities a new race-based, if not racist, approach to deal with not only Japanese in the United States but also foreign Japanese after the conclusion of the military phase of the war. Good enemy Japanese could be identified and utilized, as good Nisei citizens were, for the goal of spreading America's power and its brand of democracy. Or, as the *New York Times* suggested, "Japanese-American Yanks" could best teach defeated Japanese what America stood for because of their shared lineage. Insofar as anti-racist perspectives presumptuously associated Nisei with Japanese nationals, it still functioned as a form of essentialist thinking and practice that denoted racial sameness among them while also suggesting racial inferiority to white Americans. Hence, race still mattered in the acceptance of loyal Nisei citizens into white-dominated America—and later that of democratized Japan into the US-controlled Asia-Pacific—albeit in a more subtle and insidious manner. The state-backed rise of this liberal racism in post-1943 America foregrounded the prevalence of assimilationism that demanded cultural and ideological conformity as a precondition for acceptance, whether as minoritized members of the postwar US national community or as a junior US ally in Cold War East Asia.[32]

Nisei's Complicity with New Americanism and Colorblind US Militarism

After February 1943, the loyalty registration led to the enlistment of certifiably loyal Nisei men. Japanese American citizens, who supposedly possessed the right "mind and heart" to desire to fight for the defense of the lofty universal ideals instead of their blood emperor, offered the perfect material for the US propaganda machine to develop a lead character in the twin tales of America's disavowal of biological racism and its embrace of colorblind democracy. As a major trope for a new non-racist America, the all-Nisei 442nd Regimental Combat Team (RCT) was activated while the WRA and the War Department busied themselves screening Japanese Americans for release from confinement, military service, or segregation, based on their individual responses to the loyalty questionnaire. Starting in June 1944, the segregated army unit was deployed to the European theater; the 100th Infantry Battalion, consisting of Nisei men from Hawai'i, had been in combat since September 1943 before being attached to the 442nd RCT.[33]

This new phase of US counter-propaganda entailed not only Nisei soldiers as a nationalist ideological symbol but also Japanese American leaders as knowledge producers. Their pro-US behavior and public utterance tends to obfuscate their complex motivation and constant psychological struggle, as well as what it meant to be Nisei in the inter-imperial context where the clashing statist ideas of being Japanese and being American significantly influenced every facet of their lives. Similar historical conditions existed in the wartime worlds of Japanese Americans on both sides of the Pacific despite being polarized into two competing ideological positions. Just as Japan had a ready-made reservoir of resident Nisei clothed in nationalist garb, the United States had its own pool of ethnic Americans who volunteered to serve as self-styled super-patriots. Like Takizo Frank Matsumoto and John Tatsuki Fujii in Japan, loyal US Nisei leaders outside the incarceration camps enthusiastically offered their services for America's propaganda machine. Whereas Matsumoto was the acting president of the Nisei Association of Nippon (NAN), his counterpart, Mike Masaru Masaoka, was the national secretary of the Japanese American Citizens League (JACL). Comparing the trajectories of Masaoka and his JACL allies with their nemeses on the other side of the Pacific allows for a fuller and more nuanced understanding of the loyal Nisei's response beyond their ostensible conformity to the state-sanctioned definition of colorblind Americanism.

Calling himself "Moses," Masaoka was the self-proclaimed savior of Japanese America, who stood at the forefront of the JACL's endeavors for "constructive cooperation" with the US government and military through the entire incarceration saga and beyond. Born in Fresno but raised in Salt Lake City under Mormon influence, Masaoka was not a typical Nisei who grew up in an ethnic enclave of a Pacific Coast state, nor did he have to go to a WRA camp. The JACL leader was well known as an outstanding orator and was a member of the debate team at University of Utah. On the eve of the Pacific War, Masaoka assumed the role of chief spokesperson for the Nisei organization. In May 1941, on behalf of the JACL, Masaoka authored the "Japanese American Creed," which states in part:

> I am proud that I am an American citizen of Japanese ancestry, for my very background makes me appreciate more fully the wonderful advantages of this Nation.... She has permitted me to... worship, think, speak, and act as I please—as a free man equal to every other man.... I am firm in my belief that American sportsmanship and attitude of fair play will judge citizenship and patriotism on the basis of action and achievement, and not on the basis of physical characteristics.... I pledge myself to... defend her against all enemies, foreign or domestic; to actively assume my duties and obligations as a citizen, cheerfully and without any reservations whatsoever.[34]

This creed anticipated the wartime anti-racism of American government officials, encapsulated in FDR's February 1943 statement, which turned a blind eye to the long history of institutionalized racism and instead placed upon each Nisei's shoulders the responsibility of "proving myself to be worthy of equal treatment and consideration" as a US citizen. It also meant that Masaoka's assimilationist rhetoric, which became the official stance of the JACL during the war, created a perfect synergy with the objectives of the US propaganda machine after 1943. For his part, Masaoka volunteered as the first Japanese American to serve as soon as their military status was reinstituted. In response, the US Army made him the unit publicist for the 442nd RCT—a deliberate move that enabled him to produce glorified accounts of Nisei GI's patriotic sacrifices for public consumption. A news dispatch from the war front, published in the virulently anti-Nisei *Los Angeles Times*, described the segregated Japanese infantry as "one of the most decorated units of its size in American military history."[35] Another dispatch reported the Nisei's heroic rescue of the Texas "lost battalion" behind enemy lines, celebrating how the rescued white soldiers welcomed Nisei comrades in arms as "honorary Texans."[36] Whereas NAN's Matsumoto took the lead in "fighting enemy propaganda" in Japan through his exposé on villainous US racism against Japanese Americans, JACL's Masaoka cranked out stories of Nisei's dedications to the US war effort and the nation's anti-racist embrace of them as American patriots par excellence.

These Nisei's parallel roles as producers of war propaganda knowledge is even more salient when JACL leader Bill Kumpei Hosokawa is compared to John Tatsuki Fujii of Japan's Dōmei News. Between 1939 and 1940, Seattle-born Hosokawa worked with Fujii at an English-language newspaper called the *Singapore Herald*, which was clandestinely financed by Japan's foreign ministry. Fujii took over the editorship of this propaganda paper when its previous editor Hosokawa moved to Shanghai. In the Chinese city, Hosokawa joined forces with another Nisei journalist named Kazumaro Buddy Uno.[37] Unlike Fujii and Uno, Hosokawa still held US citizenship, and having sent his pregnant Nisei wife back home, he managed to return home to Seattle just a month and a half before the attack on Pearl Harbor. Handpicked by the WRA as founding editor of the *Heart Mountain Sentinel*, one of the camp newspapers, Hosokawa then propagated the JACL's policy of constructive cooperation with the US authorities, which included following government exclusion orders, accepting its definition of loyalty, and contributing to America's war effort, including military service out of the incarceration camps. Hosokawa's demonization of Nisei draft resisters at Heart Mountain is well documented as an infamous example of JACL's overzealous complicity with the government's policy of inclusionary racism against Japanese Americans under the guise of colorblind Americanism.[38]

Even though Hosokawa, and Fujii and Uno, ended up seemingly opposite paths, these leading voices of Nisei patriotism on the two sides of the war-torn Pacific shared much in common. For these and other educated Nisei, Japan had been where they could pursue their professional careers as journalists and writers beyond the confines of the parochial ethnic press, since American racism made it impossible for them to find employment in the mainstream print media or academia.[39] Before the war, seeking employment and residence in the United States or Japan often had little to do with their loyalty to these countries, for their sense of connection to their birth country or ancestral land was always complex, ambivalent, and vacillating. What mattered most was which country seemed to offer better opportunities for their personal lives and careers rather than their firm ideological commitment to either regime. Indeed, Hosokawa's writings in Japan-sponsored press in Singapore and Shanghai were not significantly different from the pro-Japan pronouncements of Fujii and Uno, despite his obsessive iterations of Americanism after his return.[40]

What distinguished the former from the latter was that, whereas Hosokawa began to anticipate an irreversible rupture in US-Japan relations as early as 1940 and managed to take the last transpacific steamship back to the United States, his former colleague Fujii had made no such preparation. Yet, Fujii confided he continued to feel more "American" than "Japanese," thus continuing to enjoy socializing with white American expats at a Singapore bar even on the night before Japan's attack on Pearl Harbor.[41] Uno's case seems even more like happenstance. He was led to believe that he had inadvertently lost his American citizenship when the Japanese army unexpectedly conscripted him. Despite the army's decision to discharge Uno one day later to better utilize him as a military publicist, the US Nationality Act of 1940 deemed foreign military service as a cause of disfranchisement. This unfortunate bureaucratic mix-up by the Japanese army, as historian Yuji Ichioka notes, compelled Uno to "consider himself a Japanese citizen and to shift his loyalty more in favor of Japan" after 1940.[42] Whatever they might have thought about their relationship to Japan and the United States, it became mandatory for them to declare undivided national allegiance after the fateful day of December 7/8, 1941. Depending on where they were situated at that juncture, the clear-cut loyalty they were subsequently compelled to profess bound them to a specific function: serving as a cog in the propaganda machine of imperial Japan or the United States.

Still, many Nisei propagandists and knowledge producers acted on their own volition to take part in the psychological warfare of their country of residence. Here, the related concepts of overcompensation and hyperidentification best explain the overall mechanism of these Nisei's self-propelled complicity and public display of (super)-patriotism. Theorizing about the exceptional military heroism of Nisei soldiers in the European theater, historian Takashi Fujitani argues: "overcompensation or hyperidentification is one reasonable response to the contradictory ways in which national subjects are interpellated as both equal and as less than equal. This is the mechanism that drove many Japanese Americans toward military heroism and death."[43] Whereas Fujitani speaks specifically of domestic US race relations, his theoretical insight is easily applicable to the behavior of Nisei in the transpacific propaganda war, especially their respective quest for acceptance and legitimacy as the minoritized/otherized subject of each warring state.

Just as Matsumoto had for the case of the NAN and the Nisei in Japan, Masaoka flipped the negative meaning of being Japanese American in the United States into something beneficial and exceptional through hyper-identification with the anti-racist war aims of the United States. In post-1943 America, combined with an act of state coercion, like military draft, this self-induced complicity—or constructive cooperation—not only foregrounded the well-documented tale of the 442nd RCT in the European theater but also perfectly harmonized with the official blueprints of the OWI and US Army's Psychological Warfare Branch in the Pacific theater.[44] There, many Nisei enlistees and civilian recruits were involved in anti-Japan leaflet propaganda, which exemplifies another manifestation of their hyper-identification and complicity with US anti-racist militarism.

Nisei in US Military Intelligence Service and Its Leaflet Propaganda

In the Asia-Pacific, Japanese Americans played a crucial role in the Military Intelligence Service (MIS), a section of War Department G-2. In addition to their roles as interpreters, translators, and interrogators, they were integral to the extensive leaflet propaganda program the US military waged to undermine Japanese morale and induce early surrender. Before the summer of 1945, the MIS encompassed many Japanese American linguists, who worked as cultural brokers and knowledge producers in the background of the US propaganda war. These Nisei non-combat soldiers, amounting to over six thousand by June 1946, underwent intensive Japanese-language training first at the Presidio in San Francisco and then at Camp Savage (later Ft. Snelling) in Minnesota before engaging in collecting, analyzing, and disseminating intelligence on the battlefront. Hundreds of these Japanese American linguists were also loaned to the OWI Overseas Branch (OWI-OB) and the OSS Morale Operations Branch (OSS-MOB), even though the latter agencies also recruited Nisei civilians and selected Issei as their own language experts.[45] Unlike their counterparts in the 442nd RCT, the activities of Nisei MIS members and civilian linguists were highly classified, but their role as cultural brokers vis-à-vis the Japanese enemy anticipated what would be subsequently expected of them during the US military occupation:

interpreting the inscrutable mind of defeated Japanese (or prisoners of war) so that white Americans could "use 'psychology' to augment their guns and regulations in influencing Japanese behavior," as an internal policy directive declared as early as 1943 for the management of post-defeat Japan.[46]

A large contingent of wartime MIS linguists were former residents of Japan who had often had years of Japanese schooling experience. Yet, once they returned to the United States prior to December 1941, many of these Nisei were identified as "Kibei"—deemed the most dangerous subset of Japanese Americans after Japan's attack on Pearl Harbor.[47] Because the United States hopelessly lacked white citizens—considered trustworthy—who had a grasp of this enemy language and psychology, the US Army had decided to utilize a selected group of these Japanized Nisei as early as June 1941 for MIS work in preparation for the coming war against Japan despite the prevailing mistrust of the Japan-educated Kibei.[48] Just as segments of the army brass demonstrated pragmatic thinking relative to the advantage of Nisei military service for psychological warfare even during the mass removal of West Coast Japanese Americans, the same instrumentalist perspective rationalized the recruitment of bilingual Nisei from the supposedly most dangerous elements of Japanese America.[49]

For the same reason, one of the MIS's first Japanese-language instructors, Burbank-born John Fujio Aiso, was a highly educated Nisei lawyer, who had studied and worked in the Japanese empire before the Pacific War. Although he is celebrated as a quintessential Nisei patriot inducted into the Military Intelligence Corps Hall of Fame in 1991, Aiso's prewar experience in Japan was not so different from those of Tatsuki John Fujii and Buddy Kazumaro Uno, who have been labelled co-ethnic traitors. Studying Japanese law at a Japanese university after pursuing his degrees at Brown University and Harvard Law School, Aiso had worked for the British American Tobacco Company in Japanese-controlled Manchukuo from 1937 through 1940 before coming back to the United States for a medical, not political, reason. There, Aiso was "acquainted with" the Manchukuo vice minister of industry Kishi Nobusuke—later charged with but never tried for Class-A war crimes who went on to collaborate with the US Central Intelligence Agency and became the prime minister of Japan during the late 1950s. In fact, it was Kishi who gave Aiso "permission . . . to [help] operate" the Mukden-based British firm when he served as its chief legal counsel.[50] Combined with national security concerns, such dubious backgrounds of many MIS members rendered their wartime activities a seldom publicized topic of press reporting, unlike the heavily propagandized exploits of the 442nd RCT Nisei soldiers. Nonetheless, Aiso and many other Nisei linguists whom he trained at the Presidio and Camp Savage played a critical role in generating propaganda knowledge. Japanese American MIS members offered to the United States what Americanized Nisei, like Masaoka, could not: the ability to reach enemy audiences directly with a message in their native tongue.

Nisei MIS linguists constituted a driving force of the US army's psychological warfare, especially leaflet campaigns, in the Asia-Pacific theaters. As 442nd RCT members were deployed to the battlegrounds of Italy and fought as exemplary American soldiers after the late fall of 1943, the MIS and the OWI-OB launched Japanese-language leaflet campaigns with the help of Nisei military linguists and civilian recruits. Aside from shortwave radio broadcasts from San Francisco and Honolulu (later Saipan and Manila as well), which had only a very limited reach, if at all, to enemy audiences on the battlefield or on the home front, US propagandists considered the leaflet campaigns to be the most effective method of undermining the morale of Japanese soldiers and civilians.[51] Oftentimes, relations between the MIS and OWI-OB were tenuous as the former, for example, tended to refuse to offer the service of Nisei linguists to the latter in the Southwestern area of the Pacific (under General Douglas MacArthur's command). Yet, in other Asia-Pacific theaters of US psychological warfare, especially the China-Burma-India (CBI) Theater, many contingents of Nisei MIS members found themselves working in OWI-led operations of anti-enemy leaflet and broadcast propaganda. Headquartered in Denver and then San Francisco in 1945, the OWI-OB's Japanese division had its own outposts in Honolulu and later in Saipan and Manila, as well as branch offices in New Delhi (India), Kunming, and Chungking (China).[52]

Based in Ledo, India, OWI's Assam leaflet operation exemplified how Nisei cultural brokers—both MIS members and OWI recruits—functioned in the overall machinery of propaganda knowledge production. Nisei linguists served multifaceted roles as intermediaries: they brokered relations between US military brass and white officers and servicemen on the ground; between US forces and Japanese soldiers; between white propaganda workers and Japanese prisoners of war; and between US policymakers and Japanese nationals during the wartime psychological warfare and even after. In March 1944, OWI dispatched to Ledo a team of nine Japanese American linguists, which consisted of "selected" MIS members "with backgrounds in newspapers, broadcasting, and commercial art." Included in this eclectic group were leftist Japanese Americans, such as Karl G. Yoneda, who had had experience in labor organizing and compiling propaganda newspapers sponsored by the American Communist Party before the war. Born in Southern California but reared in Hiroshima, Yoneda was a quintessential Japanized Kibei from whom Americanized Nisei, like Masaoka, wished to distance themselves as much as possible. Another Nisei MIS linguist in the OWI Ledo group was Clarke Kawakami, who had worked in Tokyo for Japan's Dōmei News Agency from 1933 to 1939 before moving to London and then to Washington, DC, as its overseas correspondent. After the outbreak of the war, Kawakami managed to swap his professional affiliation from the now-defunct Dōmei to the *Washington Post* and then utilized his journalistic background and expertise on Japanese society as an MIS agent for US psychological warfare.[53]

Albeit being placed under the supervision, if not surveillance, of white OWI agents, Nisei linguists in Ledo made their mark as indispensable cultural brokers. Deployed at the frontlines of the CBI Theater, the OWI Assam outfit was saddled with the responsibility for producing Japanese-language leaflets to induce imperial army soldiers to surrender. Initially, white OWI experts attempted to guard their authority in the knowledge production process by relegating Nisei members to the simple task of translating the leaflet narratives that they originally wrote in English. This racialized authority had been put in place in the hierarchical apparatus of the MIS/OWI, where white suspicions and sense of superiority rationalized the policy of bringing Nisei linguists—just like the 442nd RCT infantrymen—under the command of white officers/superiors. Indeed, an architect of the MIS Language School, Lieutenant Colonel John Weckerling had already warned: "the [Nisei] translators will be in a prime position to do great harm in the event that he is, as a matter of fact, disloyal. In the absence of white officers or soldiers, with at least a smattering of Japanese, in a position to check their actions, the G-2 will be at their mercy."[54] Paradoxically, the lack of linguistic ability on the part of the white overseers gave Nisei linguists much leeway to negotiate their institutionalized subordination; sometimes their "smattering of Japanese" rendered white officers at the mercy of their Nisei staff in the context of everyday work routines.[55] Equipped with a native-level command of Japanese, for example, Yoneda had no hesitation in criticizing the leaflet narratives produced by his white superiors, protesting: "[T]he Japanese just don't think that way."[56]

Eventually, white OWI administrators conceded and allowed the Nisei to take the lead in drafting most leaflets. According to an official report, dated January 1945:

> When the team began work in the Japanese language, leaflets were written first in English by the American editorial staff. They were then translated and retranslated. Generally the inadequacy of this method became apparent. Too often the retranslation bore only a general resemblance to the original English, dictated awkwardness in the Japanese—awkwardness in phraseology, and in thought pattern. Many of the early leaflets "sounded strange" to the POWs who checked them. At present all leaflets are written originally in Japanese (with some exceptions).[57]

Likewise, in the MIS-controlled leaflet campaign in the Philippines, similar interventions by Nisei linguists led to this high command directive: "It is recommended that in the future Japanese-Americans collaborate on the preparation of surrender propaganda. Very few Caucasians have the necessary insight in the Oriental way of thinking to produce effective propaganda."[58] White military administrators came to share the view in the context of theater-wide leaflet campaigns that Nisei were not simply language specialists who translated mechanically. They brokered the understanding of the enigmatic "Oriental way of thinking" for white Americans through the close reading of enemy personal documents, like handwritten diaries and letters, and face-to-face interrogation of war prisoners.

Yoneda offered a vivid account of his experience in the OWI Assam operation, explaining the process by which the surrender leaflets and other propaganda prints were produced by a handful of Kibei/Nisei in Ledo:

> I first drew up a draft and took it to the stockade where about ten Japanese POWs were detained. I gave them cigarettes and chocolate, and they became very friendly. They gave me valuable advice on the draft. Clarke Kawakami translated the leaflets I wrote in Japanese into English. Then Kenji Akune, Sam Sasaki, or Alex Yorichi delivered them to G2 Headquarters for approval. A Burmese named Simeone printed the leaflets on a portable Davidson press. The final steps were airdropping the leaflets over enemy lines in Northern Burma and broadcasting the texts to the enemy from our camp radio shop by Kenji (Kenny) Yasui.[59]

Fig. 2.2 Kenji Yasui (left) and Karl G. Yoneda (right) with white members of the OWI psychological warfare team in Assam, India, in August 1944. National Archives and Records Administration.

The Kibei agent discussed details on other propaganda techniques that he and his fellow Japanese Americans devised in Ledo.

> Another set of flyers was addressed to wounded and sick enemy soldiers in the jungle. According to POWs, many were dying there because no medical treatment was available. Our leaflets carried photos of Japanese POWs with eyes covered to disguise identities. The message of the leaflets was that "anyone who comes over to our side will receive humane treatment in strict observance of international law." We reproduced parts of diaries taken from dead enemy soldiers who had expressed anxiety, hunger, and longing for loved ones back home. We also extensively used Japanese poems and proverbs.[60]

As Yoneda's recollections show, one of the major "contributions" that Nisei cultural brokers made on the battleground to the "propaganda techniques developed during the 1944–1945 North Burma campaign" stemmed from their ability to entice Japanese prisoners of war to participate in the leaflet campaign. Even though Nisei linguists were far more knowledgeable about the enemy language and way of thinking than their white colleagues and superiors, they were the first to recognize that "none would know the Japanese army as a Japanese soldier knows it."[61] Hence, in August 1944, a six-member "POW creative group" was organized to make leaflet propaganda more effective, thanks to Yoneda's aforementioned efforts. He and other Nisei linguists bridged the gap between the US authorities and the Japanese prisoners. As an Assam field report of February 1945 acknowledged, "[t]he POW propaganda group could not have been developed without...Nisei staff. The need for the POW group was first felt by these men, and they made the original selection of POWs for the group."[62] While "spending a major portion of his time with the POWs at the stockade," one Nisei MIS sergeant—most likely Yoneda—served as the director of this group. His "vitally important" work entailed "the responsibility to train [the prisoners] in leaflet writing and layout" and "supply continuous daily stimulation to the group, as well as editorial direction and control."[63] Other Nisei linguists also visited the stockade to speak with the cooperative prisoners when necessary; white staff could not do any such work other than occasionally accompanying their Nisei colleagues.

The Nisei's intermediary role—brokering between white officials and enemy Japanese—anticipated the position these cultural brokers would occupy and how they would function in post-defeat Japan. As another military command praised Nisei linguists, their "attempts to make friends with the POW [and] to talk with him at length" reveals the exceptional ability that Japanese Americans seemed to possess in manipulating the enemy mind for the benefit of US military governance that emphasized a façade of benevolence.[64] It was an ability that white administrators would later value in the context of the military occupation. Impressed with positive implications for the "administration and reorientation of the Japanese people following their surrender," John Emmerson—State Department's Japan expert who worked with the Assam group—hailed the POW psychological warfare as an ideal policy blueprint for the postwar governance of the enemy nation. "The metamorphosis which occurs in the mind of a Japanese prisoner of war," Emmerson explained before the congressional committee in the spring of 1945, "suggests to us what may happen to the Japanese people," helping to "prepare them for the consequences of their defeat."[65] Backed by such positive official assessments, similar OWI/MIS programs of

Nisei-supervised POW psychological warfare were organized in Honolulu, Manila, Saipan, and beyond, which aimed to drop tens of thousands of propaganda leaflets over the Japanese archipelago after the US takeover of the Philippines and the Marianas.[66] The work of Nisei cultural brokers directly targeted enemy civilians, attempting to manipulate Japanese minds through the sweet words and images of anti-racist US benevolence.[67]

Among a variety of new propaganda themes were the influential visual representations of Japanese American soldiers and civilians, who encapsulated the ideas of America's destructive military might as well as its humane compassion. Because the US seizure of Saipan and Guam secured direct access to the Japanese homeland after the summer of 1944, American airplanes began to spray the archipelago with deadly bombs and kind-worded leaflets.[68] With an aim at undermining the morale of ordinary military conscripts, and then of civilians, US propaganda leaflets—more elaborate and sophisticated than their battlefront counterparts—generally conveyed these messages: the dismal prospect of Japan's war effort; the deceptions and trickeries that the militarist cliques had employed to keep ordinary soldiers and civilians of Japan misinformed and misguided; their patriotic mission to take back Japan from those corrupt leaders and rebuild it for them and

Fig. 2.3 Nisei linguist and white officer holding an information discussion with Japanese prisoners of war, Queensland, Australia. 1945. US Army Photograph.

their families; and the kindness, care and abundant food that they would receive under benevolent US custody or tutelary occupation.[69] Frequently, one reference or another to Japanese Americans sneaked into these tactical messages.

Many leaflets, for example, described the accomplishments of the 442nd RCT Nisei soldiers in Italy and France, specifically their altruistic actions that saved others' lives. During 1944, this theme was consciously, albeit rather implicitly, juxtaposed against the stories of Japanese brutality toward allied POWs, civilian captives, and local peoples of the occupied areas. Rather than exhibiting a "revenge motive," Nisei producers of these leaflets were specifically instructed to contrast the atrocity narrative with the "material on Japanese-American troops and their fine fighting record with allied forces of many nationalities" in order "to offset Japanese use of the race theme."[70] The domestic US anti-racist publicity campaign buoyed the overseas leaflet propaganda on Nisei military heroism. Between 1943 and 1944, the former had already generated many useable accounts from the battlegrounds of Italy and France. The glamorization of Nisei's martial virtue and compassion peaked in October 1944 in Bruyères, France, where Nisei troops liberated the "lost battalion," a Texas National Guard outfit of 211 white soldiers who were caught behind enemy lines, at the cost of over eight hundred Japanese American casualties, or almost half of the 442nd RCT's roster. With these stories, the OWI and MIS found no shortage of material for its overseas leaflet operations against the Japanese enemy. Mike Masaoka, the 442nd RCT's unit publicist, was responsible for crafting much of the propaganda narrative prototype on the ground for both the domestic media and overseas propaganda outlets. The knowledge he had generated was then reproduced by Nisei MIS/OWI staffers with additional local bents.

Aside from "factual" reports on Nisei's military accomplishments and humanitarianism, some Japanese-language leaflets elucidated the reciprocal colorblindness and compassion of white Americans vis-à-vis their Japanese American comrades-in-arms. Published in a fictitious propaganda newspaper titled *Jisei* (*Current Development*), which was distributed throughout the CBI Theater, one example carried the picture of smiling Nisei soldiers in western Italy being served hot coffee and doughnuts by young white women of the American Red Cross.[71] Another fictitious newspaper, *Makoto* (*Truth*), quoted well-known Hollywood actor and comedian Joe E. Brown, who lauded the "swell, loyal" members of the segregated Nisei outfit in

Fig. 2.4 "US citizen Japanese Nisei soldiers of Hawaiian regiment are served coffee and donuts by the American Red Cross in Western Italy." A propaganda photograph taken from *Jisei*, June 24, 1944. National Archives and Records Administration.

Italy.[72] Considering the central goal of US propaganda leaflets, a narrative of white America's goodwill to Nisei served to implicate the humane and fair treatment enemy Japanese could enjoy should they chose to seek capitulation to and rehabilitation under the US forces. Racial conflation was still a hallmark of America's anti-racist message.

In propaganda news reportage, the white (American) embrace of Japanese (Americans) reached its height when the wounded 442nd RCT infantrymen returned to Hawai'i in June 1945. According to a two-page weekly propaganda newsletter titled the *Rakkasan Nyūsu* (*Parachute News*):

> More than one thousand Nisei members of the 100th Battalion from Hawai'i have been decorated with the Purple Heart (military decoration for soldiers injured or killed in action).... The first group of wounded Nisei soldiers were recently granted a vacation and returned to Hawai'i...from Europe. When they arrived home, Honolulu citizens paid them a heroes' welcome, covering them with wreaths of flowers.[73]

Produced by Nisei MIS linguists of the Allied Translator and Interpreter Section (ATIS) attached to the US Army's Psychological Warfare Branch in Manila (South-West Pacific Area), two million copies per week of *Rakkasan Nyūsu* issues were literally parachuted down on Japan and Japanese troop concentrations from B-29 bombers between March and August 1945. As in the Assam POW program, these ATIS Nisei took advantage of the service of nineteen Japanese prisoners under their control.[74]

During the Battle of Okinawa (April-June 1945), OWI/ATIS leaflets aimed to dispel Japanese fears associated with the impending American invasion and military occupation through skewed representations of benevolent Nisei fighting men and the anti-racist United States that embraced them. The last wartime issue of the *Rakkasan Nyūsu*, for example, printed a close-up photograph of a Nisei MIS member holding his long-lost little nephew in occupied Okinawa, right next to the story of Okinawan civilians' joyful response to post-defeat American generosity. Even though no explanation was given for this image, the symbolism of the Nisei linguist is not unambiguous. To highlight the co-ethnic soldier's compassion and the altruistic nature of US military occupation, the opposite side of this letter-size leaflet offered a detailed report on the beginning of the Soviet attack on Japanese troops and the atomic bombings of Hiroshima and Nagasaki, with President Truman's warning about national annihilation if the Japanese continued to reject America's war justice. In a succinct way, the photograph of the Nisei sergeant embodied non-racist compassionate Uncle Sam who was ready to embrace and even lift up Japan—just like his Okinawan nephew in his arms—once the nation decided to atone for its sins and threw itself on the mercy of the father-like United States.[75]

To help foster positive ideas about the inevitable coming of American military rule, US propaganda went so far as to portray the experience of Japanese Americans in the incarceration camps as a precedent for the "happy normal life" that would await Japanese people after their defeat—presented as "liberation"—under the US governance. Entitled "Manzanar, a Japanese village," another *Rakkasan Nyūsu* report described the WRA camp in a California desert as an orderly community, where some ten thousand people have "lived in 36 residential subdivisions with large farms" since 1942. Given Japan's earlier, albeit failed, attempt at propagandizing the "savage" killing of two Nisei at "Mansana," the Nisei OWI/ATIS authors' choice of this particular "village" was not coincidental. According to the leaflet, the WRA camp functioned as a "complete self-governing body," which consisted of "stores, schools, community halls, libraries, churches and temples, museum, hospitals, and a movie theater." There were the police and fire departments under the "sole control" of Japanese residents. Life in the Manzanar "village" was presented as so comfortable that many people decided to remain there even after the exclusion order was lifted—a twisted representation when considering the real reason was the internees' fear of racist violence in mainstream America and dismal prospects after forced removal, property losses, and prolonged imprisonment.[76]

This issue of the *Rakkasan Nyūsu* was full of enchanting imagery that reinforced the skewed renditions of the incarceration camp experience

Fig. 2.5 "Nisei Sergeant meeting his nephew again." A propaganda photograph taken from *Rakkasan Nyūsu*, August 11, 1945. National Archives and Records Administration.

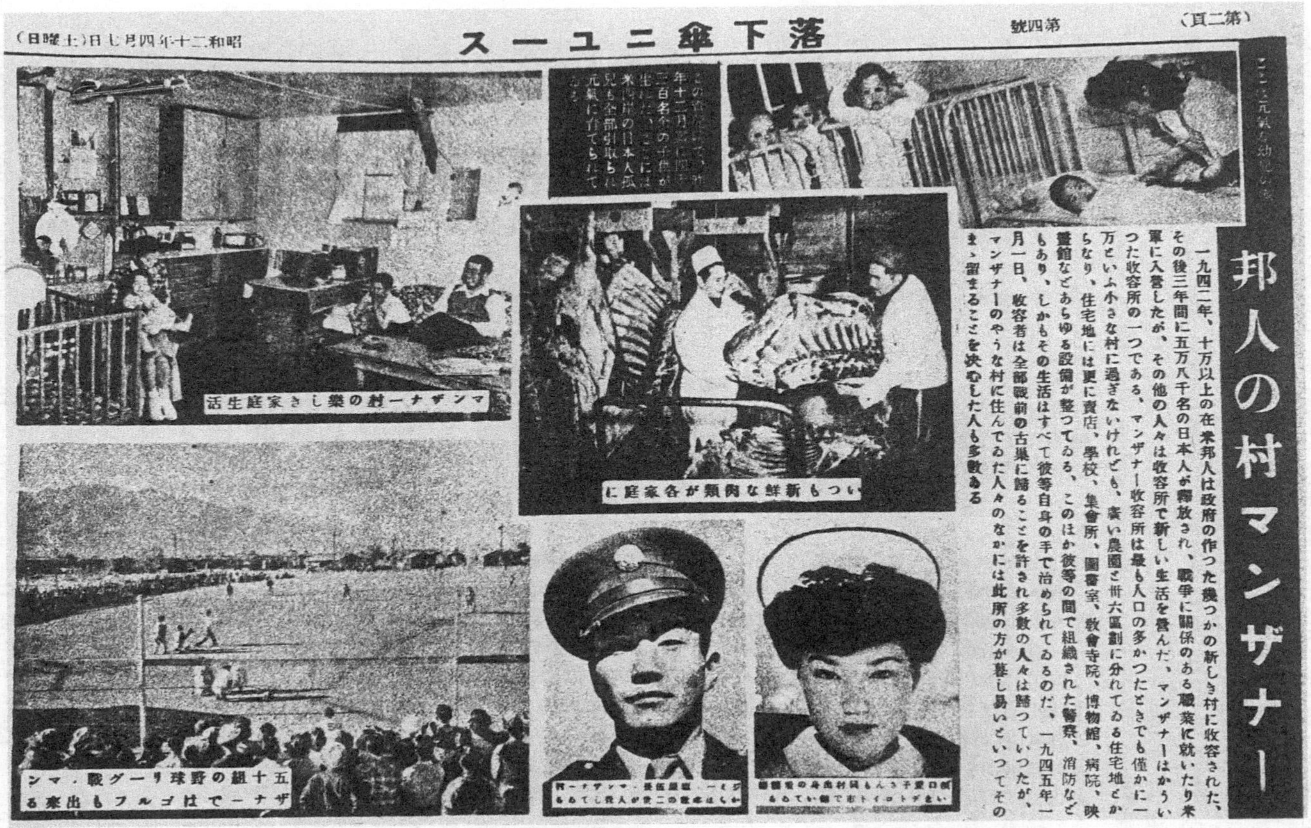

落下傘ニユース　第四號　（第二頁）　昭和二十年四月七日（土曜日）

邦人の村マンザナー

一九四二年、十万以上の在米邦人は政府の作つた幾つかの新しき村に收容された、その後三年間に五万八千名の日本人が釋放され、戰爭に關係のある職業に就いたり米軍に入營したが、その他の人々は收容所で新しい生活を營んだ。マンザナーはかういつた收容所の一つである。マンザナー收容所は最も人口の多かつたときでも僅かに一万といふ小さな村に過ぎないけれども、廣い農園と卅六區劃に分れてゐる住宅地とからなり、住宅地には更に賣店、學校、集會所、圖書室、教會寺院、博物館、病院、映畫館などあらゆる設備が整つてゐる。このほか彼等の間で組織された警察、消防などもあり、しかもその生活はすべて彼等自身の手で治められてゐるのだ。一九四五年一月一日、收容者は全部戰前の古巣に歸ることを許され多數の人々は歸つていつたが、マンザナーのやうな村に住んでゐた人々のなかには此所の方が暮し易いといつてそのまゝ留まることを決心した人も多數ある

マンザナー村の樂しき家庭生活

いつも新鮮な肉類が各家庭に

五十組の野球リーグ戰・マンザナーではゴルフも出來る

Fig. 2.6 "Japanese Village, Manzanar." A propaganda photograph taken from *Rakkasan Nyūsu*, April 7, 1945. National Archives and Records Administration.

common in post-1943 US domestic propaganda. Included in the story of the "happy normal life" under white American benevolence were snapshots of Nisei internees playing baseball; a well-decorated room with young Nisei parents and their two children; and Japanese American workers carrying big blocks of frozen beef. These pictures underscore a high level of material and emotional fulfillment that the residents purportedly enjoyed inside the Manzanar village under the benevolence of "Uncle Sam...a loyal master," as described in a 1942 propaganda film.[77] The captions for the last two images explain how "joyous" the family life was in Manzanar with "fresh meat always available to each household." An image of plump babies with a Nisei nurse also explains that many orphans were being cared for well in the camp—an idea that must have had special appeal to many Japanese civilians whose husbands and family members were killed in action somewhere overseas. Certainly, they had not seen so much beef, or meat of any sort, for quite some time.[78] These were what vanquished Japanese—civilians and combatants alike—could expect and indulge in once they submitted to the rule and care of Americans.

The use of Japanese American themes to prophesy a bright future course for defeated Japan became more explicit during the Battle of Okinawa. Sprayed all over Japan around the same time as the *Rakkasan Nyūsu* issue, another leaflet dispatched heartfelt handwritten messages by Hawai'i's Issei to Japanese audiences regarding "the worthiness of American democracy" for a postwar Japan.[79] Right after the Okinawa campaign ended in June 1945, OWI's Honolulu outfit had Nisei linguists prepare a new leaflet "series on Nipponese in Hawaii as indirect opposition to Japs racial propaganda line."[80] This particular series, which focused on ordinary Japanese Americans, dovetailed with a new "preliminary plan for leaflet campaign against Japan." It aimed to "reduce the mental obstacles [of Japanese civilians] to surrender." Adopted in the early summer of 1945, this phase of propaganda specifically recommended the use of the Nisei theme for "show[ing] humane treatment by Occidentals" after surrender, since it would "show that Americans do not hate the Japanese as a race."[81] Importantly, this guideline mirrored an earlier policy directive that had identified the "theme" of "Americans of Japanese Descent" as helpful for "shift[ing Japanese] attention from immediate difficulties to the possibilities of rehabilitation" in order to "facilitate the work of the occupation troops."[82] Even before the war ended, the propaganda leaflets already anticipated how Japanese American linguists and civilian workers would be utilized as a poignant example and an invaluable broker for the rehabilitation of vanquished Japanese—through the assimilation of democratic ideas as loyal Nisei had done—under the tutelary control of the occupying US forces and white Americans.

"Free Japanese Movement" and Japanese Americans as Teachers of Democracy

As the invasion of the Japanese homeland looked increasingly imminent in the spring of 1945, the Joint Chiefs of Staff of the US armed forces, the State Department, and OSS worked out a new two-pronged program, which institutionalized the democratizing role of Nisei vis-à-vis enemy Japanese beyond the realm of propaganda. In this development, Japanese Americans outgrew a one-dimensional symbol of US anti-racism in OWI and MIS leaflets; they were expected to establish the basis of a "liberal government" in the land of their fanatic ancestors by serving as semi-native teachers of democracy and civilized conduct. In March 1945, a high-ranking OSS official rationalized this approach purely in essentialist racial-cultural terms: "The presentation of ideas, consistent with the psychological pattern of Japanese thought, would be given credence in Japan when presented by the Japanese."[83]

This casual statement, which emphasized blood and cultural ties as a precondition for the smooth transmission of ideas to the enemy, stemmed from the policy proposals offered by white experts on Japan and Japanese culture. John Emmerson was perhaps the most influential, for he had actual experience observing and supervising the POW-generated leaflet propaganda in the CBI Theater as a State Department policy expert. In the final year of the war, Emmerson emerged as a major point person for military strategists when it came to the question of how to understand and control the Japanese minds.[84] From the principle advocated by Emmerson of using "friendly Japanese" in order to control hostile ones, a specific project emerged during the last months of the Pacific War: a "free Japanese movement" that confounded enemy Japanese (albeit rehabilitated ones) and the two generations of Japanese Americans in accordance with their racial background.

In June 1945, a "free Japanese movement" was adopted formally as a State Department project, but it had originally been put together by the OSS's Morale Operations Branch (OSS-MB) that included many Japanese

American staffers. Comprised of sixty-eight civilian and loaned MIS agents, the branch had over half of the entire Japanese staff in OSS, so it served as a center of knowledge production about the enemy, along with the agency's Research and Analysis Branch (OSS-RAB).[85] As historian Brian Hayashi's study details, these Asian American OSS staffers were instrumental in formulating covert operation plans that combined espionage, subversion, and/or "black propaganda"—the dissemination of disinformation purportedly produced by the enemy or its allies themselves.[86] A "free Japanese movement" was somewhat different from OSS's standard endeavors. By recruiting "[s]elect members of the Eisei (Issei), Kibei, and Nisei and Sansei in this country," the proposed project aimed to carry out "the re-education of Japanese war prisoners, training them for the time when they could return to Japan (in the immediate post-war period), cognizant of the advantages of a more liberal and democratic form of government." It was expected that these POWs "might even be trained for administrative positions during American occupation."[87]

The March 1945 draft plan for this program was approved by the OSS-MB leadership, but the agency decided to let the State Department take over further planning and implementation of co-racial indoctrination. The use of Japanese POWs by OSS's Japanese American agents did not fit the definition of black propaganda for which the agency was responsible—one that was supposed to come from non-US sources. Even though OSS brass felt that it could not openly operate an anti-militarist Japanese organization for re-education purposes, the agency was eager to clandestinely support the State Department with a loan of its own "competent Nissei [sic] or Issei interrogators and translators" as well as "two or three thousand dollars to cover initial expenses."[88] Reliant on the brokering role of Nisei and Issei recruits, the "free Japanese movement" also assumed in an unspoken way the cooperation of liberal-minded or anti-militarist Japanese within the enemy home islands. These silent liberals and moderates, like "reconditioned Japanese prisoners," could be steered towards assisting the civil administration of postwar Japan under the US military government. Some of these potential collaborators would consist of those who had been previously "abroad and [did] know something of Western psychology."[89] Others would be prewar Issei returnees and Nisei "strandees"—like Takizo Frank Matsumoto and Kiyoshi George Togasaki. Indeed, for this reason, the OWI and MIS began to plan on English-language broadcasts directed particularly towards those Nisei who worked as radio monitors and translators in the imperial Japanese forces. It was anticipated that some of them might consider an action against Tokyo—if not actually organize them into "a nucleus for a Japanese underground."[90]

Despite the administrative initiative of OSS, this covert POW operation was essentially the brainchild of John Emmerson, inspired by his earlier collaborations with Nisei MIS linguists. A prominent member of the white "Japan hand" crowd, this career diplomat had previously served in the American embassy in Japan; hence, he was a familiar face to leading Nisei strandees and other Japanese with an American background in Tokyo. In 1942, after a five-year stint in the now enemy capital, Emmerson's foreign service career took him to Lima, Peru. There, he helped orchestrate local anti-Japanese agitation that portrayed Japanese Peruvians as transplanted enemy agents—a notion that xenophobic Peruvian politicians exploited when they assisted the US-led kidnapping, trafficking, and incarceration of Japanese Latin Americans in the enemy alien internment camps stateside.[91] Emmerson then spent the latter years of the Pacific War in the CBI Theater. In the early phase of the Assam POW leaflet campaign, he oversaw the activities of Nisei MIS agents as a "policy supervisor" for the OWI outlet there. This experience led to his next assignment as an American emissary to Mao Zedong in Yenan, China. There, Emmerson and a former Nisei member of the Assam team interviewed both exiled Japanese communists and prisoners of war and rendered support for their POW-generated leaflet propaganda.[92] His famous "Yenan Reports" were subsequently referenced heavily by military strategists, propaganda planners, and diplomatic officials alike.

Emmerson's view of the Japanese typified the wartime and postwar liberal instrumentalist thinking that was still marked by a deep sense of superiority and yet was seemingly embracing and benevolent at the same time. Typical of inclusionary American racism of the time, this white Japan hand expressed little to no sympathy for any of the Japanese with whom he worked or those he sought to recondition for propaganda or postwar occupation. Whether Nisei citizens, Japanese Peruvians, or imperial Japanese, they were a means to the suppression of enemy belligerence and to maintain (white) American control and supremacy, as his work in Lima, Ledo, and Yenan demonstrated. The notion of racial sameness ran deep underneath his thinking and attitude toward diverse peoples of Japanese heritage.[93]

Viewed from Emmerson's instrumentalist perspective, being racially Japanese predetermined one's undemocratic disposition, as revealed in the manner of his agitation against Japanese Peruvians; yet he was tolerant enough to vouch for the possibility of their reorientation (or assimilation) under the proper guidance and tutelage of whites—an idea that underlay his enthusiastic support for the POW leaflet campaigns. Like other self-styled white experts on Japan, Emmerson offered know-it-all explanations about what can be termed the national character of the Japanese, whom he described as "not a critical individual" being only capable of doing "little thinking for himself." The white Japan expert also proclaimed that the Japanese held a "fundamental feeling of inferiority" toward the "physique of (white) Americans and...our superior mechanical civilization," which had paradoxically functioned as "a mainspring of Japanese hostility to the West."[94] Mired in the deep-seated sense of inferiority that was masked by a fanatical racial pride, according to Emmerson's colonialist psychoanalysis, the uncritical Japanese minds would be hard to manipulate by white men, whether with the threat of physical violence or force of logical persuasion. This manipulation required the kind of indirect control that the Assam POW program had successfully devised: the use of Japanese middlemen under white supervision, which was designed to induce a trickledown effect of co-racial indoctrination.

In his numerous expert reports and congressional testimonies, Emmerson was very vocal about and insistent on the advantage of using "Japanese subjects in the United States" not only for the goal of enticing the enemy to capitulate but also for that of governing the defeated and rehabilitating them effectively in a postwar context. In view of the anticipated US occupation mandate, Emmerson recommended assembling first-generation Japanese Americans into "a genuine Japanese organization," which would not only "assist (white) civil affairs officers especially during the early stages of military occupation" but also "be useful both in the planning and execution of rehabilitation and educational programs."[95] Although he tended to limit his discussion to the usefulness of Japanese immigrants in the United States (usually referred to as "friendly Japanese") in the context of his State Department policy proposals relating to civilian governance, Emmerson also expressed the need for the said Issei organization to "welcome the support of...the (Nisei-dominated) Japanese-American Committee for Democracy in New York and the Japanese American Citizens League."[96] In May 1945, the Joint Chiefs of Staff took notice of this draft plan, and after three months of deliberations, the central US military command opted to incorporate Emmerson's ideas into its comprehensive strategic plans against Japan on the eve of its defeat.[97] The joint OSS-State initiative for the free

Japanese movement was part and parcel of the US preparation for the postwar governance of enemy Japanese through the medium of "friendly Japanese," where the differences in citizenship status and cultural upbringing were confounded under the tenacious belief in racial sameness.

Even though the war ended before the mobilization of Issei and Nisei in the United States (and in Japan) materialized, Emmerson's brainchild offered a more important rationale than simply a language expert shortage for the involvement of Nisei MIS and civilian linguists in the military occupation of Japan. "Race or ancestry" still mattered when it came to the question of how to control Japanese foes even though the United States had so fervently attempted to downplay these concepts in the new definitions of Americanism—and in propaganda narratives on Nisei war heroes based on it. In no uncertain terms did America's wartime racial liberalism propagate the presumed divide between Americans and Japanese as reconcilable through the assimilation of the former's brand of democracy by the latter, albeit under white supervision. At the same time, this anti-racist thinking ironically helped preserve a conventional belief in the mythical power of blood ties in facilitating such a shift in the vanquished through the agency of Nisei cultural brokers. Therefore, as a military official already predicted a few months before the war's end, "the people of the Japanese race," like Nisei, were expected to act as "the most effective group" to help white military officials and civilian administrators to navigate and negotiate the exotic cultural milieus and enigmatic psychological intricacies of the defeated for the next phase of the race war: military occupation and democratization of defeated Japan.[98] Yet, racial sameness was not the only factor that determined the multifaceted relations of power in the occupied enemy land. With the emphasis on the colorblind citizenship that distinguished between Nisei conquerors and vanquished Japanese, that pivotal theme of US wartime propaganda remained as crucial, if not more so, through the occupation period under the colonial conditions of post-defeat Japan.

Brokering a Race War: Japanese Americans in the Pacific War and the Occupation of Japan. Eiichiro Azuma, Oxford University Press. © Eiichiro Azuma 2026. DOI: 10.1093/9780197781432.003.0003

PART II

MILITARY OCCUPATION AND THE DUPLICITY OF MINORITY CITIZENSHIP

3

Military Governance and Japanese Americans in Occupied Japan

> Many Problems are being solved here, because the nisei boys in uniform are cooperating to the utmost. We are spreading news of democracy...and many other good things of life, which the Japanese people...never knew about....We are planting the seeds for a New Japan under the kind surveillance of the US.[1]
>
> Tom S. Shiinoki, December 9, 1945

> They [Japanese Americans] are making a name for themselves here [in Japan]...but not the way you expect or want it....Well, I suppose we can be proud of the combat Niseis, but we're going to be ashamed of the occupation Nisei. Doesn't seem possible, does it?[2]
>
> Joe M. Takita, January 14, 1947

These divergent points of view, expressed by two Japanese American soldiers, equally captured the complexity of their experience in Japan during the US-led allied military occupation between August 1945 and April 1952. It is estimated that over ten thousand Nisei served in occupied Japan, the vast majority of whom were assigned to the roles of military linguists and bilingual civilian staffers in the US occupation forces and military government under General Douglas MacArthur. Their story was largely unknown until the 1990s, unlike the legendary all-Nisei 442nd Regimental Combat Team (RCT) in Europe. Since 1943, celebratory accounts of Japanese American combat soldiers formed a major aspect of US propaganda that attempted to repudiate blood-will-tell racism and popular support for the mass incarceration of Japanese Americans that this racism facilitated. Due to the security-classified nature of their activities, Nisei members of the Military Intelligence Service (MIS) in the Pacific theater did not receive much publicity. Yet, the fiftieth anniversary of the end of the Pacific War finally released a floodgate of publications and video productions that projected the same anti-racist agenda beneath a veneer of a glorified narrative of minority patriotism.[3] Accompanied by numerous stories about Nisei's exceptional valor and patriotism, this emergent master narrative explains that their work as Japanese-language specialists accelerated the termination of hostilities with imperial Japan by at least two years—a claim originally made by one of General MacArthur's aides. It also notes, albeit without explication, that Nisei linguists went on to help quickly transform former "enemies into friends" during the military occupation.[4] Thus, a public understanding of the hitherto little-known role of Nisei military linguists in occupied Japan is shaped almost exclusively along the lines of Shiinoki's statement.[5]

Part II unravels how the conflicting statements of the two Nisei linguists reflect the dual realities in which Japanese Americans were expected—and aspired—to act, as both emancipating democratizers and punitive war victors in occupied Japan. To understand what lay behind their ambivalent emotions and contradictory behaviors, it is necessary to examine the fluid meanings of race, citizenship, and culture in relation to a drastic shift in the status of Nisei linguists. Within just a few years, they went from being inmates in the wartime incarceration camps of their own country to becoming indispensable cogs of the democratizing military forces in their ancestral land. Since this shift resulted from the top-down imposition of the state policy mandate of colorblind Americanism, it is important to recognize that conventional biological racism still permeated dominant American mindsets and institutions under the guise of rising racial liberalism. Indeed, while some segments of the armed forces became open to the idea of embracing loyal Nisei citizens, the military overall continued to maintain a preexisting structure of racial hierarchy as in general US society even after 1945. Nonetheless, occupied Japan also formed a unique space where domestic race relations and conventional institutional arrangements were confounded with extraterritorial conditions of militarized colonial domination. This situation amplified the ambiguities and contradictions associated with the shifting meanings of race, citizenship, and culture relative to minoritized members of the US occupation forces.

American by citizenship and yet Japanese by race, transnational Nisei embodied the complexities of their position in their defeated ancestral country. On the one hand, they remained a racialized minority relative to their white comrades and superiors within the confines of the expeditionary military government. Insofar as the army personnel all shared US citizenship, what mattered most in that institutional context were one's racial background and cultural heritage defined by it. On the other, when it came to their relations to vanquished foreign Japanese, Nisei US soldiers enjoyed the privilege and power of colonial overlords who lived above and beyond local legal constraints or norms, including the existing structure of the Japanese government. Their possession and practice of US imperial citizenship against rightless Japanese nationals in a colonial condition coincided with their racial subordination under the transplanted white supremacy within the US military government in occupied Japan. The reconfiguration of the bounds of race, citizenship, and culture in these dual contexts characterized the process in which these Japanese Americans forged their relationships to other US citizens with no racial commonality, as well as their racial compatriots with no citizenship ties during the occupation period.

With a focus on their maneuvering within the white-dominated military institution on foreign soil, Chapter 3 examines the inner workings of the occupation regime, as well as Nisei's place and essentialized roles in it. An extension of America's sovereign power to a foreign area, the US-controlled military government in occupied Japan replicated domestic state apparatuses and asymmetrical social relations in accordance with the logic of white supremacy and conditional minority acceptance. Japanese American subordination to white command officers was therefore a pervasive theme, and they were almost always relegated to the positions of semi-native informants and excavators of enemy knowledge on behalf of white policy planners. At the same time, because they were supposed to mediate between the languages and psychologies of white Americans and enemy Japanese, Nisei linguists occupied a liminal position despite their US citizen status, having been expected to perform prescribed tasks in accordance with white Orientalist expectations. Despite the pervasive theme of domination, the military brass and white administrators on the ground were always dependent on the Japanese American intermediaries.

Following Japan's capitulation, thousands of young Japanese Americans were dragged into this quagmire while reclaiming their citizenship privilege as uniformed US military linguists and civilian occupation staffers across the Pacific. Their work as cultural brokers generally had the effect of pigeonholing them; yet, at times, Nisei linguists could take advantage of their middleman standing due to their racial ties to the enemy, by acting as frontline enforcers and symbols of democratization to conquered Japanese. This chapter explains their complicated roles, positions, and experiences within the varied apparatuses of the US military government in occupied Japan. Furthermore, its democratization project relative to defeated Japanese constituted a crucial and necessary context for the rehabilitation of all US-born individuals of Japanese ancestry, including hitherto ostracized Kibei, disloyal "renunciants" from WRA camps, and even treacherous wartime "strandees."

Origins of Nisei Cultural Brokers in the Militarized Asia-Pacific

The initial group of Nisei linguists who entered defeated Japan consisted of members of the Allied Translator and Interpreter Section (ATIS), which "suppl[ied] (white) officers and enlisted (Nisei) language personnel to the various headquarters, units, and government agencies" throughout occupied Japan.[6] By December 1945, the total number of ATIS military linguists there totaled 2,667, over 90 percent of them were Nisei. Initially, most were veteran linguists transferred from wartime outposts in the Philippines, the Marianas, and Okinawa, but they were soon replaced by fresh recruits from the United States. These newcomers went through no more than nine months of intensive training at the army language school in Fort Snelling, Minnesota, and at the Presidio in San Francisco after late 1946.[7] Their numbers eventually surpassed the 6,000-mark by the end of the occupation. There were also a few thousand civilian Nisei translators and interpreters hired by Douglas MacArthur's General Headquarters (GHQ) of the occupation government. While some civilian Nisei, including women, came from the United States on assignment, the majority were Japanese Americans who had been stranded in wartime Japan (strandees)—in addition to over a thousand Nisei who had been repatriated after their renunciation of US citizenship in the stateside incarceration camps (renunciants).[8] From August 1945 to April 1952, a cumulative total of over ten thousand Nisei men and women stayed and worked in Japan as part of the American military government.

The origins of these Nisei cultural brokers in their vanquished ancestral land can be traced to the political exigencies and pragmatic thinking of white intelligence and law enforcement officials at the outset of the Pacific War. They felt helpless when they grappled with the overlapping threats of the inscrutable enemy race inside and outside the United States as the outbreak of war looked more and more possible. From the late 1930s, the Military Intelligence Division (MID) of the War Department, the Office of Naval Intelligence (ONI), and the Federal Bureau of Investigation (FBI) engaged in surveillance on Japanese America, as the ethnic community was considered a central outpost of imperial Japan's espionage and fifth column activities.[9] With neither linguistic ability nor the appropriate physical appearance to conduct this work undetected, white federal agents had an imminent need for organizing culturally endowed experts in intelligence and surveillance vis-à-vis suspected Japanese spies and saboteurs who appeared to have been in hiding among their co-ethnics.

The practical challenges of surveilling Japanese Americans propelled the agents to recruit select ethnic Japanese—usually members of the local Japanese American Citizens League in California and its sister organization in Honolulu.[10] Out of desperation and necessity, these white intelligence experts emerged as the first group of federal government officials who reconsidered the meanings of race and citizenship relative to national loyalty when they relied on the service of Nisei informants.[11] The greater emphasis that white intelligence agents placed on the loyalty of select Japanese American citizens over their racial standing foreshadowed the systematic manner in which the United States Army decided to recruit Nisei MIS linguists in the summer of 1943 not only for battlefront intelligence but also for the future management of the racial enemy under US military occupation. This instrumentalist thinking came to be shared by military propaganda officials and experts on Japan affairs, like John Emmerson, who recommended Nisei's brokering roles in an occupation context months before the end of the hostilities.

However, to turn this idea into an actual policy, it was necessary for the higher-ups of the Roosevelt administration to realign the relationship between race and citizenship vis-à-vis the question of how to determine Nisei's political allegiance. The first step was President Roosevelt's redefinition of Americanism, which declared it was "a matter of the mind and heart . . . not a matter of race or ancestry" in early 1943.[12] This presidential proclamation underscored the primacy of citizenship and detached race from the evaluation of one's patriotism—the reversal of general US policy that had sustained the race-based incarceration of native-born Nisei citizens in the name of military necessity.

It was not coincidental that the Office for Emergency Management (OEM) within the Executive Office of the President called for the "training of Japanese-Americans for post-war services in the Far East" at almost the same time as the official declaration of colorblind Americanism. The OEM was a liaison agency that coordinated national defense measures with the military. Dated January 5, 1943, its memorandum demanded: "most serious considerations be given to" that training guidelinc, with an additional mandate that "appropriate government agencies... dealing with post-war affairs... act upon it at once." This directive was meant to override "the rather startling objection raised against it by the Division [Bureau] of Far Eastern Affairs of the State Department" (hereafter BFEA).[13] In line with the new definition of national loyalty, the gist of this policy recommendation was incorporated into a formal directive authored by Office of War Information (OWI) Director Elmer Davis; his letter was distributed through the executive branch of the federal government and the military on February 4, three days after Roosevelt's public proclamation on Americanism.[14]

While Davis's official directive left out the most egregious aspects of OEM's "bitter attack" on the BFEA, the former's January 5 memorandum presented a scathing critique of the latter's "amazing misunderstanding regarding the definition of 'American' and the method by which Americans are made and always have been made." Put together by Japan experts in the State Department, the BFEA's objection to the use of Nisei in occupied Japan was two-fold. First, the foreign service officials felt it "difficult to find any American officials willing to work on equal terms with a Nisei or accept his advice in questions... as a white man." Second, these Japan hands were certain that the leaders of defeated Japan would not appreciate what "an American official of the Japanese race" had to say or do, because the former "looked down on" the latter and viewed the Nisei as "traitors to Japan."[15]

In response, the OEM memorandum lambasted the BFEA for distinguishing Nisei from "Americans," declaring "Nisei *are* Americans, and nothing in American law, American custom or American consciousness says anything else" (emphasis original).[16] Valorizing a pluralistic notion of American nationhood, it argued that, just like Americans of European ethnic backgrounds, Japanese Americans would be of "inestimatable [sic] value to us because of their knowledge of the language, customs, and aspiration of their [Japanese] counterparts." If white military and civilian officials were to neglect such "advantage" and refuse the service of Nisei "on the basis of the preconceived opinions [about them] rather than on [their] expert knowledge of the Orient," it would be futile to try to "settle the peace" and "expect that peace to last." Put simply, as the memorandum stressed, "We are fighting an ideology, not a race, and part of that ideology is its theory of racial superiority."[17] Originating from the inner circles of the Executive Office, this high-level support for Nisei's brokering role in post-defeat Japan paved the way to a recruitment and training program for Nisei's "post-war services in the Far East" by the War Department in the fall of 1943.

It is interesting that the BFEA had attempted to block this policy guideline, which brought about an equally intriguing response from the OEM. What was at stake was not only the contestation between different ideas of race and citizenship among top government policy makers. It was also an institutional turf war in which a group of self-proclaimed Japan hands in the diplomatic circles strove to preserve their monopoly on the role of expert and policy-making power when other agencies, especially OEM and OWI, challenged them by representing Nisei as semi-native experts on enemy Japanese. Of course, the latter still operated with essentialist thinking by assuming mysterious bonds between Nisei and Oriental enemies, as articulated in OEM's memorandum. On the other hand, the BFEA's white Japan hands were desperate to safeguard their racial privilege by dismissing their potential Nisei rivals as ineffective because of their bonds to the enemy. Thus, Joseph C. Grew, the last US ambassador to imperial Japan, a special advisor to Secretary Cordell Hull and the most prominent figure in the foreign service circle of Japan hands, led the BFEA's failed assault on the OEM proposal for the training of select Nisei for postwar occupation.[18] However, Davis's formal directive of February 4 effectively nullified BFEA's resistance.

In August 1943, the War Department positively responded to the OEM/OWI guideline, subsequently adopting it "[b]y the order of the Secretary of the War" in late September.[19] The Office of the Provost Marshal General was charged with identifying Nisei MIS linguists for "civil affairs duties" in post-defeat Japan. After proper training, those Japanese Americans would be "placed in minor key positions" in order to "assist materially in the westernization of the Japanese, as these men would form a bridge between the mentality of their ancestors and American mentality and manners."[20] Here again the consistent theme of Nisei's brokering role loomed behind the essentialist thinking of military planners, who assumed being of Japanese ancestry automatically enabled them to understand the enemy mentality and promote positive transformations in them. Another, less pronounced idea was also manifest in the cursory expression: "minor key positions." This second theme resonated with the thinking of white experts on Japan in the State Department, who wanted to keep out Nisei because of their "preconceived opinions" about the race-based untrustworthiness, if not inferiority, of Japanese Americans. While Nisei could no longer be excluded from "civil affairs duties" in occupied Japan, much less military service, they had to be confined to "minor" positions. Despite the public pronouncement of colorblind Americanism, racial hierarchy was still alive in the minds and hearts of most white Americans, including the military brass.

Despite the Secretary of War's approval of the Nisei training program, many uniformed army officials expressed a strong apprehension about their recruitment that relied solely on the War Relocation Authority (WRA)'s "loyalty registration" system. Dismissing the test as "merely an evaluation of a short, four-page questionnaire" combined with a simple check of FBI records and outdated military blacklists, the army's counter-intelligence group demanded that Japanese American recruits for training "be subject to a more thorough check," including a complete background investigation.[21] Nisei's cultural attributes had the potential to threaten US national security and interests, they still felt, since these recruits could serve as a pathway of sensitive information to enemy combatants and hostile civilians. Even though their ability to decipher Japanese documents and comprehend the enemy's minds constituted a central reason to utilize select Nisei in the first place, that cultural quality remained a source of concern and lingering suspicion.

Perhaps due to the prevalent distrust of Japanese Americans within the army commands, "no requests for clearance of (Nisei) officers or enlisted men" were submitted until after the end of August 1945—when General MacArthur, Supreme Commander of the Allied Powers (SCAP), and his General Headquarters (GHQ) in Tokyo desperately began to seek Nisei linguists regardless of their qualifications for occupation duties.[22] Therefore, the special training for Nisei "civil affair officers" did not take place before the end of the war despite the Secretary of War's much earlier directive. For this reason, those dispatched to occupied Japan initially turned out to be ordinary MIS linguists from the recent battlegrounds.

Notwithstanding the prevalence of race-based suspicion, the imminent need for semi-native informants and cultural brokers in the enemy land convinced the US military authorities to rely on all groups of Japanese American citizens, including those formally classified as disloyal, for procurement of military linguists. To many Nisei who had just experienced devastating wartime imprisonment, the military occupation of Japan looked like a godsend opportunity. It provided these Nisei—mostly in their twenties with no work experience—with lucrative employment as interpreters and translators for the GHQ and for many military and civilian agencies throughout occupied Japan. In the continental United States, many Nisei needed to rebuild their lives from scratch after their release from the WRA camps. Although those in Hawai'i had escaped the mass incarceration, they, too, faced an economic pinch as the military began discharging combat soldiers who subsequently returned to their old jobs after hostilities came to an end. Whether as brand-new or returning enlistees, the work of occupation linguists paid the bills and would also fulfill their agenda of national inclusion. After the summer of 1945, job opportunities for Japanese linguists were abundant. Given the prevalence of white assumptions about Nisei's cultural expertise, those positions were theirs to monopolize. Indeed, the US Army specifically

Fig. 3.1 The first contingent of Nisei Women's Army Corps linguists being briefed by a white language officer, General Headquarters, Tokyo, Japan, ca. January 1946. National Archives and Records Administration.

recruited linguists from Japanese communities on the West Coast and Hawai'i, publishing frequent job announcements in local ethnic newspapers.[23] From January 1946, two hundred Nisei members of the Women's Army Auxiliary Corps (WAAC: later WAC) were brought over to work as linguists for GHQ's Tokyo office, although they soon had to leave enlisted status due to the army directive to remove all WAC members from the Pacific theater.[24] Due to the dearth of qualified US citizen personnel, non-WAC Nisei women also found positions as War Department civilian linguists throughout the Japanese archipelago.

Rehabilitation of Marginalized Nisei as Patriotic Americans

A long-vilified sub-group of the second-generation Japanese Americans, Japan-educated Kibei (literally those who returned to America) were the biggest beneficiaries of the US military's desire to recruit semi-native cultural brokers for the occupation. The hitherto marginalized elements of Japanese America particularly found this new opportunity attractive not simply from an economic standpoint but also for the goal of improving their own status within Japanese America. During the war, their familiarity with the enemy language and culture made Kibei look like the most dangerous sub-group of Japanese Americans—so much so that a naval intelligence officer deemed them "guilty until proven innocent."[25] Although some of these marginalized Nisei were selectively recruited for MIS/OWI operations in the Pacific theater, the pre-1945 US propaganda machine focused on—and glamourized—Nisei members of the 442nd RCT who were US educated and more Americanized. Wartime military service did not benefit Kibei linguists much, and their desire to rehabilitate their birthright citizenship remained largely unaddressed under the overshadowing stigma of disloyalty that stemmed from their prior acculturation and/or education in prewar Japan.

Once the military occupation of Japan commenced, the GHQ's demand for qualified cultural brokers swelled to the extent that work as military linguists became a main source of government employment for Japanese Americans. Kibei and other Nisei with prior exposure to Japanese culture and language emerged as the most desired ethnic sub-groups for that line of work in the eyes of the army brass. Moreover, serving as military linguists offered many Japanized Nisei a means of proving their loyalty and patriotism by taking advantage of their unique bicultural attributes. After August 1945, the military use of Japanized Nisei citizens made a small but significant crack in the widely held assumptions about the indivisibility of culture and citizenship, making it possible for Kibei and other stigmatized Japanese Americans to boast the value of their US citizenship and patriotism ironically based on their Japanese cultural upbringing. This realignment of relationality foreshadowed how postwar America would celebrate the "success" of Japanese Americans on account of their heritage culture (like Confucian work ethics) through the racially essentialized formulation of them as a "model minority" in the mid-1960s.[26]

Still, during the first year of the occupation, the US military authorities in Japan remained hopelessly short of citizen linguists, thereby continuing to rely on local Japanese officials to compile formal GHQ reports as late as September 1946.[27] A few thousand Kibei were the greatest beneficiaries of the situation. For example, a Hawai'i-born man, who was accepted into the army language school's class of September 1946, spent his formative years (1917–1936) in prewar Japan, had been wholly educated there, and had even received four years of Japanese military training while in high school. After returning to Hawai'i, this Kibei had also worked as a Japanese instructor at an ethnic language school. All these attributes, according to the official wartime yardstick, would have automatically made this man "presumed guilty of disloyalty" and subjected him to arrests and detentions by the FBI and the Justice Department right after the attack on Pearl Harbor. Yet the instrumentalist change in the thinking of the military brass allowed him to successfully apply for special training at the army language school. He was still placed under seven months of surveillance while learning to be a front-line agent of US military governance. As the long investigation produced no negative information on him, this Kibei's deep knowledge of Japanese language and society led the military brass to believe his deployment in occupied Japan was warranted. A confidential internal report stated: "That Subject was a Kibei and an instructor in a Japanese Language School enhances his value as a linguist."[28]

An intelligence report on another Kibei with a similar background (twenty-three-year residence and five years of military training in prewar Japan) also justified his assignment as a military linguist with positive renditions of his "long residence in Japan," which "should not prove a discredit but rather an asset for occupation duty."[29] For the same reason, another Japan-educated Nisei found not only his application for the class of December 1946 accepted right off the bat but also his training shortened by a few months. This man had applied for the MIS back in early 1944, which had met an outright rejection, for his Japan background had then rendered him untrustworthy.[30] In a matter of just a few years, the vilified traits of Kibei status were formally recognized as the most important characteristics for their acceptance as US citizen-servicemen, although they were to be pigeonholed into the role of cultural brokers, not the status of "normal" Americans.

Kibei were not the only beneficiaries of instrumentalist thinking among the military higher-ups. Faced with the imminent need to procure qualified linguists for the management of vanquished Japanese, the US authorities went on to salvage another sub-group of second-generation Japanese Americans who had been deemed disloyal and inimical to national security. In the class of June 1946, for example, there was a Nisei language student with dual citizenship who had once requested expatriation to Japan in 1944. When deliberating on his admission into the army language school and then on his deployment to occupied Japan, the confidential army file stressed: "the fact [that] Subject withdrew expatriation request was given serious consideration." In the end, the authorities recommended this Nisei's enlistment based on his "excellent military records" and the satisfactory result of surveillance during training.[31]

Similarly, another Nisei enlistee had failed the loyalty registration and stayed at the Tule Lake Segregation Center with a pending request for expatriation to Japan. In February 1945, this young man reversed his decision to renounce his US citizenship. Yet, his classification as disloyal remained intact despite repeated requests for release from Tule Lake in May and August 1945, because he was still classified as "a potential danger to military security." In a year's time, however, this Tule Lake segregate successfully applied for training at the army language school and graduated with flying colors as an "outstanding student." The internal security report offered the following as the rational for recommending his tour of duty in occupied Japan: "Surveillance at this station for 5 months indicates that Subject is loyal and trustworthy."[32] What propelled this 180-degree change was not the man's behavior or attitude; it was the measures that the US authorities depended on to determine what made an individual "loyal and trustworthy" or, in this case, specifically whether he had "an asset (cultural capital) for occupation duty."

It is tempting to celebrate this development as a case of America's multiculturalist progress; yet, it is necessary to take a close look at how the white army leadership salvaged the marginalized Nisei by purging the stigma and fear of disloyalty. As the individual cases revealed, that process entailed the reversal of the meaning assigned to a Japanese cultural background or ethnic heritage culture. The selection and training of military linguists for occupation also subjected Kibei and renunciants to constant monitoring and surveillance, illuminating the depth of distrust and the conditional, if not purely instrumentalist, nature of cultural tolerance. When Nisei were enlisted for linguist training, the Office of the Provost Marshal General closely reviewed an individual case file compiled during the war. Once the applicant passed that hurdle, he would be placed under the watchful eyes of multiple white personnel at the army language school, where school administrators and faculty, as well as resident intelligence officers, monitored the behavior and speech of the Nisei student, searched his personal effects, and even examined his diary and correspondence.[33] Another form of loyalty test on this racialized minority, the formal process of "clearance" of Nisei for "positions of trust" thus lasted several months if not longer before they could finally commence their work as uniformed army linguists in Japan, albeit still under the command and surveillance of their white superiors. The test never ended, and all Nisei were cognizant of it—hence the unending need to prove themselves whether stateside or in Japan.

In fact, the multilayered system of surveillance of Nisei linguists revealed deep-rooted white suspicions under the façade of officially imposed antiracism. Sharing racial and cultural commonality with the enemy remained a major cause for concern and distrust, and a solution to the problem lay in the structural subordination of Japanese American servicemen that would ensure constant supervision of them by white superiors. Insofar as they acted simply as semi-native middlemen keeping an eye on enemy nationals and furnishing useful information for white superiors without policy-making authority, the potential harm they could cause would be minimal and well contained. Of course, this has been always the way in which minority national inclusion (or assimilation) has taken place under white America's inclusionary racism. The racially lop-sided structure of the US military government in occupied Japan recreated a miniature version of a white-dominated pluralist America that wartime and postwar renditions of colorblind Americanism aspired to uphold.

The Precarious Positions and Duties of Nisei Occupation Troops

Under the conflicting forces of race-based suspicion, cultural antipathy, and colorblind extolment of birthright citizenship, several thousand Nisei MIS linguists were generally confined to the lower ranks of the military hierarchy during the war and in occupied Japan. In the theater of operation, not only did they work under white commissioned officers, but also they usually found themselves "escorted" by white soldiers, either for their "protection" or surveillance.[34] In general, most Nisei linguists held the rank of Technician Fourth Grade (T/4: equivalent to Sergeant) or lower, with no command authority—similar to what was normally awarded to the likes of cooks and mechanics—despite their highly specialized skills and several months of special training at the army language school.[35] In the military organization, even when Nisei linguists were not institutionally segregated, the consistent theme was race-based subordination, which these Japanese Americans grudgingly accepted because institutional integration looked like a better deal than exclusion or incarceration.

Still, a Nisei MIS sergeant confided his sense of indignation to a friend back home. By comparing his position to "a number of the enemy Japs" with whom he had come into contact on the battlefield, the linguist expressed "pity for them," because "in a way they are just the tools of fate—so analogous to we Nisei who wear a uniform." Speaking of the "plain facts made known to us officially," he deplored, "many branches of the service still don't accept Niseis—the signal corps and navy, for instance," even though "we work three times harder" than white enlistees. To him, the enemy soldiers who had no choice but to demonstrate total obedience resembled the Nisei servicemen who had to put up with "inwardly biased" institutional treatment.[36]

The resignation that this linguist expressed mirrored what they felt their past experience had taught them while growing up as minority Americans in a racially hierarchized system, be it general society or in the military. Whether being enlisted from an incarceration camp stateside or from Hawai'i's martial-law regime, Nisei servicemen knew all too well that their every move and utterance were under scrutiny. Hence, a public display of discontent, much less that of protest, was out of question for most. Furthermore, the state of being subordinate—or being "the tools of fate" as the linguist put—to the will and interests of white superiors was one in which the two generations of Japanese Americans had acquiesced since the prewar years. Having grown up in Hawai'i under the domination of white-controlled sugar business, this Nisei sergeant indeed had the firsthand personal/family experience of race-based containment at the lowest rung of social and economic hierarchy as a source of plantation labor. In the US West, the situation was not much different for prewar Nisei youths; most had to eke a livelihood in a preexisting ghettoized ethnic economy due to their overall exclusion from the mainstream economy.[37] In light of pervasive racial containment and pigeonholing in the US socio-economic system, it is not farfetched to compare the treatment of Nisei military linguists with the lived experience of Japanese Americans in general, yet another example of minority working-class/labor history under white supremacy.

A continuation of the longstanding US institutional practice, the wartime precedent in the armed forces set the basic pattern of the lopsided integration of Nisei's military labor into the SCAP/GHQ and the occupation forces in defeated Japan. Essentially, Japanese Americans functioned to extract raw data from native enemy sources as co-racial interlocutors. The responsibility to produce learned political knowledge—that is, to decide what information was pertinent and then formulate a policy based on it—continued to rest with white administrators and commissioned officers. The pervasiveness of their subordination within the military structure was evident in the fact that a team of twenty-five Nisei court interpreters for the Tokyo war crimes tribunal were placed under the supervision of a twenty-two-year-old white ensign, the lowest rank for a naval officer.[38]

Assigned to oversee the training of locally hired Japanese censors for the Fukuoka Civil Censorship Detachment (CCD) in the initial year of military occupation, a veteran linguist recalled with bitterness: "I was placed in charge of the [training] school unofficially, but because I was only a T/4, officially the position was given to a (white) WAC Captain, . . . who except for being an officer did not have the qualifications for the position. . . . How unfair it was for me!" When this white woman meddled in his running of the school "with her lack of knowledge of the Japanese language," the linguist "got disgusted with her interference," prompting him to request a transfer to Tokyo. According to him, "all Nisei soldiers [in his outfit] performed jobs that called for an officer or officer grade . . . position" without being so recognized.[39] As another Nisei linguist noted, "the caucasian personnel who works with the nisei, and who writes their papers on the basis of the reports or findings made by nisei gets credit for his accomplishments

Fig. 3.2 Nisei linguist interpreting the questions of a white staff attorney who interrogates a possible prosecution witness for the International Military Tribunal for the Far East, Tokyo, Japan, September 1946. Courtesy of the Seattle Nisei Veterans Committee and the US Army, and permission by Densho: The Japanese American Legacy Project, ddr-densho-114-167.

while no due credit whatsoever is given to nisei [sic]."[40] Many Nisei linguists were understandably "downright contemptuous of the (white) officers' language ability" and resented "being discriminated against," but they could not do much about it.[41]

A small division of SCAP/GHQ, the Office of the Civil Property Custodian (CPC) presents a poignant example of how such asymmetric relations between white officers and Nisei linguists were thoroughly institutionalized inside the military government structure. Charged with the control and disposition of enemy and allied properties and assets, CPC required far less involvement of Japanese American linguists than other divisions, like the Civil Intelligence Section (CIS) and Civil Information and Education Section (CIE). Yet, Nisei still accounted for almost 9 percent of its 109 American personnel as late as the spring of 1950. Of the upper seven job grades assigned to US citizen staff, the top three consisted exclusively of twenty-seven white members, including three women. They constituted about one-quarter of the aggregate American staff at CPC. Its Nisei members, all non-officers, were distributed between the fourth and seventh ranks in terms of their work classification and pay grade—with only one in the fourth, five in the fifth, one in the sixth, and two in the seventh. It means that 88 percent of Japanese American staff were concentrated in the lowest three echelons of the CPC labor force while only 34 percent of their white counterparts served in the same ranks. The highest-ranking Nisei in this division was a licensed attorney working simultaneously as counsel to the US Treasury Department, who later became one of the few foreigners authorized to practice law in postwar Japan and presided over the American Chamber of Commerce in Tokyo. Even this Nisei—with such outstanding qualifications—found it impossible to move above the status of middle-level personnel in the racially hierarchized structure of the occupation government.[42]

A close analysis of GHQ's 1951 command roster further reveals the near absence of Japanese Americans in the administrative management and decision-making apparatus. Towards the end of military occupation, the already shrinking GHQ still had 870 commissioned officers with the rank of lieutenant or above across thirty-nine sections. Eight Nisei officers accounted for a tiny fraction (less than 1 percent) of the top management of the military government; seven were concentrated in the G-2 section (intelligence), whereas one was in the office of Commander-in-Chief, who most likely served as the interpreter for General Matthew Ridgway (successor to MacArthur) and his staff.[43] As foremost GHQ historian Takemae Eiji notes, "discrimination kept most (Nisei) from rising higher than lieutenant (and captain)" despite their vital functions.[44] Indeed, four Japanese American captains held service credits a few times higher than white commissioned officers, but these Nisei only reached the second lowest rank as commissioned officers. The other four were lieutenants—the lowest officer rank.[45]

Because every aspect of military occupation work entailed some form of interaction with Japanese nationals and/or the translation of Japanese-language documents, Nisei linguists were assigned to all sections of SCAP/GHQ and the US armed forces all over the Japanese archipelago. According to army historian James C. McNaughton, "the Nisei became essential to the day-to-day function of military government and throughout country (Japan)."[46] He continues: "Their duties most often took the form of liaison with Japanese local government officials to supervise the carrying out of

SCAP directives," which took place not only inside Tokyo but also in every prefecture, every city, and even small towns.[47] In charge of purging feudalistic ideas and militaristic individuals from the native government apparatuses, schools, and mass media for the goal of democratization, the Civil Information and Education Section (CIE) and the Government Section (GS) under SCAP found Nisei linguists particularly indispensable for their operations. Part of the Legal Section (LS), Japanese American interpreters were also involved in the International Military Tribunal for the Far East (Tokyo war crimes tribunal) and the interrogations of Japanese civilians and soldiers who repatriated from the former colonial and occupied territories of imperial Japan.[48]

Moreover, what white occupation administrators found useful in the Nisei intermediaries was their racial commonalty—physical appearance included—with the inscrutable enemy. The GHQ brass opted to rely on Nisei linguists for covert information gathering among Japanese nationals. This provided a background for the continuation of the Nisei's disproportionate presence and their pivotal work in the intelligence-related apparatus of the American military government. Under the command of General Charles Willoughby who also controlled the military arm of intelligence (G-2) in occupied Japan, the SCAP/GHQ's Civil Intelligence Section (CIS), with its Counter Intelligence Corps (CIC) and the Civil Censorship Detachment (CCD) as the core, retained hundreds of Japanese American linguists during the occupation period, and beyond. For the same reason, almost all Nisei commissioned officers in Japan belonged to G-2.[49]

Even though US primary sources are scarce with regards to CIC personnel and their activities, other sources—particularly Japanese leftists who had their own information-gathering machine—provide a glimpse into the CIC's organizational structure and the Nisei's place and roles in it. In Fukushima prefecture, the regional CIC headquarters were initially established inside a restaurant building and then moved to a more unassuming location on the premise of a local factory. The personnel initially consisted of seventeen US military members, with seven being white officers. Later, the outfit had twenty-one confirmed members; seven white commissioned officers under a Major Andrew; seven Nisei enlistees, including three warrant officers; and six un-uniformed agents, three of whom were Japanese American. The last group operated out of their own private residences without reporting to the CIC office. A dozen Japanese nationals also worked

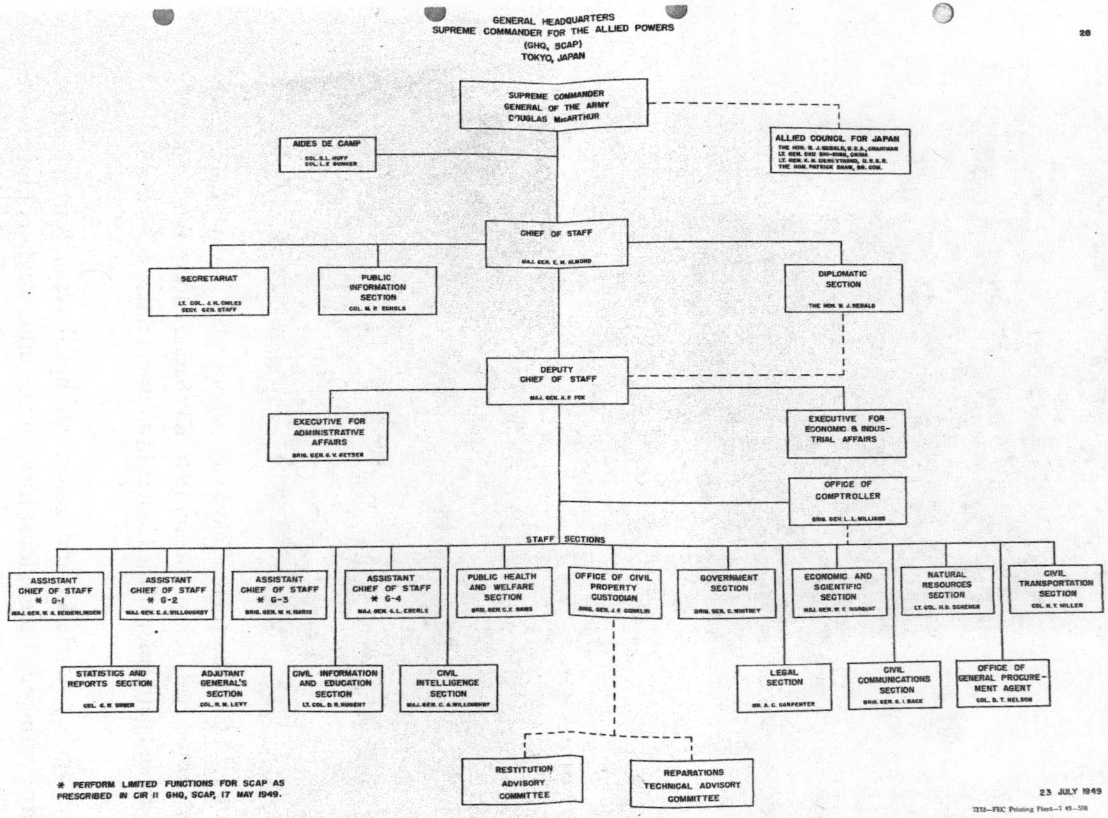

Fig. 3.3 Organizational Chart of General Headquarters, Supreme Commander for the Allied Powers, Tokyo, Japan, May 1949. National Archives and Records Administration.

Fig. 3.4 First Graduates of the Tokyo CIC School, 441st Counter Intelligence Corps, Norton Hall, Tokyo, January 1946. Kay Sasaki Papers, Box 1, Folder 7. Courtesy and permission of the Hoover Institution Library & Archives.

for the agency as clerks and gofers. Bilingual Nisei warrant officers directly commanded these local hires, while other soldiers likely served as interpreters for white superiors. In sum, over half of the Fukushima CIC was composed of Japanese Americans—both uniformed and plain-clothes undercover agents—although the leadership was overwhelmingly Caucasian. This arrangement seemed to have been the norm, for out of the twenty members at the Shizuoka CIC, eleven were similarly Japanese Americans.[50]

The CIC work enabled some Nisei to climb the ranks in the military and even make a career as counter-intelligence experts after the end of the occupation. Due to their time-consuming endeavor to create an information gathering mechanism, many CIC Nisei were desired to "stay (semi)permanently in the particular area with which they [we]re thoroughly acquainted." A native of Yuba City, California, Kay K. Sasaki "f[ell] into this category," according to the local CIC headquarters.[51] Except for his one-year stint in wartime Korea, the Nisei thus spent the entire duration of US military occupation in Japan as a CIC's "Special Agent in Charge," who also played the role of "Chief Translator" in its sub-detachments in Toyama, Kyoto, and a few other Kansai locations.[52] In Toyama, where he spent a total of two years and a half, Sasaki was involved in "Operation Baker" to develop a clandestine informant network of local Japanese nationals against communists and other subversives.[53] He was also said to have "carried out most of the interrogations besides supervising administration." Because of his excellent command of Japanese, Sasaki could handle interrogations "on his own, without the aid of an (native) interpreter." "Alert," "quick," and "accurate" in decision-making, Sasaki became indispensable to local CIC operations, and his influence so far-reaching that he could "demand the respect of officials in Toyama-ken (prefecture)" during delicate operations. Because he "performed his duties in a superior manner" as his white commander lauded, Sasaki achieved an unusually quick promotion for a Nisei in the military ranks: from Private to Seargent and from Warrant Officer Junior Grade to Chief Warrant Officer within less than three years.[54] His example shows how the intelligence work offered a special niche and rare opportunity for some Japanese American linguists because of their racial connections to the enemy. Building upon his success as a CIC agent, Sasaki continued to work for the counter-intelligence divisions of the US Army and served as an advisor with the Military Assistance Advisory Group in Vietnam during the early 1960s. Likewise, a not insignificant number of CIC members stayed on with the US military or transferred to the Central Intelligence Agency after their work in occupied Japan.[55]

It is important to note that Nisei's near-monopoly in the linguist positions in occupied Japan did not mean they all possessed bilingual fluency. Having had little prior experience with Japanese Americans, white administrators generally accepted the prevailing myth that Nisei possessed cultural knowledge and language skills simply because they were Japanese in ancestry. Neither could many whites tell whether their Nisei interpreters were carrying out their jobs properly. However, among MIS leaders who were concerned about the effectiveness of Nisei's work, there was a consensus about the gloomy prospects for obtaining a sufficient number of proficiently bilingual Nisei. According to a survey of 3,700 Nisei considered for language-related intelligence duty during the war, only 3 percent were thought to have the necessary linguistic abilities. About 4 percent were "proficient and another 3 percent fair," who "could be used only after a considerable period of training."[56] The rest—some 90 percent of tested Nisei—turned out to be utterly unfit for the work intended.

Still, the military occupation of Japan dramatically increased the number of Nisei linguists on active duty—but the overall level of their competency most likely deteriorated even further. The first contingent of ATIS members consisted of seasoned veterans, many being older Japan-educated Kibei, who came from the cream of the crop in the top 10 percent of bilingual Japanese Americans. Once they left for the United States, a good majority of Nisei enlistees who replaced them had a hard time performing the level of linguistic work required for the governance of the defeated enemy. Their duties included the translation of complicated legal, scientific, and administrative materials, as well as technical duties as censors, political liaisons, and court interpreters. Fluency in archaic bureaucratic jargon as well as colloquial slang and dialects was required for these tasks, and such diverse forms of written and spoken Japanese were difficult to master by way of intensive classroom learning alone.

Lamenting the difficulty of procuring qualified staff for censorship of postal mail and daily media outputs, an official army report brusquely noted: "Too many (Nisei) personnel, recruited statewide and in Hawaii in 1945, were incapable of performing their censorship duties." In unusually acerbic language, the report registered deep disappointment and frustration, arguing that it was not possible to "derogate sufficiently" those linguists "hired to fill specific positions, who were utterly incapable of doing so."[57] In his letter, a Nisei linguist actually confided to a friend how unprepared he was for the work to which he was assigned in Yokohama: "The army is trying to use me as a [sic] interpreter, but they are now finding they have made a grave mistake. I can do all right when they (Japanese people) speak of simple ordinary things, but when they start in on how to do a job of engineering!"[58]

State Department Japan expert John Emmerson explained a fundamental problem that was painfully obvious but unfathomable to white Americans whose judgment was clouded by cultural essentialist thinking. He observed: "Hundreds of loyal, conscientious nisei soldiers struggled with their Hawaiian and Californian Japanese learned after school and were too proud to admit the breakdowns that frustrated and distorted communication."[59] Heritage language acquisition among second-generation ethnic Americans could hardly be comparable to native-level fluency even after several months of training at the army language school—all the more reason why the formerly despised Kibei looked invaluable to concerned occupation officials and white Japan hands alike. As a female Nisei linguist recalled, "the translators (often) worked in teams consisting of Kibei and Nisei." According to her, "[t]he Kibei could read the Japanese but their translation was sometimes faulty; the Nisei, often college-educated, would translate this translation into standard English."[60]

Without enough qualified Kibei to be had, the only viable solution lay in the employment of Japanese nationals fluent in English, as well as American-born strandees and some postwar Nisei renunciants. The use of these native informants proved to be far more effective than that of enlisted Nisei linguists for essential occupation tasks. Educated Japanese nationals, including disenfranchised Nisei strandees, generally possessed better bilingual skills as well as cultural knowledge and technical expertise. For example, the CCD ended up employing Japanese nationals "in a ratio of over 6,000 to 550 US personnel."[61] However, their lack of US citizenship and/or past collaboration with Japan's militarist regime still made these native translators and interpreters dangerous in the eyes of white American occupiers, especially intelligence officers, who suspected that "no friendly natives" could ever exist in Japan—a land full of inscrutable "potential enemies."[62] For the same reason, Nisei renunciants were "ousted" from linguist jobs in the spring of 1947 once sufficient replacements became available from the pool of fresh graduates from the army language school in Minnesota. Meanwhile, American-born strandees whose US citizenship had been restored became eligible for enlistment and/or normal security clearance to serve as uniformed military linguists and Army's civilian staffers from January 1949 on.[63]

Regardless of the actual skills and qualifications, citizenship status generated a clear line of demarcation in terms of wages and benefits. In the summer of 1946, most enlisted Nisei linguists and civilian US personnel

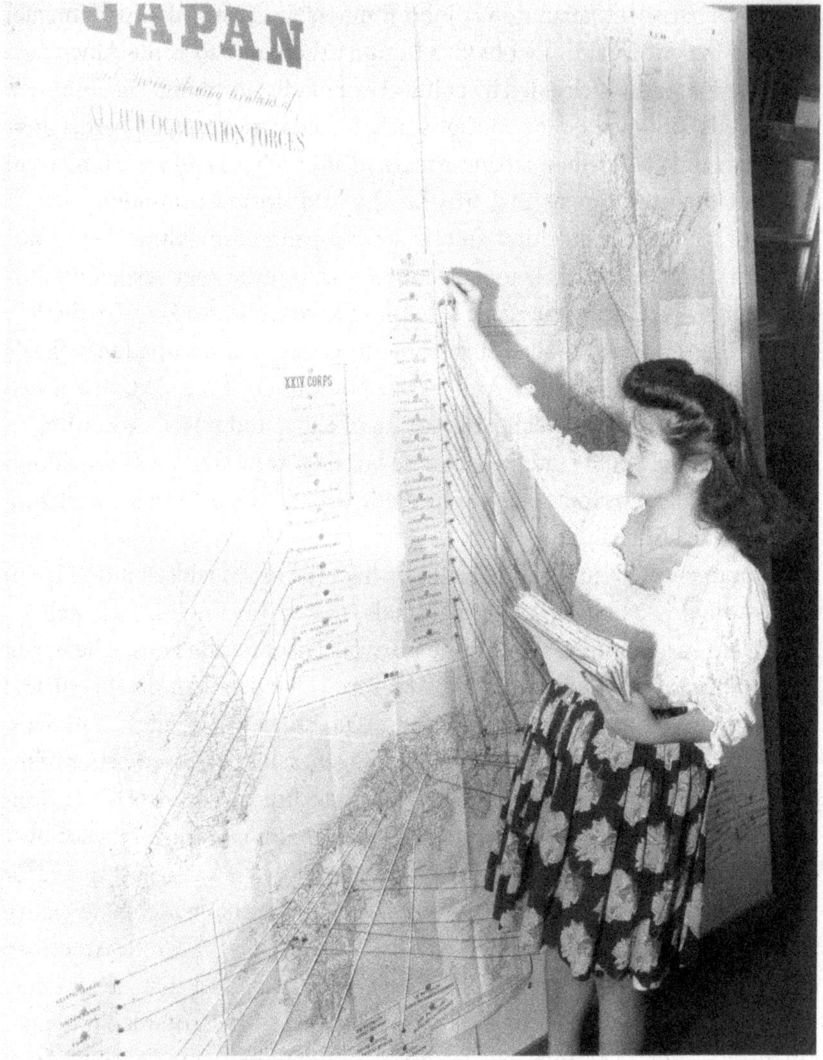

Fig. 3.5 Nisei Clerk-Typist, General Headquarters, Tokyo. This woman was a strandee who found a GHQ position after the reinstitution of her US citizenship, September 1946. Courtesy of the Seattle Nisei Veterans Committee and the US Army, and permission by Densho: The Japanese American Legacy Project, ddr-densho-114-148.

received a monthly salary of 3,500 yen or more from the GHQ. Local native hires, including renunciants and disenfranchised strandees, got only 500 yen paid for by the Japanese government. Moreover, the latter could not ride public transportation reserved for occupation personnel, eat subsidized nutritious foods at military canteens, or shop for daily necessities at PX stores. One Nisei soldier, who called renunciants "Tule bastards," explained how some of them tried repeatedly to sneak into "'[almost empty] GI trains'...to avoid [boarding] the packed, lice-infested regular coaches"—only to be "booted out by (Nisei) soldiers" who "occasionally beat them up" for punishment. Many of these non-citizen Japanese Americans had no family to stay with in Tokyo. Hence, the GHQ initially had to set up a makeshift dormitory for them by commandeering an office building, where rows of army beds were laid out for them to sleep at night. Upon her repatriation, one female renunciant could not find her Japanese relatives in Hiroshima so she "stood in line for 2 days to get a return [train] ticket here [Tokyo]" before finding a job as an English typist. "Some young buds," this young woman noted about other renunciants, were "working as labor gang foremen."[64] Aside from the much lower pay and inferior labor conditions, these accounts of renunciants' struggle present a stark contrast to the privileged experience of Nisei servicemen and civilian GHQ staffers.[65]

The majority of Nisei military linguists were day-to-day supervisors of local hires, including strandees and renunciants. Inside the office, bilingual native translators, as well as non-citizen Nisei, did most of the tedious work of deciphering handwritten letters, going over daily newspapers, and translating thousands of government papers into English. In the Tokyo CCD, the mail censorship section alone had over five hundred Japanese censors (called "examiners"). On one floor that handled personal correspondence, there were thirty large tables, each of which had ten censors seated to work. A Japanese censor remembers she went over as many as three hundred postcards and letters each day.[66]

Historian Takemae Eiji succinctly explains the civil censorship process:

> Japanese examiners scoured this material diligently, referring questionable, objectionable and sensitive items to their American (Nisei) supervisors, who ordered a full or partial translation of the suspect text, words, dialogue or scene.[67]

Based on the materials translated by their subordinates, Japanese American linguists then compiled English-language reports and summaries for their

Fig. 3.6 CCD Japanese national employees inspecting private letters and postcards for subversive contents inimical to US occupation aims in July 1947. Materials of interest are referenced to GHQ supervisors and translated into English for review by CCD American personnel, many of whom were Nisei. US Army Photograph taken from Douglass MacArthur and his General Staff, *Reports of General MacArthur: MacArthur in Japan: The Occupation: Military Phase* Volume I Supplement (Washington, DC: Government Printing Office, 1966), plate no. 76.

Fig. 3.7 A Nisei female GHQ employee and military linguists at work, Tokyo, Japan, September 1946. Courtesy of the Seattle Nisei Veterans Committee and the US Army, and permission by Densho: The Japanese American Legacy Project, ddr-densho-114-146.

white overseers. Their positioning between clueless white administrators and rightless Japanese nationals made it possible for Nisei occupation troops to replicate the exploitative practice of taking sole credit for the work completed by others—the same practice that they had complained about under racial subordination within the military structure.[68] Situated between the two cultural worlds that were presumed to be qualitatively different and incompatible, most Nisei served to broker the transaction of unadulterated data without the power to give meaning to it—a role reserved only for white superiors.

Non-citizen Nisei as Japan's "Native" Brokers

The analysis of Japanese American brokering in occupied Japan would not be complete without a discussion of how some Nisei ended up acting as "native" ideological and political brokers for the defeated regime due to the loss/absence of US citizenship. Whereas many ordinary wartime strandees eked out a daily living by working as locally hired non-citizen translators, educated and older elements of the resident Nisei population in Tokyo were not only spared from similar hardships, but were also able to access much better employment and career opportunities under US military occupation, albeit still as Japanese nationals. Some of the key leaders of the Nisei Association of Nippon (NAN), the central organization of American-born Japanese during wartime Japan, continued to occupy important positions in the post-1945 print media due to their command of English and cultural ability to negotiate with GHQ personnel. During the war, US-born individuals had taken charge of anti-enemy propaganda in their native tongue through state-controlled news outlets, such as the *Nippon (Japan) Times*, Dōmei News, and Radio Tokyo. When the GHQ reorganized and placed these entities under its censorship program, many resident Nisei newspapermen and journalists slotted into the management and top editorial staffs of domestic news agencies, yet this time as publicists of democratic ideologies for the occupation regime.

Los Angeles-born Goro Murata, news editor of the *Nippon Times*, remained at the helm of the English-language newspaper, while Tamotsu Murayama also assumed executive positions there. Kiyoshi George Togasaki took over the management of the same newspaper after Japan's defeat. Murata and Murayama were veteran Nisei journalists, who had had the experience of working for Japanese American vernaculars in California before coming to Japan during the 1930s. San Francisco-born Togasaki had been one of the most respected elder Nisei in prewar Japan, and he had been a prominent figure in the information (intelligence) section of the Japanese foreign ministry as well as the overseas division of Radio Tokyo during the Pacific War. After the arrival of US occupation forces, they rose as "native" movers and shakers in the censored print media, cranking out English-language news reports in support of US-led democratization.[69]

Acting as local collaborators in promoting the GHQ's publicity agenda, other foreignized Nisei also helped to transmit democratic knowledge through public discourse in occupied Japan. Split into two separate entities under a SCAP directive, the successors to Dōmei News employed a significant number of Nisei staffers, including the first international section chief of Kyōdō News. Some others fluent in Japanese also entered the higher echelons of regular domestic dailies as foreign news editors and division chiefs.[70] Although they were no different from other Japanese nationals in terms of their legal standing, American-born journalists created an ethnic niche in postwar Japan's mass media due to the cultural capital that they had preserved through their involvement in Japan's wartime propaganda machine. Taking advantage of their US background, they survived the tumultuous collapse of the Japanese empire by switching allegiance to the military domination of their birth country. This transition was surprisingly smooth and uneventful. In the eyes of American occupiers, the work of self-motivated native facilitators from within the ranks of the vanquished were beneficial and culturally legible. Moreover, these Nisei Japanese nationals were convenient to political and industry leaders of post-defeat Japan, who lacked the cultural and linguistic expertise to respond to and negotiate the demands of the reorientation program imposed by GHQ.

On account of their native middleman status, a small group of resident Nisei enjoyed opportunities in the national politics of occupied Japan. Ex-NAN leaders had cultivated a close partnership with high-ranking officials of imperial Japan's central government, especially those in the foreign ministry, internationally minded statesmen, and military brass. Combined with a US background, their personal relations to Japan's political insiders put them in a position to mediate the negotiations between the vanquished and the occupiers on behalf of the former—particularly through informal/clandestine channels. Just as white GHQ officers expected US Nisei military and civilian linguists to serve as semi-native brokers vis-à-vis an inscrutable enemy, Japanese government officials found this particular group of resident Nisei useful and reasonably trustworthy for the daunting task of conveying their wishes and demands in cultural terms legible to the occupiers.

Former NAN President Takizo Frank Matsumoto was a case in point. Born in Hiroshima and reared in Fresno, California, this chief voice of Japan's racial propaganda was not a Nisei in the sense that he never held birthright US citizenship. Yet, he had been always viewed—and self-identified—as a prominent leader of the Japanese American community in Tokyo since the early 1930s. Matsumoto had a wide range of friends and allies in Japan's diplomatic circles and national politics, especially future Prime Minister Miki Takeo and his cronies. Miki urged Matsumoto to run successfully for a seat in the national Diet in the first democratic general election of 1946. Another close ally of Matsumoto's was Fukushima Shintarō, a former diplomat who had been the Los Angeles consul and then a member of the Japanese embassy in Washington, DC, before the Pacific War. When Matsumoto pursued his graduate studies at Harvard in the late 1930s, the diplomat had befriended him, and they worked together on a pro-Japan propaganda campaign in the United States.[71] In 1947–1948, Fukushima served as a secretary to Japan's prime minister and then as a deputy chief cabinet secretary in charge of diplomacy (dealing with the Allied Powers); Matsumoto assumed the position of the parliamentary vice-minister for foreign affairs.[72] Owing to their American backgrounds, both individuals possessed crucial cultural expertise that made them so politically desirable that they played the role of formal Japanese government representatives vis-à-vis SCAP/GHQ.

In partnership with his allies, Matsumoto also engaged in informal and even illicit brokering. In July 1947, he spearheaded the establishment of "Service Center Tokyo," a private concern that was also known as Keimeisha in Japanese. Under the appearance of being an intercultural and business liaison with Americans, this so-called consultation firm actually lobbied for the cancellation of the ban on and release of high-profile Japanese leaders purged from public service/office due to their being charged with war crimes.[73] Although Service Center Tokyo was the brainchild of Matsumoto and Fukushima, its five-person board of trustees included Togasaki and Murata along with Matsumoto and two of his Japanese friends (one being a US-educated former immigrant). The company's prospectus professed: "Long years of association with the American people during our residence in the United States place us in a unique position," which "should serve to

Fig. 3.8 A long-term leader of Nisei in Japan, Takizo Frank Matsumoto (left) receives welcome leis from kimono-clad Nisei women in Honolulu. Representing postwar Japan, he was a part of the first delegation of Japanese National Diet members to the United States, March 9, 1950. Courtesy and permission of *Nippu Jiji* Photo Archives, *Hawaii Times* Photo Archives Foundation and Hoover Institution Library & Archives, J1108.001.

assist in liaison work between the Allied Forces headed by the United States and the Japanese people." This statement gives a glimpse into the in-between positions of Matsumoto and other US-born individuals (strandees), who could no longer call themselves Nisei due to their wartime enemy collaborations but still claimed their special brokering role on the basis of what they had continuously boasted as a "special talent" rooted in their US upbringing.[74]

Although very few written sources are available because Matsumoto's Nisei wife allegedly burned everything after his death, Service Center Tokyo is credited with having contributed to the release of several prominent politicians and business leaders as the result of Matsumoto's backdoor deal-making with high-level GHQ officials. All English documents—petitions for release, affidavits, and the like—were prepared and typed by Takizo's Portland-born wife, Mary Ayako Matsumoto. Their son recalled the Matsumotos often visited the residences of top GHQ officers, particularly Jack Napier's house. This man was a Government Section executive officer responsible for matters relating to political purges.[75]

Combined with his bilingual fluency and cultural knowledge of American-style negotiations, what made Matsumoto so effective as a broker was his

Harvard background. Having completed a master's degree at Harvard Business School in 1938, Matsumoto could claim and capitalize on his membership in the exclusive university clique. He flaunted the name of his alma mater when identifying himself publicly, and he rejoiced at the opportunity to speak at the Harvard Club in Tokyo and connect with members of the occupation authorities shortly after he was appointed the vice-minister.[76] Many of the GHQ brass, especially top-level expert administrators, were Harvard graduates, including such powerful figures as Charles L. Kades and Milo E. Rowell of the Government Section (GS).[77] As a top Japanese official recalled, Matsumoto was said to have "enjoyed the full confidence of [those in the] GS."[78]

One white GS staffer echoed the statement from the conquerors' perspective: "No other Japanese could match Matsumoto's knowledge of the complex interrelationship between the Japanese government and GHQ. That was the source of his great influence in both Japanese and American circles."[79] The same official called the Nisei an "English-speaking ambassador of goodwill who had the confidence of all Japanese political factions and all sections of GHQ."[80] Thus, it was no surprise that Matsumoto's Service Center Tokyo was highly regarded among Japanese leaders, particularly the old guard under the threat of being purged, as a de facto "office of negotiations with SCAP"—the go-to place if they needed to avoid the long arm of GHQ's vengeful justice.[81] Needless to say, it was more than plausible that Matsumoto enjoyed hefty monetary rewards in return for such clandestine brokerage as he himself once confided to a GHQ official.[82]

Japanese Americans as Knowledge Producers for GHQ Democratization

Just as Matsumoto did for the Japanese government, some US Nisei in occupied Japan performed other roles besides supervising native workers as military linguists. Japanese American GHQ staffers occasionally acted as producers of critical knowledge for the GHQ decision-making process. In CIE's Religions and Cultural Resources Division (hereafter RCRD), a Nisei named Francis T. Motofuji played the role of chief knowledge producer in the capacity of one of the two "Field Liaison Officers" (later upgraded to a "Religious Advisor"). Born and raised in Hawai'i, he graduated from the University of Hawai'i before enlisting in the MIS in 1943. The seasoned linguist was better educated than many of his fellow Nisei GIs, and he had a strong penchant for tedious research and a genuine interest in Japan's literary tradition, philosophy, and folk rituals. Indeed, after his occupation stint, Motofuji pursued graduate study in Japanese language and literature and obtained a master's degree from University of California at Berkeley and a doctorate from Stanford University. Known for his translations of traditional *Kabuki* plays, novels, and a pioneering study on Japanese cinema, this Nisei linguist went on to hold a faculty position in Japanese at UC Berkeley after 1964.[83]

In mid-1947, Motofuji successfully applied for a position at RCRD to work as a Field Liaison Officer that covered Shintoism and Buddhism while another officer, a Caucasian, dealt with Christianity. According to his job description, the Hawai'i Nisei was expected to:

> Advise the [Division] Chief... on all matters pertaining to the Buddhist, Shinto and all other non-Christian religious organizations and institutions in Japan with special reference to the establishment of religious freedom, separation of religion and state, and the elimination of militarism and ultra-nationalism in Buddhist, Shinto and other religious doctrines and practices.[84]

The work would involve frequent travel and conferences with Japanese religious leaders and local government officials, as well as "extensive field work in relation to the implementation and explanation of SCAP religious policies."[85]

This important position was not meant for a Japanese American when it was initially conceived. Given the need for the high level of language command and subject expertise, "a well-qualified person" was deemed "vitally necessary." The officer in this position was also supposed to handle the all-important question of state Shintoism, the epitome of imperial Japan's undemocratic character that GHQ wished to replace with the principle of the freedom of religion. From the beginning, the CIE brass had specific Caucasian personnel in mind, a naval officer who had studied at Tokyo Imperial University before the war.[86] Yet, this scheme fell through, and Motofuji was hired instead, albeit at a significantly lower grade than the one reserved for the white officer. Yet, the Nisei rose up the ranks at an exceptional pace, for, as his white boss marveled, "Mr. Motofuji has been performing the duties of the position in an outstanding manner."[87] He reached the original job rank set for the position of Field Liaison Officer by May 1948, and his title was expanded to Religious Advisor on Shinto and Buddhist affairs two years later.[88]

During his term from mid-1947 through 1951, Motofuji represented his division to confer regularly with Japanese government officials at the educational ministry and other agencies about "administrative, legal and technical" issues in the subjects of Shintoism and Buddhism.[89] The Nisei also liaised with representatives of these religious groups and observed and evaluated how the SCAP directives and related policy mandates were being received and implemented at the grassroots level. Between September and December 1947, for example, Motofuji travelled to the northern regions (Hokkaido and Tohoku) and southwestern regions (Shikoku and Kyushu) of Japan, that is, almost half of the Japanese archipelago. Motofuji interviewed local allied military government officials in charge of education and religious matters, met with Japanese bureaucrats and religious leaders, attended their laypersons' meetings, and visited shrines, temples, and organizations and schools. In the following year, his field research covered religiously important pockets of central Japan, as well as Kyoto and the southern end of Japan's main island.[90]

Motofuji emerged as a major producer of firsthand knowledge about religious conditions in occupied Japan. This is the type of knowledge that other experts, especially those based in Tokyo and/or armchair intellectuals, could not generate. The Nisei's supervisor at RCRD, Naval Lieutenant William K. Bunce, was unusually familiar with Japan for a white American because he had worked as an English teacher in rural Japan during the 1930s. Existing studies relate Bunce's close relationship to and dependence on a Japanese professor of religion as a major source of information, but they overlook the research the Nisei provided for Bunce's decision-making.[91] Whereas the Japanese professor and other native advisors furnished Bunce with academic advice and/or Tokyo-centered perspectives, Motofuji authored many field reports on the state of religious activities in rural Japan and grassroots responses to the top-down reform initiatives on religious freedom.

The Nisei religions officer was also a vital transmitter of official GHQ knowledge to Japanese religious leaders and local government officials, as well as regional CIE agents. While they all received common SCAP directives relating to religious reforms, they implemented the Tokyo-originated policy mandates according to their own interpretations and adjustments to specific local conditions. As a representative of the CIE headquarters, Motofuji had the power to evaluate and correct how things were being done in each locale and to steer the manner of policy enforcement in a proper direction. That power, albeit disproportionate to his mid-level institutional rank, could be wielded, because Motofuji had direct access to both local CIE officers and Japanese nationals on the ground. An analysis of Motofuji's reports revealed a certain set of themes ("problems") with which he and supposedly his boss were preoccupied: forced contributions to Shinto shrines and Buddhist temples; support of local government or public servant for religious institutions, especially Shinto shrines; public commemorations of the war dead and the construction of memorials for them with public funds (including "forced contributions"); and public school activities concerning religious establishments. At the heart of these issues lay the separation of church and state. Given the historical problem of state Shintoism in Japan, Motofuji's reports also dwelled on the "violations of the Shinto Directive of December 15, 1945."[92] The Nisei detailed concrete examples of how such violations had taken place and how they were being rectified by local occupation personnel (and him if necessary). Motofuji thus served as an important overseer and enforcer of the central occupation mandates.

At the same time, the Nisei agent played a critical role as the GHQ's eyes for local officials, who might overstep the boundaries of what they should/could do in the context of democratization. In other words, Motofuji had the prerogative of not only interpreting the properness of what was done by local US officers but also rectifying it if he deemed necessary. In October 1947, for example, Motofuji exerted his disciplining power vis-à-vis overzealous local reform agents in Hokkaido. He noted: "The zeal of the CI&E officers of the team, particularly as concerns Shinto, is such that the undersigned suggested it would be well to keep in mind the principle of the freedom of religion."[93] Within CIE, Motofuji's principled understanding of democratic norms related to religion and state made him a vocal advocate for the abolition of Yasukuni Shrine, the symbol of state Shintoism that had housed all the souls of Japan's war dead and venerated them as national heroes/gods. Motofuji stood up, albeit in vain, against his white superiors in RCRD—especially William Woodard, Bunce's right-hand man who determined that the shrine for the war dead was a legitimate religious institution.[94]

Perhaps this Nisei religious advisor—who fulfilled multifaceted functions as an occupation knowledge producer, its transmitter, and a ground-level enforcer—was an exception to the norm, but there were a few other Japanese American linguists like him who worked as subject experts and knowledge producers within various GHQ apparatuses. For example, the Nisei with higher education were frequently employed for research work that was language-intensive or culturally focused. Like Motofuji, many became academic experts on Japan/Asia later. CIE's Public Opinion and Sociological Research Division employed two Japanese Americans, who worked as Social Science Research Analysts: Tamie Tsuchiyama and Iwao Ishino. These Nisei woman and man had prior research experiences inside the Poston WRA camp.[95] Yet, as Motofuji's absent presence in the existing scholarship illustrated, white administrators like Bunce tended to reduce the Nisei's work to a semi-native source of raw data, even though they could play a larger role. Despite all they did, such Nisei experts were still structurally confined to the status of invisible middleman brokers working behind the scenes within the military government.

Nisei as the Agent and the Symbol of Tutelary Democratization

In addition to Nisei's multifaceted work within GHQ, they played another role as co-racial facilitators of democracy in occupied Japan. Many were compelled to act as living proof that people of damned ancestry could still become acceptable members of the civilized world under the generous guidance of white Americans. As military linguists, Japanese Americans mostly labored in the background of America's epochal democratization effort. Yet, many individual Nisei had been moved by essentialist expectations that they had a special responsibility as Americans of shared ancestry with those to be reformed "under the kind surveillance of the US." Indeed, this is why one of the first occupation linguists proudly declared, "We are spreading news of democracy . . . [and] are planting the seeds for a New Japan."[96] Similarly, a Nisei WAC linguist was quoted as saying, "We have Japanese faces, but we are Americans. . . . By our example we will have to show [the Japanese] what a woman of Japanese background can be like—how she acts—when she has lived in a democratic country and had the advantages offered by such a country. It's going to be a big job—but we all know it and we are going to do our best to be successful at it."[97]

Fig. 3.9 Nisei linguists and their white boss "selling democracy" to Japanese children. From *Tips: Troop Information Program Service* 2, no. 21 (1947), p. 384. National Archives and Records Administration.

Another Hawai'i-born linguist wrote his friend back home about his sense of mission embellished with a story of calculated kindness to the conquered, especially the new generation that would carry forward the future of a democratic Japan. He noted:

> Whatever candies I have been buying at the PX for months and whatever was sent from home, I have been accumulating them. I have enough to make several hundred kids in Japan happy for Xmas. . . . This may be a rather poor way to have the kids associate Democracy with candies, but it's a means to an end. These youngsters are just as innocent and naïve as any tot in Hawaii or in the states, and by the proper guidance they can be made to follow the proper road and become the leaders to rebuild Japan into a Democratic nation.[98]

As iconic teachers of US-style democracy, some Japanese American occupation troops also found themselves operating in the spotlight set up by GHQ, having to act as frontline publicists for its reorientation program by which to remake defeated Japan into a non-western/non-white democracy. Featured in a reputed woman's magazine, three Japanese American servicemen and a female Nisei GHQ staffer offered a Democracy 101 lesson to their racial cousins just about one month before the historic general election of April 1946. It was the first time ever that Japanese women could vote as equal citizens of modern Japan. Addressing a Japanese female readership, one of the most targeted populations in the effort of democratization, these Nisei youths offered a roundtable discussion on marriage, family life, gender relations, women's education, and their careers, among other topics, from an "American" perspective.[99] Juxtaposed against examples of these Nisei's own experiences as rights-bearing individuals, their critical observations of Japanese thinking and behavior underscored a central theme of GHQ's reorientation program—that is, to stamp out the "authoritarian" (feudalistic) attitude that had allegedly rendered prewar Japanese people the mindless hordes that militarists could easily brainwash into "an extreme nationalism and a glorification of war."[100]

This roundtable specifically urged female Japanese readers to appreciate their status and the rights they held as equal constituents of the household and self-reflective citizens of society—the new set of privileges that benevolent Americans brought to them for the first time. One Nisei linguist shared a story he had supposedly heard from a white soldier friend, who tried to give up a seat for a Japanese woman while riding a train. That woman called for her husband, who nonchalantly proceeded to take the seat while leaving his wife standing in a jolting car. While a Japanese moderator exclaimed "what a shame!," another Nisei GI calmly pointed out: "these problems cannot be rectified unless [Japanese are] taught (how to behave in a democratic manner) from first grade in a coeducational environment."[101] Turning to the regrettable state of Japanese wives after lambasting feudalistic husbands, a female Nisei panelist criticized how the women of her ancestral land were still "bound by traditional family customs...without being able to act according to reason instead of emotion."[102] Both women and men were at fault, the Nisei's anecdotes therefore illuminated, and it would require all individuals to "absorb democracy into every facet of their daily living (and practice) rather than simply trying to understand it as something taught as a school subject."[103] These Japanese Americans came off as being not only empathetic but also familiar with the culturally specific challenges that people of their ancestral land faced in their process of democratization. While still reifying the basic tenet of binaristic Orientalist thinking, this roundtable typified how occupation Nisei were presented as a model of democracy in action to their racial cousins in the heavily censored media under the US military rule.

Based on their own belief in racial and cultural commonalty, Japanese nationals, especially liberal-minded ones, also began to look at Nisei occupation troops as especially beneficial for the democratization ("Americanization" to them) of their country. One of the first visitors to the United States from defeated Japan, a female Christian leader acknowledged the valuable work carried out by Nisei occupation troops in "the construction of a democratic Japan." She pleaded for more Japanese Americans to come and work in the land of their ancestors to give a helping hand.[104] Another Japanese, a YMCA leader, echoed the expectation for Nisei's further "contributions to Japan's democratic progress in education, culture, and politics."[105]

A well-known painter put a unique artistic spin on how Nisei could serve as a new yardstick of ideal Japanese womanhood in the age of "Euro-American (read democratic) lifestyle." In his opinion, the beauty of the "new Japanese woman" must be articulated through the switching of their clothes from "traditional" to "western" in everyday life. To him, the tightly bound Japanese clothing represented the chains of feudalistic household customs, whereas the loosely worn western dress signified—and enabled—more freedom in the woman's individual thinking and behavior. Yet, due to a difference in body shape and living habits from "Euro-Americans," the painter argued that it would be a daunting task for Japanese women to switch to the new lifestyle. Having grown up in American society, Nisei women would serve as an inspiration for their racial sisters in Japan when these "new women" were compelled to figure out how to adopt an alien clothing practice, and indeed an entirely new modus vivendi and operandi as democratic citizens under US-led national remaking. The cultural and material realities of Japan's democratization required a new aesthetic in the physical representations of Japanese women, he argued, and there was no better reference than Americanized Nisei women who worked, played, and asserted their equality to men in western clothes.[106]

Under prevailing racial and cultural essentialism on both sides of the equation, SCAP/GHQ even attempted to exploit the Nisei's experience of mass incarceration as a useful lesson for Japanese nationals in its educational reform program. In this example, imprisoned Japanese Americans symbolized the power of transformative US democracy that made outstanding loyal citizens out of racially Japanese people. During the war, America's propaganda machine flipped the racist episode with a progressivist narrative that the incarceration camps offered Issei and Nisei not only a "happy normal life" but also a "training ground" for practicing democratic self-governance under the benevolent supervision of white administrators. At the same time, the WRA and JACL collaborated in publicity campaigns to portray the mass removal of West Coast Japanese having the positive effect of dismantling parochial ethnic "islands" to facilitate their mass Americanization. Purportedly, thus, the racial incarceration camps promoted the cultural assimilation and democratization of Japanese people in America under militarized tutelary confinement.[107] With this contrived narrative of the wartime mass incarceration, the oxymoronic symbolisms of Japanese Americans as exemplary democratic Japanese could make even more sense, for Nisei linguists and civilian GHQ staffers were deemed a product of that very recent transformative experience in confinement and white supervision. The positive rendition of the race-based incarceration offered a parallel to how defeated Japanese were being democratized en masse "under the kind surveillance of the US" armed forces.

From this alchemy of wartime racist history, there emerged a perspective that the educational program inside the WRA camps should serve as a historical precedent for similar race-centered reforms in and democratization of occupied Japan. Not only did Nisei's wartime experience become a crystal ball for Japan's bright future, but it also constituted the very knowledge base from which GHQ's efforts at democratizing Japan's education were drawn. In this sense, wartime race politics engendered in the WRA camps served the goal of the US occupation government on the other side of the Pacific, illuminating the continuities and intersections of vulgar/biological racism and polite/assimilationist racism. It also clearly shows that Nisei's work as liaisons and knowledge producers unfolded within the long tradition of white Americans' idealized view of rehabilitation and reform relative to racial minorities. This line of thinking provided a background for GHQ's desires to hire former white WRA camp administrators and educators and, conversely, for the latter's decisions to apply for or accept an invitation for employment in occupied Japan.[108]

To begin with, CIE sought to recruit selected former custodians of the Japanese incarceration camps for data collection and an analysis of family structure, social system, and religion in Japan. Out of ten researchers on the agency's "to recruit" list, four social scientists had had the experience of researching or writing about Japanese American internees during the war. They included Alexander H. Leighton, Edward H. Spicer, Andrew Lind, and Leonard Bloom [Broom]. The first two managed and conducted field research in the Poston WRA camp in Arizona, while the latter two studied Japanese American "relocation," its impact on family and community relations, and Nisei's "assimilation." While Leighton and Lind were experts on social psychiatry and behavioral science, and sociology, respectively, the other two were trained cultural anthropologists.[109] It is notable that Leighton had already published a widely read academic study titled *The Governing of Men: General Recommendations Based on Experience at a Japanese Relocation Camp* (1945), which offers scholarly discussions of and remedies for social and psychological problems that both Japanese American internees and white camp administrators grappled with. A contemporary scholarly review of the book recommended that Leighton's book "should be studied carefully by persons who are involved in the government of occupied territories . . . every one who takes his responsibility in a democracy seriously."[110]

Although none of these high-profile scholar-experts accepted a job offer from GHQ, a few mid-level WRA camp administrators, particularly architects of camp education systems, decided to provide the US occupation authorities with their expertise on and hands-on experience of assimilating Japanese Americans into white America's democracy. In 1947, Hubert C. Armstrong served as the Director of CIE's Research Unit, which was charged with the responsibility to "accumulate, translate, evaluate, correlate, and maintain a file of background and current information and data."[111] With a background in child psychology and administrative work in the Oakland Public School system, Armstrong spent several months in 1942 at the Poston incarceration camp during the formative period of its school system. His role was as specialist in education and psychology, and he had close connections to Leighton as well. This self-proclaimed practitioner of Dewey-style progressive education was a quintessential white liberal of the time who wished to see Japanese as "individuals" and "persons" rather than from the standpoint of "prejudice tied up to the word 'Japanese,'" or "as under the single classification of Japs."[112] As he argued in his wartime correspondence with his former Nisei students and Leighton, Armstrong believed that "the whole problem is a cultural one and not a biological or racial one."[113] It meant, first, that Japanese persons were assimilable, and second, that if they chose to be acculturated to the value of democracy, they should be accepted with open arms—whether they were citizens or resident aliens (or, by extension, defeated foreigners).

Not only did this culturalist thinking make it possible for Armstrong and other white liberals to distinguish Nisei from enemy "Japs" during the war; it also allowed them to see the possibility of turning the latter into the former in their disposition and behavior under America's tutelary occupation. Indeed, Armstrong's 1942 letter to a like-minded educator anticipated the kind of grandiose ideas that would later propel him to cross the Pacific. In it, he stressed the importance of democratic education—one by which to empower Nisei to break away from the chains of "conventional Japanese culture" that their parents' generation had foisted on them. Such transformative power of education would facilitate the "Americanization of Japanese, especially Nissei (sic)" in the incarceration camps—and logically in occupied Japan.[114] It is not difficult to find a similar line of thinking in CIE's official policies and programs. For example, while attempting to stamp out the influences of Japan's feudalistic tradition, CIE declared that its objectives were to popularize education, lead all Japanese to "form a habit of independent thinking and peaceful cooperation," and "let them...help each other towards the elevation of their own culture."[115] Nevertheless, Armstrong's ideal of experimental progressive education in Japan was frustrated by the reality of military governance. His superior, "a weak fearful military man with a relatively low rank (Lt. Colonel)," did nothing but "scare" staffers and make a fuss over "petty things," rendering CIE's morale "very low." Dejected, Armstrong resigned from his position in early 1948.[116]

Kenneth M. Harkness was another former camp educator, who joined GHQ in February 1946 for the "elevation of culture" in occupied Japan. A former missionary educator and graduate of Columbia Teachers' College, he previously worked at the WRA's Tule Lake center as the superintendent of education for its internal school system. At CIE's Education Division, Harkness played the role of the curriculum and textbook officer and special consultant until September 1950.[117] His job had direct impact on Japanese school children and their learning process, since his unit oversaw the contents of state-authorized textbooks and curricula and promoted "reorientation ... by means of (a) the formulation of recommendations on policies and measures ... at all school levels; [and] (b) the sharing of professional resources and giving of assistance with regard to the compiling ... of educational materials."[118]

Whereas Armstrong faced all sorts of roadblocks within the military-dominated GHQ bureaucracy and became disenchanted with the routine of data collection and report-writing without direct involvement in pedagogical developments and content-matters, Harkness could bring to the table what he had learned about educating Japanese people and the process of their cultural reform, or reorientation, in US incarceration camp. This perhaps explains why this former camp educator stayed in his job until CIE's intervention into the Japanese school system began to diminish.[119] Harkness's work in occupied Japan, albeit far larger in scale, represented an extension of his wartime activities as a practitioner of assimilationist progressive education, insofar as the Americanization of Japanese American internees resembled the democratization of the whole Japanese nation if these projects were deemed essentially a matter of cultural uplift, or "elevation."

It is also important to note that Harkness's stint at the Tule Lake camp made him better prepared and suited for his post-1945 work vis-à-vis foreign/enemy Japanese. After the spring of 1943, Tule Lake became a segregation center for those internees whose answers to the loyalty questionnaire were unsatisfactory and hence branded as un-American or pro-Japan.[120] His educational experience with Japanese Americans considered disloyal (formally a part of the undemocratic foe) must have bolstered in him an enhanced sense of mission, confidence, and commitment to GHQ's enemy reorientation program.

Perhaps reflecting his perspective and background that mixed up incarcerated Japanese Americans and occupied Japanese nationals, Harkness's textbook unit had all Nisei staff, including his personal secretary (most likely a repatriate from Tule Lake), in addition to a few local Japanese hires. Such personnel composition was unique, because all other units in the Education Division had no Nisei staffers in the specialist category; the only other three Nisei in the entire division were female civilian employees, whose status was bilingual "secretary" to white officers in command.[121] During Harkness's long tenure, two to three Nisei "textbook analysts" always worked directly under him, with minimum staff turnover. They reviewed textbook manuscripts submitted by publishers and the Japanese ministry of education, translated them into English for Harkness and other CIE brass, and help identify inappropriate contents for removal or revision according to GHQ's mandate of democratization. Because the work required a high level of Japanese-language command and security clearance, neither white military linguists nor bilingual Japanese nationals were deemed desirable for this job. Hence, Japanese American textbook analysts were college-educated, cream-of-the-crop Nisei linguists from the beginning.[122]

Given the difficulty of finding capable personnel among Japanese American occupation troops with cursory language training, CIE held a national search for special Nisei agents in late 1945 while it was at work on recruiting Harkness from California. Isao J. Doi and Davis M. Shiroma were hired as textbook analysts in January 1946. Meanwhile, accepting the position with rank of "highest civil service status" in the military government, Harkness arrived in Tokyo one month later. Doi was a graduate of University of California at Berkeley and Shiroma educated at the University of Hawai'i.[123] Later in 1948, when Doi left the position for graduate study, two Nisei replacements were hired: Dixon Y. Miyauchi, a graduate of Reed College, and Kenneth K. Yasuda, a University of Washington alumnus who was attending Columbia University for post-graduate study.[124] It is likely that Yasuda was personally recruited by Harkness, since the former was an internee at Tule Lake. At one point during the war, Miyauchi worked for the high school at the Minidoka camp in Idaho.[125] Unlike ordinary Nisei linguists, they all had backgrounds suitable for specialist duty as textbook analyst under the command of the former white camp school superintendent.

A core element in CIE's school reorientation, Harkness's textbook reform efforts benefitted from his previous experience in Tule Lake and use of Nisei specialists. It revealed the uncanny resemblance and synergy between the wartime US attempt to Americanize incarcerated Japanese Americans and its postwar program of democratization under military domination. The former also offered a training ground for semi-native Nisei democratizers like Doi, Yasuda, and Miyauchi to be recruited for the latter. What linked the different histories of Japanese American incarceration and US military occupation were liberal white ideas, which privileged culture (as held by individuals) over race (as defined biologically as a collective body), even though these ideas still had the effect of lumping together all constituents of the Japanese race—foreign and domestic—in terms of the need for the "elevation of the[ir] culture." This curious mixture of individualizing and homogenizing ensured that white America could circumvent the post-Nazi stigma of blood-will-tell racism and yet preserve the existing asymmetrical order of races and nations in the name of group cultural differences. Furthermore, Harkness's example elucidates another inevitable development in which the reformed US citizen Japanese, like Nisei GHQ specialists, were seamlessly integrated into the machination of US tutelary colonialism, which targeted foreign Japanese. Harkness's textbook unit was a microcosm of such development; it was where the white boss and his Nisei staffers were united, albeit hierarchically, through their shared belief in white American cultural superiority, thereby constituting an important cog in the machinery of multiracial US militarism and its hegemony in Cold War East Asia.

CIE had another former camp educator named Rolling C. Fox, who had direct influence on the American-style democratization of the Japanese school system as an on-the-ground executor of reform in Tokyo and its surrounding areas. Between 1943 and 1945, Fox served as the principal of Manzanar High School, which some 1,400 Japanese American inmates attended at its peak. He was credited with "complet[ing] the organization of the [full-fledged] high school program" similar to that "found in any public school" outside the Manzanar WRA camp.[126] During his tenure as principal, Fox also completed his UCLA doctoral dissertation in education based on his work at the camp high school. In 1946, he applied for a job at GHQ's Civil Affairs Section and was hired as the chief education officer for the Kanto Civil Affairs Region, which covered Tokyo and its neighboring prefectures. Characterized as a "roving educational ambassador," Fox was able to make allies with many Japanese bureaucrats and conservative teachers, and yet he was also fiercely combative with the leftist Japan Teachers' Union. Exemplified by his failed attempt to bring in the military police to squash agitating teachers, Fox's vision of democratic education worked well under undemocratic conditions, such as inside wartime incarceration camps in the United States or under military occupation in post-defeat Japan.[127]

For that reason, Fox was popular among pro-US Japanese officials and in the conservative educational establishment.[128] Japan's Ministry of Education found his Manzanar experience directly relevant to its program of educational reform, thus translating Fox's entire dissertation into Japanese and published it as a part of the special research study series for domestic teachers and reformers. His UCLA dissertation discussed the organizational structure and personnel of the Manzanar High School; curriculum building; and student guidance policy, among others—all intended to facilitate the democratization of racially Japanese adolescents in confinement. To the Japanese translations of Fox's work, the education ministry added its own introduction, which stated: "readers can learn how Japanese Americans have become such a highly respected group [in the United States] by exhibiting the (democratic) qualities no less impressive than (white) Americans." It further contended: "This is the result of the education that (white) Americans (like Fox) offered Japanese and Japanese Americans inside the segregated internment camps during World War II."[129]

Countering the increasing influence of radical leftist teachers in occupied Japan, Fox was also commissioned to write a separate treatise titled "Essentials in Modern Japanese Education." Duly translated into Japanese, the 1950 publication explicated: "the meaning of democracy"; a "guide for the development of an effective educational system"; the organizational structure and functions of the board of education and other supervising entities; duties and qualifications of principals and teachers; and school curricula and extracurricular programs. Fox's central contention was consistent with his total disregard of the problem of the violent power that had sustained democratic education in the incarceration camps and then under military occupation. The white educator emphasized "the liberty that makes democracy possible must be restricted for the public good" while cautioning how "talks of democracy are often mixed up with propaganda of undemocratic minorities."[130] Combined with his slight of the oppressive structure under which reforms were imposed, Fox's lack of empathy for "minorities"—be they a political group or an ethnic group—reflected the common attitudes of WRA camp administrators, US occupation authorities, and Japanese government officials. These people had no problem with celebrating an imprisoned racial minority as a paragon of America's colorblind democracy, on the one hand, and democratizing rightless foreigners under colonialistic military domination on the other.

These trans-historical developments across the Pacific were fused into a narrative that reified a widespread image of Japanese Americans as an exceptional kind of democratizers for the defeated Oriental foes. First, after the military's relocation program dismantled the ethnic islands of Little Tokyos, the likes of Rolling Fox rehabilitated the hyphenated ethnic Americans in the WRA camps to turn them into acceptable assimilated citizens.[131] Then, the US army granted an opportunity to them to prove their patriotism through military service and earn accolades as national heroes. Finally, the occupation of Japan gave them an additional opportunity to claim a special honor to help democratize the people of their ancestral land in the exact manner in which they had been supposedly reformed through coerced assimilation into white America. Viewed against this narrative, Nisei's statements like "We are spreading news of democracy" foregrounded more complex realities. Contrary characterizations, such as "we're going to be ashamed of the occupation Nisei," captured other aspects of such realities. By examining those realities that the existing narrative fails to tell, we can better appreciate how the varied articulations of America's inclusionary racism, its militarized benevolent colonialism, and forced assimilation and democratization influenced the behavior and thinking of this racial minority in the land of their ancestors as in their birth country.[132]

Brokering a Race War: Japanese Americans in the Pacific War and the Occupation of Japan. Eiichiro Azuma, Oxford University Press. © Eiichiro Azuma 2026. DOI: 10.1093/9780197781432.003.0004

4
Nisei Occupation Troops and Minority Imperial Citizenship

> Believe me, those Americans of J[apanese] ancestry who are now here do not have too easy a time with the J[apanese] who view them as disloyal but whose loyalty to America is clear and yet I'm sure they often realize that many Americans think of them as J[apanese] and not as Americans. They have a tough time here—but they have what it takes.[1]

A high-ranking GHQ official, who had worked in a wartime Japanese American incarceration camp, shared his observations about the difficulties he thought Nisei occupation troops were undergoing in their ancestral land. As this sympathetic white administrator noted, their troubles stemmed from the misperceptions that both mainstream Americans and Japanese nationals held relative to "Americans of Japanese ancestry." In the context of relational racial and national formation, Nisei US citizens in occupied Japan still had "what it takes" to survive and navigate the maze of clashing meanings, expectations, and powers. What enabled the occupation Nisei to push forward was their imperialized US citizenship backed by its military might, even while they continued to seek acceptance and equality in white America as a racial minority.

This chapter examines the overlapping processes of racial, national, and imperial formation among Japanese American servicemen and civilian workers in occupied Japan between August 1945 and April 1952. In the dynamics of triangular relations that also involved white American conquerors and enemy Japanese, Nisei cultural brokers underwent a radical transformation in their status, consciousness, and practice. Occupied Japan constituted a historical moment and transnational colonial space where many Japanese Americans underwent life-changing experiences. During their sojourn in Japan, they were able to enjoy the power of American citizenship, even as they continued to come to terms with the burden of being racially Japanese following the mass incarceration. Outside the established structure of US race relations where the ideas of race and related hierarchy were more rigidly defined and guarded by federal and state legislation, Nisei in occupied Japan could produce and practice nuanced meanings of Japaneseness beyond the minoritized position to which they were confined at home. This aspect of Nisei experience unfolded concurrently with their struggle within the institutional context of the occupation forces that preserved the domestic logic of white domination.

In the entanglements between conquering Japanese Americans and vanquished Japanese nationals, the former's citizenship came to have unexpected implications and significance. The transnational experience of militarized Nisei compounded their domestic struggle for racial equality with their uncritical embrace and enforcement of US imperial power and injustice against foreignized others. Nisei democratizers took for granted their privileged position relative to their Japanese staff, and few hesitated to avail themselves of the power that stemmed from their legal standing as citizen-members of the conquering military forces. In post-1945 Japan and other foreign occupied areas, the inclusive US citizenship functioned as minority imperial citizenship, rendering Japanese Americans (and other minoritized US citizen-soldiers) an integral part of global American military domination. The Nisei's practice of this citizenship vis-à-vis enemy Japanese revealed many troubling aspects of their experience, which one soldier acknowledged they were "going to be shamed of."[2]

Examples of how Nisei embraced and resorted to that citizenship ranged from the personal to institutional. Many Japanese American linguists enjoyed backdoor access to social privileges and business connections that allowed them to realize substantial material gains and receive special treatment from the Japanese whom they translated for. Their activities often involved coercion and exploitation, since these Nisei had the upper hand due to their affiliation to the conquering military forces. Some Nisei capriciously abused the Japanese workers they supervised, or they took advantage of the women they called worth only "a box of candy."[3] Other Japanese Americans belonged to certain branches of the occupation government that required them to routinely enforce the power of US citizenship against Japanese leftists and others deemed inimical to US interests. An illicit use of physical violence and extralegal abduction were sometimes a part of their de facto job descriptions as undercover US intelligence agents.

The colonial context of US military occupation was crucial, indeed indispensable, for understanding the rise of minority imperial citizenship among Japanese Americans. What is particularly ironic is that this citizenship was an inevitable consequence of Nisei's pursuit of white acceptance under the inclusionary Cold War racial liberalism of the United States. The anti-racist aspect of citizenship facilitated their national inclusion inside US society (including in the military). Across the Pacific, its twin sister of imperial minority citizenship turned Nisei soldiers and civilian linguists into primary enforcers of colonial domination and occasionally abusers of extraterritorial power against the co-racial enemies over whom they presided as cultural intermediaries in occupied Japan.

This duality of postwar American citizenship was responsible for the Nisei's tumultuous relationship with Japanese nationals. Of course, the vanquished had their own prejudices and acts of injustice, too. Even after the collapse of imperial Japan, the remnants of their imperialistic nationalism and racist thinking, accentuated by a longstanding disdain for Nisei, was as resilient as white supremacy under the guise of official US anti-racism and Japan's democratization. The military occupation thus offered a transimperial colonial environment, where these historical subjects from the two rival empires met with differing sets of ideological baggage, identities, and aspirations. This space was made up of a divided world consisting of asymmetrically ordered national societies, in which different formulations and meanings of race, citizenship, and culture clashed with one another. One set of these categories was constituted and reified in the US national context and brought over to vanquished Japan that still maintained another set—its imperialistic racism, nationalist consciousness, and essentialist cultural thinking. Inhabiting and crisscrossing these two worlds in occupied Japan, Japanese American linguists maneuvered through the interstices and grey areas of the contending ideas and social relations. There, Nisei middleman brokers developed a specific understanding of who they were and what they could and should do as American citizen-soldiers with Japanese racial background.

A product of post-1943 US anti-racist nationalism and militarism, minority imperial citizenship enabled Nisei US soldiers and civilian workers to perform the role of colonial overlords, stern disciplinarians, and yet sympathetic benefactors of defeated Japanese. At times, Nisei linguists strategically invoked racial invisibility to take credit for the success of the occupation aims without being associated with reports of its negative aspects. At other times, Nisei's emphasis on intra-racial difference elucidated their possession of a legal American identity that gave them uncontested power over Japanese nationals. Either way, they could elevate the collective image of American-born Japanese as valuable members of the US armed forces and the global empire that it sustained while solidifying their national identity as assimilated Americans. This function of minority imperial citizenship simultaneously gave birth to the polarized identities of Japanese Americans as a model minority in inclusive postwar America and as chief executers of the US military violence abroad. This chapter sheds light on a grossly understudied transnational aspect of post-World War II Japanese American experience that exemplifies the duplicity and multifaceted articulations of Nisei's postwar citizenship.

Capitalizing on Racial Commonalty with the Enemy

A few years in occupied Japan provided several thousand Nisei military linguists and a few thousand civilian personnel attached to the military government with a revolutionary racial experience. In the land of their ancestors, these young men and women had the uncontested powers and privileges that victorious US citizens enjoyed in the semi-colonial context of military occupation. Because of their shared race and cultural heritage with the occupied, Nisei enjoyed advantages that were not available to other Americans. For example, they were able to carve out new economic niches in the context of Japan's postwar reconstruction. Although the initial American policy sought to deprive Japan of industrial capacities as a safeguard against an attempt to rearm itself, the rise of Communism in East Asia propelled the United States to reverse that course.[4] Instead, it had to set the Japanese economy back on its feet, albeit under the continuous control of the US military and industrial capitalism. As a result, many Nisei acted as brokers between American and Japanese commercial interests. In September 1945, one linguist already predicted a "wide open field for Nisei in Japan: engineering, doctoring, foreign trade, etc." This Japanese American later extended his tour of duty by eighteen months "with a sole purpose of getting into the import and export business."[5] In September 1947, that opportunity officially opened up as General MacArthur lifted the ban on foreign trade with occupied Japan.

Under the terms dictated by the American military regime, three types of Nisei linguists reaped tangible benefits as postwar bilateral trade expanded. First, some individuals who lacked their own resources to start an international enterprise worked as resident representatives for US-based corporations, including Nisei-owned concerns in Hawai'i and California. George Aratani, a Los Angeles Japanese American leader, capitalized on the services of Nisei linguists-turned-purchasing agents with whom he had been personally acquainted since the war, thanks to his job as a civilian instructor at the MIS language school. In cooperation with Aratani, Tad Yamada, a former MIS linguist, set up a small office in Tokyo in 1951 as a distributor of US-made medical and scientific devices. This operation developed into a major company called AMCO. Another graduate of the army language school, Bill Kasuga, helped launch Kenwood—an audio equipment business—as Aratani's business agent in Tokyo. Based largely on his transpacific MIS network, Aratani's company subsequently thrived in three areas of US-Japan trade: the import of Japan-made chinaware under the Mikasa brand and of Kenwood products, as well as the export of AMCO equipment to Japan.[6]

The second group of Nisei linguists consisted of individual investors and business proprietors. Intending to cater to the needs of American and foreign residents under the restricted and segregated world of occupied Japan, many enterprising Nisei found profit-making opportunities. After discharge from the military, they established firms with capital infusion from other Japanese Americans as well as their own investments. What would become a thriving dry-cleaning and linen supply company in postwar Japan was started by a Hawai'i-born linguist who took advantage of his stint and newly created connections in Tokyo. Born in 1914, Naotaka Roy Hiroshige was a seasoned battlefront linguist, one of the first ATIS members to enter Yokohama with MacArthur's General Headquarters (GHQ) from the Philippines in late August 1945. Before his wartime service, he had graduated from the University of California with a degree in business administration and had been a part owner of "one of the largest [dry-cleaning businesses] in Honolulu and the Territory of Hawaii." With this background, Hiroshige was "entrusted and was responsible for the laundry and dry-cleaning for ATIS organization [and] GHQ." After his discharge, he returned to Honolulu to resume his role in the management of "Davenroy Drycleaners" under a partnership with another Nisei.[7]

His experience in Tokyo made Hiroshige cognizant of an untapped profit-making opportunity for establishing "the most modern, most sanitary, and efficient dry-cleaning and laundry plant" in order to meet the demands of "foreign ships and planes that touch Japan," "hotels and restaurants," "Visitors and traders coming to Japan," and "Occupational Forces and personnel." According to the Hawai'i Nisei, existing Japanese-owned laundry businesses were barely mechanized and "not capable of measuring up to American standard[s] in production, sanitation and quality of work." He proposed to GHQ that he would build a brand-new plant in the vicinity of Tokyo' main airport and the port of Yokohama with "80% machine and 20% hand work," the opposite of a standard Japanese set-up that depended mostly on manpower. Hiroshige's application for business license guaranteed "the introduction of American made equipments and machine plus the technical knowledge," a task for which he argued he was already best prepared.[8] Just as he had taken charge of supervising a Japanese workforce as an ATIS linguist conversant in the local language, Hiroshige was able to manage Japanese employees for the washing, drying, and ironing of clothes and linens for occupation personnel as well as foreign expatriates and visitors.

Having worked in the heart of GHQ, he also benefited from his personal relationships with and access to white administrators with decision-making authority. In Hiroshige's case, he could arrange face-to-face meetings with top officials in GHQ's Foreign Investment Board (FIB), which had the power to authorize and deny business applications from foreign business investors. When he visited Japan in early 1950 to file his application, Hiroshige managed to get "many courtesies extended to" him by FIB personnel and felt comfortable enough to press them for a quick decision in a rather unbusiness-like manner.[9] In July 1950, a license was issued for the proposed company with the requisite of $100,000 start-up capital, at least 55 percent of which Hiroshige promised to bear initially. Less than three years after the start of its Japan operation, Davenroy Drycleaners organized a linen supply operation to dominate the local market.[10] Just like their Hawai'i business operation, the Tokyo-based firm was so prosperous that it put Hiroshige and his partner "among top [Nisei] earners" in Japan, according to the Japanese American Citizens League (JACL)'s newspaper, *Pacific Citizen*. Underscoring the importance of occupation military experience as a factor in their business success, the JACL house organ noted that the Japanese Americans who had come to Japan before the war (strandees) were contrarily "not listed as a 'high tax-paying individual.'"[11] Although they, too, were American-born, their loss of US citizenship generally prevented them from carving out business niches or having backdoor access to white GHQ administrators.

The third group of enterprising Nisei became "claim merchants," who negotiated on behalf of Japanese businesses with GHQ authorities regarding problems of unpaid bills and fraud by foreign traders. During the military occupation, foreign merchants, especially buyers of Japanese goods, often exploited a deficient claim resolution system controlled by GHQ's Economic and Scientific Section (ESS) by fabricating outstanding debts and undelivered/defective merchandise. These opportunistic foreigners knew that Japanese would have an uphill battle in dealing with ESS. As a Japanese government auxiliary to ESS recalled, most of the 2,300 claims filed at ESS came from foreign buyers and identified Japanese merchants and manufacturers as defendants. Due to their lack of power and English language ability, Japanese businesses often resorted to remedying problems informally by relying on the intermediary work of Nisei claim merchants, including those linguists who worked on claims on a part-time basis. As the Japanese official speculated, the cases that involved these Nisei likely exceeded ten thousand, over four times more than the officially submitted claims.[12]

Although many Nisei linguists viewed it as a sideline job to earn extra income while in Japan, others became professional brokers upon discharge from active duty. Once the Korean War began in June 1950, many of these Nisei found another niche mediating between US military purchasing officers and Japanese merchants in the transaction of war materials and supplies for combat troops.[13] Japanese traders were well aware that Nisei claim merchants and brokers enjoyed backdoor access to pertinent GHQ personnel through their prior military connections. Not only did these Nisei effectively communicate the Japanese concerns and wishes to the white American authorities, but they also facilitated business deals and/or expedited the settlement of disputes, albeit often through bribes and other illicit means. In this sense, these Nisei were as much cultural brokers as they were unscrupulous influence peddlers.

Abusing Racial Commonalty with the Enemy

Understandably, the conduct of some Nisei brokers often bordered on criminal. Just like foreign merchants, these Japanese Americans frequently preyed on their clients, who had little recourse against members of the allied powers. Of course, Japanese merchants and business owners were no less guilty of frauds and deceptions, but under the rigidly established order of power, the vanquished could hardly fight back against those of allied nationalities on equal ground since the latter enjoyed the privilege of operating their businesses and pressing their claims above the severely curtailed sovereign power of occupied Japan and its judicial system. In the interstices of the two legal regimes and segmented matrixes of power, Nisei functioned as semi-native colonial masters who found plenty of profit-making opportunities. According to a Japanese official who could finally publish his firsthand observations after occupation censorship was lifted, these "devilish" Nisei "first deceived Japanese into believing that they had understanding and sympathy based on shared blood. Yet, once their intrigue became apparent (after swindling fees and commissions), they followed up with a threat to their (Japanese) clients, brandishing the authority of occupation personnel."[14] Such racketeering reflects a dark side of Nisei niche-making in postwar US-Japan trade and highlighted how much they could gain by manipulating their status in occupied Japan. Whether ethical or not, the business of brokering brought some Nisei significant economic returns and prepared others for future career opportunities in bilateral commercial relations.

During the GHQ/SCAP's reign, Japanese merchants who dealt with foreign traders opted to share a list of the "most crooked Nisei triad," professional swindlers of a sort, because of the widespread damages inflicted by them. One of these Japanese Americans, identified as "M," was included for allegedly cheating one of Japan's top publishers out of three million yen by proposing that he would assist the firm in obtaining the right to sell their magazines in occupied Okinawa. The same Japanese American also cheated a Japanese scientist out of a valuable patent and millions of yen when he promised to procure necessary capital for a new business on security of the latter's patent and an advance investment as collateral. In both instances, the colonial justice system of occupied Japan offered the Japanese victims no chance to recover funds and other losses; they were even less capable of bringing these matters up for scrutiny due to the shady nature of the original arrangements with the illegitimate Nisei broker.[15]

Inside GHQ, some Nisei staffers exploited their middleman status for personal gain "like... big time racketeers," according to one disgusted linguist. In his letter home, this righteous Nisei complained about one "interpreter in an engineer outfit [who] threatened Japanese contractors [with] the loss of jobs and future jobs if he weren't paid so much a day in yen." This forced bribery had to happen for the Japanese to continue their business with GHQ, and they ended up "hardly making a profit for themselves." The crooked linguist also smuggled "valuable stones into America" in cooperation with another Nisei accomplice. The letter writer had plenty of stories to tell, albeit much smaller in scale, but other examples of his fellow Nisei's misconduct suggest the prevalence of similar problems. Working as an army base guard, another Japanese American serviceman "charged Japanese laborers so much money to go in and out the gate." A more creative Nisei racket involved two soldiers who played "bad soldier" and "good soldier" to extract money from Japanese nationals. The former engaged in the underground sale of cigarettes to a Japanese national, and another acted as a Counter Intelligence Corps (CIC) agent to confiscate the goods from the buyer. "After selling the [same] cigarettes several times," the letter writer lamented, "you could see they were making [a lot of] money."[16]

Sometimes Nisei linguists mixed up their dedication to their work with the abuse of their powers, which they rationalized in the name of their service to the overall aims of the US military occupation. For example, a Nisei sergeant at the Fukuoka Civil Censorship Detachment (CCD) was described as a "wheeler-dealer" by his co-ethnic colleague, who still approved of his questionable treatment of local Japanese residents. The sergeant was responsible for recruiting bilingual Japanese censors for the outfit's work, but he was troubled by low employee retention due to the less than desirable wage scale for qualified native workers. To tackle this problem, this Nisei linguist used his local connections and authority to coerce Japanese farmers into selling fresh vegetables at wholesale prices or lower, which he periodically made available to new recruits as an incentive to stay on the job. This Nisei's local connections included a powerful businessman in the region, and he made the man's daughter-in-law his mistress even though her husband, an imperial naval captain, was still alive in detention. When the husband returned home, the Japanese businessman was compelled to send his own son away to live in Tokyo so that his daughter-in-law could continue to satisfy the sexual and other needs of the Nisei sergeant as his kept woman—these deplorable actions by both parties were taken to prolong their mutually profitable relations. Moreover, with no consideration for the illicit nature of the whole thing, the sergeant's colleague at the same outfit wholeheartedly approved of the Nisei's exploitative behavior:

"This ability to purchase vegetables at low cost kept many Japanese workers on our staff!"[17] The "undemocratic" behavior of the sergeant was tolerated because it did not cause any damage to US properties or GHQ's operations, as his fellow linguist contended. In fact, what the sergeant did was viewed as a positive contribution if not patriotic deed, for his "wheeler-dealer" act kept the number of Japanese staffers sufficient for CCD to continue its operations uninterrupted.

GHQ generally turned a blind eye to the prevalence of these problems in the ranks of its uniformed staff, not least because negative publicity about occupation troops was kept out of public discourse as much as possible. The activities of crooked Nisei were also much harder to detect in occupied Japan than those of white or Black soldiers, since covert transactions were carried out in Japanese without the need for a third-party middleman or potential witnesses. Unless a case of Nisei's misconduct involved embezzlement of army properties or a complaint from a white American victim, they tended to remain unexposed. However, once cases of Nisei's misconduct were deemed injurious to GHQ's interests, they were swiftly brought into the SCAP's military justice system—generally in a much harsher manner than those involving white servicemen.

The court-martial of a Nisei MIS lieutenant is a case in point. During the first few years of GHQ's reign, this linguist was the highest ranked Japanese American in the Tokyo headquarters of the Civil Information and Education Division (CIE), working as a chief liaison officer/translator for David Conde, director of the Motion Picture and Theatrical Branch (MPTB). A New Deal civilian bureaucrat, Conde was a left-leaning liberal who embraced the opportunity to purge the Japanese of a militarist and feudalistic mindset by foisting on them censored movies and stage performances. With the ban on traditional *samurai* dramas and other forms of feudalistic film representations, MPTB clashed with Japan's film industry—the management and production staff alike. Under the complicated bureaucracy of the military government, Tokyo CCD, a part of Civil Intelligence Section (CIS), was also charged with the task of civil censorship that often overlapped with CIE's jurisdiction, thereby creating rivalry and contestation between that agency and the latter's MPTB.[18]

In these multifaceted entanglements of institutional interests and agendas, Conde's Nisei liaison positioned himself as a powerful advocate on behalf of Japan's film business within his own MPTB/CIE while realizing a large amount of monetary and other rewards for his illicit service. In order to safeguard his role as an inside broker for Japanese business interests, the crooked lieutenant endeavored to deter the rival CCD—especially its staff Nisei censor—from interfering with his brokering activities in the process of MPTB's decision-making relative to the cinema ban and censorship. What made this Japanese American liaison officer so much more powerful and influential than others with the same institutional standing was the degree to which both his white chief and Japanese stakeholders had to depend on him in negotiating their respective desires. Japanese filmmakers and production staff despised this middleman Nisei's acts of self-serving manipulation and relentless profit-making. But the industry brass knew only too well that his outlandish demands had to be accommodated at all costs.[19]

In due time, this Nisei's misconducts came to SCAP's attention, prompting an official investigation off and on between March 1946 and June 1947. Until his arrest, this linguist frequently demanded that Japanese film companies organize lavish *geisha* parties for him and his Nisei buddies. In March 1946, the military police got a hold of pictures of these parties with attendants, including company executives and employees, *geishas* and maids, and some Nisei linguists. All the Japanese in the pictures—some fifty to sixty people, including a who's who of Japan's film industry—were summoned to the GHQ building for two days of interrogations.[20] This first round of investigation did not produce enough evidence to prosecute the interpreter or remove him from his position because the Japanese most likely kept their mouths shut about the bribery allegations. Yet, the military police put the Nisei under close surveillance from this point on. According to a fellow linguist who ran into him after the investigation, this man continued to "act like a *shogun*"; the lieutenant had such power and influence in Tokyo's entertainment quarters that he could "arrange with the madam [for anyone] to stay with one of the girls." At one of the *geisha* houses where the crooked Nisei entertained the unsuspecting linguist for a reunion, the former told the latter that he would do his old friend a favor, taking the puzzled linguist to a backroom. To his surprise, there was a young girl—barely an adolescent—whom he was told he could have for fun. The girl was blubbering, "I don't want to do it, I don't want to do it." Disgusted with what was presented to him, this linguist called the crooked Nisei "a disgrace," but he also conceded: "that was the way he was."[21]

Under the colonial conditions of military occupation, these acts of native exploitation did not cause the lieutenant's downfall. His arrest took place when his misconduct appeared to have had negative effects on US citizens and/or GHQ. In July 1946, some four months after the initial investigation, Conde's resignation from CIE tilted the balance of power in favor of CCD under anti-communist General Charles A. Willoughby, who had viewed the MPTB chief as too liberal. Thereafter, CCD intensified control over the work of film censorship, and so did its counter-assault on CIE/MPTB.[22] In November, Willoughby's Army G-2 section started to build a strong case against the corrupt Nisei interpreter with information furnished by its subdivision of CCD, which obtained a lead to a tangible case of his acceptance of 50,000 yen for doing a Japanese briber a favor.[23] By March 1947, additional information poured in about the Nisei's complicity with film companies in skirting CCD's film censorship.[24] The final blow came from the wife of the lieutenant, who had just moved from Hawai'i with their two small children to join him in Tokyo. The Nisei had previously had one of the film companies provide a Japanese actress as his mistress with whom he had cohabited. With her husband missing on so many nights—presumably with his mistress—the Nisei wife had enough and requested GHQ investigate.[25] Soon after, the linguist was finally brought to a general court martial.

Perhaps aiming to send a strong message to other Nisei linguists, the military court handled the case severely. The Japanese American lieutenant was convicted of accepting more than 130,000 yen ($2,000) and lavish entertainment in bribes from Japanese picture studios and of cohabiting with a Japanese woman despite being married to a citizen wife. Found guilty of "conduct unbecoming an officer and a gentleman and a discredit to the military service," the Nisei defendant was sentenced to a one-year confinement at hard labor, forfeiture of all pay, and dismissal from the army. The punishment was quite harsh considering three Nisei defendants who stabbed a Japanese worker to death outside a Tokyo dance hall for no good reason were acquitted in the appeal.[26] Thoroughly disgraced and ostracized by his compatriots, all that awaited the convicted Nisei was total oblivion.[27]

Whereas GHQ/SCAP's justice generally operated according to the logic of US domestic race politics, Japanese law enforcement could not do much under the occupation's colonial conditions. Yet, after its end, some Nisei culprits were brought to Japan's vengeful justice. Publicized in reputable Japanese dailies and magazines, an arrest and subsequent flight of a prominent Nisei businessman in Tokyo bordered on a conspiracy theory involving alleged international spy rings and prostitution rackets—with his pivotal role as a cultural broker and political fixer wrapped into one.

An owner of a Japanese food trading company in San Francisco, this Nisei established a medical import company in Tokyo in 1950 (not to be confused with AMCO); he was one of the first group of US traders to enter the post-defeat Japanese market.[28] His Tokyo-based business introduced "a complete line of (latest) drugs, pharmaceuticals and sundries to service the foreign community including the American clinics" in occupied Japan.[29]

While running this lucrative business and raking in a lot of money, the entrepreneur cultivated connections with Japan's political leaders and GHQ officials, allowing him to wield power in the underworld dubbed Tokyo's "foreign concession." Allegedly, this Japanese American played a significant role in setting up and running international gambling and prostitution operations at a five-star hotel near the GHQ building where the main office of his medical import business was also located. Illegal drug dealers, CIA and other foreign intelligence agents, and a wide variety of unsavory characters purportedly gathered at the establishment known as the "Mandarin Club" under this Nisei's control. There, several other Japanese Americans regularly worked as bilingual pimps, who arranged one-night stands between Japanese "club service girls" and "foreign guests," including businessmen, military officials, and foreign government representatives and diplomats. In partnership with outlaw white elements in Tokyo, the California Nisei businessman was said to have pulled the strings behind the scenes of these multifaceted illegal operations.[30]

Whether he was the racketeering leader and fixer that Japan's media reports made him out to be is not as important as the fact that the Japanese police proceeded to crack down on the Mandarin Club and arrested him shortly after the end of US occupation, that is, the return of sovereign power to Japan. In July 1952, Tokyo policemen raided the club's premises, although insider information enabled the racketeers to prepare for the law enforcement investigation in this instance. After a brief suspension of its operation, the underground casinos at the Mandarin Club were in full swing again to make the Japanese law enforcement even more determined to put a stop to its illicit businesses. In early 1954, another raid resulted in the arrest of the suspected Nisei owner for violations of Japan's foreign currency control regulations. Apparently, he had run a side-business of illegal money exchange and lending catering to the demands of Japan's political and business leaders. When these dignitaries visited the United States and/or engaged in import-export transactions, the crooked Nisei lent them a large sum of US dollars out of his bank account in California. During the military occupation, Japan had maintained strict restrictions on the outflow of foreign currency due to economic difficulties. According to the police, the Japanese American had secretly loaned his clients $6,500 in exchange for Japanese yen payments. His profit from the interests and commissions as well as other illegal activities was said to have reached 170 million yen, or over $472,000.[31]

Japanese newspaper reports suspected that this Nisei's control of drug imports from the United States was possible because of his cozy relationships with high-ranking Japanese bureaucrats and a government minister. The police also discovered a stash of illegal firearms at the Nisei's residence in central Tokyo. Arrested with him were notorious figures of Japan's underworld, including Kodama Yoshio, who had served as a secret agent for the Japanese army in China and later became a CIA collaborator and power broker in postwar Japan's organized crime. This episode ended with the parole of the Nisei ringleader, who subsequently fled to California and stayed out of the reach of Japan's sovereign power. Some other Japanese Americans, who had purportedly played the role of pimps for white customers at the Mandarin Club, also fled Japan after their boss absconded, reportedly leaving the service girls in disarray without the Nisei's brokering roles.[32] The truth lay deeper, as the accused Nisei maintained his innocence and dodged a conviction; yet, the sensationalized press reports helped solidify the negative perceptions that the Japanese public had already developed about the Nisei's extraterritorial privilege and their propensity to use it in every "criminal" way possible.[33] Indeed, as a Hawai'i-based ethnic periodical lamented, the association of "[s]ome of Nisei businessmen [in Japan]...with gamblers, smugglers and other notorious dealers" led to "the rising tide of anti-Niseism" there by the early 1950s.[34]

Practice of Flexible Invisibility

Besides access to a variety of profit-making opportunities, another advantage that Japanese Americans enjoyed in occupied Japan included the ability to fade out of public view when negative perceptions arose regarding the general conduct of occupation troops. Because of the ambiguous boundaries of race and citizenship, Nisei cultural brokers could circumvent scrutiny and criticism from the military brass and the American public about what was transpiring in Japan. This racial invisibility made it possible for Nisei to preserve a positive image as benevolent democratizers particularly in US domestic discourse. In the immediate postwar years, much of the critical discourse regarding the US occupation of Japan derived from the problem of fraternization between American soldiers and local women. The military authorities were primarily concerned about such pragmatic issues as the spread of venereal diseases among the occupation troops, the need to maintain proper distance vis-à-vis the vanquished, and the rise of anti-American sentiment among the native population. For other white Americans, this fraternization had direct implications for the existing social order and power relations in the United States.[35]

The sexual domination of enemy women by US soldiers created a dangerous situation where accepted notions of proper racial boundaries and hierarchical order were being compromised, albeit outside the United States proper. Even worse, to the chagrin of those on the home front, "the single, young, American officers and non-coms" often brought back "a changed and bias[ed] opinion of American life," as one irate white woman in Los Angeles wrote to the State Department. "[H]ow can American women face a re-adjustment which calls for a complete reorientation of values, culture, social steadiness?" she wondered. According to her, the "changed" racial perceptions held by returning male soldiers were intertwined with other racial disruptions on the home front: the coming of "Japanese brides of [white] American soldiers and illegitimate Eurasian orphans."[36] Fundamentally, the uncontrolled intercourse between American men and Japanese women imperiled the integrity and purity of the white race.

In occupied Japan, the problem of fraternization invited more critical scrutiny than in Europe, precisely because these relationships were deemed to erode racial differences. Interracial fraternization—the loathsome act of "miscegenation"—symbolized the outright transgressions of established racial boundaries, hence the very basis of social order. Just as Southern states dealt with the Black problem by legally banning interracial marriage, California and many other western states had passed anti-miscegenation laws against Asians (Japanese included) before World War II to penalize attempts to undermine the biological foundation of white supremacy.[37] The same negative interpretation, which misrepresented the question at hand simply as a race issue, was prevalent in the media coverage of "occupation babies" whose racial identity and citizenship status would be murky and hence perilous to society, as the letter writer suggested. Viewed as a serious threat to the white power structure, interactions between US servicemen and Japanese women—including formal marriages—tended to be frowned upon stateside during the occupation years.

In response to these concerns, GHQ implemented a policy of "non-fraternization" that lasted much longer than in occupied Germany.[38] In its effort to prevent racially undesirable enemy nationals from crossing the national border, the US Congress initially denied foreign Asian wives the right to come to the United States with their soldier husbands even after the passage of the first War Brides Act of 1945.[39] Despite official bans and public censure, allied male personnel continued to fraternize with Japanese women, because, as one Nisei crudely noted, "[f]or a bar of candy you can get them."[40] Most servicemen treated these desperate women as a cheap, convenient outlet for their sexual needs. The number of occupation babies skyrocketed, which reinforced negative publicity and perceptions in the United States.[41]

Despite the policy, Nisei men fraternized with local women as much as white and Black Americans did. When those in military uniform engaged too obviously in a "public display of affection toward Japanese women,"

Fig. 4.1 Nisei occupation troops dancing with Japanese women, September 1946. Courtesy of the Seattle Nisei Veterans Committee and the US Army, and permission by Densho: The Japanese American Legacy Project, ddr-densho-114-469.

some Nisei ended up being court-martialed, imprisoned, and fined.[42] However, if they took off their uniforms and behaved somewhat discreetly, Nisei could easily blend into the local Japanese population—an option that was not available to most other occupation personnel. Their Japanese physical features and linguistic skills allowed them access to all sorts of Japanese women—in brothels, cabarets, and bars, as well as in more reputable places, many of which were off limits to occupation personnel.[43] The extent of this access is exemplified by the fact that three Nisei linguists were married to Japan's top movie actresses—and had already had babies with them—by 1947.[44]

Most linguists were not as committed to marriage, instead viewing local women as "a plaything or little sincerely just good friends," however.[45] It was not uncommon for some veteran ATIS members on new assignments in occupied Japan to (try to) compensate for homesickness with an idea of "strolling down Ginza odori [sic] (ō-dōri: large street) with giggling geisha girls clinging on to both my sturdy arms."[46] A similar idea captivated many new recruits from the United States. Ever since initial news about the occupation reached the MIS language school in the fall of 1945, one Nisei linguist recalled, "[c]lassroom discussions continued to center on sexual adventures" in Japan; many linguists eagerly anticipated their tour of duty in their ancestral land as "adventure, opportunities for romance, and sexual exploitation."[47] Once they found themselves in Japan, some Nisei, especially inexperienced younger men, "quickly became obsessed with sex."[48] One irate Issei mother complained after "discover[ing] what their son did" in Japan during his two-year stint as an occupation linguist: "He did not save a penny although he was getting $200 a month.... On weekends... he... spent time with geisha girls.... I asked him if other Nisei led the same sort of life, he said most of them did. Some even had two mistresses and lead 'interesting' lives [sic]." The same source added: "Since the war, there has been an increase in sex crimes and other offence among Nisei" in Japan.[49]

Thus, Japanese Americans were no less engrossed than other American occupation troops with fraternization, fatherless babies, and various sexual transgressions in Japan. Of course, many Nisei linguists had sincere intentions when they went out with local women, and a not insignificant number of Japanese American occupation troops ended up marrying Japanese women. Notwithstanding the SCAP's effort to "clamp down and discourage" GI-Japanese marriages, almost 73 percent of the 823 authorized nuptials involved Nisei occupation troops in November 1947, although other groups of Americans marrying local women had begun to increase at a faster pace following the liberalization of the war bride immigration policy in that summer.[50] At the same time, some sources speculated, through a selected examination of Japanese family registries and other official records, that Nisei were just as responsible for the cases of child abandonment as were white or Black Americans.[51] In 1949, a Tokyo newspaper reported a tragic case of a murder suicide, which involved a 24-year-old Japanese woman and her 2-year-old baby. She became despondent when she learned that her Nisei lover and father of her baby was about to return to the United States without telling her.[52]

Nevertheless, most media discussions reported on the interracial nature of American-Japanese intercourse and the mixed racial identity of "Eurasian" and "Negrasian" babies. Thanks to this focus on the purported perils of racial mixing, Japanese Americans were generally absolved from discussions of accountability or guilt.[53] Similarly, stories of sexual assaults and unprovoked attacks by allied personnel were usually portrayed—and understood—as acts committed by white and especially Black soldiers, reflecting anti-Blackness embedded in both US white supremacy and imperial Japanese racism.[54] Being of Japanese ancestry, Nisei could and often did simply vanish under the façade of racial(ized) conflicts and power relations.

In the colonial context of occupied Japan, Nisei constantly crossed ambiguous boundaries of ancestry and citizenship, which dictated all aspects of social relations there. They always sought to enhance the positive value of their racial and legal attributes for the goal of promoting their inclusion in the US citizenry. Their ability to disappear in the local crowds without becoming a problem explained a unique aspect of their everyday behavior that can be characterized as the practice of flexible invisibility. Consciously or unconsciously, Japanese American linguists resorted to this practice when they found it convenient to exploit racial commonalty with the local population. It enabled them to safeguard a hard-earned identity as a loyal model-minority citizen while enjoying various profits of their imperial citizenship, like other US conquerors.

Hyper-Disidentification and the Performance of Intra-Racial Difference

Despite the advantage of racial sameness and the politics of flexible invisibility they often enacted in occupied Japan, Japanese Americans were compelled to bring constant attention to the value of birthright citizenship while disavowing the weight of racial ancestry. Such calculated actions resulted in the performance of intra-racial difference among various contingents of Nisei in occupied Japan: military and civilian linguists, long-term resident Nisei since before the war (strandees), and renunciants who were deported to Japan after the end of the hostilities. This performance frequently took the form of mistreating Japanese nationals in a phenomenon best explained by the concept of "hyper-disidentification," the flip side of "hyper-identification" that wartime Japanese Americans like Mike Masaoka and the 442nd RCT members had publicly displayed in accordance with the dominant (re)definition of Americanism. The occupation Nisei's performance of intra-racial difference pointed to manifestations of the same racial politics, with one notable distinction. In the wartime United States, the emphasis on the Americanness of Nisei citizenship dictated the terms of their hyper-identification with the US war effort and its white mainstream. That emphasis aimed to ensure Nisei's national belonging despite, or rather because of ongoing race-based exclusion, that is, the mass incarceration.

In occupied Japan, different contingents of Nisei felt it necessary to constantly distinguish between themselves and non-citizen Japanese (or anyone associated with them). As much as GHQ linguists and other loyal Nisei were deeply entrenched in the US military government, the visual/physical confusion with their consanguineous foes could well jeopardize their hard-earned identity as acceptable US citizens. Thus, Nisei's hostile actions against local Japanese represented an attempt to arrest the recurrence of race-based exclusion by way of hyper-disidentification. Given the prevalence of anti-Japanese hatred in white America, many Japanese Americans almost intuitively found it imperative and most effective to deter the race-based denial of their American identity through the performance of aggression and a display of scorn towards Japanese nationals—to be seen, read, heard, and appreciated by their fellow white soldiers and officers. Seen from this standpoint, some Nisei's mistreatment of Japanese nationals was part and parcel of their broader aspirations and collective practices in Japanese America since the Pearl Harbor Day.

In transnational and triangular relations of race and citizenship, Nisei's ongoing practice of hyper-identification with white America was augmented by that of hyper-disidentification with the foreign consanguineous others in occupied Japan. The overall colonial conditions of occupied Japan determined the relations between Nisei US citizens and defeated Japanese nationals. Under the circumstances, the former's tendency to dissociate from the latter revealed their ongoing effort to gain access to the full privilege of US citizenship. Yet, that citizenship came to denote a violent character against foreign enemies rather than the national mottos of liberty, equality, and democracy that Nisei's hyper-identification had pursued in the US domestic context. This explained an example of how minority imperial citizenship took hold among non-white soldiers, which produced colonial enforcers of the US military might and its geopolitical agendas out of assimilated ethnic Americans in Cold War East Asia.[55] Paradoxically, or perhaps logically, the US government even attempted to reinforce and safeguard the imperial citizenship of Nisei military linguists vis-à-vis the behaviors of other Allied Powers that clashed with America's domestic anti-racism.

In occupied Japan, the relationship between race and citizenship was constantly called into question under the entanglements of multiple imperial powers that carried their own brands of race politics. In particular, America's inclusionary racism came into conflict with the policy of Anglo-supremacist Australia and other contingents of the British Commonwealth Occupation Forces. In the early years of allied military occupation, Japanese American linguists often bore the brunt of the transpacific "White Australia" policy. Because GHQ loaned Nisei language experts to other occupation powers due to the lack of competent bilingual personnel, many Japanese Americans worked under the command of non-US allied forces that maintained their own imperial racisms that came to contradict America's professed colorblind agenda. In this sense, occupied Japan formed a site of contestation for overlapping foreign imperialisms and their racisms, and some contradictions revolved around the status and treatment of Nisei US citizens. There, Nisei's position and the value of their citizenship became even more fluid and destabilized. Understandably, many Anglo-supremacist Australians were not enthusiastic about treating Japanese Americans any better than despised Japanese enemies.[56] In 1949, the worsening situation finally propelled Nisei in Japan and their compatriots stateside to collaborate in a transpacific effort to assert the equal value of their birthright US citizenship against another racist empire that shared the multilateral colonial space in the defeated enemy land.

Learning about numerous instances of blatant discrimination against Nisei occupation troops, Mike Masaoka, the national JACL director, pressed Washington to intervene on their behalf while lodging a direct protest against "an intolerable situation" with the Australian government.

Yet, the crux of Nisei's discontent lay not in the injustice of white supremacy against the Japanese race per se; it was how the Australian troops arbitrarily distinguished between "Caucasian Americans" and "Americans of Japanese ancestry" in denying the latter due access to certain facilities and activities in the areas of occupied Japan under Australian command. In the letter, Masaoka said nothing about discrimination against non-citizen Japanese, nor did he explicitly disapprove of biological racism among Australians.[57] What JACL wanted the US government—and Americans in general—to be concerned about was the devaluing of birthright US citizenship along racial lines at the hands of a foreign power. Washington was compelled to concur, since Masaoka's protest defined the issue at hand in line with the post-1943 US anti-racist mandate of colorblind democracy for all loyal Americans, a mandate that was no less relevant in a Cold War context. Thus, even though the military unit brass had been initially hesitant to respond to individual Nisei complaints, the State Department promptly acted in support of the JACL once Masaoka's letter came in. The formal US government action helped ease the discriminatory treatment of Japanese American citizens by the British Commonwealth Forces in occupied Japan.[58]

Instead of challenging racism in the universalist language of justice or racial equality, the Japanese American protest drew from the narrow definition of their citizenship-based rights, or the violation thereof. In occupied Japan, the success of their struggle against white Australian discrimination helped further solidify the polarized definitions of being Japanese: those who were citizens and privileged members of an allied power, and those who were legal subjects of the defeated nation and hence rightless in the eyes of victors, including Japanese Americans. This government-sanctioned differentiation buoyed the Nisei's ill-treatment of their racial cousins as well as their appreciation for the imperial nature of US citizenship. Yet, it kept them generally acquiescent to white officers and soldiers who continued to act racially superciliously on a personal level. Insofar as their integration into the military structure ensured them equal privileges with other Americans as well as a separate status from Japanese nationals, Nisei linguists seldom considered that their lower organizational standing in GHQ would seriously demean their citizenship—whether equal or imperial. For this reason, their struggle with racial discrimination tended to reinforce—or indeed often manifested itself as—an exaggerated performance of intra-racial difference rather than an outright objection to white prejudice or action stemming from it.

In order to achieve their goal, it was essential for Nisei linguists to control the terms of their relationship to native Japanese, trying to infuse a clear understanding of intra-racial difference into the minds of their white colleagues and superiors. Therefore, in their daily encounters with local Japanese, many Nisei calculatedly behaved in an aggressive manner to illuminate their status as victors and, most importantly, their primary allegiance to the United States, not race. Nisei sociologist Tamotsu Shibutani, who himself served in occupied Japan, described this Nisei behavior by quoting a frank observation of his co-ethnic comrade:

> Some of these guys (Nisei soldiers) have always been squawkin' about getting' pushed around in the States. They heard about discrimination and all that crap from the time when they were kids. Now this is the first time they're "King Shit." They can push guys around, and the other guys can't do a fuckin' thing. So now they take it out on the Boochies (referring to local Japanese).[59]

According to Shibutani, there was a causal nexus between Nisei misconduct against Japanese nationals and a high degree of racial awareness. "The very men who identified themselves with the Japanese 'race' were," he noted, "the ones who treated them more harshly."[60] That is to say, the more the Nisei were concerned about their racial ties to defeated Japanese, the more roughly the former tended to act toward the latter. These Nisei could also behave obliviously to the plights of the vanquished in order to create a mental distance from those with whom they fretted they were automatically identified due to their common ancestry. In a private letter dated November 1945, one Nisei linguist shared his thoughts on Japan and Japanese people in a contemptuous way. "I just wonder why in the hell these people ever had the leaders push them around as they did," he exclaimed. After describing "Situation here is lousy as hell," this soldier went on to bemoan: "I'm ashamed to think I am a descendant of the Japanese" although he took solace in "considering [him]self an American [citizen]." His letter then offered a lengthy description of how a "great many" Japanese women had "no morals," claiming that they were only worth "a box of candy" and he "wouldn't trade [his Nisei girlfriend] for all the girls in Japan." Men and children were no better, just "begging for cigarette and candy," according to him. Indeed, this Nisei was especially disgusted with Japanese men, "old or young," remarking: "I feel like beating the hell out of some of them."[61] No trace of human kindness or compassion could be detected in his letter or in descriptions of his behavior and thoughts. A fear of intra-racial association permeated his—and other Nisei's—rancorous attitude towards the people of his ancestral land.

Conversely, as Shibutani explained, those Nisei who were more confident in their "American" identity could sometimes afford to publicly exhibit "deep sympathy" for local people, "not so much because they were Japanese but because of their conviction that human beings should not be subjected to such suffering and indignity."[62] In different correspondence, dated around the same time, another Nisei linguist observed the similar "lousy" situation in occupied Japan, but his response starkly contrasted with the November 1945 letter writer. Speaking of some starving Japanese who loitered around the military mess hall to get waste food, this letter writer claimed that he and a few other Nisei GIs did "everything in their power to give it to them before it goes into the garbage can." The linguist continued, "Hakujins (white people) chase them away but Nisei boys will even get to gether [sic] opened cans of milk and put together all they can from what's left and then give it to the Japanese people."[63]

Predicated on similar human sentiments, the charitable deeds of Nisei servicemen were also occasionally reported in news media. The examples included a civilian linguist who spearheaded the organization of a "boys club" for positive cultural and social activities in Japan's countryside; and the Nisei GIs who started a donation campaign for a Japanese actress disabled due to a train accident.[64] Even though a number of Japanese Americans performed random acts of kindness for Japanese nationals, especially women and children, Shibutani observed that the individuals who transcended the fear of intra-racial association constituted a minority.[65] Even the aforementioned Nisei GI who had endeavored to pass uneaten food on to starving Japanese later began to express callous contempt for Japanese women, whose "intelligence," he spat out, "[was] very, very low."[66]

Since Nisei supervisors of local workers were not only in constant contact with their co-racial others but also exposed to the scrutiny of their white superiors, the loudest complaints about supercilious Nisei behavior came from those Japanese workers. The military linguists seized the opportunity to disentangle themselves from vanquished Japanese by making an exaggerated display of their power and status through abusive acts. When he was on assignment in Japan, a Los Angeles Nisei journalist frequently "heard native Japanese who have worked under Nisei describe how conceited their supervisors were."[67] Shibutani also found that some Nisei "seemed to enjoy ordering about laborers, forcing them at times to perform unreasonable tasks."[68] Court-martialed for extreme examples of abuses and other offenses, one such Japanese American linguist concurred with Shibutani's observations, testifying how "strict" he was on his crew of twenty-five local laborers whom he denigrated as "so dumb and lazy." Working under a white sergeant, this Nisei private admitted he "use[d] to... kick them and also gave them (violent) warnings." He knew "for sure they hated" him, but he did not care because he was not there "to spare the rod."[69]

The negative feelings of Japanese employees toward aggressive Nisei overseers ran deep, although the censored media rarely publicized this until the end of US military rule. Translated by CCD, private letters of Japanese laborers often complained about mistreatment by Nisei linguists. One example read: "We were forced to work just like so many coolies from 08:00 to 11:30 and from 12:30 to 16:30 without a single minute rest, roughly scolded by the (Nisei) interpreters. I felt bitterly miserable."[70] Right after the end of military occupation, an English-speaking Japanese national who had worked for GHQ registered his intense abhorrence of "Nisei's wickedness toward Japanese people." He even declared that "no Americans of other ethnicity would be disliked by people of their ancestral land so intensely as Nisei."[71] Some Nisei, especially civilian office linguists, were critical of the behavior of enlisted Japanese Americans. A female Nisei staffer at GHQ deplored the manner in which many soldiers took advantage of their "superior status" to "behave insolently," thereby tarnishing the image of all Japanese Americans in Japan, in her opinion.[72] John Aiso, one of the few Nisei commissioned officers, echoed the woman's point and mourned that misbehaving individuals tended not to return to the United States, since they so enjoyed a privileged lifestyle in occupied Japan.[73]

This penchant among many Nisei in Japan for consanguineous racial hostilities culminated in extreme linguistic denigration of the local people. In this instance, Nisei appropriated discursive aspects of wartime white racism in order to publicly distinguish between Japanese enemies and Japanese Americans. Even after the war, many Nisei continued to refer to the people of Japan using derogatory references and qualifiers, yet at the same time they emphasized their contrarily democratic and moral dispositions. Some of the common epithets used by Nisei against foreign Japanese included:

"Nip," "Jap," "gook," "boochie," "dumb," and "ignorant." These terms appeared frequently in their daily conversations and letters.[74] Back in the United States, the Japanese American print media similarly juxtaposed "Nips" and "Japanese Americans" in news stories and reports about occupied Japan.[75] Not only did such transpacific collaboration result in a shared sense of intra-racial superiority, but it also helped further dichotomize a public understanding of Japanese identity into polar opposites of good and bad, of dominant and subordinate, and of domestic and foreign. Only after the outbreak of the Korean War did Japanese Americans become less inclined to use wartime hate words against Japanese nationals. In tandem with the emergence of communist Chinese and Koreans as the new Oriental menace, the general American perception of the Japanese shifted dramatically by the mid-1950s, thereby diminishing Nisei's defensive postures for better.[76]

While distancing themselves from Japanese nationals, loyal Nisei US citizens on both sides of the Pacific strove to highlight a clear line of demarcation between themselves and foreignized Nisei: renunciants and strandees in occupied Japan.[77] These groups of American-born Japanese were vilified and ostracized by mainstream Japanese America, not only because their citizenship was lost or their legal status murky but also because they were too heavily tainted by negative symbolism of self-proclaimed disloyalty to the United States and active complicity with the treacherous enemy during the war. Many Japanese Americans viewed renunciants and strandees as major liabilities to their hard-earned hold on the claim that they were patriotic US citizens.

In the fall of 1946, the *Pacific Stars and Stripes* printed a letter from one Nisei serviceman about "how repatriates (and strandees) should be shunned and treated roughly for denouncing their citizenship [sic] during the war and claiming it after the war." This opinion piece catalyzed "quite a battle of words" by other Nisei letter writers—"both pro and con"—in the army newspaper.[78] Another episode, recalled by a white GHQ administrator, involved two Nisei who grew up together in Los Angeles's Little Tokyo and "played ball on the gas house team when [they] were in knee pants." The white officer had a chance encounter with these Nisei at a Tokyo bar; while one was a US serviceman, the other turned out to be a strandee, who confided that he had served in the Japanese army and was trying to figure out a way to regain his American citizenship. A few days later, the administrator ran into the Nisei serviceman, asking him about his friend's loss of citizenship and his desire to regain it. Despite their longstanding friendship, this Japanese American spitefully responded to the sympathetic white man: "No sir, those guys made their choice, now let 'em stand by it. I respect a fellow a lot more if he admits he was on the wrong side and takes his medicine than I do somebody who always wanted to be on the winning side."[79] The hatred toward co-ethnic traitors ran deep in the minds of many Nisei—in occupied Japan or stateside. Indeed, until the end of the 1940s, it was not uncommon to see wartime strandees referred to as "Nip draftee," "Nip GI," "turncoat," and the like in ethnic news reporting due to the perceived dubiousness of their national allegiance.[80] Often called "Tule bastards," renunciants fared no better as far as Nisei's hostilities were concerned.[81]

JACL leader Mike Masaoka vowed not to assist these disloyal elements in occupied Japan when they made desperate pleas for the restoration of US citizenship often through their family members and friends stateside. In a confidential JACL memorandum, he noted coldheartedly: "Personally, I can't see why we should go all out to help these people."[82] Under his leadership, the national JACL remained "neutral" on the question of formal assistance for renunciants during the occupation period. Strandees' requests for JACL support were handled only on a case-by-case basis after 1947.[83] Individual Nisei linguists in Japan were no kinder. Some accused GHQ of being too "lenient," as it gave these "traitors" "civilian jobs with good ratings, shelter, and food," which the "Yellow-bellied Japs" did not deserve in their opinion.[84] An Issei returnee lamented how some Nisei servicemen denigrated strandees as "treasonists" and verbally tormented them, saying things like: they "will never ever be able to return to the United States." In the first two years of occupation, this observer noted, the rift between enlisted Nisei and strandees was so wide that the former treated the latter as total "flops."[85]

Because of intense hostilities from their own compatriots, these ostracized Nisei were also hard-pressed to dissociate themselves from things Japanese on their part for gaining national and ethnic (re-)acceptance. Their performance of intra-racial difference likewise entailed linguistic denigration of Japanese nationals, which aimed at exculpating their denied Americanness in a pathetically exaggerated manner. Reported in a Los Angeles Japanese American paper, one episode involved a young man who revealed a 180-degree change in attitude from the defeated into the conqueror once he received confirmation of his US citizenship. This former renunciant started to call Japanese persons around him "Jap, Jap" to the extent that one white serviceman became so annoyed that he corrected the man to say "Japanese." Another renunciant frequently masqueraded as a Nisei conqueror, yelling at local railway employees in English with derogatory language like "goddamnit" and "SOB!"[86]

The postwar letters that one female strandee sent to her Nisei friends and siblings back home showed how hard she worked to construct an impression of an unbridgeable gap between herself and Japanese people with whom she had lived, studied, and worked in the very recent past after getting a job at the US occupation forces. According to her, "[i]t is so pitiful to see the cold and hungry Japanese looking into the brightly lit and warm canteens (where she now lived as a GHQ civilian linguist)." Then this strandee added unabashedly: "I just [think] they are getting what they brought upon themselves" as if she was completely oblivious to the fact that she had been as guilty of contributing to Japan's war effort as those "cold and hungry Japanese."[87] Nor did this writer demonstrate much sympathy for distressed Japanese women of her own age, who had to prostitute themselves to American servicemen for daily survival: "it is distasteful to me to see these soldiers with their arms around the Jap girls.... It seems so cheap."[88] After all, as her letter to a sister noted, "I have no love for the Japanese" because "these people are not my people."[89] Another letter further illuminated her heightened sense of distance and difference: "God—what did you create man for? What is the purpose in all these people? Japs everywhere.... What are their lives worth?"[90] Perhaps, combined with her rancor for frequent mistreatment of Nisei strandees by Japanese nationalists and police during the war, this discursive dehumanization of "Japs everywhere" in occupied Japan showed the extent of her desperation for acceptance as a Japanese American. On this shift in the attitude of many such strandees, one contemporary observer succinctly noted: "the Nisei strandee during the wartime was a pitiful lot.... After the war, when they re-instated their citizenship, they became proud Americans. Thus, they looked down upon the Japanese as inferior."[91]

This strategy of consanguineous differentiation was also gendered due to American Orientalist sexism, whereby a Japanese woman was meant to be a readily available "sex kitten" to any conquering male soldier. Analyzing a "tremendously popular, semi-pornographic" cartoon series on Japanese women under military occupation, historian Naoko Shibusawa argues that the images of the Japanese "Babysan" reflected "the fantasy of a heterosexual

Euroamerican man."[92] That fantasy did not discriminate between American-born and foreign-born. In fact, a popular cartoon series titled *Babysan's World* includes a depiction of such callous confusion with which every Japanese American woman must have been troubled in occupied Japan. One GI apparently mistook one of the Nisei for a native "Babysan." This uniformed white serviceman looked bewildered by the response he received after reciting a Japanese punchline from a book titled "How to Speak Japanese." Standing firm with her arms on her waist, the native-looking woman yelled at him: "Listen, bud—I'm just visiting here, too. I was born and educated in Frisco!"[93]

Comical as it may look, such an encounter with the objectifying gaze and propositions of US military personnel must have been a daily occurrence, especially for strandees and renunciants who had no visible sign of being American, like military-issued clothing or identification. Indeed, for Nisei Women's Army Corps linguists, wearing "the American uniform" was so important, since it served as "a shield against racial antagonism by white male soldiers."[94] The female Nisei's performance of Americanness by way of denigrating "cheap" native women had this dimension of trying to safeguard themselves from racialized sexual harassment in a colonial context of military occupation.

Japanese Americans as Democracy's Disciplinarians

It is ironic that Nisei's struggle for acceptance and equal rights in US race relations had to be complemented by the mimicking of, and even the outdoing of, white colonial practices in a transnational context. Yet, Nisei's embrace of imperialized US citizenship came with a heavy price—the paradox of simultaneously making them the oppressed and the oppressor. That was the very mechanism that sustained the dual identities of Japanese Americans as promoters and detractors of democracy in occupied Japan. Nisei occupation troops, especially Counter Intelligence Corps (CIC) agents who engaged in covert operations, constantly played the role of democracy's disciplinarians vis-à-vis defeated Japanese.[95] This aspect of occupation Nisei's activities was where the most violent and oppressive nature of their imperial citizenship revealed itself systematically beyond the parameter of individual actions. That Nisei CIC agents were compelled to serve as the watchful eyes and long arms of America's anti-communist extralegal suppression underscored how deeply the punitive power of minority US soldiers were integrated into GHQ's machinery of forced democratization.[96] Embedded in the inclusionary citizenship of postwar America, that power was institutionally sustained and exhibited in the form of formal military orders and/or white superiors' direct commands, which minority soldiers, especially Nisei servicemen, found extremely difficult to defy. Indeed, given the profound trauma of wartime suspicions and exclusion experienced by Japanese Americans, surrendering themselves unconditionally to the call of duty was most necessary for dispelling any lingering doubts about their loyalty to the United States.

In occupied Japan, the demand for unqualified national allegiance left many Nisei—CIC agents and others alike—in a dilemma, since they were sometimes expected to carry out deeds that were dangerous, unpleasant, morally questionable, and even outright dirty on behalf of their white comrades and supervisors. Nisei sociologist Tamotsu Shibutani reported an example of this dilemma which he personally witnessed while on duty. At a military barrack near Tokyo, a white mess sergeant took a fancy to a young Japanese server, but he could not communicate his desire to have sex with her due to the language barrier. The sergeant charged his Nisei kitchen staffer with the task of translating his proposition: that the young woman would get ten pounds of wieners should she spend the night with him. In this instance, the Nisei could avoid becoming an accomplice in the exploitation of the woman. Taking advantage of the white man's ignorance of the Japanese language, the Nisei told her "that the sergeant was infected with a venereal disease and that he intended to rape her," sending the woman running.[97]

Although it was sometimes possible for Nisei soldiers to negotiate personal pressures from their superiors based on their conscience and ingenuity, official military orders were harder to dodge. Disobeying a formal assignment would constitute a violation of the military regulations and subject Nisei servicemen to a court-martial or even dishonorable discharge. Most Nisei troops hoped to avoid such a situation not only for their self-interest, but also for the good name of their fellow Japanese Americans who were supposed to be unqualifiedly loyal. Nisei members of CIC likely faced such a dilemma constantly because of the very nature of their work. These agents who were expected to function as semi-native undercover operatives dominated covert intelligence activities, particularly in the leftist circles of enemy Japanese. For that reason, GHQ's Civil Intelligence Section, including CIC, had a much larger number of Nisei linguists than other branches of the military government.[98]

Nisei CIC agents were often commanded to carry out dangerous and problematic operations against suspected Japanese communists and other individuals deemed inimical to the American military government and US Cold War agenda. When they were assigned to the task of infiltrating or keeping an eye on subversive groups—a task that white intelligence agents escaped due to their physical differences—such Nisei were put in constant and imminent danger. For example, in May 1950, Nisei CIC members were stoned by communist demonstrators when they were assigned to observe a labor union rally. Two years later, during a communist gathering in commemoration of the thirtieth anniversary of the party's establishment in Japan, two Nisei CIC agents were discovered, "surrounded by hostile Japanese," and severely beaten.[99]

At the behest of their white bosses, some Japanese Americans also executed unlawful arrests and clandestine imprisonment of local civilians. Although neither US government sources nor Nisei MIS oral histories discuss the subject because of their security classification and, no doubt, a desire to save face, Japanese sources suggest that Nisei linguists were extensively involved in illicit operations of these kinds—which frequently included blatant violations of what little legal limits existed for the official activities of GHQ personnel.[100] These examples underscored the enormous amount of power that Japanese Americans exerted over Japanese nationals, as well as crystallized the costs of national inclusion that Nisei had to live with. Their desire to prove unwavering national allegiance created a Faustian bargain in which some undercover operatives participated—whether willingly or not—in the darkest chapters of the military occupation. Some Nisei were so repulsed by these duties that GHQ was compelled to dispatch a request to the army language school that "no more sensitive linguists" be assigned to "intelligence work" that they "cannot handle." In July 1947, almost fifty linguists were removed from this line of work for being too "sensitive."[101]

Still, a great many Japanese Americans responded to the call of duty faithfully as loyal citizen soldiers. One well-publicized case of Nisei involvement in a CIC covert operation was a major blunder that inadvertently exposed the inner workings of American intrigue against Japanese leftists. It entailed the abduction and alleged torture of Kaji Wataru and the subsequent extralegal detainment of this renowned socialist writer for over an entire year. A onetime collaborator with the Office of Strategic Services (OSS) in China during the Pacific War, Kaji emerged as a major critic of the US military occupation of Japan after 1945.[102] On November 25, 1951, special agents of a secret "Z Unit" under Lt. Colonel Jack Y. Canon forcibly took custody of him.[103] Canon was initially interested in enticing Kaji to work for GHQ as a double agent through his influence in Japan's leftist circles. The Korean War also made Kaji an attractive candidate as a double agent, since he had personal connections to Communist China's leadership; he had cultivated these connections when he had engaged in anti-militarist propaganda in Yenan. Yet, the leftist's dogged refusal led Canon to treat Kaji as a treacherous saboteur, subjecting him to long hours of interrogations about his connections to Chinese communists, which the victim characterized as "torture." In this episode, more than a dozen Nisei members took turns interpreting for Canon and his henchmen, still trying to convince the Japanese to collaborate by furnishing information beneficial for US military operations in war-torn Korea. Nisei agents were also ordered to keep an eye on the detainee every minute, force-feed him when he went on a hunger strike, and administer medical treatment to keep him alive.[104]

A week of unbearable mental anguish and deteriorating health propelled Kaji to attempt suicide by swallowing cresol. He failed but was rendered bed-ridden and was useless for espionage work; Kaji instantly became a liability to the powers that be. The leftist knew too much about the US army's extralegal activities in Japan. Even worse, with the military occupation ending in a few months, the uncensored leftist Japanese press would surely make Kaji a celebrity spokesperson for an anti-US political movement. Freeing the detainee was therefore out of the question. As his condition improved by February 1952, Kaji was transferred to a secluded location outside of Tokyo, where he lived in solitary confinement under the full-time supervision of three Nisei jailers for the next ten months. Kaji was finally released after Canon's Japanese cook managed to leak information on his whereabouts to the Japanese media.[105] Stories spread about the "kidnap," "torture," and "incarceration" of Kaji, exposing the integral roles of Nisei agents in the scandal as well.[106]

Published memoirs by Kaji as well as Japanese servants and a Korean agent employed by the Z Unit provide a glimpse into the Nisei's importance and troublesome roles in this and similar extralegal clandestine US counterintelligence operations in occupied Japan. Under the command of Jack Y. Canon, who bragged about killing two hundred Soviet agents in occupied

Japan, the unit comprised twenty-six members; of these, sixteen were Japanese Americans—mostly of warrant officer and sergeant ranks. Along with four white higher officers and agents (including Canon), two Nisei members possessed the authority to carry a gun, investigate, and arrest Japanese nationals without restrictions. Empowered by Japan's national police agency and Willoughby's G-2, their special privileges allowed them to place the local law enforcement under their command, if necessary, not to mention freely overriding its authority.[107] Identified by Kaji, his torturers were among these CIC Nisei, who served as Canon's interpreters and enforcers of violence according to his command.

The conversations that Kaji recalled having with his tormentors revealed these Nisei's precarious position and moral ambivalence. For example, as if trying to absolve himself of guilt for the illegitimate operation, one of Canon's Nisei interpreters apologetically said to bruised Kaji during an initial interrogation: "I am just interpreting." When the Japanese leftist reprimanded him for a "shameful" act at their second encounter, the same Nisei embarrassedly stated that he was "simply a lowly employee with no authority."[108] Likewise, during his confinement, two of the three Nisei jailkeepers often expressed their dislike of their work as they chitchatted with the captive. One Nisei would say, "Gosh! I really hate this job," and another would respond: "This is not a task I can be proud of; frankly we are no different from kidnappers."[109] Their lack of enthusiasm showed in how they routinely shortchanged their duties when they were not under the watchful eyes of their white superiors—a cause for eventual information leakage. At the same time, these Nisei still made sure to keep their mixed emotions hidden from the white officers who occasionally ran a check on the compound. The third Nisei, as Kaji observed, genuinely took pride in being a "dedicated servant" to his white bosses, and thus always took the initiative to keep a close eye on his prisoner.[110] Whatever their personal thoughts and feelings were, all three Nisei—and many other Japanese Americans in the occupation forces—believed that there was no alternative but to quietly carry out their assigned tasks regardless of what they entailed.[111] Their credibility as loyal American citizens was at stake, and the defense of that public image through the display of unwavering allegiance took precedence over all other concerns.

In 2002, a Japanese journalist conducted a rare interview with one of Canon's Nisei agents that illuminates the extent to which the principle of "loyalty at any cost" was still embraced and practiced by that Japanese

American. Most likely, this is the third Nisei whom Kaji referred to as the "dedicated servant" back in 1952. In the 2002 interview, the former Z-Unit agent justified his integral role in the persecution of Kaji with no hint of regret: "I went to Japan as an American.... We simply worked according to the US strategy to prevent the spread of Communism in the world."[112]

This view was echoed by many of his fellow MIS veterans, ex-CIC members included, who similarly gloated over their achievements and patriotism in their contrived oral histories. A publication of an MIS veterans' organization does not allude to the downside of their uncompromised loyalty. It unabashedly lauds Nisei's contributions to covert operations: "The CIC mission was that of detecting and preventing subversive activities directed against the Occupation Forces in Japan.... The CIC Nisei were very much involved in highly sensitive operations.... Many sensitive operations were carried out successfully because of direct involvement of CIC Nisei."[113] Stories of extralegal violence, destruction, and conspiracy, present in many Japanese eye-witness accounts, are nowhere to be found in the rather self-serving recollections.[114]

The simplified narratives of Nisei's military contribution and success fail to reveal the ambivalent character of their historical agency in occupied Japan. They neglect to mention that the linguists partook in the oppressive power of the United States through their embrace of legal belonging, functioning as a component of minority imperial citizenship. Subsuming these disturbing episodes under a celebratory narrative is tantamount to ignoring Nisei's struggles to deal with the daunting problems of race and citizenship under the continuously racist regime that presented itself as anti-racist. It is also equivalent to neglecting their dilemmas of enacting tutelary US militarism under the mask of the altruistic democratizer. An analysis of Nisei's complex experience sheds light on how the minority soldiers' quest for domestic national inclusion made them like complacent, if not enthusiastic, executors of the US military power against non-western foreigners abroad. This explains a rarely studied aspect of the transpacific process in which Japanese Americans became a so-called model minority. At the crux of this process lay the workings of minority imperial citizenship, which shored up the multiracial armed forces of self-styled democratizers in postwar World War II Asia-Pacific and beyond.

Nevertheless, it is important to note that Japanese victims of US minority oppression were not completely powerless or innocent of racial politics of their own. Despite his communist persuasion and prior working relations with Japanese American OWI/OSS agents in Yenan, Kaji Wataru considered Nisei occupation troops fundamentally no different than other Japanese in accordance with the blood-based thinking so characteristic of Japan's imperial racism. His essentialist hyper-identification was well articulated in his public "appeals to Japanese Americans," published soon after the communist was rescued from US military captivity. Reminiscing about past collaborations with Nisei linguists in creating propaganda leaflets in wartime China, Kaji stressed "the close blood ties that you, Japanese Americans, share with us, Japanese nationals," before lamenting that they were "doing white men's dirty work to promote the latter's (American) imperialism."[115] In his opinion, Nisei had betrayed the indissoluble racial kinship by standing on the side of US/white oppressors. Hence, Kaji added: "General Japanese perceptions of Nisei are being exacerbated day by day."[116]

Despite being embellished with leftist lingo and expressions, Kaji's published appeals resembled wartime Japan's propaganda when he told Nisei to "render support for the struggle for independence and liberation that their own blood had been fighting" instead of acting as US imperialism's "tool." Nisei were urged to "revolt against racial discrimination and overcome third-class citizen status" of the white American empire.[117] Juxtaposed against the notion of Nisei's racial betrayal, Kaji's frequent mention of "blood ties," "common ancestry," and "kindredness" anticipated how other Japanese nationals would also strike back at the American-born "race traitors." Vanquished Japanese, too, still managed to practice politics of intra-racial differentiation as a way to retaliate against Nisei's use of their imperial US citizenship, albeit under the constraints of American military domination.

Japanese Reprisals and Nisei's Criminalization

Like Kaji, many Japanese nationals were quick to find Nisei's (mis)conduct as an egregious instance of betrayal to their racial brethren to whom they should have been more loyal than to white men. This perspective provided a background for the rampant vilification of Nisei in post-defeat Japan—or "anti-Niseism."[118] No sooner had the end of military occupation removed GHQ censorship than Japan's print media generated a flood of scandalous stories about "criminal" deeds of presumably Japanese American individuals in newspapers, magazines, and books. Many of these stories were exaggerated, and others were mixed with wild speculations. In the minds of many Japanese, the idea of "Nisei" conjured up the particularly negative images that these biased press reports corroborated, and vice versa. The public imaginations of vilified Nisei typically involved: gangsters, swindlers, and panderers as well as thieves of all kinds. While stories of the first group were correlated with the demonization of predatory business brokers and claim merchants, extensive coverage in the news media of alleged Nisei burglars and robbers led to their general criminalization in postwar Japan's public discourse.

Indeed, during the 1950s, Japanese media reports frequently assumed that violent crimes were committed by Japanese Americans with a common characterization of perpetuators as "Nisei-esque" (*Nisei-fū*).[119] This curious analogy drew from anecdotes of "Nisei soldiers who threatened the Japanese at gunpoint, entered Japanese homes with their heavy boots and shoes,... (and) were associated with gamblers, smugglers and other notorious dealers."[120] Conversely, many Japanese crooks consciously masqueraded as Nisei soldiers to evade the law by taking advantage of the latter's imperial citizenship. In a widely publicized case, a group of Japanese outlaws pretended to be CID/CIC agents to rob Japanese merchants, while other criminals stole money and valuables from unsuspected women by promising a marriage and nice life in America. In another case, a young burglar refused to speak Japanese during police interrogation and instead reportedly stated in broken English mixed with some Japanese words: "Me, CID Osaka come back; watakushi very very tsukareteimasu (I need to return to Osaka CID; I am very very tired)."[121] Similarly, a Japanese bank robber wore clothes resembling US military gear and threatened clerks and customers with a gun by screaming some unintelligible English words. Even after his true identity was revealed following the arrest, the Japanese press continued to depict the man as "Nisei-looking," supplemented by a discussion of how difficult it would have been for the police to deal with lawbreakers of allied citizenship should this criminal have actually been a Japanese American.[122] It provided the very reason that some Japanese criminals opted to perform a "Nisei-esque" act, since they knew all too well that local law enforcement hesitated to take up a case involving foreign Japanese, especially US military personnel.

The criminalization of Nisei by Japanese nationals was intertwined with their sober recognition of the colonial conditions under which they had to endure the extralegal rule of the transpacific American military empire as much as it was an expression of racial-nationalist resentments towards occupation Nisei. Thus, as many Nisei endeavored to distance themselves from the defeated with whom they were supposed to rule as cultural brokers, Japanese nationals responded by otherizing American-born Japanese in a highly vindictive manner. Published in an ethnic monthly back home, one Nisei's grievance succinctly explained how their ancestral land disowned Japanese Americans as criminalized co-racial others. This linguist-turned businessman in Tokyo bitterly complained:

> The anti-Nisei feeling reported in certain quarters in Japan seems to have reached a point of hysteria. In a report of armed thugs trying to break into the home of Prime Minister Shigeru Yoshida, I quote from a local paper, excited Japanese press reports first described the intruders as "foreigners" resembling Nisei. What manner of physical features makes a Nisei in Japan look like a foreigner![123]

Of course, from the Japanese standpoint, Nisei's foreignness and disorderly conduct rested with their citizenship status. The notion of Nisei as outlawed aliens formed an important aspect of the Japanese response to their defeat and the negative effects that Nisei's imperial citizenship generated against them.

Stuck in the shifting grounds of meaning and power associated with citizenship and race, Japanese Americans experienced the opposites of what occupied Japan offered them: status of semi-colonial oppressors backed by their birthright US citizenship and that of semi-native brokers reified by their Japanese heritage. Under the US military domination, these contradictory positions and roles determined what relationships they formed with other Americans and foreign Japanese, as much as what benefits and burdens they were exposed to in the war-devastated ancestral land. Some episodes, like Nisei linguists' involvement in extralegal intelligence and military violence, were neither recorded in official history nor registered in public memory, since they could be deemed repulsive and inconsistent to their quest for positive recognition. Yet, Nisei's possession of US citizenship's imperial power did not spare them the vindictiveness of vanquished Japanese. Just as inclusionary US nationalism managed to harmonize the oxymoronic ideas of colorblind democracy and Nisei's perpetual subordination to white America, Japan's post-defeat racial nationalism renounced criminalized Nisei while co-opting Japanese Americans when profitable and convenient despite the tilted power relations. These represented a complicated landscape and clashing forces which young Japanese Americans negotiated constantly in occupied Japan.

Brokering a Race War: Japanese Americans in the Pacific War and the Occupation of Japan. Eiichiro Azuma, Oxford University Press. © Eiichiro Azuma 2026. DOI: 10.1093/9780197781432.003.0005

PART III

NISEI MILITARY HEROISM AND JAPAN'S REARMAMENT

5

Mythologizing Japanese American Soldiers in Defeated Japan

As World War II wound down, Japanese American combat veterans who had served in the 442nd Regimental Combat Team (RCT) were welcomed as heroes and featured in army reports and American newspapers. But in occupied Japan, few people heard of their heroic exploits until around 1949. This was no accident but was a direct result of differing US military orders. Stateside, a June 1945 War Department directive on "Nisei publicity" advised concerned officials to "give full public relations treatment to the activities of American soldiers of Japanese descent in the United States Army" with a special emphasis on their "combat duty"—that is, their "heroic" actions in battle.[1] This was an extension of the wartime anti-racist propaganda campaign intended to counter the rise of racist attacks and movements against Nisei and Issei returning to the West Coast from the incarceration camps.[2] In occupied Japan, marked silence prevailed on the same topic for the first few years of the reign of Douglas MacArthur (Supreme Commander for the Allied Powers/SCAP) despite the ubiquitous presence of Nisei occupation troops. This curious "absent presence" stemmed from the propaganda policy of MacArthur's General Headquarters (GHQ) against Japanese militarism. The demilitarization of defeated Japan aimed to strip the nation of any and every capacity to wage a war, which entailed the complete destruction of Japan's armed forces and related industries and social apparatuses, as well as the promotion of anti-militarist and pacifist sentiments in every single Japanese national. Notwithstanding these structural and psychological rehabilitation efforts by GHQ, post-1948 Japan suddenly witnessed a surge in public discourse on Nisei's wartime military heroism. This radical shift, prompted by the drastic SCAP policy change commonly referred to as "the reverse course," paved the way for the rearming of postwar Japan as a junior US ally in Cold War East Asia that was being engulfed in actual armed struggles between divided Chinas and Koreas.

To rehabilitate the meaning of state armed forces and national military service and its connections to race and democracy in Japanese minds, the US military authorities drew on the precedent of wartime psychological warfare by exploiting an array of (mis)representations and useful symbolisms regarding World War II Nisei soldiers. Yet, the occupiers were not monolithic in their views about the utility of the Nisei's military myth, as multiple forms of contestation emerged: MacArthur and his GHQ reformist-civilian staff versus the Pentagon's top army brass; GHQ in Tokyo versus US Eighth Army in Yokohama; and SCAP/liberal administrators versus hawkish military officials within GHQ. Furthermore, this public relations campaign entailed more than top-down impositions on the powerless natives by the military occupation regime. Influenced by the officially sanctioned stories about Japanese American war heroes, despite the widespread dislike of Nisei linguists, leading circles of Japanese society, especially those who developed a political stake in US-led national rebuilding, engaged in their own version of Nisei glorification. Meanwhile, Japanese Americans—in Japan and back home—volunteered to play a significant role in this complex process of Nisei's martial mythologizing. These three strains of discursive formation (the occupiers, the occupied, and Japanese Americans) unfolded in tandem and converged at the most pivotal moment of the occupation: the remilitarization of Japan in early 1950. Transplanted from the ideological battleground of US race politics to that of occupied Japan and Cold War East Asia, the story of Nisei's martial heroism helped shore up the shift toward rearming rehabilitated Japan with its democratized citizen-soldiers, who supposedly shared the same blood and cultural mores with their racial cousins in US army gear.

Chapter 5 traces the convoluted politico-cultural processes of occupied Japan and the United States that gave birth to and solidified the trope of Nisei fighting men as a model for postwar democracy and new soldiers in a free Japan after 1948. An analysis of the disparate agendas and interests that the US military authorities, Japanese Americans, and post-defeat Japanese leaders held form an important aspect of this chapter. The problem of race, which the occupation government wished to downplay vis-à-vis the weight of citizenship and cultural affiliations, flaunted its presence on many occasions by complicating the course of the three-way entanglements and contestation over the meanings of being Japanese, being a soldier, and being democratic. As an ideological symbol, Nisei soldiers were indispensable in cementing these meanings in service of the shared goal of rearming Japanese nationals. Yet, because of the disparate and even contradictory agendas and interests, it was easy for these meanings to be manipulated and for the three parties to be kept apart. Looking at how race, citizenship, and culture informed the transnational competition for the proprietary rights to the legend of the Nisei soldiers, this chapter unravels how the notion of Japanese soldierhood became rehabilitated in occupied Japan around the myth of these Japanese American war heroes. The exigencies of Cold War geopolitics required the United States to remilitarize its disarmed enemy as a subservient ally between 1948 and 1951, just like previously despised Nisei under white American commanding officers in the US armed forces.

Suppression, Importation, and Resurrection of the Nisei War Heroes in Occupied Japan

In the initial phase of MacArthur's reign, discussions of Nisei martial achievement and valor were hard to find in public discourse, for US occupation authorities endeavored to cast military-related subjects in a negative light. According to formal explanations of imperial Japan's demise, which other allied powers agreed upon, it was the militarists and military institutions that had sunk the nation into the depths of insane aggression and eventual self-destruction. Japanese people—albeit being ignorant and mindless—were also victims of the military leadership and associated institutions as much as they shared responsibility for waging a war in Asia that led to death and devastation for countless people. As initial steps toward their collective atonement and rehabilitation, the Japanese were told to disavow militarists and their supporters who had duped the nation into fighting a murderous war, while also renouncing practices and ideas that had ties to Japan's military ("feudal") traditions. Thus, as the imperial forces were being dismantled and former military leaders and their associates brought to justice, symbols of Japanese militarist virtue and ideology, such as *kendō* and *bushidō*, were officially prohibited and purged from the public sphere of occupied Japan.[3] Purportedly, Japan's traditions—especially the feudalistic way of thinking and behavior—had made up the common racial/national traits that had rendered "Japaneseness" the antithesis of a civilized, democratic soldier who would fight for justice and liberty instead of committing wanton destruction and pillage.

Under the machinery of occupation censorship controlled by the Civil Information and Education Section (CIE) and the Civil Censorship Detachment (CCD), motion pictures, stage performances, and publications could not feature positive images and narratives of military-inspired themes, including feudalistic *samurai* dramas, lest those give Japanese audiences a message contrary to the goal of reorienting them toward peace and democracy. As early as November 1945, GHQ issued a strict ban on any films deemed to be "infused with militarism," "nationalistic," "portraying feudal loyalty or contempt of life as desirable and honorable," "approving suicide either directly or indirectly," and "depicting brutality, violence or evil as triumphant," among others.[4] Military personnel—especially fighting troops—as film characters were also to be struck out of public representations as much as possible. Whether it was in a Japanese or American medium, the "glorification of the war" and "war heroes" also received resounding official disapproval during the first few years of the occupation so that defeated Japanese would not receive a confusing message.[5] Discourse on Japanese soldierhood could appear in censored literary works and public commentaries only if they explained that Japan had been defeated because it had been an evil empire. Depictions of Japanese military life were strictly designed to illuminate all sorts of tragedies that Japanese people had experienced on a personal level, as well as their collective guilt as a nation.

Under this comprehensive censorship, "Japanese-American characters were (generally) off limits" to avoid confusion and controversy.[6] Although postwar racial liberalism in the United States continued to take full advantage of Nisei's military heroism to disavow blood-will-tell racism in the domestic context, the story of the all-Nisei 442nd RCT was completely absent from Japan's tightly controlled public discourse until mid-1948—with a few exceptions. On December 7, 1945 (Pearl Harbor Day), CIE purposefully distributed information on "how Japanese-Americans are used in our army" in the context of retelling a "(hi)story of the Pacific War" on the first major anniversary to mark Japan's war responsibility after its defeat. "20 photographs of... the destruction of Manila and Japanese atrocities" accompanied the story along with more reports on "Japanese criminal acts on American prisoners." The purpose of disseminating information about Nisei World War II soldiers was obvious: to juxtapose the brutality of imperial Japanese forces and the righteousness of democratic American forces in the most striking manner; it was not to generate a positive impression of

Japanese-looking soldiers. Yet, perhaps due to deep-seated distrust of the enemy within GHQ brass, even such a prescribed usage of Nisei soldiers was seldom seen in occupation propaganda after this one instance until a radical shift in 1948.[7] Nisei occupation troops were expected to function as stern but benevolent human agents in delivering "news of democracy" in their day-to-day interactions with local Japanese rather than through media-produced narratives of their military accomplishments.

In the enemy reorientation program, one subject concerning Japanese Americans occupied an important place, however. Given the magnitude of negative press coverage in wartime Japan about their mass imprisonment, GHQ had to circulate a counter-narrative on the non-racist, if not anti-racist, character of the wartime incarceration. A day after the four-year anniversary of Japan's attack on Pearl Harbor (Japan time), the ninth day of December 1945 marked the beginning of a full-scale media campaign under the US occupation authorities to instill war guilt and disdain for militarism into the post-defeat Japanese consciousness under the title: "Shinsō wa kōda" ("Now It Can Be Told"), and its spin-off "Shinsō bako" ("Truth Box")—weekly radio installments that were repeatedly rebroadcast nationwide almost every day until January 1948. A Nisei linguist named Frank Baba was deeply involved in this press censorship/propaganda.[8] Accompanied by the print versions of anthologies that followed the broadcast, the radio program articulated the US positions concerning what caused the war and MacArthur's policy toward defeated Japan in a simple question-and-answer format. Having been implemented during the first two years of the occupation, the propaganda broadcast—and its associated publications—were designed to create a definitive mental break between the war-mongering, anti-American past of the Japanese nation and its peace-loving, pro-American future. In recent years, right-wing Japanese historians and pundits have criticized this program as a poignant example of how the United Sates imposed its warped interpretations of history on Japanese people, depriving them of national identity and pride in their own culture and tradition.[9] Even Takemae Eiji, the foremost Japanese historian of the allied occupation, conceded "there was some truth in that assertion," but he also contended that post-defeat censorship had a "liberating" effect compared to the thought control engaged in by the Japanese government in the 1930s.[10]

In the radio program and its associated publications, the question of the "Japanese (American) relocation" received measurable coverage. Modeled after the OWI's rationale developed in its 1942 film, the formal GHQ answer carefully circumvented the involvement of racism in the whole saga. It was simply a matter of political exigencies, the program asserted, since the US army had to be concerned about the concentration of Japanese populations in the Pacific Coast states; residents of German and Italian ancestry did not present a similar problem, since they were dispersed throughout the United States. According to the official narrative, race played no role whatsoever in the decision to remove Japanese Americans en masse from the West Coast and imprison them in the incarceration camps. Despite initial confusion and inconvenience, the "relocated" Japanese were supposedly well taken care of, and their human dignity preserved. "It is important to note that the relocation centers were never internment camps," the official explanation emphasized, "because nobody was subjected to any form of punishment, persecution, or violence." Once there was no military necessity, American people quickly embraced Issei and Nisei with sympathy and goodwill, and this "brilliant" example of American racial tolerance was "unprecedented" in human history. "Not only did Nisei soldiers prove themselves that they deserved no shame from their own country through their (military) contributions," so the GHQ propaganda stressed, "but America also showed them that it had absolutely nothing to be ashamed of."[11] Until 1949, Nisei war heroes did not receive any more attention than this type of cursory reference or passing mention in the grand narrative of America as an "unprecedented" anti-racist power.

For the same reason, the representations of wartime white American conduct that might infer an involvement of racial hate and violence were subject to occupation censorship even when such representations were deemed perfectly acceptable in the US domestic context. For example, a "heroic" story of a "bad boy" white GI, who received a medal of honor posthumously for "having singled handedly [sic] killed a hundred Japs," had "all references to the killing…deleted" in a censored version of an imported Paramount film production. In the same 1945 movie, an image of a poster showing the words "Wipe the Japs off the Map" also got censored out before commercial release in occupied Japan.[12] All these were done according to the recommendations of CIE and CCD to present American (white) soldiers as peace-loving and humane, not trigger-happy murderers of a racialized enemy as wartime Japanese propaganda had portrayed.

This effort to sanitize "America" in the public imagination, which constituted the flipside of depicting things "Japanese" in a negative manner, even compelled US military censors to object to a newsreel report on the destructiveness of a harmful pest known in Japan as "Amerika shirohitori" (fall webworm).[13] Rather than the content of the report itself, the censors took issue with the prefix "Amerika [America]," which "might develop into an objectionable dialogue" among Japanese concerning the pest's supposed origin: the United States. Thus, in the early phase of US occupation censorship, the calculated disavowal of anything negative about America, especially its racism and destructive power, had to be packaged with the wholesale disavowal of Japanese feudal traditions and their innate brutality, under the banner of democratizing the enemy nation. Considering the heavy weight of the essentialist assumptions that automatically equated being Japanese with being militaristic, an alternative idea that someone with Japanese blood, like a Nisei 442nd RCT member, could be a civilized soldier was still deemed too confusing and hence dangerous to be brought into occupied Japan.

While the occupation government was hesitant to take advantage of the readily available trope of the Nisei war hero, the first notable attempt to put it in direct service for the democratization of Japan surfaced among Japanese American leaders back home. In March 1948, as a part of ongoing domestic anti-racist propaganda, the Department of the Army decided to posthumously honor the patriotic sacrifice of one Nisei 442nd RCT member, Sadao S. Munemori, who had been killed in Italy while trying to save his comrades by hurling himself on an exploding grenade. The public display of honor took the form of renaming an army transport ship after him. The dedication ceremony was held at Brooklyn Army Base with many white military leaders as well as Nisei veterans and community representatives. In the US domestic print media, the event drew extensive coverage.[14]

As this display of racial acceptance by the armed forces unfolded merely six years after the President had authorized the treatment of the same people as an "enemy race," Mike Masaoka and his colleagues in the Japanese American Citizens League (JACL) were ecstatic, and they entertained the idea that they should blow up the public relations value of the event to the fullest. Their central agenda was still domestic-centered with a view to combating lingering anti-Japanese sentiment in the US popular consciousness and facilitating more substantial inclusion of Japanese Americans into white America. In order to achieve their goals, Nisei leaders specifically aimed to link Munemori's honor to the theme of US wartime propaganda, which had dissociated Nisei soldiers from the enemy Japanese as a paragon of America's tolerance and democracy.[15] The message that the JACL wanted to reinforce was that race did not make the Japanese American a hero or a villain; it was their dedication to democracy and freedom, entrenched in their US citizenship and upbringing, that had also distinguished them from their racial compatriots—who were under American tutelage for their own democratization.

On March 10, 1948, six days before the ship-naming event, Mike Masaoka sent a letter to the Secretary of Army, requesting the rerouting of the USAT *Pvt. Sadao S. Munemori* to the Pacific as a "telling token of democracy and racial understanding at work."[16] According to the Nisei leader, it would be even better if the ship was sent to Yokohama with a full load of relief materials, since such an action would come across as a definite "gesture of good will toward the people of Japan." It would be a tangible form of benevolence that would come not only from the United States but also from the anti-racist trope of the Nisei war hero emblazoned on the transport ship.[17] The JACL's attempt to revive this propaganda theme for their own domestic racial agenda received instant support from many politicians and reputable media. Representative William W. Bradley of California, for example, declared: "it would be of inestimable value in further cementing Japanese and American friendship and understanding."[18] On March 20, the *New York Times* approvingly editorialized on Masaoka's proposal, even recommending that the *Munemori* be "manned by his old Nisei companion-in-arms and sent to Japan" to valorize its symbolic meaning. The editorial concluded: "Patriotism and (military) heroism are passports across every frontier."[19]

The rerouting of the transport ship did not materialize, not because the army rejected the rationale but because no ships could be diverted from the Atlantic to the Pacific at that juncture.[20] While turning down the JACL's request, some segments of the military brass in Washington were intrigued by the utility of Nisei military symbolism half a globe away across the Pacific. During 1948, however, the valorization of martial virtue and heroism, which the *New York Times* thought had universal appeal, did not yet look suitable for occupied Japan, especially in the eyes of MacArthur and many left-leaning "New Dealers" in GHQ, as well as the State Department's "Japan Crowd." As they saw it, the Japanese masses were not prepared to appreciate "[p]atriotism and (military) heroism" in the way Americans could, as they were still mired in feudalistic thoughts and, worse, getting increasingly influenced by combative communist ideas.[21] A military-related subject, if mentioned at all, might still be best subsumed under a broader narrative of Nisei assimilation and their embrace of a democratic lifestyle and capitalist mode of economic activities. The JACL's proposal nonetheless revived an interest in the potential utility of the mythologized Nisei military experience in some segments of the army brass in Washington, which simultaneously spearheaded the relaxing of occupation censorship despite SCAP's misgivings.[22]

A few months after the *Munemori* affair, important developments took place in Washington, DC, and Tokyo. In June 1948, the Department of the Army commissioned Hollywood producer and director Robert Josephs to create a documentary film titled "The Nisei Story," which was "centered on the resettlement of wartime evacuees of Japanese ancestry in the Pacific Coast."[23] With the enthusiastic support of the JACL and the Nisei Veterans Association, Josephs also recorded various aspects of Japanese American community life in Los Angeles, including their economic recovery and social activities as full-fledged members of democratic capitalist society. The film also featured the heroic struggles of the local JACL when many Nisei still met resistance to their resettlement in California. In sum, it was a film about postwar America's anti-racism in action narrated and performed by Nisei citizens. The army headquarters intended to distribute the film to "Far Eastern occupied areas in the Pacific, especially in Okinawa, Japan, and Korea."[24]

In the fall of 1949, while this film was still being shown throughout East Asia "under US Army auspices," another ten-minute "documentary" on the post-internment life of Japanese Americans was produced by the department's reorientation branch in New York specifically for "orientation and educational purposes in Japan." Designed to eradicate the residual influences of wartime anti-US propaganda "by Japanese militarists," the 1949 film planned on "portraying to the people in Japan how... the Nisei fit into American life" through the visual presentation of "the facts... without using 'sugar-coating' for the benefit of the... Japanese audience."[25] This marked an important moment where the moving images of Nisei US citizens literally became the embodiment of colorblind American democracy, which ironically dispatched to vanquished Japanese a message that their racialized minds and colored bodies had the capacity of absorbing and mastering democracy just as their US-born compatriots were doing on the silver screen.

Around the same time with the first transnational army propaganda film, in July 1948, a Nisei GHQ staffer named Lt. Walter Y. Mihata acknowledged the value of imported United News footage on the burial of "two Nisei

[war] heroes at Arlington," characterizing it as "one of the best 'good will' propaganda subjects that has been noticed by this section."[26] This Nisei linguist was affiliated with the Civil Censorship Detachment (CCD) in Tokyo, and he played a significant role in that division due to his superb command of Japanese. According to Mihata, the solemn ceremonies featured close-up shots of white army dignitaries and Issei parents, which he praised as "particularly impressive." Even if it might not be a special sight in American eyes any longer, what would maximize its propaganda value relative to people of Japan was the scene where General Jacob L. Devers, former Commander of the US Sixth Army, humbly handed over folded American flags to the aged mothers of the Nisei 442nd RCT members killed in the historic rescue of the Texas "lost battalion" in wartime France. The visual image of the towering white commanding general offering full honors to these feeble Japanese elders would not only disrupt the traditional Japanese sense of hierarchical social relations, but it would also counter the commonly held idea of beastly white men dominating the yellow race. Hence, the CCD Nisei agent raved: "The commentary in Japanese...was effective in pointing out the impressive ceremony as ample evidence of the tolerance and understanding of democracy in the United States." This newsreel was shown at over 80 percent of the 2,027 movie theaters throughout occupied Japan in the summer of 1948.[27] This development provided a significant background for the submission of an application for permission to publish the first ever Japanese-language articles on the 442nd RCT in occupied Japan.[28]

It is important to note that this "good will propaganda sequence" in the United News newsreel was originally censored and processed by Mihata.[29] A veteran MIS linguist from Hawai'i, Mihata was perhaps the first GHQ insider who positively capitalized on the existing trope of the Nisei war hero by (re)defining its propaganda value for Japan in the language of "good will," that is, examples of "tolerance" and "democracy in the United States," not in terms of equal citizenship as had been in the US domestic context. As this Japanese American censor saw it, "good will" propaganda was supposed to neutralize feudalistic Japanese thinking and impressions of the colonial/racial characteristic of US military occupation, which GHQ would have no reason not to embrace. In addition, what made Lt. Mihata successful in bringing important changes to the occupation reorientation program was the Department of the Army's concurrent film projects on Nisei, which reinforced his message with a powerful push from outside GHQ's command hierarchy.

Soon after the nationwide showing of the Arlington ceremony newsreel in Japan, Washington's army brass authorized the first formal burial, with full military honors, of a Nisei war hero, another 442nd RCT soldier, in the home village of his Issei parents in Kumamoto prefecture. In September 1948, his body was transported from an army cemetery in Italy by a military vessel, and it was received at the Yokohama pier by a local army honor guard, an army band, and the chaplain representing the commanding general of the US Eighth Army. After cremation, the Nisei's remains were hand-carried by a soldier escort to his family in rural Japan for his final rest. This localized reenactment of the Arlington ceremony, which took place in Yokohama, was reported in the domestic print media of occupied Japan.[30] The Japanese press did not hesitate to point out that this show of respect to a soldier of Japanese ancestry was possible due to "the good will of the US army authorities."[31] Incidentally, or perhaps by design, the army reporter, Pfc. Lawrence H. Sakamoto, who most enthusiastically wrote about this episode in the *Pacific Stars and Stripes*, was the very Nisei who had just applied for the publication of his essays on the 442nd RCT in occupied Japan.[32] Both Mihata and Sakamoto originated from Hawai'i and most likely knew each other well. This seems to suggest the presence of behind-the-door maneuvers by some Nisei occupation troops when the mythical tale of the Nisei war heroes first entered the public discourse of occupied Japan in mid-1948 in the context of the policy change by the Department of the Army in Washington to which SCAP/GHQ in Tokyo acquiesced.

Equally importantly, this trope catalyzed serious negotiations between GHQ and vanquished Japanese, generating another phase of the three-way struggle over the fluid meaning of the Nisei war hero. The fundamental problem lay in the paradox of communicating the colorblindness of US democracy to Japanese nationals in terms of the common heritage (lineage and culture) that they shared. Put differently, it was not far-fetched for Japanese nationals to claim ownership over the symbolism of the Japanese American war hero by pointing to same heritage—and the immutable racial and cultural qualities that resulted from it—that they shared despite the difference in citizenship status. Seen from the standpoint of this possible rhetorical hijacking, Japanese American military heroism could look like the manifestation of superior racial qualities, albeit perhaps aided by the Nisei's US upbringing. Even though imperial Japan lost the war, it was possible to conclude that Japanese race and culture still prevailed in the Nisei soldier success story, thereby asserting Japan's superiority and hence perpetuating key aspects of its imperial racism that was supposed to be no more.

The possibilities for this self-serving rhetorical hijacking may well explain an attempt by some Japanese nationals who worked in the local motion picture industry. This case of counter cultural production transpired in mid-1948 when many important changes were simultaneously taking shape within the US occupation regime. Coinciding with the US Army's first film project on the Nisei, a group of Japanese cultural workers in Tokyo, including Issei returnees from California, sought to develop their version of an "anti-racist" movie based on their own rendition of the Japanese American past. In June 1948, cultural workers and businessmen affiliated with the Tōhō Film Studio drew up a blueprint for a motion picture on the history of Japanese in America; they focused on the "family education" of Issei parents, which was purportedly responsible for "producing members of the legendary 442nd RCT." According to a draft script, the story would begin with the prewar experiences of immigrant parents, who had helped build California agriculture and raised outstanding Americans out of their US-born sons and daughters despite many "obstacles." Then, the unelaborated "incidents" that the two generations of Japanese in America encountered during the war would pave the way to the film's ending, which would delineate how Nisei and their children Sansei—both proud outcomes of Issei education—were contributing to the construction of a democratic America.[33]

Newspaper reports on the project summarized what one Japanese production staffer, a former Issei Hollywood film worker, described to his immigrant friend in Los Angeles in private correspondence.[34] Well informed about the heroism of Nisei servicemen due to his connections to the Japanese ethnic community, the letter writer and other former immigrants collaborated with Tōhō producers and actors to organize a film project team. As one of the news reports revealed, their preliminary scenario carefully circumvented the detailed examination of racial discrimination in Japanese American history by adopting such generic descriptions as "obstacles" and "incidents."[35] This was done because the occupation authorities would surely censor those scenes out of the storyline if they were too obvious. Nonetheless, this film would be all about white racism and the Japanese struggle against it, if only covertly. Indeed, the proposed project would not be able to avoid discussions of race when narrating specific aspects of the prewar "obstacles" and wartime "incidents" that engulfed Issei and Nisei.

For example, California's Japanese farmers had always been subjected to the state alien land laws, which had denied them landownership and tenancy since the 1910s. Contrary to the benign descriptions of the wartime Japanese American experience in occupation propaganda, a Japanese-generated interpretation would necessitate critical considerations and negative articulations of race factors. The mistreatment, if not outright oppression, of Issei and Nisei by the West Coast public was inseparable from the ensuing wholesale incarceration.

Indeed, during the prewar period, Japanese immigrants and their supporters in Japan had already produced a systematic narrative of the former's group experience in the US West with the interrelated themes of "perseverance" and "triumph." Their narrative had focused on the dialectical relations between race-based discrimination and Issei's endeavors to overcome it through the use of their ethnic cultural capital, that is, the collective ethics of hard work and the proper upbringing of their American-born successors in accordance with selected Japanese cultural norms.[36] This grand narrative of ethnic history doubtless dictated the writing of the 1948 Tōhō film script, which specifically valorized the value of Issei's "family education" for Nisei war heroes.[37]

So framed, the proposed motion picture would undermine a pivotal theme of official US propaganda. Given its primary focus on ethnic family education, the film's conclusion—the rise of democratic Nisei and Sansei—would inevitably lead viewers to a different causal interpretation. It was not so much America's anti-racism as it was the legacy of Nisei's cultural upbringing that formed the foundation of their resolve, tenacity, and hence their accomplishments as American patriots par excellence. That cultural upbringing was not Americanization; it was a form of Japanization by their Japan-born parents, who had fought white American racism as imperial Japan had done. In the end, as this narrative was designed to unfold, the symbolism of Nisei war heroes would carry very opposite implications vis-à-vis the officially endorsed occupation narrative. Instead of white America's tolerance or its democratic society's embrace, the Japanese national character and cultural traditions supposedly accounted for the wartime success of Japanese America. By reversing the relations of power relative to race and culture, at least in discourse and representation, this Japanese film project was fundamentally subversive to SCAP/GHQ's objectives and their control of the defeated nation.[38] These dangerous implications would be hard to overlook once the film script became substantive enough to articulate what "obstacles" and "incidents" actually meant. Along with financial and logistical difficulties, it was perhaps this political ramification that caused the project to stall even though initial presentations of it to CIE officials brought about their "enthusiastic approval," according to the bureau's Nisei staff linguist.[39]

Although the planning for the film did not leave the circle of cultural workers and businessmen in the Tōhō Film Studio during 1948–1949, this episode crystallizes the ambiguous position and meaning that the Nisei held in occupied Japan—both as a trope and knowledge producers. Any positive representations of their bodies and dispositions would create possibilities of rhetorical manipulation for the benefit of not only the occupiers but also the occupied. The former, who privileged citizenship status and nurture (cultural Americanization), claimed ownership of Nisei behavior and their accomplishments as quintessentially American. Moreover, the US authorities and Nisei occupation troops both knew that defeated Japanese would never become "Americans," although they should strive to emulate their US-born racial cousins through the adoption of new ideas and institutions during US-induced democratization efforts. People of Japan would forever be foreign disciples of American democracy—a junior ally at best, as they were soon to become in Cold War East Asia.

On the other hand, many Japanese nationals continued to take for granted racial and cultural bonds as a source of their collective strength despite the defeat, thus trying to assert, if implicitly, a dogged belief in Japanese superiority through the officially approved symbolism of the Nisei war hero. As historian Yukiko Koshiro explains, the demise of imperial Japan did not put an end to Japanese imperialist thinking and racism, which had aggrandized immutable blood bonds and essentialized cultural qualities. Not only did these ideas survive military defeat, but they also adapted well to the new reality of US geopolitical hegemony.[40] Seen from this standpoint, public discourse on the Nisei formed an important site for continuous racial and cultural struggle between Americans and Japanese, and between the United States and Japan during the military occupation and beyond. Like the Tōhō filmmakers, many other Japanese were eager to co-opt the US-generated Nisei military trope to bolster their repressed sense of pride as a race despite, or perhaps because of, total subordination to the US military after the defeat. In this struggle, the participants were not limited to white Americans and Japanese nationals. As Masaoka's proposal in the *Munemori* affair or Lt. Mihata's behind-the-door maneuvering showed,

Japanese Americans performed a pivotal role by setting the Nisei war hero on a pedestal in their own self-serving way.

Why, then, did all these parties suddenly become so interested in the public representations of Japanese American soldiers in mid-1948? What happened to US occupation policies during the middle of that year gave historical specificity to the utility of the Nisei martial myth that the occupiers extolled. Ahead of the departure from GHQ's earlier "liberal" reforms, known as the "reverse course," the third month of 1948 marked the beginning of the "Kennan Restoration," supported by top State and Defense Department officials in Washington. Historian Takemae Eiji describes this as "a shift away from such 'destabilising reforms' as the purge, reparations, the dismantling of the (Japanese) Home Ministry, police decentralisation, *zaibatsu* dissolution, and liberal trade unionism" that had been carried out under MacArthur's Tokyo GHQ.[41] The joint State-Defense efforts to undermine SCAP's liberal programs in the areas of social and economic policies were accompanied by the ascendancy of anti-communist elements within GHQ, especially its intelligence chief General Charles Willoughby, who had close connections to the surviving leaders of Japan's imperial armed forces as well as conservative Japanese elites—often with Nisei Counter Intelligence Corps (CIC) agents as intermediaries.

Among many developments in occupied Japan that followed the Kennan Restoration were an organized campaign to suppress resident Koreans as radicals and communists; the replacement of the democratic-socialist cabinet by incumbent Premier Yoshida Shigeru and his conservative cabinet; and the departure of the most ardent proponents of liberal reform from GHQ.[42] These developments helped revive Japanese imperial racism (and even militarism) after a post-defeat hiatus and boosted the idea of rearming Japanese people for the defense of democracy and capitalism. Therefore, the three-way entanglements over the Nisei military trope in 1948 cannot be divorced from the larger geopolitical context of the US-Japan joint endeavor to turn postwar Japan into a "bulwark against communism" in Cold War East Asia. The triumph and establishment of the People's Republic of China in October 1949 only reinforced this chain of events.

However, the Nisei's military symbolism was always open for various, even conflicting, renditions and narratives in the service of divergent agendas. From 1950 on, the relations of power and control over the Nisei martial mythology started to veer from the conquerors to the conquered in occupied Japan. Moreover, its original linkage to US national discourse of anti-racism became increasingly overshadowed by the theory of Japanese superiority. This discursive shift in, or rather, the discursive hijacking of the Nisei war heroes was an important component in the reverse course in US occupation policy from demilitarization to remilitarization of vanquished Japan.

Nisei Military Heroism and the Problem of Rearmament in Occupied Japan

In occupied Japan, such three-way entanglements for the meaning of the Nisei military trope were visible in the realms of public discourse and actual politics during the months of February to April 1950. This development revolved around two highly publicized events, which helped ignite local Japanese interest in the glorified story of the 442nd RCT. The rise of the Nisei war narrative at this juncture was specifically tied to the question of Japan's rearmament that engulfed both the occupiers and occupied in the period between the communist takeover of China in October 1949 and the outbreak of the Korean War in June 1950. The dramatic change in East Asian geopolitics and the corresponding reverse course in US occupation policy precipitated the full-scale entry of Nisei soldiers into political propaganda in occupied Japan from late 1949 onward. That trope helped turn the former enemy into a US military ally and regional bulwark against the rapidly spreading perils of Communism in Cold War East Asia.

This does not suggest the presence of some vast conspiracy or a well-calculated design by specific groups or individual masterminds on the US or Japanese side. Whether it was intended by specific instigators or not, what was most important is that the celebration of the Nisei martial myth in occupied Japan had a discursive and ideological effect of shoring up the larger political shift in the direction of rearming Japan. The way in which Japanese nationals co-opted that trope in 1949–1950 illuminated a national structure of thought in occupied Japan, which had the capacity to compromise US mandates of disarming vanquished Japanese. When the US authorities and Japanese leaders were compelled to sell the idea of rearmament to the public, Japanese nationals generally appreciated new democratic values and the idea of peace over militarism imparted to them not only by the GHQ's reorientation program but also through the traumatic memory of their own wartime sufferings. Yet, many still held onto the blood racism and cultural nationalism of a bygone era. This situation foregrounded the complex national psyche of defeated Japanese where the Nisei martial mythology functioned as qualitatively different ideological symbols than in the domestic discursive space of the United States. In occupied Japan, that structure of thought made it possible for the Nisei war heroes to metamorphose into model Japanese soldiers, when the demilitarizing nation was suddenly confronted with the need to rearm itself. Even though people and leaders of occupied Japan had no real negotiating power to alter the course, their warped appropriation of the Nisei military myth helped smooth the full-on shift in US policy mandate from total national disarmament to remilitarization.[43]

During the critical years of 1949–1950, the presumed nexus between being a Japanese soldier and being atrocious and evil in US-controlled public discourse was increasingly confounded by the representations of Japanese American servicemen as model soldiers. Nonetheless, this unfolding did not disrupt the basic US policy of democratizing the enemy or the postwar structures of power while it enabled remnants of Japanese imperial racism to thrive under the ascendancy of paternalistic US imperialism and its polite racism. Given the pervasiveness of imperial racial thinking that emphasized the primacy of blood ties, the consequence of the mythologizing of Nisei war heroes in occupied Japan entailed the conflation of Japanese Americans and Japanese nationals. It led to the reversal of the values associated with race and military service. Just as assimilated Nisei US citizens could become exemplary American soldiers despite their damned heritage, it follows that Japanese nationals could take up arms as democratic soldiers of a new Japan as long as they had been properly reoriented, if not Americanized, under tutelary US occupation. Such conflation still took hold within the bounds of GHQ's enemy reorientation mandate, insofar as Nisei's democratic dispositions were deemed helpful, if not indispensable, for producing good soldiers capable of civilized and humane conduct. By that time, vanquished Japanese had already gone through several years of systematic rehabilitation to become "democratized" according to the yardstick set by the American military authorities. Thus, it was not deemed preposterous for Japanese people to be able to appropriate 442nd RCT war heroes and celebrate the Nisei's accomplishments.

As the Cold War was about to turn hot in East Asia with the communist domination of continental China and northern Korea, America's desire to rearm Japan surfaced first among the uniformed and civilian military officials at the Pentagon. In January 1948, Secretary of Army Kenneth C. Royall suggested that the United States make Japan "serve as a deterrent against any other totalitarian war threats which might hereafter arise in the Far East."[44] The following month Defense Secretary James V. Forrestal ordered Royall to study the feasibility of Japan's rearmament—the question to which the latter responded in the affirmative by May 1948. Meanwhile, in October, the National Security Council, with the support of President Truman, called for a Japanese police force of 150,000 to offer "some degree of military assistance" to the United States.[45] The Joint Chiefs of Staff (JCS) followed suit by putting remilitarization on the official agenda in March 1949, but without a definitive timeline. Half a world away in Tokyo, GHQ was not immune to these developments despite MacArthur's personal objections.[46] By December 1948, liberal New Dealers affiliated to its Government Section had been ousted while anti-communist hawks, like General Willoughby of the G2 intelligence division, had tightened their grip on GHQ through its CIC. With the establishment of the People's Republic of China in October 1949, the tide accelerated for Japan's rearmament despite SCAP's resistance. In July 1950, two weeks after North Korea attacked South Korea, MacArthur finally ordered the Japanese government to establish the 75,000 strong National Police Reserve—the precursor of the present-day Self-Defense Forces of Japan.[47]

Under these international and domestic political intrigues for remilitarization among American political and military leaders, an initial rise of conservative Japanese interest in Nisei military heroism could be traced to a thirty-day Japan tour of a white American named Earl Finch in February-March 1950. Often called the "godfather of the 442nd RCT" and a "one-man USO," Finch had acted as a benefactor to hundreds of World War II Nisei soldiers at an army training camp in Mississippi before their deployment in the European theater when anti-Japanese sentiments had been still running high in 1943–1944.[48] Masquerading as a private sojourn of an American businessman, Finch's Japan trip coincided with the JCS's visit to Tokyo in the early months of 1950. Whereas the political tug of war between JCS and SCAP over the question of Japan's rearmament was going on without public knowledge, Finch drew substantial media coverage in Japan as he traveled from Tokyo to Kyoto/Osaka, and back between early February and early March.[49] While former members of the 442nd RCT in Japan and MIS linguists organized welcome receptions in his honor, the Department of the Army (not SCAP/GHQ) helped arrange a series of highly publicized personal meetings between Finch and

Japanese dignitaries, including Prime Minister Yoshida Shigeru and Tokyo Governor Yasui Seiichirō. The latter also held a special reception for the American guest at his official residence. Some former members of the 442nd RCT, who currently worked for GHQ and the Eighth Army, accompanied Finch at these meetings.[50]

Page Two PACIFIC STARS and STRIPES March 2

ALL JAPAN EDITION

FINCH GREETED—During his recent visit to Osaka, Earl Finch (center), "godfather" of the wartime 442d Infantry Regiment, renewed accquaintances with several members of the unit now serving with the 25th Infantry Division. He is shown with (left to right): Sgt. Tom Uchiyama, 25th Quartermaster Company; Maj. Stelin C. Moore, Kinki Civil Affairs Region; Earl Finch; Cpl. Biyozo Uyehara; and Pfc. Thomas Y. Ono, who are assigned to division headquarters. (U.S. Army Photo)

Fig. 5.1 Earl Finch (center) with former members of the 442nd Regimental Combat Team while stationed in occupied Japan. *Pacific Stars and Stripes*, March 2, 1950. US Army Photograph. Courtesy of the *Stars and Stripes*.

Finch's "private" tour of occupied Japan revealed much about the tense relations between the Pentagon and GHQ, between the JCS and SCAP, and between liberal New Dealers and hawkish military officers within MacArthur's GHQ over the question of Japan's remilitarization. The propaganda use of the Nisei war heroes elucidated the deep rifts among these US government constituents in a transpacific context. Preoccupied with the broader geopolitical threat of communist expansion, the Pentagon was less concerned with the goal of enemy reorientation in occupied Japan—especially after three years of what appeared to be overall successful military governance. On the other hand, MacArthur's personal views aligned with reform-minded occupation administrators, many of whom were not career army officers, as they considered their utmost task to help rehabilitate enemy Japanese by eliminating their militarism and its future resurgence. More bellicose GHQ brass, like Willoughby, understood the strategic needs for *realpolitik* and thereby came to support developments that might buoy the cause of a rearmed Japan against communist expansion. Commanders of the Eighth Army that provided security for the greater Tokyo region were also favorably disposed to similar strategic thinking. Propagandizing the evil nature of Japan's martial traditions or its military organization was not their assigned role; providing defense against the spread of Communism was. For these reasons, Major General Floyd L. Parks, Chief of the Public Information Division of the Army in Washington, initially brokered communications between Finch and Japan-based 442nd RCT veterans, specifically those affiliated with the Eighth Army headquarters in Yokohama.[51] Thus, it is appropriate to argue that Finch's visit was organized by the Pentagon, not GHQ, and it was carried out under the aegis of the Eighth Army. This pattern of bypassing GHQ's central authorities with the blessing of the Pentagon and/or the Eighth Army characterizes how the positive renditions of the militarized Japanese bodies and deeds pervaded post-1949 Japan through the dissemination of the Nisei's martial myth.

Under the joint efforts of the Pentagon and the Eighth Army, Finch's visit of early 1950 made a lasting impression on the minds of many Japanese, especially political and social leaders. In the context of explaining who this unknown white man from Mississippi was to a Japanese audience, the press reports and other sources needed to provide an abbreviated story of the legend of the 442nd RCT's wartime heroism. Then, Finch was particularly credited with his "humanitarian friendliness to the Nisei," as one Japanese dignitary put it.[52] During his month-long tour in Japan, Finch's frequent calls at local orphanages and grammar schools were portrayed in domestic newspapers as an expression of his general good will to Japanese people, undifferentiated from Nisei US citizens. Press accounts similarly included references to his generous gift of candies and other goodies to Japanese children—yet another example of Finch's "humanitarian friendliness."[53] By the conclusion of his Japan visit, the Nisei's benefactor reportedly received "piles of letters from Japanese people" in appreciation of his generosity. Purportedly, over thirty people came to his Osaka hotel each day to thank him in person. A farewell event for Finch drew as many as five thousand Japanese schoolchildren, who sang the Star-Spangled Banner in his honor.[54] Stories of Finch's support for "his (Nisei) boys" and contrived reports on his goodwill gestures to children of Japan were not hard to deem interconnected through none other than the targets of his "humanitarian friendliness" being Japanese in an all-encompassing manner.

Finch's visit paved the way for several developments that promoted the cause of Japan's rearmament. First, he provided a major catalyst for the sudden Japanese craze for the 442nd RCT—a psychological development that the United States could subsequently exploit for a smooth transition to the remilitarization of anti-communist Japan. The 34-year-old Mississippian personified a white America that had embraced members of the Japanese race according to the formally advertised principles of colorblind American democracy.[55] Many Japanese indeed conflated his "noble and unselfish acts" toward Nisei soldiers with the US occupation policy toward people of Japan.[56] This perception was reinforced by another popular characterization of Finch as a generous white/western "Santa Claus," who presented all sorts of gifts to Japanese children. In the local Japanese eyes, Finch's "noble... acts" had the effect of illuminating the racial commonality between young Nisei soldiers and Japanese children more than their difference between US citizens and Japanese nationals—both the recipients of white American "generosity."

Perhaps more significantly, the visit of the "godfather of the 442nd Combat Team" enabled many Japanese people to appropriate the Nisei's success story and glory for their own achievement of democratization. This curious rhetorical leap was articulated in the conversation that Finch had with Prime Minister Yoshida. At the meeting, as Finch recalled, the premier shared his good grasp of Nisei's martial achievements, which he praised as contributing to the promotion of mutual understanding between Japanese and Americans. "People of Japan now take pride in the military heroism of

Nisei soldiers," Finch elaborated on the meaning of Yoshida's remarks, "as if it was theirs to celebrate."[57] The evangelist of America's anti-racism paradoxically awakened in the minds of the occupied the essentialist thinking that allowed them to presumptively identify with the achievements and accolades of Nisei war heroes solely on racial grounds.

During Finch's tour, a similar rhetorical leap was detectable in Japanese understandings of the white man's benevolent gesture toward the 442nd RCT servicemen. While Japanese nationals often developed a dislike of Nisei linguists based on their encounters, many people also likened the positive stories of their racial cousins with their own trajectories since the defeat. Finch's embrace of Nisei 442nd RCT soldiers enabled defeated Japanese to indulge themselves in an enticing dream of being recognized and accepted as democratized equals by white Americans despite the reality of military domination and semi-colonial social relations between the conquered and the conquerors. For example, one of the letters that Finch received from a random Japanese expressed a "heart-felt appreciation" for his acts toward Nisei soldiers, because the letter writer felt: "Had it not been for your humanitarian warmness and friendliness, it seems it would have been impossible for our country to achieve democracy so quickly."[58] This line of thought allowed Japanese nationals to measure their "progress" in mastering democracy in terms of the accomplishment of Nisei soldiers, both of which were supposedly made under the guidance of white Americans, be it Douglass MacArthur or Earl Finch. Whereas the chairman of Japan's chamber of commerce declared that "Finch's kindness was a contributing factor to the brilliant war record of the Nisei" at his welcome reception, Prime Minister Yoshida elaborated on the same point: "The Nisei's wartime record has captured the imagination of Japanese and helped in Japan's progress toward democracy."[59] The comparison of Nisei war heroes and rehabilitated Japanese led to the frequent confusion of the two groups of Japanese—victorious US soldiers and subjects of the vanquished enemy empire—in Japan's public discourse.

After early 1950, this form of racial conflation characterized emergent public views on the question of Japan's rearmament. Nisei's military record looked like living proof that people of Japanese background could be civilized soldiers if their dispositions were capable of generating appropriate action for justice and humanity. What followed Finch's visit further compounded these processes in which the Japanese American war heroes were rendered as a mirror image of soldiers of a new Japan in subsequent

Japanese discourse and consciousness. In April 1950, the Tokyo metropolitan government sponsored a massive outdoor gala to celebrate the patriotism of 442nd RCT Nisei by inviting former members who were currently stationed in Japan. This public display of the Nisei war heroes in the heart of Tokyo was the brainchild of Governor Yasui and his special counselor, Kimura Ki, a popular novelist and literary scholar.[60]

These individuals were typical of turncoat leaders of Japan, who unabashedly switched imperial gear with democratic dress in the context of post-defeat regime change. Yasui had been a longtime insider to Japan's political establishment since the 1920s, serving as a home ministry bureaucrat affiliated with the oppressive police authorities and then as a top security officer and provincial governor in colonial Korea. When imperial Japan started state-sponsored colonization in Manchuria, Yasui took charge as colonial ministry head. This government insider survived the post-defeat political purge by GHQ, since he happened to be associated with a minority army faction that had been marginalized by General Tōjō Hideki and his henchmen. In 1947, Yasui was elected governor of Tokyo, beating out a socialist contender. In that context, he had no qualms about switching his allegiance from Japanese imperialism to US-led democratization.[61]

Another turncoat Japanese, Kimura, had a similar trajectory in Japan's cultural industry and academia. He was often regarded as supporting the proletariat cause, but at the same time, Kimura had been no stranger to the prewar intellectual and cultural developments that had offered discursive support for imperialism. He had been also a familiar name to Japanese America during the 1930s, having authored a semi-fictional tale of the first Japanese immigrant woman in California. In that novel, which later served as the basis of a popular 1940 movie, Kimura had contributed to the co-optation of Issei history in service of Japanese colonialism, especially its project of migration-led agricultural colonization in Manchuria. Kimura was responsible for a rhetorical leap by which to conflate the experience of first-generation Japanese Americans (a racialized minority) with that of imperial Japan's settler colonists (colonial masters). His 1935 publication misrepresented the Issei pioneer woman as the first female settler colonist of a "new Japan" in America, who purportedly exemplified what imperial subjects of the 1930s were supposed to do as agricultural colonizers in Japan's Manchurian frontier.[62]

After the defeat of the empire, Kimura extolled US-imposed democracy and liberty in his writings. During MacArthur's reign, the Japanese writer hailed the American general as "the best military leader since Napoleon." Kimura also became the head of the Freedom Publishers Association, which consisted of Japan's top publishing houses. In the face of the GHQ purge, these press collaborators with the former militarist government lobbied for their survival under Kimura's leadership. Soon after the end of US occupation, Kimura turned again, being accused of starting to produce "anti-American discourse."[63] Not only could the likes of Kimura and Yasui navigate the clashing waves of imperial colonialism and post-defeat democratization, but they also maintained the long-standing blood-will-tell thinking characteristic of imperial Japan's racism. Yasui, for example, was quoted as attributing his interest in the story of Nisei soldiers to their being "Japanese in blood" despite being "American in nationality."[64] From their standpoint, Japanese Americans always belonged to the Japanese race and nation, thereby feeling naturally compelled to contribute to Japan's cause, whether imperial expansionism or anti-communist democratization. Kimura and Yasui typified some Japanese nationals who managed to adapt to and negotiate the changing demands of the time without much of a moral compass or a sense of shame. Their attitude toward Nisei war heroes revealed how that chameleon-like behavior manifested itself in the context of the debate on Japan's rearmament.

Some ten years after the publication of the book on the Issei woman pioneer, Kimura put forward the idea of a gala for the Nisei 442nd RCT veterans, convincing Governor Yasui to sponsor the event under the auspices of the Tokyo metropolitan government. Kimura's interest in the Nisei war heroes drew from the same idea of immutability of blood ties and cultural superiority. As he later contended, his appreciation of Japanese American war heroes had to do with the positive moral influence that their story could have on Japanese youths whom he viewed as having turned decadent and effete since the defeat.[65] Aiming to positively influence those youths, Kimura was credited as Japan's first author to put together a book-length publication on World War II Nisei servicemen. His involvement in the glamorization of Nisei war heroes also motivated him to take up another book project on Pfc. Sadao S. Munemori, the first Nisei recipient of the Medal of Honor, which he did not complete despite conducting a research trip to Los Angeles.[66]

Inspired by Kimura's biased presentations, Governor Yasui decided to organize massive festivities to disseminate the hitherto neglected saga of their racial compatriots to the home public. In late 1949, Yasui sent a letter to General Walton H. Walker, Commander of the US Eighth Army, to request permission for such an event.[67] Apparently, there was initially "some criticism and objections against [Yasui's] plan" among central government elites, but Walker's positive response silenced the detractors and critics within the Japanese government.[68] Two weeks before Finch's widely publicized visit, Yasui's project officially got rolling. On the occasion of a grand welcome party organized by Finch's "boys" in Tokyo, Yasui made a formal announcement for "a garden party under cherry blossoms" for former members of the 442nd RCT. Some Nisei veterans, who worked in Japan, were asked to form an advisory committee to cooperate with Kimura and other Tokyo government officials to prepare for what would become a major pageant with six hundred American and four hundred Japanese guests, as well as eighty former 442nd RCT members as the guests of honor. The Eighth Army Public Information Office offered logistical support for the planning.[69] Notably, Yasui and the US army largely bypassed GHQ, especially SCAP, which had been critical of Japan's rearmament, suggesting the presence of an ulterior motive on the part of those involved in the glorification of the Japanese American military mythology.

On April 15, 1950, the historic fete featured these war heroes at one of the emperor's former gardens in central Tokyo—under cherry blossoms in full bloom—with both white American and Japanese dignitaries lauding the Nisei guests of honor. After performances by swing jazz ensembles and traditional Japanese dance and music troupes, the festivities ended with the Japanese American veterans singing the 442nd regiment song, "Go For Broke."[70] In addition to newspaper reporting, the public radio station broadcast some of the proceedings, and a newsreel was produced and shown at movie theaters nationwide. With the backing of the city of Tokyo, the newly established "Association of Thanks to the 442nd RCT [sic]" also planned on compiling a Japanese-language pamphlet "describing the[ir] distinguished services . . . not from the military point of view, but from that of loyalty to democracy." The material was slated for distribution to primary and secondary grade schools throughout Japan. There was even an attempt to erect a special memorial for the 442nd RCT in Tokyo.[71]

Drawing on widespread media coverage, this fete reinforced and extended the domestication of the celebrated Nisei soldiers as Japanese heroes beyond the circles of government officials and social leaders in occupied Japan. In their speeches, both white and Japanese guests stressed

Fig. 5.2 Former members of the 442nd Regimental Combat Team at a garden party sponsored by the Tokyo metropolitan government in honor of their military heroism, April 15, 1950. *Scene: The Pictorial Magazine* 2, no. 2 (1950), p. 55. Courtesy of the Japanese American National Museum (gift of James H. Kurata, 97.8.7).

the anticipated role of Nisei soldiers as a "bright link in the chain of American-Japanese relations"—an idea that Finch had also stressed in his public utterances.[72] Yet, as news reports illuminated, Japanese speakers did not fail to incorporate racial comments to their flowery orations. Governor Yasui, for example, added this sentence after exalting the Nisei's mediating role in bilateral relations: "the friendly ties between the United States and Japan would be further enhanced in the future by blood ties borne by the Niseis."[73] Reportedly, he also nonchalantly characterized the Nisei's "record in the last war" as the "pride of all Japanese," but he was completely oblivious to how that war had actually made the two sides seek to destroy one another just a few years earlier.[74] Here, again, racial conflation enabled Yasui and other Japanese to claim proprietary rights to the wartime experience of Nisei US soldiers as their own to the effect of normalizing the unprecedented celebration of the foreign (if not enemy) troops at a former imperial garden. As many Japanese came to see it, the all-Nisei 442nd RCT was a Japanese story, no longer simply an American saga.

Members of the 442nd combat team in Tokyo were feted recently at a Shinjuku Garden party in one of the biggest international gatherings ever held in Tokyo. An honored guest was Col. Gordon Singles, wartime commander of the 100th battalion.

Fig. 5.3 Nisei 442nd RCT veteran (second from right) and a former white commander (next to the Nisei) with Japanese actresses (to the left) and Tokyo Governor Yasui Seiichirō (far right), April 15, 1950. *Scene: The Pictorial Magazine* 2, no. 2 (1950), p. 55. Courtesy of the Japanese American National Museum (gift of James H. Kurata, 97.8.7).

To most Japanese, who had been taught to abhor the military institution and service as symbols of the shameful imperial past, the notion of a fighting soldier of Japanese race as an agent of democratic change and international friendship was a novel revelation—an idea that began to take root in their consciousness during Finch's visit and further reinforced following the April 15 gala. "The dozens and dozens of Japanese who spoke to me," Colonel Sidney F. Mashbir indeed recalled, "had a chance to discover for the first time what a man of Japanese blood, trained in the ideals and principles of democracy and brought up in a Christian civilization, could turn out to be."[75] According to the army's foremost Japan expert who had commanded Nisei linguists in the Pacific theater, many Japanese came to see in Nisei soldiers "the personification of the American ideals of democracy."[76] The coupling of Nisei's Japaneseness and democratic soldierhood formed a logical background for Tokyo's formal decisions to "seek the assistance of Nisei occupation troops as training officers" for enlisted men of the National Police Reserve.[77]

During these developments, uniformed Nisei servicemen enjoyed to the fullest their fifteen minutes of fame, where they were publicly honored by both US military brass and Japanese leaders as lynchpins of US-Japan friendship, key messengers of democracy, and symbols of a rearming Japan. Japanese Americans had no reason to take issue with all the flowery accolades about them. They eagerly performed the role assigned to them in media discourse and at public events. When Earl Finch visited Japan, Lt. Walter Y. Mihata, former CCD censor, reportedly told "Japanese people" that they, "too, owe[d] Mr. Finch a debt of gratitude, for through his services to the Nisei, he has raised a great respect for the Japanese as a whole."[78] A Nisei staff writer at the English-language *Mainichi* daily news was so ecstatic about the Tokyo garden party that he ran a five-part series on the history of the 442nd RCT narrated by a former president of the 442nd Veterans Club employed at the Eighth Army headquarters in Yokohama.[79]

After the spring of 1950, the self-mythologizing of the Japanese American war heroes pervaded Nisei activities in occupied Japan, which were subsumed neatly under a new phase of militaristic democratization efforts. One of the most striking examples appeared in a popular Japanese magazine for middle-schoolers (aged 13 to 15). Not coincidentally, when the Korean War was about to take place, one Nisei linguist was invited to "speak directly" to Japanese youths as a former 442nd RCT member in the magazine's "roundtable with a Nisei about the Life in America." There, a certain Captain Nishimura shared his thoughts on "how Nisei [World War II] soldiers developed such an outstanding mind and body" as to become the US war heroes that "President Truman personally commended." To this question, the Japanese American purportedly stated: "we are the same Japanese as you (young readers of Japan) are." Born and raised in Hawai'i, Nishimura drew a parallel between his personal experience and his audience's, explaining how he had attended Japanese school every day after public school and had grown up with Japanese foods, ancestral cultural mores, and a love for Japanese martial arts.[80]

At the same time, the Nisei linguist told magazine readers that "the bravery (of the 442nd RCT fighters) stemmed from our everyday experience" in America. He emphasized the importance of "independent thinking and self-reliance," "good-neighborliness," and humanitarianism—American values that Japanese people tend to lack and hence should learn from the Nisei war heroes who were "the same Japanese." This rhetoric elucidated the inherent abilities and real possibilities of absorbing those values for Japanese youths. At this point, the roundtable had another speaker, an accompanying white GHQ officer, who expanded on the Nisei's articulations in terms of the broader goal of the US military occupation. The officer summed them up by describing Nisei's ethnic experience as "experimentation in democracy" that was being foisted on Japanese school children.[81] This example reveals the integral place that the theme of the Nisei military accomplishment came to occupy by the middle months of 1950 in GHQ's political program of democratization and its publicity campaign relating to rearmament.

Outside the limelight of media reports and public commendations, most Nisei occupation troops silently played their assigned role as model democratic soldiers with Japanese faces and bodies. It was mostly others—white Americans and Japanese nationals—who interpreted and explicated the meaning of the ideological symbol and narrated a racialized military tale suitable for defeated Japanese. Generally, Japanese Americans were content with being a useful public icon so long as that simplified representation could buoy their primary goal of promoting further integration into postwar US citizenry and society as full-fledged Americans. Their pivotal concerns remained consistent since the war years. Considering the bitter experience of the mass imprisonment in the very recent past, their group rehabilitation as model (minority) American had been a central focus in their identity politics and public behavior, whether inside or outside the United States. How Nisei in occupied Japan responded to the mythologizing of their military exploits drew from the collective ethnic agenda bound to US race relations and their fragile position within them. For this American racial minority, the preoccupation with national belonging and equal citizenship defined the basic character of their transnational military experience. This is precisely why they were simultaneously so eager to embrace minority imperial citizenship, with all its intrinsic violent power and oppressiveness, despite the ostensible contradiction of being democracy's symbol and being facilitators of US imperial domination.

Nevertheless, some Nisei servicemen went on to play roles greater than the silent performer of the predetermined ideological trope. They felt it beneficial to take the initiative in disseminating the self-serving image of the Nisei war hero in occupied Japan for their overall goal of US national inclusion. At the same time, doing so also led to personal gains, because it created an opportunity for business and political partnerships with Japanese supporters of Nisei glorification, like Kimura Ki, who had their own stake in the matter. The two events of early 1950 put the legend of Nisei military heroism in the service of the new policy mandate of rearming Japan. Moreover, the Pentagon-backed visit of Earl Finch and the Tokyo-sponsored garden party also revealed public iterations of an ongoing partnership between Japan's cultural workers and some Nisei occupation personnel, albeit for divergent agendas and goals.

Brokering a Race War: Japanese Americans in the Pacific War and the Occupation of Japan. Eiichiro Azuma, Oxford University Press. © Eiichiro Azuma 2026. DOI: 10.1093/9780197781432.003.0006

6

Nisei and the Cultural Politics of Remilitarization

During the early months of 1950, the public acknowledgment of the Nisei war heroes in occupied Japan proliferated in conjunction with the rise of its rearmament as a major political agenda there. Key public events—Earl Finch's visit and Tokyo's glamorization of the all-Japanese 442nd Regimental Combat Team (442nd RCT)—signified pivotal moments in which the Nisei military trope was used politically to argue for the Americanness or Japaneseness of their national heroism. This battle had been fought behind the scenes since the arrival of a former 442nd RCT soldier named Lawrence H. Sakamoto in occupied Japan. What precipitated the Japanization process of the Nisei war hero in its initial phase was the work of this Hawai'i-born Japanese American who had no desire or intention to aid such a development.

Unlike many other Nisei in occupied Japan, Sakamoto possessed only rudimentary conversational Japanese and had no military language training. He was brought over to work for the army newspaper, the *Pacific Stars and Stripes* in Yokohama. Even though his day job kept him mostly in the English-language bubble, Sakamoto's chance encounter with Japan's leading literary critic Kimura Ki ignited a battle over the ownership of the Nisei war hero narrative in the binational context of US-governed Japanese society. Despite his low rank in the military hierarchy and his work outside of GHQ's reorientation program, Sakamoto provided Kimura and other Japanese cultural workers with vital information that helped dissolve the presumed contradiction between being Japanese and being a soldier of democracy. He was also personally responsible for a literary output in translated Japanese on the Nisei martial mythology that could directly reach the ordinary masses of occupied Japan. Therefore, rather than functioning solely as the objects of politico-ideological projections by others, some occupation Nisei, like Sakamoto, acted as important knowledge producers for their own mythologized martial pasts, albeit for quite different goals and purposes than the occupation authorities or their Japanese supporters.

Shifting perspective from top-level political developments to popular discursive formations, this chapter traces the convoluted processes through which Sakamoto's partnership with Kimura paved the way for transpacific contestation that involved GHQ censors, a Hollywood movie studio, Nisei World War II veterans, and the Japanese American Citizens League (JACL) on the US side. The ultimate stakes of the 442nd RCT story, namely that these Japanese Americans were war heroes who proved the claims of American race-blind democracy, were challenged and even imperiled in occupied Japan. The reasons that the foreign land became the unlikely stage for this contestation over the meaning of Nisei's martial virtue demonstrate the continuous theme of their post-1943 experience in the propaganda war and the history of inter-imperial relations between the United States and Japan: whether citizenship or race should define Japanese American identity, their national belonging, and the democratic character. In the key moment of the reverse course in US occupation policy, Sakamoto inadvertently entered the discursive space of occupied Japan to serve as a pivotal broker and agent in the production of knowledge about Nisei war heroes and their Issei parents. White Americans and Japanese nationals endeavored to put their own spins on this knowledge in accordance with their conflicting perspectives and agendas. This struggle over cultural symbols and binational meanings surrounding the heroic Nisei soldiers formed a crucial background for the social and political processes that buoyed the rearming of disarmed Japan and defeated Japanese in 1950 that the previous chapter has examined.

Lawrence H. Sakamoto and the Japanization of the Nisei War Heroes

Born in Honolulu, Private First-Class Lawrence H. Sakamoto worked as a staff writer for the *Pacific Stars and Stripes* (*PSS*) and had been a member of the US Eighth Army's Public Information Office in Yokohama since early 1948. Prior to the war, Sakamoto had briefly worked at the *Honolulu Star-Bulletin* after graduating from University of Hawai'i, so he had some experience as a journalist before taking up a position at the army newspaper in occupied Japan. Sakamoto was also a 442nd RCT veteran, one of the first from Hawai'i to volunteer to fight in Italy, where he was wounded and awarded with the Purple Heart.[1] Sakamoto had planned to enroll in the

Army's MIS Language School after being discharged from the Nisei regiment in 1946, but he decided to stay in Honolulu to work on a pet project: to compile a pictorial record of the 442nd RCT and MIS Nisei servicemen between the summers of 1945 and 1946. Embracing the official (re)definition of Americanism proclaimed by President Roosevelt in early 1943, Sakamoto took intense pride in the patriotic contributions that he and his brothers-in-arms had made in the struggle against not only foreign enemies but also domestic racism. He wanted the American public to know their story and accept Japanese Americans as full-fledged citizens bearing equal rights and national loyalty.[2]

Sakamoto was one of the numerous Nisei soldiers who had internalized the lofty, if not naïve, ideal of colorblind democracy and their special role in spearheading it—first inside the United States and then across the Pacific in occupied Japan. In his 1943 letter from an army training camp, Sakamoto described his own understanding of military service in this somewhat dramatic manner:

> We realize our task ahead of us.... When the smoke of battle clears someday, there will he stand, proud and happy that he's an American soldier—a direct contributor to Freedom and yet there will another lie lifeless, but a towering symbol of an undaunted spirit—Yes, he's a member of the 442nd Combat team.[3]

Published in mid-1946, Sakamoto's *Hawaii's Own: Picture Story of 442nd Regiment, 100th Battalion and Interpreters* was one of the first English-language books on the Nisei World War II military heroes.[4] Sakamoto was listed as its publisher, and a Nisei *Star-Bulletin* reporter as writer and another 442nd RCT veteran as illustrator. Yet, the 103-page book showed heavy editorial control by Sakamoto, since the listed author was not a veteran so information drew from the publisher's own experience.[5] The narrative of *Hawaii's Own*—composed mostly of factual descriptions of battles—was built on the orthodox thesis summed up by the Foreword, ostensibly penned by the white editor of the *Honolulu Star-Bulletin*. It reads:

> "*Hawaii's Own*" is more than a story of heroism in danger, and of thrilling achievement under the stimulus of battle. It is a story of steadfast courage in the face of skepticism, and of quiet determination to prove to their Territory, and to Americans everywhere, that Americans of Japanese

> ancestry in Hawaii are loyal, dependable citizens of the United States.... Once again it is proved that the quality of American citizenship is not in race but in the training of its people in the traditions of American democracy—and how to preserve that democracy.[6]

At the time of *Hawaii's Own*'s publication, Sakamoto, like other Nisei veterans, was still preoccupied with the task of getting the American public to accept the anti-racist definitions of Americanism and Nisei's equal citizenship.[7] This narrative—barring references to American citizenship—could easily be applied to soldiers of a democratic Japan, who also had been "in the training...in the traditions of American democracy" under tutelary US occupation. To demonstrate that enlightened white Americans had been on their side, Sakamoto's book included a separate chapter on Earl Finch—an obscure figure at that time—and his colorblind support for Nisei 442nd RCT troops at an army training camp in Mississippi and beyond. Notably, Sakamoto's celebratory account of this white American hero directly influenced his future literary collaborator, Kimura Ki. As a special counselor to Tokyo Governor Yasui Seiichirō, the Japanese writer took the initiative in organizing the April 1950 garden party for Finch's 442nd RCT "boys" when the politician learned of Finch's plan to visit Japan. Indeed, even before getting to know Sakamoto in person, Kimura avidly read the Hawai'i Nisei's pictorial book.[8]

In early 1948, after *Hawaii's Own* was enjoying a positive reception in his home territory, Sakamoto reenlisted in the military and was assigned to a position as publicist with the US Eighth Army headquarters in Yokohama. Aside from needing to find a well-paying job, he had another reason for this move. Sakamoto's mother in her seventies was living alone in Kumamoto prefecture in southern Japan. His new work enabled him to "rejoin my mother and my (deceased) father after ten long years of waiting." Before World War II, it was not uncommon for aged Issei to retire in their home village and/or for their remains to be sent back there after death for burial. Sakamoto's mother carried back her husband's ashes to their family cemetery in rural Kumamoto before the war intervened. In a moving *PSS* guest column, Lawrence explained: "while mother lived through the last war, I was on the other side of the globe fighting Germans. I reenlisted in the Army to come to Japan to be near my mother."[9] After they reunited and visited his father's grave, which they "decorated" with "wild flowers" and "an American cigarette," Sakamoto felt "the purpose of my visit was

Fig. 6.1 *Pacific Stars and Stripes* reporter Lawrence H. Sakamoto (far right) interviewing Japanese athletes returning from the United States. *Pacific Stars and Stripes*, September 5, 1949. US Army Photograph. Courtesy of the *Stars and Stripes.*

complete."[10] Yet, he soon found another purpose: to transplant an enchanting saga of Nisei soldiers and their parents, like the Sakamotos, onto his ancestral land.

An initial inspiration for disseminating the 442nd RCT story to the Japanese public came from his chance encounter with Kimura. Confident that the Nisei story could facilitate democracy not only in Hawai'i but also in Japan after his meeting with Kimura, Sakamoto developed a strong interest in introducing Japanese people to the transformative power of their group experience by publishing a Japanese version of his 1946 treatise with the help of the renowned Japanese writer/literary scholar. It would also allow his mother to receive the proceeds from his writing, Sakamoto expected, and for that reason he later named her as the copyright holder of all his publications.[11] No evidence suggests that he had a hidden intention or connection to the army's intelligence and propaganda sectors, although he did assist CCD censor Walter T. Mihata's initiative in the propaganda use of the Nisei martial myth through his *PSS* reports on the burial of a fallen Nisei war hero in Japan.[12]

After mid-1948, Sakamoto endeavored to get his *Hawaii's Own* and related written pieces published in Japanese with the backing of Kimura and other collaborators in Japan's local publishing world. On August 19, a formal request was filed at GHQ for "permission to write and sell articles for publication" of a magazine article, "Nisei–American," based on *Hawaii's Own*. The twenty-six-page article, according to Sakamoto, would discuss "my experiences in the war and my feeling of what it means to be born a Nisei." Because members of the occupation forces were not allowed to engage in paid business activities, Sakamoto explained that the remuneration of 20,000 yen would be sent to his mother in Kumamoto.[13] Inside GHQ, his application was first directed for clearance by CIE, which recognized its educational value "to be deserving of separate (special) consideration as the literary work to be published" by January 1949. Then, six months later, the Foreign Investment Board followed suit with its endorsement, stating Sakamoto's "application is desirable in that it will contribute to cultural development in Japan."[14] When the SCAP granted formal permission in July 1949, Sakamoto had jumped the gun based on insider information from his GHQ Nisei friends, and he had already put out a condensed version of *Hawaii's Own* in a Japanese monthly (see Table 6.1). The two-part article, ostensibly "co-edited" by Kimura and Sakamoto's mother, was actually more than a simple translation of Sakamoto's English publication, since the essay series not only adopted Sakamoto's first-person narration of the battlefield experiences in Europe but also incorporated his mother's recollections of war experience in Japan as well as Kimura's long opening interjections.[15]

Kimura's introduction, which he presented as "essential for [Japanese] readers to understand the real value of the [Nisei war] story," framed the manner of rhetorical artifice in which to Japanize the entire storyline. The Japanese writer began by recalling the excitement that he had felt when he had first learned of Sakamoto's story. "Wow, those are our compatriots, Americans of Japanese ancestry!" Kimura proclaimed. "That was my response, because after all we are Japanese and we are not ashamed of having our [outstanding] blood." Kimura then expounded on the inseparable

Table 6.1 List of books and selected articles on Nisei soldiers published in occupied Japan between June 1949 and December 1950

June and July 1949
Sakamoto Kijiyu and Kimura Ki [坂本きじゆ・木村毅]. "Amerika no Nisei shukun monogatari Dai-442 butai," nos. 1–2 ("Story of American Nisei's Heroism: 442nd Regiment") [アメリカの二世殊勲物語:第四四二部隊(一)(二)]. *Seikatsu bunka* (*Lifestyle and Culture*) [生活文化] 10, nos. 6–7 (1949): pp. 64–69, 62–69.

July 1949
Sakamoto Kijiyu and Kimura Ki [坂本きじゆ・木村毅]. *Amerika no Nisei shukun monogatari Dai-442 butai* (*Story of American Nisei's Heroism: 442nd Regiment*) [アメリカの二世殊勲物語:第四四二部隊] (Tokyo: Ōbunsha, 1949).

Kimura Ki [木村毅]. "Dai-442 butai (442nd Regiment) [第四四二部隊]." *Chūgaku jidai* (*Middle Schoolers*) [中学時代] 1, no. 3 (1949): pp. 16–19.

March 1950
Rōrensu Sakamoto [坂本ローレンス] (Lawrence Sakamoto). "Nihon no chi to Amerika no kokoro: Nisei Butai Itari Furansu tensenki" ("Japanese Blood, American Heart: Record of Nisei Regiment in France and Italy") [日本の血とアメリカの心:二世部隊伊太利フランス転戦記]. *Bungei Shunjū* [文芸春秋] 28, no. 3 (1950): pp. 116–39.

June 1950
Orville Shirley; translated by Nagata Shigeshi [オビィル・シャーレィ著、永田稠訳]. *442 Butai: Nisei butai monogatari* (*442nd Regiment: Story of Nisei Regiment* [original title: *Americans*]) [四四二部隊:二世部隊物語] (Tokyo: Tokyo-dō, 1950), with a forty-four-page appendix by the translator.

October 1950
Rōrensu Sakamoto [坂本ローレンス] (Lawrence Sakamoto). *Nisei Butai: "Edifice to Victory"* (*Nisei Regiment*) [二世部隊] (Tokyo: Sumiyoshi Shobō, 1950).

December 1950
Kimura Ki [木村毅]. "Minshushugi no eiyū: Ben Kuroki monogatari" ("Hero of Democracy: Story of Ben Kuroki") [民主主義の英雄・ベン黒木物語]. *Kingu* (*King*) [キング] 26, no. 12 (1950): pp. 178–88.

nature of blood ties to Nisei's inherent cultural heritage. According to him, the "proud blood of our compatriots," which had survived in the bodies of US citizens, made it possible for Nisei to "flourish as soldiers of the [American] republic."[16]

What made war heroes out of Japanese Americans was their Japanese character etched in what could be called "the spirit of the suicide battalion" (*tokkōtai seishin*)—that is, the determination to sacrifice their lives for the good of humanity. In the past war, Kimura argued, misguided soldiers of imperial Japan practiced this in a destructive way, because their actions were not predicated on the "universal moral principle of humanism." Nisei soldiers, on the other hand, "exhibited the (blood-infused) Japanese character" in accordance with such universal moral precepts, thus inducing the world to acknowledge their greatness. Nisei solders, Kimura concluded, embodied the harmonization of Japanese traditional "*bushidō*" (the way of *samurai* warriors) with western ideals of "knighthood." The records of the 442nd RCT would teach Japanese people how their beaten nation might be able to recover positive aspects of their traditions by resuscitating the *bushidō* spirit—one that had been formally outlawed by the occupation authorities.[17] Purportedly, this magazine article instantly "became the talk of our country's journalism," prompting the publisher to hastily put together a book version that showcased the story of the perfect "fusion of Japanese character and American humanism" in the Nisei war heroes.[18]

Published in the summer of 1949, the first ever Japanese book on the Nisei war heroes featured the co-authorship of Kimura Ki and Sakamoto Kijiyu, Lawrence's Issei mother.[19] Drawing from *Hawaii's Own* and the wartime experiences of the Sakamotos, Kimura wove the personal accounts into the formal battle stories of the 442nd RCT as well as wartime Japan. The Japanese writer also accentuated the sentimentalized narrative with his own analysis of why Nisei soldiers had excelled. What Kimura especially glorified were Lawrence's dedications to his birth country and his ancestral country, and the outstanding "Japanese" character of Nisei US soldiers, like him, which of course was instilled by Issei parents, like his mother Kijiyu.

Kimura depicted Lawrence in terms of conventional Japanese moral precepts, which bordered on the elevation of hitherto stigmatized martial virtues in occupied Japan. After the outbreak of the Pacific War, as the story goes, the Issei mother and the Nisei son became separated between Japan and Hawai'i, for Kijiyu had traveled to her home village in Kumamoto prefecture to bury her dead husband's ashes. Lawrence, the youngest of the five siblings, was worried to death about his mother who was separated from her children because of the war. Yet, when the call came for volunteers for the 100th Infantry Battalion (later a part of the 442nd RCT), the Nisei opted to serve his birth country despite "making an enemy out of his ancestral land" where his mother was stranded.[20] Lawrence's act of prioritizing the interests of his country over that of his kin corresponded to an age-old theme in *bushidō*, where the exigencies of Japanese feudalism distorted the original Chinese Confucian priority of filial piety and instead placed more emphasis on one's loyalty to his political master. GHQ censors might have failed to catch the *bushidō* analogy, but Japanese readers would never miss the point—one that would be repeated as Kimura's dramatic narration unfolded.[21] Fighting in separate outfits of the 442nd RCT in

Europe, Lawrence was eventually injured, and his Sansei nephew—Kijiyu's grandson—was killed in action. These tales of sacrifices further valorized the sublimity of Sakamoto's quintessentially *samurai*-esque behavior according to the precept of *bushidō* without articulating them.[22]

Kimura also argued for a causal nexus between what he termed "the Japanese character plus X" and the unparalleled heroism of Nisei soldiers. Along the basic occupation guidelines, the Japanese author discredited the legitimacy of the "*old* Nippon spirit" that had supposedly undergirded the atrocious and inhumane conduct of imperial soldiers in the past war.[23] Yet, that spirit should not be entirely dismissed, because Kimura showed he believed that it entailed some positive contribution to humanity. It was exactly the remnants of the Japanese spiritual heritage that Nisei war heroes like Sakamoto embodied, but Kimura suggestively qualified: "They (Nisei soldiers) must have had something more." Then he added the following explanation:

> They were reared in America. Not only have they transformed and re-forged the Japanese character in them; they have also overcome [its negatives] and enlarged and elevated [its positives] so that the Japanese character could be accepted—and praised—as a form of Americanism, and much more, as cosmopolitan morality. They have given new life to (hitherto) particularized Oriental *bushidō* and elevated it to a new form of knighthood that is still alive and well in the Occidental world.[24]

By reducing the heart-wrenching story of Lawrence Sakamoto to a typical Japanese military saga, Kimura thus presented the achievement of the 442nd RCT as a crystal ball for "how we, the Japanese in the homeland, may be also able to rise from the ashes so long as we continue to search for that 'plus X'."[25] Logically, that "plus X" had been available and already instilled in many Japanese under the democratizing effects of tutelary US occupation—equivalent to the upbringing of Nisei children in the United States. It is also not far-fetched to argue that soldiers of a new Japan would look next to follow in the footsteps of these Nisei war heroes if Kimura's assertion was evaluated in the context of a debate on Japan's remilitarization.

While hijacking what was supposed to be a story of colorblind US democracy and anti-racism (Sakamoto's original vision), Kimura was intent on reaping the maximum political benefit from this literary artifice.

Thus, he went on to put together an abbreviated version of the contrived 442nd RCT narrative for a popular magazine for Japanese middle-schoolers (aged 13 to 15), who had learned mostly negative things about their own heritage and traditions for as long as they could remember since the defeat. A heavy dose of the ideological message was delivered to this future generation of a new Japan by Kimura's magazine articles:

> It has been a few years since the end of the war. The reason why I wanted to tell you the story of the 442nd RCT at this juncture was not to turn you into militarists of old days. I suspect you all have been made dejected about how Japan fought an unreasonable and scandalous war. Then, you should recall the story of the 442nd RCT. The most decorated army unit in America consists of the Nisei who share the same Japanese blood with you.... But they also have the Japanese (character) plus X.... Training in the cosmopolitan (democratic) spirit can produce the likes (of Nisei war heroes), because the Japanese have an inherent capability. There is no need to feel crest-fallen even if your father's generation might have committed shameful acts.[26]

Building on this rhetorical artifice of intra-racial/cultural conflation in martial virtues, Kimura extended his endeavor to a short biography of Ben Kuroki, a Nisei airman who had participated in high profile US bombing missions in the European theater, including the "suicidal" Operation Tidal Wave of August 1943 in Romania. Kimura described the dedicated and fearless Kuroki in terms of the "Yamato spirit" that the Nebraska-born Japanese American had purportedly embodied, even while praising Kuroki as a "champion of democracy" and "defender of peace." After this article, Kimura worked on a biography of Sadao S. Munemori, the 442nd RCT recipient of the Medal of Honor, even interviewing the Nisei's mother and other family members during a 1951 trip to Los Angeles. The initial inspiration for the story of this Nisei war hero had originated from Sakamoto's *Hawaii's Own* and the dramatized tales that Kimura had subsequently heard directly from the Nisei author and his mother.[27]

The success of Kimura's writings gave Lawrence Sakamoto an opportunity to publish his own renditions of the 442nd RCT story in Japanese, which ironically advanced Japan's hijacking of the Japanese American military legend even further contrary to Sakamoto's main objective of illustrating Nisei's undiluted Americanism. In the March 1950 issue of *Bungei shunjū*, one of Japan's most reputed monthlies, Sakamoto's English-language essay appeared in translation under the title of "Japanese Blood and American Heart" ("Nihon no chi to Amerika no kokoro").[28] The timing of its publication was crucial, as it coincided with the visit of Earl Finch and the planning for the April 15 gala orchestrated by Kimura within the Tokyo metropolitan government. Here lies the confluence of discursive contrivances and public misrepresentation of Nisei military heroism, which took place when occupied Japan was engulfed in the radical shift from demilitarization to rearmament. The partnership between Kimura Ki and Lawrence Sakamoto underpinned the complex political, social, and ideological transformations beneath the making of postwar Japan as a US junior ally in Cold War East Asia.

Whether it was faithful to Sakamoto's original writing or reflective of the unnamed translator's presuppositions, the Japanese version of his magazine article dramatized the extraordinary battle morale and fortitude of Nisei soldiers in accordance with the traditional warrior drama familiar to Japan's general public. "Japanese Blood and American Heart" carried descriptions of several notable battles and campaigns that the 442nd RCT had fought in Italy and France. Each episode offered a similar setting of extreme difficulties that Nisei soldiers had to cope with, like a greater number of German soldiers and/or superior enemy weaponry. In the end, they always prevailed, albeit with heavy casualties (selfless "sacrifices"), and they accomplished their missions according to the regiment motto, "Go for Broke." In Sakamoto's rendition, however, scenes of fearless Nisei offensives against German machine guns and fortresses resembled suicidal attacks of imperial soldiers ("*gyokusai*") in popular readings of wartime Japan.[29]

To compound this eerie resemblance, the Nisei writer characterized a midnight assault of Japanese American troops as a "*banzai* attack," explaining how their Japanese blood foregrounded their sacrifices and heroism as American soldiers of democracy, hence the title of the article. One Nisei soldier, Sakamoto wrote, started to yell "*banzai*," which led his fighting comrades to suddenly "realize what their true self was." Screams of "*banzai*" ensued from other Japanese American soldiers, who subsequently charged ahead and broke through the enemy line "like a ball of fire with a lion's roar." Soon they overcame fierce enemy resistance with only rifles and bayonets.[30] After reflecting on how and why Japanese Americans had tried so hard to hate Japanese for waging a treacherous attack on the United States, Sakamoto's conclusion revisited the theme of their "true self," arguing: "it was not accidental [for the Nisei soldiers] to scream *banzai* at that critical juncture; the blood that flows inside us made us do it!"[31] According to him, the lesson of the Japanese American military story should not be about the destruction of the Axis enemy, Germans or Japanese. It should be about, the Nisei told his Japanese readers, "the 442nd RCT as a messenger of friendship and humanity."[32]

When the Korean War finally convinced MacArthur to order the creation of the National Police Reserve in August 1950, the combined Japanizing effects of Sakamoto/Kimura's literary endeavors and Tokyo's public celebrations had already engendered a cultural industry relating to the theme of Japanese American military service in occupied Japan. While functioning as a device of psychological disarmament for pacifist Japan's remilitarization, this cultural industry included publishing and filmmaking—both of which often revealed direct signs of Sakamoto's influence. In print media, a major publication offered a Japanese translation of Orville Shirey's *Americans: The Story of the 442nd Combat Team*, one of the earliest publications on the subject.[33] Published in June 1950, the main part of this book detailed battle records of the Nisei platoons in Europe with minimal editorializing. Nagata Shigeshi, a former California Issei, took on the task of preparing the 224-page Japanese version, but it contained a forty-four-page appendix by Nagata regarding the historical background of the formation of the 442nd RCT. The Japanese translator repeated aspects of Sakamoto's discursive domestication, referring to the Nisei regiment as a "special assault unit" (*tokkōtai*)—the same term that was used for imperial Japan's *kamikaze* pilots. Like Sakamoto, Nagata praised the role of Nisei fighting troops in "solving race-based frictions of the past eighty-odd years between the United States and Japan through the sacrifices of their blood and bones."[34]

Because the Nisei military trope as presented in occupied Japan came to form a site of contestation over the meanings of being Japanese and Japanese American, pundits other than Nisei occupation troops and defeated Japanese entered into this discursive battleground with their own agendas and interests. Given the prevailing image of ill-famed strandees, Tamotsu Murayama, a self-styled leader of American-born Japanese residents in their ancestral land, found the public craze for Japanese American military heroism a good opportunity for rehabilitating his cohort of marginalized Nisei. Through his personal connections in Japan's print media, Murayama managed to publish a series of magazine articles in Japanese from September 1949 through March 1950 under the title of "Nisei story (Nisei monogatari)."

With a view to providing an expert explanation of "what kind of people Nisei really are," his eight-part treatise put a major spin on the emergent myth of Japanese American martial virtue—a characterization that would look heretical if not subversive from the standpoint of other stakeholders. Rarely did Murayama delve into 442nd RCT's combat record except for cursory references in his writings; instead, he presented a historical overview of the Japanese American experience before 1930 from which the generational cohort called the Nisei derived. As such, Murayama's narrative concentrated mostly on the activities of the Issei, or his parents' generation.[35]

Discussions of second-generation Japanese Americans appeared only in relation to two specific themes that derailed the Japanese obsession with blood ties and undermined Nisei's identity as US soldiers. When his narrative picked up Nisei-related themes, Murayama opted to examine the problem of their dual citizenship and then directed readers' attention to the sufferings of resident Nisei in pre-1945 Japan, including his own predicament.[36] Juxtaposing the ordeal of Nisei strandees with the experiences of 442nd RCT soldiers (albeit only casually mentioned), the author complicated the simple-minded celebration of Japanese American soldiers and compelled Japanese readers to reflect on their wrongdoings against the very people they were unabashedly putting on a pedestal. Murayama's treatise starts with this powerful statement:

> Nisei—these are the people who came under hostilities and suspicions, even being treated as spies in wartime Japan, and I was one of them.... While being socially persecuted, Nisei were mobilized for [Japan's] war efforts, and thousands of them were shipped over to the war front. Meanwhile, in the United States, Nisei were enlisted as US soldiers and deployed to the European and Pacific theaters, and from among them emerged the 442nd combat troops who are now revered as national heroes.... On the contrary, we, Nisei in Japan, had many of our compatriots perish on the warfront without their souls ever being consoled. And those who have survived the war are being despised as "collaborators" or "traitors." We have lost our [birthright US] citizenship and are unable to return to our birthplace, thereby living like a flock of wanderers.[37]

Published amid the mythologizing of Nisei soldiers in occupied Japan, Murayama posed a counter-normative narrative, but it quickly encountered insurmountable obstacles: GHQ's suppression and the amplified forces of Japanization from Japan's cultural workers. Even though Murayama completed a Japanese book manuscript that expanded on the magazine articles around the same time, CIE's Press and Publication Branch prohibited the book version from being published, since Murayama's narrative dwelled on a history of Japanese exclusion and institutionalized racial discrimination (white American racism) in the prewar United States. Murayama depicted this history as a crucial background for the arrival of minoritized Nisei in imperial Japan in search of educational and employment opportunities. He also identified white racism against Issei and Nisei as an important cause for the Pacific War.[38] His heterodox spin on the Nisei trope—patriotic soldiers as well as victims of American racism and Japanese oppression—failed to intervene in the controlled public discourse of occupied Japan. As GHQ silenced Murayama's counter-narrative and buried the long and ongoing history of anti-Japanese racism, the Japanese public continued to engage in historical amnesia about the oppression of resident Nisei by themselves.

In the meantime, the forces of Japanization bolstered the legend of the Nisei war heroes under the combined effects of the early-1950 public commemorations in Tokyo and publications by Kimura and Sakamoto. In October 1950, Lawrence Sakamoto finally published his own full-length book in Japanese.[39] Available sources indicate that, although he initially wanted to have *Hawaii's Own* translated, Japanese publishers seem to have persuaded him to alter the narrative from a documentary-style story of battles and military exploits to a human emotional drama that engulfed both Nisei and Issei in the tragedy of war. Nothing was more appropriate than the experience of Sakamoto's own family in this regard. Hence, his *Nisei Butai* ("Nisei Regiment": English title *Edifice to Victory*) came out as a semi-autobiographical novel that revolved around the lives of an Issei mother in rural Japan and her Nisei son—Sakamoto's alter ego—in Hawai'i and the 442nd RCT.[40]

In this book, Sakamoto's narration switches between two separate scenes and sequences of events in a transpacific context. First, the outbreak of the war has the mother and her youngest Nisei son stranded in rural Japan, where they are temporarily visiting to lay the dead father's ashes to rest. While the mother in rural Japan and the other Nisei son in Honolulu agonize over each other's well-being, the latter decides to volunteer for the all-Japanese American 100th Infantry Battalion. His "dilemma"—being torn between his sense of duty as an American citizen and an aversion to taking

Fig. 6.2 Front cover of Lawrence H. Sakamoto's Japanese-language book, *Nisei butai* (*Edifice to Victory*) (Tokyo: Sumiyoshi Shobō, 1950). Author's personal collection.

up arms against Japan where his kin lived—is never resolved as he goes to the European battlefront. The two Nisei brothers eventually die; the younger one falls victim to malnourishment and illness in Japan after confinement by the police for being a US citizen, and the older one is killed in action as he is rescuing white soldiers of the Texas "lost battalion" in France. After peace comes, the mother still grieves over the deaths of her sons, but the thought of a Sansei baby that her oldest son has left behind in Hawai'i—the baby that neither she nor her son was able to see—gives the Issei mother a cause for hope and peace of mind.[41]

Key ideological messages of the book, as far as its relevance to the broader political problems of Japan's remilitarization and Nisei's Japanization is concerned, can be found in a chapter dealing with the immediate postwar period. The Issei woman is forced to confront her Japanese nephew, who has returned from the war crippled and dejected.

Having been caught stealing her possessions, the young man is severely censured by his parents and other villagers. The former Japanese soldier bursts into a fit of anger, telling them that he regrets returning alive because they treat him like useless scum. The ostracized veteran also accuses villagers of being hypocritical, since they seem to have conveniently forgotten giving him a hero's sendoff at the time of his induction into the imperial army. "Japan is full of ignorant liars like you," he continues. The villagers respond with the standard answer authorized by GHQ: "It is because the militarists duped us."[42]

The Issei woman bursts onto the scene with equal fury, questioning him disdainfully: "What would become of the dead American soldiers who shed their precious blood for [the liberation of] people like you?"[43] She then divulges for the first time to her nephew and other villagers that she lost her oldest son in the war, who wished to "bring peace by destroying the militarists who instigated war." While telling the Japanese to "reflect on their guilt" in participating in the evil aggression—another GHQ teaching—the irate Issei woman also passes on to them the last words of her dead soldier-son: "Those who have survived, please fight hard to prevent another outbreak of war, never again."[44] From the standpoint of US Cold War policy in Asia, what message would be more appropriate for a nation that was preparing to rearm itself against war-mongering Communism in the wake of the Korean conflict? Sakamoto's writing sublimated the US mandate of balancing between the goal of enemy reorientation and the exigencies of remilitarization. Hence, GHQ officials deemed his application for the original publication project serviceable to "cultural development in Japan."[45]

Nevertheless, given multifaceted Japanese efforts to co-opt the 442nd RCT story from early 1950 onward, *Nisei Butai* could generate ideological effects that were dangerously subversive to the US occupation goal of enemy reorientation. Even though it illuminates the military heroism of her Nisei son, the book's narrative incorporates no element of foreignness in the life of that protagonist—a level of Japanization that other contemporary publications of the 442nd RCT had not achieved. The experience of the Issei woman depicted in the melodramatic story looks no different from that of a typical mother in postwar Japan who had recently lost a son(s) and/or husband. While living under American bombardment and constant lack of food, she shared the same psychological and material suffering as other Japanese nationals. Narrated from the standpoint of such an individual, albeit with a Hawai'i background, the patriotic sacrifice of her Japanese

American son was also rendered as beneficial to Japan, if not more, as it was to the United States, dissolving the critical differences between Nisei as members of the occupying power and Japanese nationals as occupied and dominated. The book concludes with the arrival of the dead Nisei's ashes in Japan for burial at the foot of Mt. Fuji—a powerful imagery of Nisei's return to his racial homeland. His persistent aversion to taking up arms against Japan even as a US serviceman also reifies the Nisei's blood ties to that country, which the narrator described as "the love for Japan that cannot be forsaken because he is bound to it by his unbreakable relation to his father and mother."[46]

These literary constructions undermined the primacy of Nisei birthright citizenship over racial affiliation that the official US liberal discourse had insisted on since 1943. Why, then, did the occupation authorities not comprehend the reactionary aspects of Sakamoto's narrative? The answer lies in the eclectic nature of the storyline that consisted of two concurrent plots with distinctive national groups of protagonists. If readers were to be primarily drawn to the experience and psychological anguish of the Issei mother, that lens would generate a line of interpretation just delineated. It is logical to assume that most Japanese readers adopted such a perspective, as they were likely to find the Issei mother more relatable. Just like other Japanese "victims" of their own militarism, she had lost family members in the last war and/or suffered from similar predicaments on the bombarded home front. Viewed through a native Japanese lens, her Nisei son would be of secondary importance, even serving as a narrative device to enhance the mental anguish of the Japanese protagonist.

Alternatively, as a left-leaning literary critic pointed out in his book review, Sakamoto's portrayals of patriotic Nisei US soldiers "entail a larger question," referring to their Japanese-style military behavior. The book reviewer linked up the "question" to Sakamoto's narrative that presented Nisei soldiers as "being stirred to the depths of their heart by an emotional charge when they rushed [the enemy's position] all crying out *banzai* in Japanese."[47] Either way, Japanese readers likely ended up co-opting the story of the "Nisei Regiment" as a Japanese war narrative—whether as one of shared suffering or as an affirmation of heroic racial military valor.

However, Americans reading this book in its original or translated form would interpret it rather differently because they would adopt a Nisei-focused lens—one that would prioritize the soldiers' decisions to emphasize allegiance to the United States and die for it. This gap could be seen in an English-language book review of *Nisei Butai*. Published in the *Nippon Times*, the review was most likely penned by a bilingual Japanese American on the editorial staff, who presented a lopsided reading of the story through a Nisei-centered perspective. The anonymous writer spoke mostly of the "mental agony" of the Hawai'i Nisei soldier in the book; on the other hand, he scarcely analyzed the meaning of Sakamoto's depictions of the Issei mother. "In short," he concluded, "the book offer[ed] much enlightenment to the people in Japan to whom the Nisei's (pro-American) action during the war was a puzzle."[48] That is to say, the Nisei were compelled to put more value on birthright citizenship than blood bonds, contrary to Japanese presumptions. These distinct nationalized readings allowed Sakamoto's eclectic narrative to elude the GHQ censors, who failed to flag the ideologically subversive elements that would be otherwise so transparent to Japanese readers.

Notwithstanding, some GHQ officials began to feel it necessary to prevent the hijacking of the 442nd RCT story by the Japanese, especially when Sakamoto's writings inspired Japanese cultural workers to organize a major film project based on his book. Sakamoto's longstanding endeavor to publicize the accounts of Japanese American military service for national inclusion paved the way for an unexpected political contest over the ownership and control of the Nisei war heroes. Neither American occupation authorities nor Japanese leaders had qualms any longer about the positive Japanese renditions of martial spirit and military heroism because it effectively buoyed the cause of Japan's rearmament after early 1950. The problem lay in the national identity of Nisei soldiers in public representations—whether it was determined by their race or citizenship.

This struggle between the occupiers and the occupied centered on a proposed movie based on *Nisei Butai*, but not the book itself that was published several months later without incident. This curious turn of events was partially a product of the dual structure of the GHQ's censorship apparatus, that is, the contentious relations between CIE and CCD. The former implemented "civil censorship" of film scripts and synopses until June 1949—and only completed film productions thereafter. CIE did not concern itself much with print materials. CCD, a subsection of the G-2 intelligence division, imposed another layer of control from a military standpoint relative to the items approved by CIE. In addition, CCD screened publications, newspapers, radio broadcasts, and postal communications before they were released to the public. This two-tiered program of comprehensive censorship started to loosen up when CCD placed book publishers under post-publication vigilance in October 1947, followed by magazine publishers in December 1947 and newspapers in July 1948. The press censorship ended altogether in November 1949, when CCD was disbanded.[49]

CIE continued post-production censorship of motion pictures until the very end of American military occupation. The Film Ethics Regulation Control Committee, an ostensibly autonomous body organized by the Japanese motion picture industry, took charge of preproduction review of scripts after July 1949; through this committee, CIE still maintained the constant monitoring of the contents of motion pictures before their production despite the façade of non-authoritarian/intrusive governance. Published between mid-1949 and 1950, the writings of Kimura, Nagata, and Sakamoto on the 442nd RCT remained basically outside of the existing censorship apparatuses that concentrated on motion pictures after 1948. This shift allowed printed materials to avoid catching the ire of the occupation authorities, whereas the 1950 film project still drew scrutiny from censors, thereby illuminating the problematic nature of *Nisei Butai*'s representations in particular and that of Japanese fascination with the 442nd RCT story in general.[50] Sakamoto's activities as a knowledge producer created a crucial context in which one last showdown transpired between US authorities and defeated Japanese over the proprietary rights of the Nisei war heroes in the final months of military occupation.

A Transpacific Film War: *Mother of Japanese Americans* vs. *Go For Broke!*

Before Sakamoto's book came out in October 1950, a film-script version of *Nisei Butai* caused a clash between Japanese cultural workers and GHQ censors in February and March. These were the very months in which the visits of the Joint Chiefs of Staff and Earl Finch, as well as Tokyo's planning for the April gala, brought public attention to Nisei 442nd RCT soldiers and their wartime exploits in occupied Japan. This film project was initially conceived in late 1949 when Tanaka Kinuyo, a leading actress dubbed "Bette Davis of Japan," visited Hawai'i and California as the first postwar Japanese entertainer to be invited to Hollywood. In Honolulu, Tanaka learned about the orthodox US narrative of Nisei military heroism from local Japanese residents and also had a chance to meet veterans of the

442nd RCT in person. Once in Los Angeles, the Japanese actress toured the city's Evergreen Cemetery where a massive memorial dedicated to the Japanese American war hero was erected. These chance encounters got her interested in the Nisei story.[51]

After returning to Japan at the end of January 1950, Tanaka negotiated the production of a commercial movie with the Shōchiku Motion Picture Company, one of Japan's major film studios.[52] Coinciding with Earl Finch's visit in early February, Tanaka announced a plan to produce a film based on Lawrence Sakamoto's *Hawaii's Own* and his family's experiences across the war-torn world. A Shōchiku executive proposed that the film would "trace into the minds of the Japanese the true meaning of Americanism," a theme with which Sakamoto concurred. The Nisei author was quoted as saying that he wished to "help steer the Japanese into firm acceptance of democracy after the occupation is finished"—the kind of rhetoric that US military authorities would not dare oppose. In fact, former white unit commanders of the 442nd RCT in the Eighth Army promised full support for the film project. Through Sakamoto's introduction, Tanaka conferred with Finch, who agreed to have a preliminary film script reviewed by his "boys" in Hawai'i.[53]

Under Shōchiku's auspices, a production team was quickly formed, consisting of seasoned producers, a well-known director, and a first-rate cast. Within one month, three different draft versions of scripts were consecutively submitted to CIE's Motion Picture and Theatrical Branch through the industry's Film Ethics Regulation Control Committee, as the Shōchiku team was "determined to produce this film" as soon as possible.[54] Switching the title from *Amerika rikugun dai-442 butai* ("American army 442nd regiment") to *Nikkei shimin no haha* ("the mother of Japanese Americans") and back to *Nisei butai*, these scripts reflected the polarized forces that stemmed from a self-induced attempt to adjust to US occupation mandates, on the one hand, and a desire to co-opt the Japanese American story, on the other. Hastily drafted between early February and mid-March, all three versions followed the main narrative scheme of Sakamoto's book version, albeit with some significant modifications. The earliest draft was cursory, perhaps serving as a prospectus for the film project. The more substantive later drafts reveal much about the film's main themes and messages, both consistent and shifting despite and because of GHQ's interventions. All in all, these script drafts entailed a noticeably heavier focus on the psychological and emotional turmoil of Sakamoto's Issei mother (to be performed by

Tanaka) than Sakamoto himself (to be performed by a popular actor named Sano Shūji), hence the initial title: the "mother of Japanese Americans." Indeed, as the "statement of purpose" composed by the production team declared, the proposed film was intended to chiefly feature "the trajectory of the [Issei] mother's spiritual development."[55] Other themes underwent significant changes between the second and third scripts due to GHQ's objections.

Indeed, CIE's response was less than enthusiastic, which prompted the production team to substantially revise the third and final draft. Although the story's lopsided focus on the Issei mother remained, the last version removed many scenes and dialogue that elucidated close relations between Hawai'i's prewar Japanese community and imperial Japan. These encompassed specific references to arrests of suspected Japanese spies in Hawai'i; Issei's expressions of positive sentiments relating to Japan's war victories in China; scenes of various activities at Japanese language schools and immigrant organizations; and ambivalent Issei feelings stuck between the United States and Japan at war.[56] These changes diminished the film's focus on the presumed primacy of race and ancestry over other forms of national belonging and allegiance, which the new language of Americanism had attempted to disavow.

The final revision of the script endeavored to make the bonds between America and the main characters tighter and more recognizable than Sakamoto's book or the earlier scripts. In the altered narrative, the younger Nisei son did not die in Japan; instead, he survived the war and was alive and well when Earl Finch's visit aroused a Japanese interest in the legend of the Nisei soldiers. The young man even had a chance to attend a welcome reception for Finch with his old friend in the occupation forces—a 442nd RCT veteran and his dead brother's comrade. The revised draft script ended with a scene of great jubilation when the Issei mother and Nisei son received a telegram notifying them they had been granted official permission to return to Hawai'i. Instead of the Nisei soldier's ashes coming to Japan for burial near Mt. Fuji, his mother and brother were going back to their American homeland to be reunited with the dead son's cremains and his Sansei baby.[57] In line with this change, the film title returned to the original: *Nisei butai* ("Nisei regiment").

Despite such significant modifications, CIE censors still took issue with it. While claiming that the agency could "only give advice and guidance when so requested" rather than approve or reject the submitted scripts according to its office function after July 1949, they issued a damning statement to the production team shortly after the final version of the script was submitted in the middle of March. It read: "The production will require a great deal of understanding of American life insomuch as the Nisei is American and…the tendency to show ties to the Fatherland (Japan) might be misunderstood unless properly handled."[58] Some cursory omissions and modified plots did not suffice to assuage the occupiers' distrust. Insofar as the film's narrative remained so racially binary that it might remind Japanese audiences of the Nisei's "ties to the Fatherland," there was a chance that the vanquished could sidetrack the proper interpretation of the Japanese American military trope and could be empowered discursively through the act of Japanization, consciously or unconsciously. CIE's lukewarm response to the Shōchiku also signaled its unwillingness to facilitate the latter's undertaking from an administrative standpoint—the message the production team duly acknowledged. The Japanese side felt it crucial to have GHQ's assistance in the areas of furnishing US military garb and equipment, but it appeared impossible to procure such necessities for the film production from seemingly reluctant American authorities.[59]

Not only did GHQ censors shun the filmmakers' request for logistical assistance, but they also dismissed the validity of its partnership with Finch and the Nisei Veterans' Club in Honolulu. Earlier, a Shōchiku representative asked CIE for permission for the production team to travel and film on location in Hawai'i and to use the footage of 442nd RCT soldiers from the US Army Signal Corps.[60] This request was met with a statement of noncommitment from GHQ. Without articulating their response to these specific requests, CIE censors simply stressed "the importance of being fully prepared before starting their production." The shooting of "a [motion] picture of this nature," according to CIE, would require "permission from the Department of Army" and commanding officers in Hawai'i and other locations. This reply to the filmmaker's requests was clearly a refusal of assistance, as was obvious to the filmmakers.[61]

Without acknowledging that Finch and his Nisei veteran friends had already informally reviewed the submitted script draft, CIE's reply also "strongly urged that the script be carefully checked for technical correctness." This statement signaled GHQ's negation of the validity of the review done already by Finch and Nisei veterans, much less their approval of the second draft. They offered no suggestions for who should check "technical correctness."[62] In the end, CIE insisted on "the advisability of securing cooperation and/or approval from proper authorities before proceeding with production."[63] This passive-aggressive bureaucratic roadblock effectively sent the Japanese film project back to the drawing board after the third script, although an interest in the 442nd RCT continued among the Shōchiku filmmakers throughout 1950.[64]

Aside from GHQ censors' misgivings about "the tendency to show ties to the Fatherland," what likely induced them to stall the Shōchiku project was the existence of a competing film project that had commenced in the United States at almost the same time. Announced at the end of January 1950, Metro-Goldwyn-Mayer (MGM)'s new film production stood decidedly against its Japanese counterpart in terms of the US military's choice of priority. A film titled "*Go for Broke!*" (442nd RCT's motto that means "shoot the works") had the full support of the Pentagon, as well as the JACL and Nisei veterans' groups stateside, from the beginning. Its first press release stated: "the filming will be collaborated by the US Army Depart., so that 'nothing will be missed' to add dignity to the story." The Army assigned a former 442nd RCT white officer to the project as "military advisor."[65] On the suggestion of the Pentagon, Mike M. Masaoka, JACL National Legislative Director and former 442nd RCT unit publicist, was invited to join the Hollywood production team as "special consultant." Whereas this JACL-centered support base for MGM initially excluded Hawai'i's Japanese Americans who were not part of the organizational structure, the island Nisei subsequently leaped on the bandwagon as the film production team chose to cast some Hawai'i-born 442nd RCT veterans.[66] This explains why the support of Finch and his Hawaiian "boys" for Shōchiku not only withered quickly but was also deemed impractical by GHQ.

Under Army-JACL oversight, *Go for Broke!* was destined to tell a visualized story of America's official anti-racism that had been already propagated in post-1943 psychological warfare. "The 442nd had lived up to their motto," an MGM press kit declared, "'*Go for Broke!*' is part of American history."[67] This "American" story focused on the actions of Nisei soldiers and their white comrades-in-arms at the army training camp and European battlefronts. Unlike Sakamoto's book or the film script based on it, Hollywood's story offered little reflection on the Nisei's psychological dilemmas, much less the torturous experiences of families divided by national borders or the scenes related to imperial Japan or enemy kin. There was no room for ambiguities or contradictions pertaining to the Nisei's undivided national allegiance to the United States. Hence, as far as GHQ censors were concerned, their show of non-commitment to the Japanese film project was a no-brainer. Indeed, when CIE shut down Shōchiku's revised draft and request for logistical assistance, the agency reminded the Japanese team that "a film dealing with the same subject was being made by MGM in Hollywood."[68]

While the Shōchiku film project faded into oblivion, MGM began shooting *Go for Broke!* in September 1950 and it premiered throughout the United States in May 1951. MGM then took the film to Japan in December 1951 as one of its main features for the New Year holiday market. According to a Japanese film expert, the Nisei-themed MGM production represented one of the first US war movies to make commercial headway in the Japanese market after late 1951 in tandem with the rearmament of the occupied country.[69] The imported film was billed as none other than "*Nisei butai: Go for Broke!*" in the Japanese market. During the first week of its release in occupied Japan, the 442nd RCT movie attracted over 48,000 people, topping other major features, like James Stewart's *Winchester '73* (46,000), Gregory Peck's *Only the Valiant* (34,000), and Randolph Scott's *The Desperadoes* (29,000). Only two other foreign films, including John Wayne's *Sands of Iwo Jima*—another "Japanese" military-themed film in audiences' eyes—drew more local people than *Go for Broke!* in the first half of the 1952 fiscal year.[70]

Studies of the ideological functions of *Go for Broke!* in US domestic race relations generally overlooked its production and reception in the context of transpacific cultural and race politics of the early Cold War era.[71] The Hollywood movie epitomized the degree to which postwar America extolled racial liberalism and universal democracy despite, or because of, the persistence of grassroots anti-Asian sentiment. *Go for Broke!* also accounted for the post-World War II continuation of America's disavowal of racism since the United States had formally presented its war aim as the defeat of ideological foes, like Nazism, fascism, and militarism. The Cold War anti-communist agenda retained the imperative of prioritizing ideology (colorblind democracy and capitalism) over race or ancestry as the underpinnings of US national identity. Hence, the MGM film prominently featured the 1943 edict of President Roosevelt that had paved the way for the enlistment of certifiably loyal Nisei men—that is, "Americanism is a matter of the mind and heart."[72] To Japanese Americans, the nationwide showing of *Go for Broke!* marked a culmination of their long-term effort to fight blood-will-tell racism with a contrived display of their uncompromised loyalty and superb military records—the effort to present a racial minority with stigmatized ancestry as model minority Americans. Fundamentally what motivated JACL leader Mike Masaoka to serve as special consultant to the Hollywood motion picture did not differ much from what had propelled Lawrence Sakamoto to take up his book project.

Yet, once the analysis of *Go for Broke!* was removed from the narrow confines of US domestic race politics and juxtaposed with what had transpired in occupied Japan in 1949–1950, the situation looked more complex. Just as Sakamoto's writings had taken on a markedly different ideological character in occupied Japan, the imported version of *Go for Broke!* (hereafter referred to by its Japanese title, *Nisei butai: Go for Broke!*) was no longer merely a device for advancing the acceptance of a once-persecuted minority into multiracial postwar America. First and foremost, the MGM production cemented the identity of Nisei servicemen as Americans and devalued their racial background and blood relations concerning questions of national belonging and patriotism. In light of the recent Japanese endeavors to hijack the 442nd RCT legend through printed materials and public commemorations, *Nisei butai: Go for Broke!* posed a formidable challenge to a rendition of the legend as a Japanese story in occupied Japan.

To the detriment of the thesis of Japanese superiority, another possible consequence of appropriation, the imported MGM movie made a point to preserve the asymmetric relations of power among races and cultures (and by extension nation-states) in representation, even though its narrative offered an uplifting tale of humanistic mutual understanding and interracial friendship between a white officer and Nisei GIs in the 442nd RCT. In fact, that very narrative of anti-racism in the film unfolded by way of magnifying a rigid racial hierarchy. Unlike the conspicuously mono-racial narration of the Japanese appropriation (either Sakamoto's translated book or the proposed Shōchiku film), its Hollywood counterpart centered on the interactions between a Texas-born white lieutenant and his Nisei platoon. The former represented a typical mainstream American who was unequivocally racist against all Japanese at first. By the end of the war, the Nisei soldiers managed to change the lieutenant's view and attitude through their exceptional valor and patriotism, and the white Texan emerged as a reformed man, an Earl Finch-esque advocate for the acceptance of Nisei as fellow Americans. Despite its liberal assertion against race-based national exclusion, *Go for Broke!* nevertheless made it known that a gradated order of race always existed between white Americans (officers) and Japanese Americans (enlisted men) despite the common US uniform in which they were dressed or the same citizenship they held and fought for. In this sense, the film was a testament to the ascent of America's inclusionary polite racism under the pretense of colorblind anti-racism.[73]

When it was imported into Japan in the final months of American military occupation, the MGM film articulated this message to Japanese audience in very specific ways. Doubtless, many moviegoers still processed the film through their Japanizing lens.[74] Yet, the political circumstances of the time rendered the ideological message more historically specific. With the Korean War raging only several hundred miles away, the geopolitical implications of the imported Hollywood movie were never lost on Japanese viewers, who were grappling with the uncertainties of their future after the impending conclusion of US occupation set for April 1952. Film critics were quick to pick up such implications in their published reviews. What especially captured their attention was the theme of multifaceted Japanese subordination. They interpreted its meaning not simply in racial terms but also in terms of post-occupation international relations. For example, some reviews and commentaries registered disappointment at how "shabby," "vulgar," and "miserable" Nisei soldiers looked vis-à-vis white officers and servicemen in the film. These self-denigrating comparisons pointed to both physical and behavioral deficiencies. Not only were the Nisei cast visually dwarfed by the Caucasian cast but Japanese American soldiers were also often portrayed as indulging themselves in gambling and petty quarrels.[75]

In no uncertain terms did the movie remind many viewers of their own status as a "people of a defeated race" who had been at the command of white Americans, just as were the "shabby"-looking Nisei characters on the silver screen.[76] Therefore, even though the valor of "our compatriots" (or "those who share[d] our blood") offered moviegoers some degree of "joy" and "pride" through their self-serving act of racial conflation, it still did not suffice to offset their feeling of "heavy heartedness" or "deep emotion," as some movie reviews attested.[77] Viewed from the vantage point of a Japanese audience whose remilitarized homeland was about to regain independence, albeit under continued American dominance, "feeble" Japanese Americans in *Nisei butai: Go for Broke!* might have well looked like soldiers of a new Japan, a nominally sovereign but essentially client state in Cold War Asia.

While the film sent a clear message to its Japanese audience about the proper relations of power under American military hegemony, some differing

Fig. 6.3 MGM movie *Go For Broke!* Japan premier advertisement, December 1951. Author's personal collection.

understandings of the wartime Nisei story were still detectable in the seemingly contradictory tones of commentaries on the imported film. One reviewer positively evaluated the visual representations of Nisei's dedication to democracy in terms of Japan's successful rehabilitation. He noted: "We, citizens of a defeated country, need to calmly observe the trajectories of these (Nisei) young men, who did not stray from the path of righteousness despite severe adversities, for doing so would surely elicit some deep emotional response from us, the Japanese who are on the threshold of a fresh start as an independent country."[78]

Published in a magazine intended for middle-school students, an extended review of *Nisei butai: Go for Broke!* sent the same ideological message directly to its readers, the future generation of a democratic Japan.

> Nisei soldiers fought gallantly [on warfronts] and contributed to the elimination of racism and hatred. We, the Japanese of Japan, should try our best to emulate them and become outstanding citizens (of the free world). If white people look down upon us (like that lieutenant in the film), we need to prove through our hard work that we are all equal and entitled to happiness. This film has taught us we, the Japanese, can do it if we strive to the best of our ability (just as did Nisei).[79]

Other critics nevertheless recognized the possibility that the Hollywood war film might resuscitate a militaristic "conceit" in some audiences through the similar race-based co-optation of Nisei military heroism. An unlikely venue for a film review, a financial magazine carried this column on *Nisei butai: Go for Broke!*: "We know they are American citizens, but what would come to the mind of a young Japanese audience after watching the battle scenes of those soldiers with the same Japanese blood? This is the first post-defeat war movie that features *Japanese* fighters."[80] While appreciating the film's "honest" characterization of US race problems, another reviewer "dare[d] moviegoers not to fantasize that the Japanese are strong in war."[81] Many others echoed this concern, presuming to or engaging in the conflation of Nisei GIs with Japanese soldiers. A major newspaper printed a review that regretted: "it is too early to show this film (in Japan), since it helps invigorate warlike Japanese with the impression that Japanese people are braver and better in fighting a battle than (white) Americans."[82] In another Japanese daily, a well-known critic/journalist wrote:

> Even though [viewers] may well have restored confidence and fortitude that they have lost due to the miserable defeat because Japan is these Nisei [soldiers]'s fatherland...there is a dangerous possibility that [this movie] may revive fanatic militarism boosted by the idea of Japanese superiority on the battle ground....This is a film not recommended for warlike Japanese.[83]

The US-made *Nisei butai: Go for Broke!* differed significantly from the aborted Shōchiku version in that the Hollywood production left little room for idiosyncratic interpretations because it lacked references to Japan or Japanese nationals. Yet, even the singular focus on Nisei's US identity and their legally constituted Americanism could still possibly allow Japanese film viewers to appropriate the Nisei war narrative based on blood ties to the "fatherland." During the critical years of Japan's rearmament in 1950–52, the US government-certified version of *Nisei butai* (MGM film) put a stop to the outright takeover of the 442nd RCT story by Japanese filmmakers. Its success was still limited, however, insofar as the remnants of imperial racial thinking could still empower some Japanese movie-viewers to apply the ethnocentric lens to domesticate "foreign" stories and actions, as warned by some film critics. Furthermore, separate from the Hollywood movie, the abolition of GHQ press censorship in 1949 gave Sakamoto's book version of *Nisei butai* a chance for rebranding the 442nd RCT saga as a Japanese story for Japan's reading public.

In the complex discursive and cultural space of 1950–52 Japan, the coexistence of the imported Hollywood film and Sakamoto's Japanese publication—with almost identical titles—left the Nisei military trope open to divergent interpretations, thereby keeping it as a site of ongoing struggle between occupiers and occupied. The stasis of Shōchiku's film project certainly marked a partial victory of GHQ/US endeavors to disavow heretical renditions of the Nisei military myth, especially its total Japanization, even when they were more likely to use it for the political goal of Japan's rearmament. As Sakamoto's intermediary role crystalized, Nisei occupation troops played a pivotal role in brokering this historical unfolding to the benefit and detriment of both sides.

In Japan, this delicate equilibrium proved short-lived. This is not only because Japanese nationals monopolized discursive control over the representations of Nisei in the domestic context after the restoration of sovereignty, but also because most Japanese Americans lost a vested position as transpacific and transnational mediators. No longer could the Nisei military linguists function as indispensable cultural brokers after April 1952, since the normal apparatuses of diplomatic and business negotiations were restored in bilateral relations with the end of Allied military occupation. The Nisei's presence or roles were not needed any longer. Furthermore, another function of Nisei cultural brokers disappeared when they ceased to act as semi-native knowledge producers in their ancestral land. Many of their GHQ bosses, especially white language officers, would emerge as academic experts on Japan trained in Asian area studies, a new institution of knowledge production in US academia.[84] As MIS brass had originally hoped for back in 1941, trustworthy "American" experts could do the work for the United States instead of the latter having to rely on the Nisei out of necessity. Hence, with the dismantling of GHQ, most Nisei linguists left behind the entrenched role of cultural broker and unceremoniously returned to the United States to merge into postwar Japanese America and rejoined a collective quest for national inclusion and assimilation into white-dominated America.[85]

Paradoxically, as the example of contestation between Shōchiku's Nisei war film and its MGM's counterpart shows, the political, social, and ideological space of occupied Japan was less regimented than in white-dominated multiethnic America. Albeit under conditions of military domination, the defeated enemy land encompassed all sorts of ruptures and struggles over the meanings of race, citizenship, and culture. For this reason, a serious analysis of those ambiguities and entanglements outside the United States reveals what the hitherto domestic-centered study of Japanese Americans cannot, including why unknown Nisei occupation troops, like Sakamoto, should be deemed as important as the likes of Mike Masaoka, who did not leave the United States. Such a transnational perspective also makes it possible to understand how the trope of Nisei US war heroes aided the complex processes that led to the resurrection of Japanese soldiers and armed forces in post-1950 Japan. Because a popularly held idea of indissoluble blood ties among the defeated undergirded the unlikely causal nexus between US minority military heroism and Japan's remilitarization, it so happened that the militarized Nisei trope generated more profound psychological effect on many Japanese than simple political rhetoric or partisan advocacy.

While the US occupation came to an end in the spring of 1952, both Japan's conservative leaders and Japanese American occupiers enjoyed the fruits of valorizing the Nisei military trope. Through it, defeated Japan managed to refashion itself as a junior US ally, and Nisei occupation troops could go back to postwar Japanese America with a more solid US identity—as another constituent of the ethnic war hero in a pluralist America. Yet, white America was the ultimate winner, because it managed to preserve the structure of white supremacy under the appearance of inclusive democracy in a US domestic context. Moreover, the United States strengthened its control over the Cold War Asia-Pacific with the self-induced participation of minoritized national subjects in that hegemonic transnational structure. In this sense, this story of minority military service and imperial citizenship served as a prologue to what would follow during the rest of the Cold War years: the continuous and expanded use of Asian Americans for US imperial objectives, including both military operations and public diplomacy.[86]

Brokering a Race War: Japanese Americans in the Pacific War and the Occupation of Japan. Eiichiro Azuma, Oxford University Press. © Eiichiro Azuma 2026. DOI: 10.1093/9780197781432.003.0007

Epilogue

Postwar Careers of the Japanese American War Heroes

During the Pacific War and the subsequent military occupation between December 1941 and April 1952, both the United States and imperial Japan relied on the cultural and ideological work of American-born Japanese US citizens (Nisei), whose dubious standing—racial, cultural, and legal—enabled them to find niches in the propaganda machines and militarist regimes of both countries despite, or because of, their unique identities and attributes. Although Japan took the initiative in mobilizing its American-born residents based on the logic of blood bonds, the United States responded to the enemy's use of Nisei by valorizing the value of their legal citizenship according to a new definition of Americanism, which was supposed to be "a matter of the mind and heart, not a matter of race or ancestry." Whereas for Japan Nisei represented America's racist past and present as victims with first-hand experiences of white imperialist supremacy, for the United States they played a pivotal role in its anti-racist racial propaganda that emphasized its colorblind democracy.

Mobilized by these self-proclaimed multiethnic empires that were fighting for mutual destruction, the Nisei on both sides of the Pacific similarly served as language experts and propaganda knowledge producers by capitalizing on their Japan-rooted cultural heritage ("nature") and US-based acculturation and upbringing ("nurture"). These state-affirmed attributes provided the background for competing meanings of culture vis-à-vis their entanglements with race and citizenship when Nisei emerged as cultural brokers of the two warring regimes. Between the ideologies of blood-based national belonging and legally constituted national belonging, bicultural Japanese Americans were stuck in the interstices of multiple categories that helped sustain the power structures and very existences of the two warring states and empires.

This slanted form of Japanese American integration into the US military machine continued into the occupation of defeated Japan, where several thousand Japanese Americans were recruited as US army linguists in addition to a few thousand ununiformed staffers for the General Headquarters (GHQ). In occupied Japan, the position of Nisei US soldiers and civilian workers resembled that of colonial middlemen—an "enlightened" class of a conquered race that assumed the position of mid-level cultural managers for white governors. What distinguished them from other Japanese was their legal standing as American citizens. That is to say, notwithstanding Nisei's perceived connections to the people of Japan, there was an unbridgeable gap: citizenship created a legally constituted difference that helped to shape their identity and position as a distinctive group of cultural brokers in semi-colonial conditions of military occupation. In the relational formation of social boundaries there, ancestry and culture played a subsidiary role in generating the gradated meanings of group identities and asymmetrical positions among white conquerors, defeated Japanese nationals, and Nisei linguists who served the needs of the former.

Indeed, in occupied Japan, allied legal status entailed uncontested power and privilege. In accordance with the realignment of social fault lines and hierarchical order in an enemy land, race and other attributes came to carry less weight—a significant divergence from the US homeland norms that were still sustained by the logic of white supremacy. Insofar as Nisei held birthright American citizenship that underpinned their superior status to vanquished alien enemies, the meaning of their racial heritage was wide open for manipulation, therefore expanding the range of Nisei's agency in terms of their relationship to local Japanese. At the same time, Nisei linguists were still placed firmly under white control within the apparatuses of the American military government and occupying armed forces. Thus, occupied Japan formed a composite of a transnational colonial space and extended domestic race relations under militarized US imperialism.

As they strove for national acceptance as full-fledged Americans in this idiosyncratic space, the contingencies of racial meaning vis-à-vis legal status helped Nisei citizens to claim a respectable place in postwar United States society. This process took place without disturbing the hegemonic understanding of proper hierarchical relations between triumphant Americans and defeated Japanese in a geopolitical context, as well as between the ruling white class and racial(ized) minorities, including Nisei, in domestic US race relations. The mutually reinforcing relations of inclusive colorblind citizenship and minority imperial citizenship, which soldiers embraced with equal fervor, are key to these historical developments and relational racial formations that involved white American conquerors, Japanese American brokers, and vanquished alien Japanese during the tumultuous years of US-led occupation. Such a transimperial experience of Japanese Americans and their complicity with US hegemony helped harmonize its Cold War militarism with conditional minority inclusion at home and tutelary enemy democratization abroad.

The legend of the all-Nisei 442nd Regimental Combat Team (442nd RCT) formed a pivotal site of contestation and mutual complicities among these parties in occupied Japan. During the latter half of the US military occupation of Japan, the invented symbolisms associated with World War II Japanese American servicemen mirrored significant aspects of the US Cold War agenda, post-defeat Japan's aspirations, and the interests of Nisei occupation troops and their compatriots back in Hawai'i and stateside. The varied public images of the 442nd RCT war heroes were subject to constant manipulations by transpacific influences and sometimes confluences. The US occupation authorities had a strong stake in disseminating knowledge about the Nisei for the management of the racialized enemy and its rearming after the triumph of Communism in China. At the same time, Japanese Americans on both sides of the Pacific strove to exert a good measure of control over the construction of ideological meanings around their own martial mythology for their own goal of furthering national inclusion. Vanquished Japanese nationals were hardly quiet bystanders on the receiving end of American discursive impositions. Many saw the possibility of appropriating the Nisei trope and recasting it as a Japanese war story in the context of political debates over Japan's remilitarization. All these parties participated in and contributed to the convoluted processes that led to the sudden ascendancy of Nisei war heroes in the public discursive space of occupied Japan between 1949 and 1952.

By examining the intricacies of the three-way interactions and negotiations, this book helped readers to understand how the established narratives of minority heroism and the inclusive citizenship that it undergirded have continued to sustain multiethnic US militarism and minority imperial citizenship outside the confines of America's domestic race politics, social justice, and colorblind democracy. That entanglement allowed both the US armed forces and Nisei and other non-white soldiers to dress themselves in the garb of emancipator and democratizer. The 442nd RCT war heroes were the first major ideological symbol for these minority US soldiers that anti-racist America embraced for fighting domestic bigotries; and then,

Nisei occupation troops emerged as the first group of the servicemen to carry the weight of minority citizenship as frontline executors of US military power under the banner of democratizing the non-western enemy.

From anonymous propagandists to background knowledge producers, and from disciplinarians of consanguineous enemies to ideologically charged symbols, Japanese Americans lived through multifaceted roles and positions in the imperialist regime(s) and negotiated the turbulent forces of the war and military occupation. In the eye of that storm lay the shifting grounds of race, culture, and citizenship that influenced their daily experiences so heavily and consistently. *Brokering a Race War* offered a glimpse into the nuances, ambiguities, and ambivalences that were so fundamental to the experience of this racialized American minority. It is a story that the nationalist orthodoxy of military history and ethnic history has failed to unveil, for it facilely celebrates the wartime and occupation Nisei as another sub-group of patriotic heroes in a colorblind America. Such a grand narrative obfuscates contradictions and ironies in the Nisei experiences that defy simple glorification or condemnation. This omission whitewashes complex human agency, particularly the constant maneuvering and struggle of Nisei occupation troops and civilian workers in the white-supremacist birth country that unabashedly touted anti-racism, and their semi-colonial ancestral home that still foisted its blood-based imperial racism.

Aftermaths of Nisei's War History

Viewed from a transimperial perspective, a post-history of this story, too, is anything but celebratory. Once the end of the military occupation sent them home from Japan, this sub-group of patriotic Nisei soldiers was mostly subsumed under the continuous mythologization of the 442nd RCT on both sides of the Pacific. Thus, although postwar US presidents have frequently extolled the emancipatory consequences of minority military service in the language of inclusive nationalism and domestic civil rights struggle, the historical records of Nisei linguists and propagandists in the Pacific War and occupied Japan were largely obscured, if not unrecognized, until the 1990s. Contrary to the vanishing of transpacific Nisei cultural brokers in public discourse, the 442nd RCT war heroes continued to matter to the United States, Japanese America, and Japan.

In post-1952 Japan, most Japanese Americans disappeared both from physical and discursive spaces except for the dialectical public imaginations of criminalized or heroic Nisei. Whereas the otherization of Japanese Americans resulted from Japanese indignation at the former's practice of imperial US citizenship as much as from remnants of Japan's imperial racism, the appropriation of the Nisei's military story was an extension of the ongoing development that derived from the discursive tug of war over Japan's remilitarization. Backed by Japan's statesmen and cultural workers, the saga of the 442nd RCT as an American story had been largely compromised under the rhetoric of blood-based co-optation. Yet, the full-scale Japanization of the Nisei war (hi)story was temporarily arrested by GHQ censors when MGM's *Go for Broke!* was imported into the Japanese market in late 1951 to the effect of squashing a subversive film project by Shōchiku. However, post-occupation Japan successfully wiped away noticeable differences between Nisei US soldiers and Japanese soldiers, thereby claiming ownership of the 442nd RCT saga and Nisei's militarized bodies as theirs in domestic discourse by 1960.[1]

Eight years after its failed movie project, Shōchiku took up the theme again—this time with a focus on the Korean War. Based on a semi-autobiographical novel titled *Hey Pineapple!* (1958) by Hawai'i Nisei Robert Nobuyuki Hongo, the Japanese film production significantly altered the storyline so that the Nisei soldiers' thoughts and behaviors, their interactions with civilians in Japan, and their combat actions against communists on the Korean battlegrounds all contributed to gross confusion, if not conflation, of Nisei identities with Japanese in the eyes of the local audience.[2] Produced in 1960, Shōchiku's *Painappuru butai* (*Pineapple Regiment*) began by misrepresenting the doings of Hongo's regiment in Korea as a story of an all-Nisei unit—another 442nd RCT story—even though the Hawai'i Nisei was a member of the 25th infantry division that consisted not only of Japanese but also Chinese, Korean, Hawaiian, and white Americans. In the original novel, the term "pineapple" referred to an infantryman from Hawai'i, but the film limited it to Hawai'i Nisei only. This misdirection led Japanese film critics to deem *Painappuru butai* "a fitting successor to 'Go For Broke,'" a film about the 442nd RCT Nisei.[3]

Painappuru butai thus reorganized Nisei-Japanese relations around the theme of intra-racial commonality and equality while downplaying the difference in citizenship or the presence of military violence and domination. Hongo's original story is full of episodes in which the soldiers visit brothels, have casual one-night stands with local prostitutes and bar girls, and enjoy drinking sprees without concern for natives in Japan (or Korea).[4] By contrast, the film's Japan-related scenes are more focused on the stories of family reunions and serious romance between Nisei men and Japanese women—some ending in tragic separations and others leading to marriages. Relations between Nisei US soldiers and foreign Japanese were normalized as being based on the ties of blood and mutual respect despite some humorous cultural mishaps stemming from different upbringings.[5] Indeed, Hongo was quoted in a Japanese magazine as stressing: "I am American by citizenship but Japanese by blood. . . . I wanted this film—a story about us Japanese—to be produced by Japanese people."[6]

In the Shōchiku film, Nisei GIs often engage in familiar practices of imperial Japanese soldiers by giving cheers of "*banzai*" and singing old Japanese military songs. Organized by an uncle of one soldier, a geisha party in Tokyo harmonizes Nisei's appropriation of Japanese militarism of a bygone era with the theme of Japan's postwar democratization. When these Nisei are invited to join in when a group of Japanese sing a popular Japanese military song of the late 1930s—*roei no uta* (field encampment song)—they request to swap the original words "divine emperor" for "free world" before singing it with drunken cheers of *banzai*:

> How I think upon the skirmish yesterday
> And of my comrade who perished in the fray
> Weltering in his blood with final breath
> Smiling he did say *banzai* to the "*Free World*"!
> How could I forget those words of his which still remain with me.

When they are at an encampment on a Korean battleground, these Nisei soldiers sing the altered "field encampment song" again, accompanied by ukulele and many cheers of *banzai*.[7]

Combat scenes in Korea replicate a similar invention of Japanized Nisei militarism, when Japanese American soldiers charge with screams of *banzai* to bulldoze Communist enemy positions—an action that even their white commanders are induced to imitate. The majority of the protagonist's platoon are killed in the end, including the Japanized white officers, but the few Nisei survivors still hear roars of *banzai* from all over the place—likely from other charging "pineapples."[8] This time-honored theme of gallant military sacrifice is easy to relate to the preexisting dogma and imagery of

Japanese military heroism (suicidal *banzai* attacks) from the imperial era. Despite the notion of fighting for the free world, not the divine emperor, the sense of unbridgeable gap between imperial soldiers and democratic soldiers is hard to maintain. Indeed, this dangerous implication looked so obvious to leftist Japanese critics of *Painappuru butai*—when postwar Japan was about to conclude the mutual security pact with the United States in 1960.[9]

The mythologizing of Nisei soldiers as Japanese fighting men was complete in that critical political moment, which was not dissimilar to the time of Japan's remilitarization. To postwar Japan, *Painappuru butai* was equivalent to what *Go for Broke!* had been to the United States, and to Japanese America. Featuring nationalized and racialized soldiers, these films served as a convenient ideological devise to achieve a controversial political goal of the time—whether that be remilitarization, the US-Japan military alliance, anti-racist propaganda, or minority national inclusion. Perhaps, for this reason, the trope of the Nisei war hero would be re-invoked periodically in Japan's public discourse after 1960, when the country has been at a crossroad, which might require the elevation of public confidence in being Japanese through the teleological tale of the (Japanized) Nisei fighting men. Whether implicitly or explicitly, their story suggests the outstanding quality of the Yamato race, from which their perseverance and eventual triumph purportedly derive.[10] This emphasis on the fundamental Japaneseness of Nisei is often juxtaposed against the unjust racism of the United States or white Americans that victimized them, thus vindicating Japan's wartime claim for fighting against it.[11] As such, the distorted memories of Nisei US soldiers have comprised an important aspect of postwar Japan's racial nationalism and its resuscitated imperial thinking.

Across the Pacific, the legend of the 442nd RCT helped Nisei linguists to merge seamlessly into the mainstream of Japanese America after the occupation was over. Back in their birth country that was enmeshed in US-centered anti-racist discourse on Nisei's military service and Americanism, these returnees from the US-occupied ancestral home could rehabilitate themselves despite their tarnished backgrounds as Japan-educated Kibei, turn-coat strandees, and even treacherous renunciants. Postwar Japanese America continued to take advantage of the nationalist/anti-racist trope of the Nisei war heroes to facilitate further integration into white America that still imposed the logic of conditional acceptance.[12] At the same time, the occupation Nisei's lopsided transnational experience and the troublesome records of their imperial citizenship were buried into the grand narratives of their assimilation into mainstream US society, their rise as a model minority, and/or their struggle for equal civil rights and racial justice in a multicultural America.

Nisei's exemplary patriotism, backed by tales of heroic sacrifices and many medals, has indeed helped silence racist disquietude and grumbling in terms of their unmatched patriotism—so much so that Japanese American activists of the 1980s utilized the very trope to push for redress and reparations for the wartime incarceration. To rally support for this struggle, for example, a documentary film called *Nisei Soldier: Standard Bearer for an Exiled People* was shown before the US Congress.[13] Then, a congressional redress bill was designated as none other than H.R. 442. When the bill was sent to his desk for signature in 1988, President Ronald Reagan was reminded of his own 1945 eulogy for a fallen 442nd RCT hero. The president himself had participated in a government-led publicity campaign against racist attacks on Japanese Americans returning from the incarceration camps: "Blood that has soaked into the sands of a beach is all of one color. America stands unique in the world, the only country not founded on race, but on a way—an ideal.... That is the American way."[14] After speaking of the achievements of the 442nd RCT, which "served with immense distinction to defend this nation... laying down their lives" for "the very freedom" denied to their families, Reagan repeated his 1945 speech, and he proceeded to sign into the Civil Liberties Act of 1988 "H.R. 442, so fittingly named, in honor of the 442nd."[15]

Although former Nisei military linguists remained silent and obscured under the giant name of the 442nd RCT through these developments, they basically enjoyed the same benefits and acceptance as they were also considered patriotic military veterans until the 1990s. The release of declassified World War II documents in 1972 led to the publication of obscure works on Nisei MIS members in the wartime Pacific; yet, most former linguists did not speak out until the fiftieth anniversary of the end of Japanese occupation.[16] While the Military Intelligence Service Association of Northern California compiled a commemorative booklet in 1991, the Military Intelligence Service Veterans Club of Hawaii organized a reunion and published its own book two years later.[17] The termination of the legally binding silence in 1996 for former members of OSS and other intelligence agencies also made it easier for former Nisei linguists to reflect on their wartime and occupation-era activities.[18]

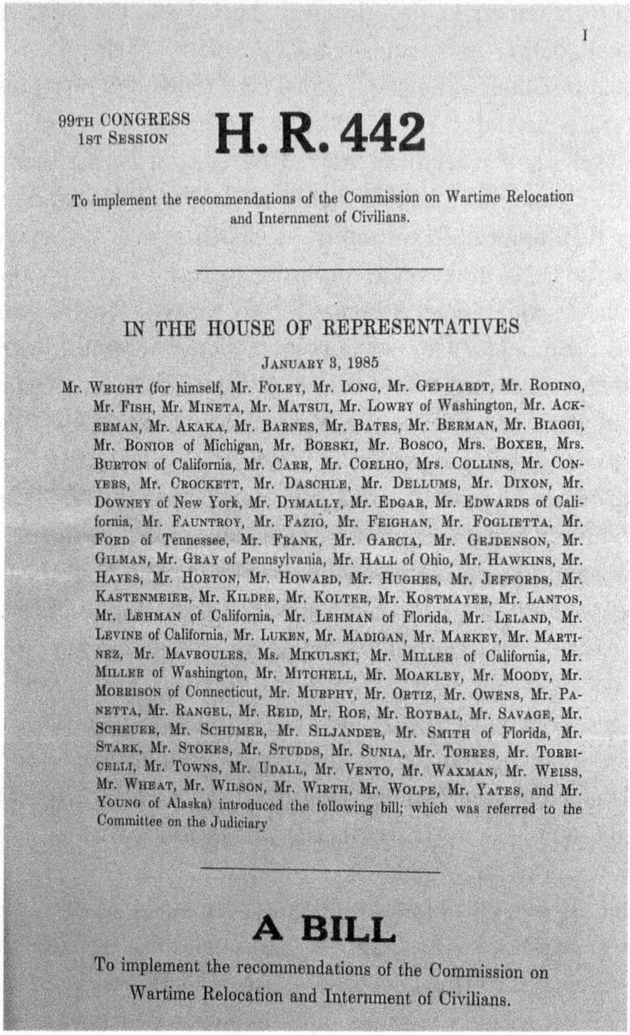

I

99th CONGRESS
1st Session

H. R. 442

To implement the recommendations of the Commission on Wartime Relocation and Internment of Civilians.

IN THE HOUSE OF REPRESENTATIVES

January 3, 1985

Mr. Wright (for himself, Mr. Foley, Mr. Long, Mr. Gephardt, Mr. Rodino, Mr. Fish, Mr. Mineta, Mr. Matsui, Mr. Lowry of Washington, Mr. Ackerman, Mr. Akaka, Mr. Barnes, Mr. Bates, Mr. Berman, Mr. Biaggi, Mr. Bonior of Michigan, Mr. Borski, Mr. Bosco, Mrs. Boxer, Mrs. Burton of California, Mr. Carr, Mr. Coelho, Mrs. Collins, Mr. Conyers, Mr. Crockett, Mr. Daschle, Mr. Dellums, Mr. Dixon, Mr. Downey of New York, Mr. Dymally, Mr. Edgar, Mr. Edwards of California, Mr. Fauntroy, Mr. Fazio, Mr. Feighan, Mr. Foglietta, Mr. Ford of Tennessee, Mr. Frank, Mr. Garcia, Mr. Gejdenson, Mr. Gilman, Mr. Gray of Pennsylvania, Mr. Hall of Ohio, Mr. Hawkins, Mr. Hayes, Mr. Horton, Mr. Howard, Mr. Hughes, Mr. Jeffords, Mr. Kastenmeier, Mr. Kildee, Mr. Kolter, Mr. Kostmayer, Mr. Lantos, Mr. Lehman of California, Mr. Lehman of Florida, Mr. Leland, Mr. Levine of California, Mr. Luken, Mr. Madigan, Mr. Markey, Mr. Martinez, Mr. Mavroules, Ms. Mikulski, Mr. Miller of California, Mr. Miller of Washington, Mr. Mitchell, Mr. Moakley, Mr. Moody, Mr. Morrison of Connecticut, Mr. Murphy, Mr. Ortiz, Mr. Owens, Mr. Panetta, Mr. Rangel, Mr. Reid, Mr. Roe, Mr. Roybal, Mr. Savage, Mr. Scheuer, Mr. Schumer, Mr. Siljander, Mr. Smith of Florida, Mr. Stark, Mr. Stokes, Mr. Studds, Mr. Sunia, Mr. Torres, Mr. Torricelli, Mr. Towns, Mr. Udall, Mr. Vento, Mr. Waxman, Mr. Weiss, Mr. Wheat, Mr. Wilson, Mr. Wirth, Mr. Wolpe, Mr. Yates, and Mr. Young of Alaska) introduced the following bill; which was referred to the Committee on the Judiciary

A BILL

To implement the recommendations of the Commission on Wartime Relocation and Internment of Civilians.

Fig. E.1 Front page of "H.R. 442," a House bill for reparations for former Japanese American internees, January 3, 1985. US House of Representatives, 99th Congress.

These publications—and many other printed and video productions—feature life histories and interviews of former Nisei linguists. Yet, their narratives tend to offer highly subjective, if not self-serving, pictures of their experiences with few traces of complexities, nuances, and ambiguities. In their testimonies, their motivations and agendas seem to stay consistent to the existing grand narrative. While shoring up the positive public view of these super-patriotic soldiers who had supposedly fought not only for destroying the foreign enemies but also for the true meaning of democracy and Americanism, the 442nd RCT myth has easily accommodated the MIS's later version without disturbing its ideological message that Nisei have striven to convey to white America since the mid-1940s. The valorization of their undiluted loyalty and military heroism, they have hoped, would permanently disavow lingering anti-Nisei discourse and racist justification for their incarceration as a "military necessity." Soon the government followed suit, putting Nisei linguists on a pedestal as paragons of colorblind democracy. Just as their 442nd RCT compatriots had received unit citations in the limelight earlier, the MIS was finally awarded the Presidential Unit Citation for its World War II valor in 2000.[19]

The September 11 attacks and the subsequent US invasions of Afghanistan (October 2001) and Iraq (March 2003) rendered the historical records of Nisei military linguists directly relevant and useful to the ongoing US military operations and subsequent occupation of the enemy lands. In 2006, the Department of the Army sponsored a publication of a massive 514-page academic monograph on Japanese American linguists in the wartime Pacific theater. Accompanied by numerous stories about Nisei's valor and patriotism, the official history explains that their work as Japanese-language specialists accelerated the end of hostilities with imperial Japan. It also unabashedly claims that Nisei linguists went on to help quickly transform former "enemies into friends" during the military occupation.[20] This emergent master-narrative offers no room for considering the problems of militarized minority transnationalism and their imperial citizenship, much less the ambiguous positions and roles that Nisei cultural brokers held under the conditions of colonialistic military rule.

Instead, Japanese American linguists have become the poster children for liberal discourse and anti-racist racial nationalism in a contemporary United States that masks its imperial tendencies. Moreover, they have symbolized a successful precedent of America's endeavor to reform and democratize the treacherous and atrocious enemy. This idea has been repeatedly invoked to rationalize the interventionist deployment and violence of the US armed forces—encompassing many non-white soldiers—all over the globe in the name of defending/promoting universal freedom and democracy. The post-2001 US interest in celebrating Nisei democratizers of vanquished Japan was inseparable from the contemporary debates on the US tutelary role in the democratization of the Middle East, for example.

In 2008, when Senator Daniel Akaka (D-HI) lobbied for federal funding for the Army's Center for Military History to compile another body of orthodoxy on Nisei linguists in occupied Japan, he proclaimed: "The book could provide lessons which can be used in the occupation of Iraq."[21]

Brokering a Race War aimed to expose the long history of the government's hijacking and exploitation of Nisei's complex experience for its military agendas. Challenging the lopsided nature of a dominant historical memory, it unraveled the Nisei's records of desperate maneuvering, including their complicity with US military domination and violence as much as their self-imposed role as co-racial democratizers. These records highlight the cost of becoming full-fledged Americans for this racial minority (and others) in the militarist regime that continues to practice a different form of colonialistic racism under the façade of anti-racism.

Indeed, as President Obama's unabashed celebration of the 442nd RCT Nisei in his civil rights speeches reveals, progressive American politics has generally failed to pay serious attention to the duality of post-World War II US citizenship—that is, its simultaneous functions for and indivisible relations of colorblind national inclusion and militarized minority imperialism.[22] The latter aspect of postwar US citizenship can be only seen by looking beyond the confines of US domestic race relations and civil rights struggles and critically examining the roles and positions of minority American soldiers vis-à-vis foreigners around them on the battlegrounds and at military bases. In his 1947 letter, one Nisei linguist in Tokyo asked: "I suppose we can be proud of the combat Niseis [sic], but we're going to be ashamed of the occupation Nisei. Doesn't seem possible, does it?"[23] The answer to this question should be clearer once the complex roles, relations, dilemmas, and complicities of the Nisei have been illuminated rather than swept up in the master-narrative of Nisei's exemplary patriotism and national inclusion. *Brokering a Race War* provided readers with vital clues for addressing that question.

Brokering a Race War: Japanese Americans in the Pacific War and the Occupation of Japan. Eiichiro Azuma, Oxford University Press. © Eiichiro Azuma 2026. DOI: 10.1093/9780197781432.003.0008

Notes

Introduction

1. Military Secretary to the Commander-in-Chief, "Weekly Military Plan for Psychological Warfare," June 23, 1945, p. 1 of "Japan Radio Plan," in box 403, OWI-BOICF.
2. Franklin D. Roosevelt to Mr. Secretary [Henry Stimson], February 1, 1943, in OF 4849 (WRA RG 107), FDRL.
3. The notion of Japanese Americans as an "enemy race" with "undiluted racial strains" underpinned the US policy of the mass incarceration of West Coast Japanese, the majority of whom were native-born citizens. See "Memorandum: Subject: Evacuation of Japanese and Other Subversive Persons from the Pacific Coast" (February 13, 1942), reprinted in Roger Daniels, ed., *American Concentration Camps*, vol. 2 (New York: Garland, 1989). On the Pacific War as a race war, see John W. Dower, *War without Mercy: Race and Power in the Pacific War* (New York: Pantheon, 1986).
4. On critical analyses of the nationalist glorification of Nisei US soldiers, see Ellen D. Wu, *The Color of Success: Asian Americans and the Origins of the Model Minority* (Princeton: Princeton University Press, 2014), pp. 72–110; and Takashi Fujitani, *Race for Empire: Koreans as Japanese and Japanese as Americans during World War II* (Berkeley: University of California Press, 2011), pp. 206–36.
5. On examples of scholarly histories that glamourize minority military service as an engine of civil rights progress, see J. Todd Moye, *Freedom Flyers: The Tuskegee Airmen of World War II* (New York: Oxford University Press, 2010); and Christopher S. Parker, *Fighting for Democracy: Black Veterans and the Struggle against White Supremacy in the Postwar South* (Princeton: Princeton University Press, 2009).
6. See a propaganda poster (Fig. 2.1) titled "Americanism is not, and never was, a matter of race or ancestry," dated February 3, 1943. President Barrack Obama made this speech at the fiftieth anniversary of the Selma to Montgomery Marches on March 7, 2015. See https://obamawhitehouse.archives.gov/the-press-office/2015/03/07/remarks-president-50th-anniversary-selma-montgomery-marches (accessed on July 20, 2025).
7. See Masayo Umezawa Duus, *Unlikely Liberators: The Men of the 100th and 442nd*, translated by Peter Duus (Honolulu: University of Hawaii Press, 1987); and Robert Asahina, *Just Americans: How Japanese Americans Won a War at Home and Abroad* (New York: Gotham, 2006).
8. See [Kenneth D. Ringle], "Japanese in America: The Problem and the Solution," *Harper's Magazine* 185 (1942), p. 492.
9. On a substantive study of Kibei, see Michael R. Jin, *Citizens, Immigrants, and the Stateless: A Japanese American Diaspora in the Pacific* (Stanford: Stanford University Press, 2022), pp. 38–83.
10. On representative works, see James C. McNaughton, *Nisei Linguists: Japanese Americans in the Military Intelligence Service during World War II* (Washington, DC: Department of the Army, 2006); Bruce Henderson, *Bridge to the Sun: The Secret Role of the Japanese Americans Who Fought in the Pacific in World War II* (New York: Knopf, 2022); Lyn Crost, *Honor by Fire: Japanese Americans at War in Europe and the Pacific* (Novato, CA: Presidio Press, 1994); Stanley Falk and Warren Tsuneishi, eds., *MIS in the War against Japan: Personal Experiences Related at the 1993 MIS Capital Reunion* (Washington, DC: Japanese American Veterans Association, 1995); "MIS in Japan," *Nikkei Heritage* 15, no. 1 (2003): pp. 4–18; Military Intelligence Service Association of Northern California (MIS NorCal) and National Japanese American Historical Society (NJAHS), eds., *The Pacific War and Peace: Americans of Japanese Ancestry in Military Intelligence Service, 1941 to 1952* (San Francisco: MIS NorCal and NJAHS, 1991); Military Intelligence Service Veterans Club of Hawaii, ed., *Secret Valor: MIS Personnel, World War II Pacific Theater, Pre-Pearl Harbor to Sept. 8, 1951* (Honolulu: MIS Veterans Club

of Hawaii, 1993); MIS-Northwest Association, *Unsung Heroes: The Military Intelligence Service Past-Present-Future* (Seattle; MIS-Northwest Association, 1996); and David W. Swift, Jr., *First Class: Nisei Linguists in World War II* (San Francisco: National Japanese American Historical Society, 2008). These film productions on Nisei linguists share the similar storylines: "Fifty Years of Silence" (1992); "Prejudice and Patriotism" (1998); and "Uncommon Courage" (2001). On earlier references to Nisei linguists, see Bradford Smith, *Americans from Japan* (Philadelphia: J. B. Lippincott, 1948), pp. 324–28; Joseph D. Harrington, *Yankee Samurai: The Secret Role of Nisei in America's Pacific Victory* (Detroit, MI: Harlo Press, 1979); and Tad Ichinokuchi, ed., *John Aiso and the MIS: Japanese American Soldiers in the Military Intelligence Service, World War II* (Los Angeles: Military Intelligence Service Club of Southern California, 1988). On a serious scholarly treatment of the subject, see also Kayoko Takeda, *Interpreting the Tokyo War Crimes Tribunal: A Sociopolitical Analysis* (Ottawa: University of Ottawa Press, 2010).

11. On works that deal with Japanese Americans in prewar and wartime Japan, see Eiichiro Azuma, *Between Two Empires: Race, History, and Transnationalism in Japanese America* (New York: Oxford University Press, 2005), pp. 135–59; John J. Stephan, *Hawaii under the Rising Sun: Japan's Plans for Conquest after Pearl Harbor* (Honolulu: University of Hawaii Press, 1984), pp. 41–54; Jin, *Citizens, Immigrants, and the Stateless*, pp. 14–37, 114–34; A. Carly Buxton, *Unthinking Collaboration: American Nisei in Transwar Japan* (Honolulu: University of Hawaii Press, 2022), pp. 17–129; A[nne]. Carly Buxton, "The Enemies among Us: Race, Trust, and Allied Internment in World War II Japan," in *Defamiliarizing Japan's Asia-Pacific War*, edited by W. Puck Brecher and Michael W. Myers (Honolulu: University of Hawaii Press, 2019), pp. 194–203; Masayo Duus, *Tokyo Rose: Orphan of the Pacific*, translated by Peter Duus (New York: Kodansha USA, 1979); and Naoko Wake, *American Survivors: Trans-Pacific Memories of Hiroshima and Nagasaki* (Cambridge: Cambridge University Press, 2021), pp. 57–66.
12. McNaughton, *Nisei Linguists*, esp. p. 462.
13. From a similar standpoint, Susan L. Carruthers critically examines the paradox of US postwar occupation in Germany and Japan, albeit with a focus on white officers and servicemen, in Susan L. Carruthers, *The Good Occupation: American Soldiers and the Hazards of Peace* (Cambridge, MA: Harvard University Press, 2016).
14. On recent works that look critically at the US military occupation of foreign territories, albeit not with attention to the role of minority US soldiers, see Kornel Chang, *A Fractured Liberation: Korea under US Occupation* (Cambridge, MA: Belknap Press of Harvard University Press, 2025); Justine F. Jackson, *The Work of Empire: War, Occupation, and the Making of American Colonialism in Cuba and the Philippines* (Durham: University of North Carolina Press, 2025); and Zach Fredman, *The Tormented Alliance: American Servicemen and the Occupation of China, 1941–1949* (Durham: University of North Carolina Press, 2022), esp. ch. 2. Chang unravels the US use of native Koreans who had worked for Japan's colonial regime for the suppression of anti-American protestors and leftist reformers under American military rule. Fredman examines the training and use of Chinese military interpreters for US occupation personnel under the auspices of Chiang Kai-Shek's regime.
15. On the application of a similar concept of governmentality to minority military service, see Fujitani, *Race for Empire*, pp. 26–27.
16. Simeon Man, *Soldiering through Empire: Race and the Making of the Decolonizing Pacific* (Berkeley: University of California Press, 2018), p. 13.
17. Azuma, *Between Two Empires*, pp. 135–51, 181–83, and also Jin, *Citizens, Immigrants, and the Stateless*, pp. 38–83.
18. See Fujitani, *Race for Empire*; Yukiko Koshiro, *Trans-Pacific Racisms and the US Occupation of Japan* (New York: Columbia University Press, 1999); and Dower, *War without Mercy*.
19. Studies of minority transnationalism tend to look at educated intellectuals, well-known artists, or committed political activists, but not common military enlistees. See, for example, David Levering Lewis, *W. E. B. Du Bois, The Fight for Equality and the American Century 1919–1963* (New York: Henry Holt and Company, 2001); Nico Slate, *The Prism of Race: W. E. B. Du Bois, Langston Hughes, Paul Robeson, and the Colored World of Cedric Dover* (New York: Palgrave Macmillan, 2014); Robin D. G. Kelley, *Freedom Dreams: The Black Radical Imagination* (Boston: Beacon Press, 2003); and Judy Tzu-Chun Wu, *Radicals on the Road: Internationalism, Orientalism, and Feminism during the Vietnam Era* (Ithaca, NY: Cornel University Press, 2013).

20. On racism and minority resistance within the US armed forces, see Thomas A. Guglielmo, *Divisions: A New History of Racism and Resistance in America's World War II Military* (New York: Oxford University Press, 2021).
21. See Michael Cullen Green, *Black Yanks in the Pacific: Race in the Making of the American Military Empire after World War II* (Ithaca, NY: Cornell University Press, 2010).
22. In reality, many minority Americans were compelled to leave their birth country in search of better economic and political opportunities outside the confines of the white supremacist regime. On examples of scholarship on African Americans' migration and (re)settlement in Liberia and other parts of Africa, see Claude Andrew Clegg III, *The Price of Liberty: African Americans and the Making of Liberia* (Chapel Hill: University of North Carolina Press, 2004); Kenneth C. Barnes, *Journey of Hope: The Back-to-Africa Movement in Arkansas in the Late 1800s* (Chapel Hill: University of North Carolina Press, 2004); and Kevin K. Gaines, *African Americans in Ghana: Black Expatriates and the Civil Rights Era* (Chapel Hill: University of North Carolina Press, 2008). On Chinese Americans in pre-World-War-II China, see Charlotte Brooks, *American Exodus: Second Generation Chinese Americans in China, 1901–1949* (Berkeley: University of California Press, 2019).
23. On the experience of Nisei as foreignized immigrants of shared ancestry in 1930s Japan, see Azuma, *Between Two Empires*, pp. 135–59; Eiichiro Azuma, *In Search of Our Frontier: Japanese America and Settler Colonialism in the Construction of Japan's Borderless Empire* (Berkeley: University of California Press, 2019), pp. 242–60; Jin, *Citizens, Immigrants, and the Stateless*, pp. 14–37; and Wake, *American Survivors*, pp. 57–66.
24. On soldiering as a form of labor, see Man, *Soldiering through Empire*, p. 11; and Green, *Black Yanks in the Pacific*, p. 31.
25. On the concepts of "polite racism" and "vulgar racism" relating to US wartime and postwar racism, see Fujitani, *Race for Empire*, pp. 25–27. Paul A. Kramer's discussion of "inclusionary racism" sheds light on the intersections of US domestic politics and colonial politics in the Philippines. Gary Y. Okihiro describes the articulations of the same variations of American racism as "racism" and "anti-racism," while Mary L. Dudziak discusses the limitations of racial liberalism in the context of an expanded scope of US civil rights in Cold War America. See Paul A. Kramer, *The Blood of Government: Race, Empire, the United States, and the Philippines* (Chapel Hill: University of North Carolina Press, 2006), pp. 5–6, 18–19, 192–98; Gary Y. Okihirio, *Storied Lives: Japanese American Students and World War II* (Seattle: University of Washington Press, 1999), pp. xii–xiii, 137–38; and Mary Dudziak, *Cold War Civil Rights: Race and the Image of American Democracy* (Princeton: Princeton University Press, 2011).
26. On equivalent concepts used by other historians, see Fujitani, *Race for Empire*, pp. 25–27; and Kramer, *The Blood of Government*, pp. 5–6.
27. On aspects of these processes, see Fujitani, *Race for Empire*; Man, *Soldiering through Empire*; and Monica Kim, *The Interrogation Rooms of the Korean War: The Untold History* (Princeton: Princeton University Press, 2019). On other works that examine racial subordination of Asian American soldiers despite inclusion, see Franklin Odo, *No Sword to Bury: Japanese Americans in Hawai'i during the Pacific War* (Philadelphia: Temple University Press, 2004); K. Scott Wong, *Americans First: Chinese Americans and the Second World War* (Philadelphia: Temple University Press, 2008); Brian Masaru Hayashi, *Asian American Spies: How Asian Americans Helped Win the Allied Victory* (New York: Oxford University Press, 2021); and Guglielmo, *Divisions*.
28. See Ilene Rose Feinman, *Citizenship Rites: Feminist Soldiers and Feminist Antimilitarists* (New York: New York University Press, 2000), pp. 1–6.
29. Brenda L. Moore, *Serving Our Country: Japanese American Women in the Military during World War II* (New Brunswick, NJ: Rutgers University Press, 2003), pp. 124–31.
30. On the discussion of minority "rightlessness," see A. Naomi Paik, *Rightlessness: Testimony and Redress in US Prison Camps since World War II* (Chapel Hill: University of North Carolina Press, 2016).
31. Some historians studying African American occupation troops have examined what it meant to be a racial minority in the military forces of a white supremacist regime in a non-white land and analyzed the impact such an experience had on Black soldiers and those on the home front. Their works offer conflicting narratives as to whether or not Black soldiers maintained a race-based perspective with which to transnationalize their opposition to US domestic racism

and foster moral bonds to foreign subjects of US military domination. Marc Gallicchio characterizes Black soldiers' attitude toward the Japanese enemy in terms of the "ambivalence" that they had felt since before the war. More critically, Michael Cullen Green explains why and how such ambivalence soon gave way to African Americans' acceptance of the US imperial project in Cold War Asia and their subsequent animosity toward East Asian foreigners, including new immigrants in a postwar domestic context. On these and other works, see Marc Gallicchio, *The African American Encounter with Japan and China: Black Internationalism in Asia, 1895–1945* (Chapel Hill: University of North Carolina Press, 2000), esp. p. 204; Green, *Black Yanks in the Pacific*; also Gerald Horne, *Facing the Rising Sun: African Americans, Japan, and the Rise of Afro-Asian Solidarity* (New York: New York University Press, 2018); Reginald Kearney, *African American Views of the Japanese: Solidarity or Sedition?* (Albany: State University of New York Press, 1998); and Yuichiro Onishi, *Transpacific Antiracism: Afro-Asian Solidarity in 20th-Century Black America, Japan, and Okinawa* (New York: New York University Press, 2013).

32. Clarence Adams, *An American Dream: The Life of an African American Soldier and POW Who Spent Twelve Years in Communist China* (Amherst: University of Massachusetts Press, 2007), p. 28. I thank Daniel Y. Kim for bringing this book to my attention.
33. Ibid.
34. Eizo Suzuki to James A. O'Brien, April 19, 1949, and "Record of Trial of Suzuki, Eizo," August 28, 1947, Kobe Base, in folder 6, box 48, MMMP.
35. On other examples of this ironic role, see Man, *Soldiering through Empire*; and Kim, *The Interrogation Rooms*.
36. On a different example of Asian American cultural brokers, see Mae Ngai, *The Lucky Ones: One Family and the Extraordinary Invention of Chinese America* (New York: Houghton Mifflin Harcourt, 2010), pp. 223–25.
37. On examples of postwar Nisei/minority struggles for equality and justice, see Wu, *The Color of Success*; Cindy I-Fen Cheng, *Citizens of Asia America: Democracy and Race during the Cold War* (New York: New York University Press, 2014); and Dudziak, *Cold War Civil Rights*.

Chapter 1

1. On an exception, Takashi Fujitani, "The Reischauer Memo: Mr. Moto, Hirohito, and Japanese American Soldiers," *Critical Asian Studies* 33, no. 3 (2001): pp. 379–402. Though it does not address the question of Japanese Americans, John W. Dower's work explains how the problem of race formed the common propaganda themes of the United States and imperial Japan. See John W. Dower, *War without Mercy: Race and Power in the Pacific War* (New York: Pantheon, 1986). For a general study of US and Japanese propaganda, see Allison B. Gilmore, *You Can't Fight Tanks with Bayonets: Psychological Warfare against the Japanese Army in the Southwest Pacific* (Lincoln: University of Nebraska Press, 1998); and Barak Kushner, *The Thought War: Japanese Imperial Propaganda* (Honolulu: University of Hawaii Press, 2005).
2. See Yukiko Koshiro, *Trans-Pacific Racisms and the US Occupation of Japan* (New York: Columbia University Press, 1999), esp. pp. 1–48.
3. On this campaign, see Eiichiro Azuma, *Between Two Empires: Race, History, and Transnationalism in Japanese America* (New York: Oxford University Press, 2005), pp. 171–83.
4. Ibid., pp. 171–72, 183.
5. Ibid., pp. 148–50; "Fighting Enemy's Propaganda," *Reimei* 1, nos. 1–2 (1943): p. 14 (English section); and Torii Hideharu, *Kokusaku tsūshinsha "Dōmei" no kōbō* (Tokyo: Kadensha, 2014), pp. 182–86, 607–8. The school was called Heishikan. See also Michael R. Jin, *Citizens, Immigrants, and the Stateless: A Japanese American Diaspora in the Pacific* (Sanford: Stanford University Press, 2022), pp. 34–36, 120–26.
6. Chōsa-bu Dai-rokuka, "Boku-bei kansō hōkoku," November 25, 1941, DAMFA.
7. "Transcript of Shortwave Broadcast (Record number T-112)," May 4, 1942, in box 637, TMFB-FBIS. On the same arguments, see "America Continues Abusing Japanese," *Japan Times*, May 6, 1942; and Foreign Office, "We Fight through the Radio," vol. 1 (1942), pp. 216–17, DAMFA.
8. See Dodo Masao, "Beikokumin no zangyakusei," *Shin wakōdo* 4, no. 1 (1943): pp. 112–16; "Transcripts of Shortwave Broadcast," April 17 and 20, 1942, July 28, 1942, September 9–11, 1942, November 26, 1943, and December 7, 1943, in boxes 636, 641, 643, 644, 686, 687, TMFB-FBIS; and "News behind the News," *Nippon Times*, December 3, 1943. On Dodo's prewar activities in California, see Chrissy Yee Lau, *New Women of Empire: Gendered Politics and*

Racial Uplift in Interwar Japanese America (Seattle: University of Washington Press, 2022), ch. 2. Another notable Issei returnee is Ebina Kazuo, a newspaperman with strong connections to San Francisco immigrant intelligentsia, who expounded on the thesis of white American treachery. In his radio addresses and publications, Ebina argued that Issei farmers had made many contributions to the development of western agriculture, and yet, thankless America drove them out of their farms and "chased [them] right next door to [the internment camp in the] valley of death." See, for example, "American Picture," October 23–24, 1942 (Record number T-106), box 646, TMFB-FBIS. On the Japanese version of this narrative, see also Ebina Kazuo, *Kariforunia to Nihonjin* (Tokyo: Rokkō Shuppanbu, 1943), pp. 241–51; and Jōhōkyoku, "Kaigai kōenshū," no. 4, December 1942, pp. 110–13, DAMFA.

9. See, for example, "Former Japanese Internee Scores Cruel Treatment Received in US," *Nippon Times*, January 27, 1943, and similar narrations in ibid., January 28, February 4 and 19, November 14 and 17, 1943.
10. See "Domei Morse," September 21, 1942, in box 644, TMFB-FBIS. On Radio Tokyo's coverage of the subject, see Takeya Mizuno, "A Disturbing and Ominous Voice from a Different Shore: Japanese Radio Propaganda and Its Impact on the US Government's Treatment of Japanese Americans during World War II," *Japanese Journal of American Studies* 24 (2013): pp. 110–19.
11. "Light from the East" (Record number 100), September 29, 1942, p. 1, in box 645, TMFB-FBIS. Aboard the first ship, Nakazawa Ken was another notable repatriate-turned propagandist in wartime Japan. Having taught Japanese studies courses at the University of Southern California, Nakazawa had also served as an English-language publicist for the local Japanese consulate before December 1941. Because of his role as Japan's apologist for its imperialist policy in China, the Federal Bureau of Investigation had blacklisted him, resulting in his swift arrest and incarceration following the attack on Pearl Harbor. After his repatriation to Japan in August 1942, Nakazawa wrote about his experience as an American prisoner while working for Radio Tokyo. His 262-page reportage offers a sensationalized account of his daily ordeals during the five-month detention as a dangerous enemy alien in Los Angeles and Montana, detailing the alleged "inhuman" treatment of him and other Issei by white prison guards and soldiers. See Nakazawa Ken, *Amerika no gokuchū yori Dōhō ni tsugu* (Tokyo: Masu Shobō, 1943), pp. 33–40, 257–60; December 15 [1942], in box 650, TMFB-FBIS; and "Morning Far Eastern Propaganda Analysis," no. 74, September 7–8, 1942, p. 1, in box 3449, and "Morning Far Eastern Propaganda Analysis," March 8, 1943, in box 3448, both in OWI-AJB. On the alleged "torture-death" of a Los Angeles Issei doctor and ethnic community leader, see also Yuji Ichioka, "The Death of Dr. Honda Rikita," in *Before Internment: Essays in Prewar Japanese American History*, edited by Gordon H. Chang and Eiichiro Azuma (Stanford: Stanford University Press, 2006), pp. 258–70.
12. "Light from the East," pp. 3–4. See also Jōhōkyoku, "Kaigai kōenshū," no. 4, pp. 79–81. On Sakanishi, see also Greg Robinson, *The Unsung Great: Stories of Extraordinary Japanese Americans* (Seattle: University of Washington Press, 2020), pp. 6–9.
13. See, for example, "Domei Morse," and "Light from the East," p. 1; and Jōhōkyoku, "Kaigai kōenshū," no. 4, pp. 79–81.
14. Takashi Fujitani, *Race for Empire: Koreans as Japanese and Japanese as Americans during World War II* (Berkeley: University of California Press, 2011), pp. 96–101.
15. On colorblind birthright citizenship and its complicated connections to Asian American experience and US race politics, see Carol Nackenoff and Julie Novkov, *American by Birth: Wong Kim Ark and the Battle for Citizenship* (Lawrence: University Press of Kansas, 2022).
16. See "Tekikoku zairyū Dōhō dainikai kōkansen kikokusha kōshū nittei-an" and "Nichibei dainiji kōkansen Teia-maru Yokohama nyūkō no sai ni okeru shochiburi ni kansuru kyōgi jikō," in *Nichibei kōkansen kankei*, vol. 6, Showa series, DAMFA. According to these guidelines, some Issei repatriates and former residents emerged as authors of propaganda books masquerading as life stories of victims of American racism. On representative publications by wartime Issei returnees, see Nakazawa, *Amerika no gokuchū yori Dōhō ni tsugu*; Kawamura Masahei, *Taiheiyō no senkusha* (Tokyo: Tōzaisha, 1943); and Aoki Hisa, *Teia-Maru no hōkoku* (Tokyo: Maeda Shobō, 1944).
17. "Tekikoku zairyū Dōhō dainikai kōkansen kikokusha kōshū nittei-an" and "Nichibei dainiji kōkansen Teia-maru Yokohama nyūkō no sai ni okeru shochiburi ni kansuru kyōgi jikō."
18. Translated or edited by Nisei staff, for example, Dodo's contributions to the English-language *Nippon Times* are plenty in late 1943 and early 1944. Between December 1943 and January

1944 alone, at least a total of seven translated editorials by the Issei propagandist appeared in that newspaper. See the following issues of the *Nippon Times*: December 3, 17, 23, and 26, 1943, and January 15, 29, and 30, 1943. Ebina's translated editorial was also published in its April 14, 1942, issue.

19. On the establishment of the NAN, see "Nisei Determined to Stay despite Worst, At Inaugural Meeting of New Federation," *Japan Times*, November 24, 1941: p. 1; *Asahi Shinbun*, November 23, 1941: p. 3; and P. R. (Acting US Political Advisor in Tokyo), "Nisei Language Personnel Residing in Japan," November 19, 1945, pp. 1–2, in box 1, DS-CGC. The NAN's history traces back to November 1941, after Tokyo assembled leaders of major second-generation organizations in the region and convinced them to disband the existing entities and form a single association for Nisei in Japan. This scheme went hand in hand with the ongoing national mobilization movement, where overseas Japanese residents, including US-based immigrants, were organized into the Central Federation for Overseas Japanese (Kaigai Dōhō Chūōkai). Their foreign-born/foreign-citizen sons and daughters were expected to form its Young People's Bureau (Kaigai Dōhō Chūōkai Seinenbu), which became the institutional backbone of the NAN. Both organizations came under the jurisdiction of Japan's foreign ministry, hence the government support for and control of its Nisei members from the outset. On a prehistory of the NAN, see Eiichiro Azuma, *In Search of Our Frontier: Japanese America and Settler Colonialism in the Construction of Japan's Borderless Empire* (Berkeley: University of California Press, 2019), p. 240.
20. General Meeting of the Nisei Association of Nippon, "Resolution," in *Reimei* 1, nos. 1–2: p. 1 (English section). This bilingual bulletin was the NAN's official publication.
21. The statistical data on Japanese American residents in Japan are taken from ibid., p. 6 (English section), and pp. 5, 12, 16 (Japanese section). The figures are considered reliable, because they were provided by foreign ministry officials when the Japanese government had a tight control of the domestic population, especially foreignized peoples like US-born Nisei.
22. On persecutions of resident Nisei, see Eiichiro Azuma, "Toward a Transnational History of Wartime Japanese Americans: Nisei and Imperial Japan's Race Propaganda," *Journal of American Ethnic History* 42, no. 2 (2023): pp. 10–15. On the internment of Caucasian and Eurasian American residents in wartime Japan, see A. Carly Buxton, "The Enemies among Us," in *Defamiliarizing Japan's Asia-Pacific War*, edited by W. Puck Brecher and Michael W. Myers (Honolulu: University of Hawaii Press, 2019), pp. 194–95, 201–2.
23. Prior to the Pacific War, NAN's leaders in Tokyo, like Tamotsu Murayama and Goro Murata, had held close relations with JACL leaders stateside, like James Y. Sakamoto and Mike M. Masaoka. They shared similar views about the role of Nisei as the transnational "bridge of understanding" between the United States and Japan before the uncompromised national allegiance to one state or the other dominated their self-representations. In this sense, their parallel trajectories suggest much about the behavior of minoritized subjects in a militarist state at war. See Azuma, *Between Two Empires*, pp. 156–57; and Yuji Ichioka, "A Study in Dualism: James Yoshinori Sakamoto and the *Japanese American Courier*, 1928–1942," in Ichioka, *Before Internment*, pp. 92–124.
24. The state patronage enabled the NAN to command instant authority and legitimacy in the eyes of many Nisei, especially those in the greater Tokyo region who needed relief from social and official persecutions in the early months of the war. Out of the estimated three thousand to five thousand English-speaking Nisei in Japan, the NAN had almost two thousand registered members in 1942. The regional distribution of the members was as follows: 830 in the Kantō region (including Tokyo), 705 in Hiroshima Prefecture, 111 in the Kansai region (including Osaka), and 328 in the rest of the Japanese archipelago. Perhaps due to regional rivalry, many of US-born Japanese in the Kansai and Kyūshū regions refrained from joining the NAN. An Osaka renegade group had an informal organization called the Young Pacific Club, although it exerted little political power because of the lack of state support. See "Business Report," p. 25; and P. R. (Acting US Political Advisor in Tokyo), "Nisei Language Personnel Residing in Japan," p. 3.
25. On these resident Nisei leaders, see Sano Shin'ichi, *Kyokai-den: Shōriki Matsutarō to kagemusha-tachi no isseiki* (Tokyo: Bungei Shunjūsha, 1994), pp. 219–22; and Azumi Suimei, "Zatsunen no kuni," *Nippon to Amerika* 21, no. 6 (1967): pp. 7–9. On the roster of the NAN leadership, see "Zainichi Nisei Rengōkai kikō," *Reimei* 1, nos. 1–2: pp. 21–22 (Japanese section).
26. Takizo Matsumoto, "A Message to Nisei in Japan," *Reimei* 1, nos. 1–2: p. 2 (English section).

27. General Meeting of the Nisei Association of Nippon, "Resolution," p. 1.
28. On imperial Japan's effort to incorporate diverse populations, including Nisei residents, into a unified imperial citizenry, see Buxton, "The Enemies among Us," pp. 194–95.
29. On their prewar insistence on a unique US background, especially birthright citizenship as a marker of intra-racial difference from the home compatriots, see Azuma, *Between Two Empires*, pp. 150–51, 156–57.
30. As Matsumoto and other NAN leaders recalled, the Japanese police frequented the organization's Tokyo headquarters to keep them in line, if not outright intimidate them, in addition to subjecting many members to "embarrassment... by arrests and by long cross-examinations." Moreover, they lived in constant fear of "attacks by fascistic thugs." See P. R. (Acting US Political Advisor in Tokyo), "Nisei Language Personnel Residing in Japan," pp. 3–4; and Ozawa Takeo and Yamashita Sōen, "Imin hyakunen sanbun-no-ichi no butaiura," *Nippon to America* 21, no. 9 (1967): p. 16. The quotes are from these sources.
31. "Business Report," p. 25; and "Zainichi Nisei Rengōkai kikō." Japanese advisors to the NAN's board of directors included the former minister plenipotentiary to Canada, foreign ministry bureau chiefs, and National Diet members. Longtime supporters of Nisei in Japan, like army General Araki Sadao, were also among them. In cooperation with these Japanese board members, the NAN pulled a major fundraising event in October 1942 to set up special scholarship funds for Nisei students who had lost contact with—and hence support from—their parents across the Pacific. On this event, see "Nisei Benefit Show to Feature Singers," *Nippon Times*, October 8, 1943: p. 4; "Benefit Show Held for Nisei Students," *Nippon Times*, October 15, 1943: p. 4; "Imin hyakunen sanbun-no-ichi no butaiura 17," *Beifu Jihō* 210 (1969): p. 10; Ozawa and Yamashita, "Imin hyakunen sanbun-no-ichi no butaiura," pp. 16–17; "Zainichi Nisei Rengōkai jigyō gaiyō hōkokusho," *Reimei* 1: pp. 16–20 (Japanese section); and "Business Report," pp. 26–31.
32. See Mikiko (Miki) Sawada, "A Message to Nisei," *Reimei* 1: pp. 4–5 (English section).
33. "Tatakau gunkoku no Nisei: Tagiru goman-nin no chishio," *Asahi Shinbun*, January 15, 1943.
34. "Fighting Enemy's Propaganda," p. 14.
35. See, for example, "Activities of Nisei since War Lauded," *Nippon Times*, June 16, 1943: p. 3. Coupled with the glorification of military service and patriotic actions of conscripted Korean and Taiwanese, this pro-Nisei propaganda functioned as a trope for total mobilization of diverse constituents of the multiethnic Japanese empire in the struggle against the Anglo-American powers and their global white supremacy. It presented an eerie parallel to how the wartime United States suddenly began to embrace soldiers of color, including Japanese Americans, as heroes of anti-racist America that was supposedly fighting for colorblind democracy and universal liberty in the world while maintaining the structure of white supremacy within its armed forces and beyond. See Fujitani, *Race for Empire*; and Thomas A. Guglielmo, *Divisions: A New History of Racism and Resistance in America's World War II Military* (New York: Oxford University Press, 2021).
36. "Business Report," pp. 26–29.
37. *Asahi Shinbun*, September 27, 1943: p. 2.
38. "Business Report," p. 29. In 1942 alone, over four hundred Nisei, especially financially strained students, also utilized NAN's job placement service for war industries and propaganda-related work as translators and foreign radio monitors. See ibid.; and Ozawa and Yamashita, "Imin hyakunen sanbun-no-ichi no butaiura," p. 16.
39. P. R. (Acting US Political Advisor in Tokyo), "Nisei Language Personnel Residing in Japan," pp. 3–4; and also, "Imin hyakunen sanbun-no-ichi no butaiura 13," *Beifu Jihō* 204 (1969): p. 9. Interrogated by a state department official a few months after Japan's defeat, Matsumoto stated that Nisei's cooperation with Japan's war effort helped "alleviate much of the police pressure on them." The quote is from the first source.
40. As discussed in later chapters, wartime Nisei "strandees" were demonized by US Nisei, especially Japanese American Citizens League (JACL) members and 442nd RCT veterans, as the most "disloyal" of all "disloyal" Nisei. They have been also largely written out of postwar ethnic memory and community history. On a rare report on them in ethnic press, see Richard T. Kenmotsu, "The Forgotten Nisei," *Pacific Citizen*, December 19–26, 1975. On JACL's postwar attitude toward the Tokyo Rose and other Nisei strandees in Japan, see Naoko Shibusawa, *America's Geisha Ally: Reimagining the Japanese Enemy* (Cambridge, MA: Harvard University Press, 2006), ch. 4.

In Japanese-language literature, many publications on the wartime Nisei experience offer both fictional accounts and pseudo-academic expositions based on the arbitrary reading of selected primary sources, questionable oral histories, and conjectures. Both forms of publications tend to narrate the Nisei experience from the standpoint of Japanese ethnocentrism that emphasizes the primacy of blood ties and hence the fundamental Japaneseness of Nisei. Yamasaki Toyoko's novel, *Futatsu no sokoku* (*Two Homelands*: 1983, 2007), typifies this narrative scheme; that work (and a popular Japanese television program based on it) came under harsh criticism and were boycotted by Japanese Americans in the mid-1980s, since it portrayed the national allegiance of many wartime Nisei as being more tightly aligned to their blood homeland than to their birth country. On this controversy, see Jin, *Citizens, Immigrants, and the Stateless*, pp. 85–92, 107–13; and http://encyclopedia.densho.org/Two_Homelands_(book) accessed on July 21, 2025.

41. General Meeting of the Nisei Association of Nippon, "Resolution," and Sen Nishiyama, "From Membership Drive Committee," both in *Reimei* 1: p. 1 and pp. 32–33 (English section). The quote is from p. 32 of the second source.
42. "Araki Emphasizes Spirit of Pioneers," *Nippon Times*, June 8, 1943: p. 3.
43. On the involvement of Nisei in Japan's propaganda and intelligence work, see Matsumoto Takizō, "Daitōa Sensō to Amerika umare Dai-Nisei no dōkō," *Zaisei* 7, no. 12 (1942): pp. 58–60; Sawada Miki, *Kuroi hada to shiroi kokoro* (Tokyo: Nihon Keizai Shinbunsha, 1963), p. 136; Masayo Duus, *Tokyo Rose: Orphan of the Pacific*, translated by Peter Duus (New York: Kodansha USA, 1979), pp. 64–69; Murayama Tamotsu, *Amerika Nisei* (Tokyo: Jiji Tsūshinsha, 1964), pp. 238, 249–50; "Imin hyakunen sanbun-no-ichi no butaiura 17," p. 10; and Kayoko Takeda, "Dual Citizen Interpreters: Consequences of Assigned Loyalties in the Aftermath of War," in *Interpreting Conflicts: A Comparative Framework*, edited by Marija Todorova and Lucia Ruiz Rosendo (Cham, Switzerland: Palgrave Macmillan, 2021), pp. 22–25. On US Nisei's involvement in the Office of Strategic Services' "black propaganda" and its intelligence programs, see Brian Masaru Hayashi, *American Spies: How Asian Americans Helped Win the Allied Victory* (New York: Oxford University Press, 2021).
44. On the question of "truthfulness" in the transpacific propaganda war, see Gilmore, *You Can't Fight Tanks with Bayonets*, p. 5.
45. Other prominent "Tokyo Roses" were Yoshie June Suyama from Vancouver, British Columbia, and Sumi Ruth Hayakawa from Los Angeles. Having worked for Japan's broadcast propaganda since before 1941, Suyama had been known as the "Nightingale of Nanking." She was a NAN board member. On the existence of multiple "Tokyo Roses" and other Nisei's work in Radio Tokyo propaganda, see Duus, *Tokyo Rose*, pp. 67–68. On the wartime work of Iva Toguri, see also Jin, *Citizens, Immigrants, and the Stateless*, pp. 124–25.
46. "Fighting Enemy's Propaganda," p. 14; and Torii, *Kokusaku tsūshinsha "Dōmei" no kōbō*, pp. 182, 184–86, 607–8.
47. See Murayama, *Amerika Nisei*, pp. 238, 249–50; "Imin hyakunen sanbun-no-ichi no butaiura 17," p. 10; and "Personals," *Reimei* 1: pp. 15–17 (English section).
48. Azuma Eiichirō, "Tokyo ni okeru Zainichi Hokubei Nisei no shidōsō to shakai soshiki keisei," in *Ekkyō suru "Nisei"*, edited by Yoshida Ryō (Tokyo: Gendai Shiryō Shuppan, 2016), pp. 28–29; and Sano, *Kyokai-den*, pp. 219–22.
49. See Matsumoto Takizō, "Kokusai senden no saikentō," *Senden* 8725 (May 1942): pp. 11–14; Matsumoto, "Daitōa Sensō to Amerika umare Dai-Nisei no dōkō," pp. 54–60; Matsumoto Takizō, "Nisei no tachiba yori mitaru tekikoku Amerika," *Bunmei Kyōkai nyūsu* 200 (June 20, 1943): pp. 1–26; Matsumoto Takizō, "Nisei yori mitaru teki Beikoku no jitsujō," *Nihon kōen* 676 (June 30, 1943): pp. 2–30; Matsumoto Takizō, "Beikoku oyobi Beikokujin," *Han-kōtsu* 44, no. 8 (1943): pp. 15–27; and Takizo Matsumoto, *The American Ventures in East Asia* (Tokyo: Meiji University Press, 1943). Some of the Japanese articles and booklets drew from his public lectures while others were based on his shortwave radio commentaries. Matsumoto's 1943 English publication provided a scholarly account of America's "fallacies" and "hypocrisy" by tracing its history of high-handed expansionist interventions in East Asian affairs and racist policies, including anti-Asian immigration exclusion. Such a history, of course, was juxtaposed against Japan's ongoing effort to defeat Anglo-Saxon supremacy and "liberate" Asia from their colonial domination. See Matsumoto, *The American Ventures in East Asia*. The quotes are from p. 7.
50. Matsumoto, "Daitōa Sensō to Amerika umare Dai-Nisei no dōkō," p. 57; and Matsumoto Takizō, "Daitōa-sen to Zaibei Nisei no shinkyō," *Bunmei Kyōkai nyūsu* 200 (June 20, 1943): p. 40.

51. Matsumoto, "Nisei yori mitaru teki Beikoku no jitsujō." This lecture was held in the heart of Tokyo on July 3, the two days after "the Day of National Humiliation (*kokujokubi*)," the Japanese equivalent to the Day of Infamy, commemorated since the implementation of the 1924 US Immigration Law that had resulted in the total exclusion of Japanese immigrants. And the timing was doubly suggestive, because Matsumoto's prediction of America's eventual defeat was made one day before the US Independence Day.
52. Ibid., pp. 5–9, 17, 27. See also Matsumoto, "Beikoku oyobi Beikokujin," pp. 20, 26–27. Another lecture that Matsumoto presented in May 1943 was also published in a booklet format, where his mother's teachings were described in more racially charged terms perhaps due to the deteriorating state of war. Instead of "must live strong," for example, the Issei supposedly told Matsumoto "not to be defeated by white beasts" and "to maintain a sense of superiority" to them. See Matsumoto, "Nisei no tachiba yori mitaru tekikoku Amerika," pp. 2–3. In another essay, Matsumoto described the idea of "Do not give in to whites; be strong" as his *father*'s dictum. See Matsumoto, "Beikoku oyobi Beikokujin," p. 19.
53. Historian Yuji Ichioka has documented the life of Kazumaro Buddy Uno, a California-born Nisei who edited English propaganda newspapers and magazines in Shanghai for the Japanese army and produced reportage on the fall of Corregidor as a war correspondent. See Ichioka, "The Meaning of Loyalty," pp. 153–56, 168–70. On Uno's war reportage, see Kazumaro Uno, *Corregidor, Isle of Delusion* (Shanghai: Mercury Press, 1942); and Uno Kazumaro, *Korehidoru saigo no hi*, translated by Shibata Kenjirō and Mochizuki Motoo (Tokyo: Seitoku Shoin, 1944).
54. His publications are Tatsuki Fujii, *Singapore Assignment* (Tokyo: Nippon Times, 1943); and Fujii Tatsuki, *Shōnan sōseiki* (Tokyo: Takubundō, 1943). On his short biography, see Fujii, *Shōnan sōseiki*, "chosha shōkai" (no pagination); John Lim, "Japanese Journalist Caught in the Whirlpool of War," *Singapore Business Times*, ca. 1985, in folder 2, box 84, JARP-Ichioka; and Kenmotsu, "The Forgotten Nisei," p. A-5.
55. See Fujii, *Singapore Assignment*; and Fujii, *Shōnan sōseiki*. In the English version, neither Introduction nor Epilogue discusses much about "Nisei," either as a reference point of his experience or a general topic. In its Japanese counterpart, those two sections are full of such references and topics, including the story of Fujii's own life portrayed as a "Nisei" (see, for example, p. 253). *Singapore Assignment* was comprised of the newspaper columns published earlier in the *Nippon Times* between April and June 1943. Its Nisei news editor Goro Murata was Fujii's old friend, and the former facilitated the publication of the latter's original essays and then a compilation of them as an English propaganda publication. The Japanese version was handled by the Dōmei News.
56. Fujii, *Shōnan sōseiki*, pp. 3–23, 257. The quote is from p. 257.
57. See Kitō Itsuko, *Hawai-shi monogatari* (Tokyo: Tōtō Shoseki, 1943), "jo."
58. Both Nisei were recent arrivals from Hawai'i to Japan. Having graduated from the University of Hawaii in 1939, for example, Miike came to his ancestral land "just before the war," according to historian John J. Stephan. See Stephan, *Hawaii under the Rising Sun*, p. 143. Kito held a position as a clerk/typist at the foreign ministry, and Miike was a staffer at the *Japan (Nippon) Times.*
59. Miike Noboru, with Takahara Shirō, *Watashi no umareta Hawai* (Tokyo: Seitoku Shoin, 1942), pp. 1–9; and Stephan, *Hawaii under the Rising Sun*, pp. 143–44. On Miike, see also Jin, *Citizens, Immigrants, and the Stateless*, p. 117.
60. Miike, *Watashi no umareta Hawai*, pp. 9, 264–65, 268–69.
61. Miike, *Watashi no umareta Hawai*, pp. 268–69. See also Stephan, *Hawaii under the Rising Sun*, pp. 143–44.
62. See "Personals," p. 16.
63. Kitō, *Hawai-shi monogatari*. The quote is from "jo."
64. Ibid., "oboegaki" and pp. 2–3. See also Stephan, *Hawaii under the Rising Sun*, pp. 138–39. Like many other Nisei in Japan, Kito did (could) not return to Hawai'i after Japan's defeat. Yet, despite being an assimilated immigrant national in their ancestral land, she lived a life that was continuously entangled with her American background. Just as her cohorts did for survival and social mobility in postwar Americanized Japan, Kito took advantage of her command of English to work as a college professor at various institutions of higher education in the Tokyo area. She also authored a textbook series under the general title of "Living English Expressions for Your Conversation." By the 1960s, Kito emerged as one of the most popular radio instructors in Japan, teaching American colloquial English on a nationwide radio educational program called "English for Millions." Known to conclude her weekly broadcast always with this signature statement: "Aloha, until next Wednesday!," the Nisei woman still held Hawai'i

dear—so much so that her radio program and published textbooks were colored with references to the mid-Pacific islands. Kito's example was not an exception; other Nisei-turned Japanese maintained an enduring sense of connections to their beloved birthplace—the acute nostalgia that Miike had dared to articulate in his wartime propaganda book.

65. "Nisei in Imperial Forces Increase: Many Apply for Positions in Front," *Nippon Times*, September 11, 1943: p. 1. On similar news account for domestic and foreign audience, see *Asahi Shinbun*, January 15, 1943: p. 3; and "Activities of Nisei since War Lauded," p. 3. On personal stories of individual Nisei soldiers, see Jin, *Citizens, Immigrants, and the Stateless*, pp. 126–32.
66. "Nisei in Imperial Forces Increase."
67. Ibid.
68. See *Asahi Shinbun*, October 12, 1937: p. 11; ibid., July 29, 1938: p. 2; and ibid., October 11, 1940: p. 7. Prewar Japanese newspapers in Hawai'i appropriated the story of this Nisei as their own hero, since Japanese America was generally supportive of Japan's war against China until early 1940. See, for example, *Nippu Jiji*, October 12, 1937 (Japanese section), and October 13, 1937 (English section).
69. See "Muraoka Stresses Nisei's Role in War," *Nippon Times*, March 11, 1943: p. 3. On examples of this rhetoric that appeared in Japanese-language discourse, see *Asahi Shinbun*, May 1, 1942: p. 2; ibid., November 15, 1942: p. 3; and ibid., January 15, 1943: p. 3.
70. *Asahi Shinbun*, January 15, 1943: p. 3; and "Tatakau gunkoku no Nisei: Tagiru goman-nin no chishio," *Reimei* 1: p. 12 (Japanese section).
71. *Asahi Shinbun*, March 24, 1942: p. 2.
72. See *Yomiuri Shinbun*, June 13, 1943: p. 3; and *Asahi Shinbun*, September 27, 1943: p. 2. The quote is from the latter source.
73. *Yomiuri Shinbun*, June 13, 1943: p. 3. On the Nisei mass enlistment, see *Asahi Shinbun*, July 25, 1943: p. 2; ibid., September 27, 1943: p. 2; ibid., November 2, 1943: p. 3; and November 15, 1943: p. 2.
74. See *Asahi Shinbun*, July 25, 1943: p. 2; ibid., September 27, 1943: p. 2; and "Warera mo rippana Nihonjinda," *Reimei* 1: pp. 14–15 (Japanese section). The quotes are from the first source.
75. See *Asahi Shinbun*, September 27, 1943: p. 2; ibid., November 2, 1943: p. 3, and November 15, 1943: p. 2; *Yomiuri Shinbun*, November 13, 1943: p. 3; and "Shinto Rites Conducted for Fallen Nisei Heroes," *Nippon Times*, October 31, 1944: p. 3.
76. See *Asahi Shinbun*, September 27, 1943: p. 2.
77. "Shinto Rites Conducted for Fallen Nisei Heroes."

Chapter 2

1. "Japanese-American 'Yanks,'" *New York Times*, January 30, 1943: p. 14.
2. See Takashi Fujitani, *Race for Empire: Koreans as Japanese and Japanese as Americans during World War II* (Berkeley: University of California Press, 2011), pp. 206–36; and Ellen D. Wu, *The Color of Success: Asian Americans and the Origins of the Model Minority* (Princeton: Princeton University Press, 2014), pp. 72–110.
3. Elmer Davis to the President, October 2, 1942, in microfilm reel 3, Papers of the US Commission on the Wartime Relocation and Internment of Civilians.
4. O[scar]. N. Solbert, "Basis for a Detailed Plan for Propaganda into the Japanese Empire," May 13, 1942, p. 18, in box 5, OWI-HRPWB. See also Fujitani, *Race for Empire*, pp. 99–100, 409n53.
5. O[scar]. N. Solbert, "Japan Plan," May 23, 1942, p. 34, in box 5, OWI-HRPWB. On this document, see also Takashi Fujitani, "The Reischauer Memo: Mr. Moto, Hirohito, and Japanese American Soldiers," *Critical Asian Studies* 33, no. 3 (2001): pp. 387–88.
6. Office of War Information (with War Relocation Authority), "Japanese Relocation," November 1943. On a good synopsis of the film, see Abé Mark Nornes, "Japanese Relocation," in *The Japan/America Film Wars: WWII Propaganda and Its Cultural Contexts*, edited by Abé Mark Nornes and Fukushima Yukio (Chur, Switzerland: Harwood Academic Publishers, 1994), pp. 216–17.
7. On these test cases and circumstances surrounding them, see Peter Irons, *Justice at War: The Story of the Japanese-American Internment Cases* (Berkeley: University of California Press, 1983).
8. Clayton R. Koppes and Gregory D. Black, *Hollywood Goes to War: How Politics, Profits, and Propaganda Shaped World War II Movies* (New York: Free Press, 1987), pp. 72–81; and "Little Tokyo USA," Twentieth-Century Fox, 1942, in Motion Picture Collection, UCLA Film and Television Archive.

9. See, for example, "Kindness to Alien Japs Proves Poor Policy," *Los Angeles Times*, December 8, 1942: p. 4; and Warren B. Francis, "Manzanar Arson Cases Disclosed: Strict Control over Japs in Their Centers Demanded in Congress," *Los Angeles Times*, December 9, 1942: p. 1.
10. On the Manzanar incident and varied narratives of the incident, see Michi Nishiura Weglyn, *Years of Infamy: The Untold Story of America's Concentration Camps* (New York: William Morrow, 1976), pp. 121–32; Brian Masaru Hayashi, *Democratizing the Enemy: The Japanese American Internment* (Princeton: Princeton University Press, 2004), pp. 107–47, esp. 134–36; Arthur A. Hansen and David A. Hacker, "The Manzanar Riot: An Ethnic Perspective," *Amerasia Journal* 2, no. 2 (1973): pp. 112–57; and Lon Kurashige, "Resistance, Collaboration, and Manzanar Protest," *Pacific Historical Review* 70, no. 3 (2001): pp. 387–417.
11. See "Army Halts Rioting by Coast Japanese," *New York Times*, December 7, 1942: p. 16; and "Troops Called to End Riots at Manzanar," *Los Angeles Times*, December 7, 1942: p. 1.
12. On a rare example of reports on loyal Nisei in Manzanar, see "Japanese Boy Scouts Saved Flag in Riot," *New York Times*, December 10, 1942: p. 18. In the ensuing weeks, the press generally published contrary stories of Japanese American disloyalty, embellished with discussions of public demands for stricter control of inmates.
13. See War Relocation Authority (hereafter WRA), *WRA: A Story of Human Conservation* (Washington, DC: GPO, 1946), p. 50. The quote is from Miike Noboru, with Takahara Shirō, *Watashi no umareta Hawai* (Tokyo: Seitoku Shoin, 1942), p. 265.
14. On the Japanese coverage of the incident, see Takamoto Hosokawa, "2 Japanese Shot to Death by US Troops at Mansana [sic]," *Nippon Times*, November 21, 1943: p. 1; and also Takamoto Hosokawa, "Harrowing Trials Are Told of Japanese in Americas," *Nippon Times*, November 16, 1943: p. 1. As the title shows, Japanese propagandists could not even give the right spelling of the Manzanar camp, which suggests how unfamiliar they must have been to the incident.
15. See WRA, *WAR*, p. 50. The WRA brass later expressed how relieved they were that "the incident provoked no particular reaction from the Japanese authorities and apparently went almost unnoticed," even though they were initially greatly concerned if the enemy might interpret and propagate the US suppression as "an attempt at mass murder."
16. The quotes are from WRA, *WRA*, p. 50.
17. Ibid., pp. 50–53. On JACL's views, see Mike Masaoka to Dillon Myer, January 14, 1943, in box 559, Entry 16, RWRA. On WRA Director Myer's "symbiotic relations" with Mike Masaoka, see Richard Drinnon, *Keeper of the Concentration Camps: Dillon S. Myer and American Racism* (Berkeley: University of California Press, 1989), pp. 72–73.
18. WRA, *WRA*, pp. 50–57.
19. On this fabricated reason, see War Department, *Final Report: Japanese Relocation from the West Coast, 1942* (Washington, DC: GPO, 1943), pp. 8–10, esp. p. 9. For a politico-legal context of why this fabrication took place, see also Irons, *Justice at War*, pp. 195–218.
20. See James C. McNaughton, *Nisei Linguists: Japanese Americans in the Military Intelligence Service during World War II* (Washington, DC: Department of the Army, 2006), pp. 23–28.
21. Roger Dingman, *Deciphering the Rising Sun: Navy and Marine Corps Codebreakers, Translators, and Interpreters in the Pacific War* (Annapolis, MD: Naval Institute Press, 2009), esp. pp. 1–23.
22. This statement, widely distributed as a 20 × 28 "OWI Poster No. 75," was initially a part of the letter from the President to the Secretary of War. See Franklin D. Roosevelt to Mr. Secretary [Henry Stimson], February 1, 1943, in folder: "War Relocation Authority (WRA)," OF 4849, FDRL.
23. On Davis's heavy involvement, see Tom Coffman, *The Island Edge of America: A Political History of Hawai'i* (Honolulu: University of Hawaii Press, 2003), pp. 86–87.
24. "Japanese-American 'Yanks.'"
25. "War Relocation Authority," ca. 1943, in box 2, OWI-RND.
26. Ibid.
27. "Operational Report," February 21, 1945, p. 2, in box 8, OWI-HRPWB. On the racial antagonism of local US military and OSS commanders, like Joseph Stilwell and Carl Eifler in the CBI Theater, see Brian Masaru Hayashi, *Asian American Spies: How Asian Americans Helped Win the Allied Victories* (New York: Oxford University Press, 2021), pp. 36–37. Eifler was said to have refrained from recruiting Nisei agents for his OSS outfit, which may explain why the OWI was the only US agency that capitalized on loaned Nisei MIS agents in the CBI Theater.
28. On an example of this silence in Issei repatriates' reportage, see Aoki Hisa, *Teia-maru no hōkoku* (Tokyo: Maeda Shobō, 1944).

29. Japan had good access to the news from the Tule Lake Segregation Center, because the inmates there were deemed "pro-Japan," hence accorded the treatment of war prisoners. Diplomats from a neutral power often visited the camp for inspections on behalf of the Japanese government. A large number of official reports from the Spanish consul in San Francisco are available at Japan's foreign ministry archives. On typical Japanese press reports of US "atrocities" in Tule Lake, see "Oppressive Acts by US at Tule Lake Are Bared," and "American Shooting of Nippon Internee Scored by Okazaki," *Nippon Times*, November 25, 1943, and May 27, 1944, respectively.
30. Clarence R. Harbert and A. B. Caldwell, "Memorandum for Colonel Miller," August 11, 1944, p. 2, in folder 4, box 1737, Entry 480: Subversive Organizations, Personnel Security Division, ROPMG-JABGF.
31. Solbert, "Japan Plan," p. 34. See also "Long-Range Policy Directive for Japan," ca. 1943, p. 7, in box 110, OWI-ROPC. Takashi Fujitani has examined the convoluted policy-making process based on this general directive. See Fujitani, *Race for Empire*, pp. 96–108.
32. On this point, see also Fujitani, "The Reischauer Memo," pp. 391–93.
33. On the most accepted narrative, see the Commission on the Wartime Relocation and Internment of Civilians, *Personal Justice Denied: The Report of the Commission on the Wartime Relocation and Internment of Civilians* (Seattle: University of Washington Press, 1997), pp. 185–212, 253–60. On the JACL's involvement in the construction of the Nisei soldier trope, see Wu, *The Color of Success*, pp. 78–84.
34. See Mike Masaoka, with Bill Hosokawa, *They Call Me Moses Masaoka: An American Saga* (New York: William Morrow, 1987), pp. 55–181, esp. p. 51. On a critical analysis of Masaoka's role, see Wu, *The Color of Success*, pp. 75–78; and Fujitani, *Race for Empire*, pp. 183–91.
35. "Jap-American Soldiers Decorated," *Los Angeles Times*, January 3, 1945: p. 6.
36. "Nisei Soldiers Helped Rescue Lost Battalion," *Los Angeles Times*, November 7, 1944: p. 5.
37. On Uno, see Yuji Ichioka, "The Meaning of Loyalty: The Case of Kazumaro Buddy Uno," in Yuji Ichioka, *Before Internment: Essays in Prewar Japanese American History*, edited by Gordon H. Chang and Eiichiro Azuma (Stanford: Stanford University Press, 2006), pp. 153–79.
38. See Bill Hosokawa, *Out of the Frying Pan* (Boulder: University Press of Colorado, 1998), pp. 14–23, 48–54; and Eric L. Muller, *Free to Die for Their Country: The Story of the Japanese American Draft Resisters in World War II* (Chicago: University of Chicago Press, 2001), pp. 64–99, esp. pp. 81–82. Hosokawa's autobiography leaves off many aspects of his life experiences that look too controversial or unsuited for a grand narrative of Nisei patriotism and victimhood.
39. On this aspect of prewar Nisei migration to Japan, see Eiichiro Azuma, *Between Two Empires: Race, History, and Transnationalism in Japanese America* (New York: Oxford University Press, 2005), ch. 6.
40. On an analysis of the writings of Hosokawa and Uno in Shanghai, see Greg Robinson, *The Great Unknown: Japanese American Sketches* (Boulder: University Press of Colorado, 2016), pp. 67–77.
41. John Lim, "Japanese Journalist Caught in the Whirlpool of War," *Singapore Business Times*, 1985, in folder 2, box 84, JARP-Ichioka; and Richard T. Kenmotsu, "The Forgotten Nisei," *Pacific Citizen*, December 19–26, 1975: p. A-5.
42. Ichioka, "The Meaning of Loyalty," p. 165.
43. Takashi Fujitani, "*Go for Broke*, the Movie: Japanese American Soldiers in US National, Military, and Racial Discourses," in *Perilous Memories: The Asia-Pacific War(s)*, edited by T. Fujitani, Geoffrey M. White, Lisa Yoneyama (Durham: Duke University Press, 2001), pp. 257–58; and also Fujitani, *Race for Empire*, pp. 182–85. The quote is from the first source.
44. In addition to the OWI/MIS campaigns, OSS carried out its own counterparts with a little over two hundred Japanese American agents. See Hayashi, *Asian American Spies*.
45. McNaughton, *Nisei Linguists*, preface, pp. 207–14; and Hayashi, *Asian American Spies*, pp. 93–111.
46. "Long-Range Policy Directive for Japan," ca. 1943, p. 1.
47. On wartime Kibei experience, see Michael R. Jin, *Citizens, Immigrants, and the Stateless: A Japanese American Diaspora in the Pacific* (Sanford: Stanford University Press, 2021), pp. 56–83.
48. McNaughton, *Nisei Linguists*, pp. 13–28, 33–37, 208.
49. [Kenneth D. Ringle], "Japanese in America: The Problem and the Solution," *Harper's Magazine* 185 (1942): p. 492. On positive evaluations of Kibei's work by an OWI leader, see

Lawrence E. Davies, "Directed to Tokyo," *New York Times*, April 1, 1945. The name of the author may have been a pseudonym of Clarence A. Davies, chief of the news and features division of the OWI Overseas Branch in San Francisco, who oversaw the operation of propaganda broadcast against Japan and many Nisei/Kibei staffers for it.

50. McNaughton, *Nisei Linguists*, pp. 10–11, 98–102; and H. B. White, "Intelligence Report: Japan and Manchuria, Who's Who in Japan," July 4, 1945, pp. 2–4, in box 7, DNONI-SECS.
51. See Edward W. Barrett to All members of the (OWI) Overseas Branch, September 12, 1945, in folder 1, box 1, RSRH-Hoover; and Richard S. R. Hubert, "The Value of an Information Service," ca. late 1945, in folder 3, box 1, RSRH-Hoover.
52. McNaughton, *Nisei Linguists*, pp. 126–27, 207–12, 289.
53. Ibid., pp. 126–27, 209, 289–90; Karl G. Yoneda, *Gambatte: Sixty-Year Struggle of a Kibei Worker* (Los Angeles: UCLA Asian American Studies Center, 1983); pp. 154–61; and Greg Robinson, *The Unsung Great: Stories of Extraordinary Japanese Americans* (Seattle: University of Washington Press, 2020), pp. 82–85.
54. John Weckerling to Carlisle C. Dusenbury, December 31, 1941, p. 4, in folder 1, box 282, CROLSTF-ODI. See also McNaughton, *Nisei Linguists*, pp. 28–31, 51–53, 146–47.
55. See Herbert Passin, *Encounter with Japan* (Tokyo: Kodansha International, 1982), p. 178.
56. McNaughton, *Nisei Linguists*, p. 289. On Yoneda's own recollections of his MIS/OWI work at Ledo, see Yoneda, *Gambatte*, pp. 154–61, esp. pp. 154–56. Yoneda's propaganda narratives came under the severe criticisms of Chinese communist propagandists—led by exiled Japanese communists and prisoners of war—in Yenan. The problems included the use of "high-class" and/or "highly politicized" languages and expressions that would put off ordinary Japanese soldiers of rural origin. See Yamagiwa Akira, "Bei Senji Jōhōkyoku (OWI) no 'En'an hōkoku': Yenan Reports by the Office of War Information (OWI), USA," *Nishōgakusha Daigaku kokusai seikei ronshū* 8 (March 25, 2000): pp. 12–15.
57. OWI-Psychological Warfare Team (PWT), "Tactical Propaganda against Japanese Troops: A Report of Propaganda Techniques Developed during the 1944-45 North Burma Campaign," January 15, 1945, p. 9, in box 404, OWI-BOICF.
58. R. G. Fergusson, "Psychological Warfare," January 10, 1945, p. 2, enclosed in "Washington Weekly Intelligencer" nos. 27 and 28, January 27, 1945, and February 3, 1945, respectively, in box 444, OWI-FMAD.
59. Yoneda, *Gambatte*, pp. 154–55. Kenny Yasui, another well-known member of the Assam Nisei MIS group, was a 1935 graduate of Waseda University in Tokyo.
60. Ibid., pp. 155–56.
61. Fergusson, "Psychological Warfare," p. 8.
62. OWI-PWT, "The Assam POW Group," February 23, 1945, p. 4, in box 403, OWI-BOICF.
63. Ibid.; see McNaughton, *Nisei Linguists*, p. 290; and Allison B. Gilmore, *You Can't Fight Tanks with Bayonets: Psychological Warfare against the Japanese Army in the Southwest Pacific* (Lincoln: University of Nebraska Press, 1998), pp. 142–43.
64. See OWI-PWT, "Tactical Propaganda against Japanese Troops," p. 11.
65. US Senate, Subcommittee to Investigate the Administration of the Internal Security Act and Other Internal Security Laws of the Committee on the Judiciary, *The Amerasia Papers: A Clue to the Catastrophe of China*, vol. 2 (Washington, DC: Government Printing Office, 1970), p. 1747. See also Joint Chiefs of Staff, "Plan to Permit Friendly Japanese to Organize for Psychological Warfare against Japanese Militarism (JCS 1351)," May 16, 1945, p. 6, in microfilm reel 5, RJCF-PT. Emmerson was also greatly impressed by the massive scale and success of Chinese communist propaganda which drew upon the integral work of reoriented POWs. See Yamagiwa, "Bei Senji Jōhōkyoku (OWI) no 'En'an hōkoku,'" pp. 8–17.
66. See McNaughton, *Nisei Linguists*, pp. 212, 405; report by Neil D. Brown, March 28, 1945, p. 5, in box 8, OWI-HRPWB; and Richard S. R. Hubert, "The O.W.I. Saipan Operation," ca. February 1946, in folder 3, box 1, RSRH-Hoover. In Kunming, civilian OWI linguist Tatsuo Arthur Miyakawa took the editorship of a Japanese-language propaganda newspaper series, which the local OWI chief desired to make "the largest unpaid net circulation of any Japanese newspaper in China."
67. Initially, US propagandists prioritized propagandizing enemy combat soldiers rather than Japanese civilians due to tactical difficulties. With the increase of Nisei MIS linguists on the Pacific battlefront after mid-1943, US commanders also desired to take living prisoners in order to extract vital military information, even though most American soldiers on the ground preferred to see "dead Japs." See Combined Chiefs of Staff, "Anglo-American Outline Plan for

Psychological Warfare against Japan," May 21, 1944, pp. 7–11, in microfilm reel 5, RJCF-PT. On the problem of allied soldiers' reluctance to take Japanese captives alive, see "Psychological Warfare," New Delhi, September 28, 1944, pp. 6–7, in box 391, OWI-BOICF. As the occupation of Japan looked increasingly imminent, the military intelligence brass anticipated that the POWs would be presented as a poignant example of US benevolence to the vanquished. Another potential benefit was that some POWs might serve as a native vanguard of pro-US reforms once they were returned home with the reconditioned mindset. See Andre Pacatte to Kenneth Mann, "Draft for Policy on Japanese Propaganda," March 24, 1945, pp. 1–2, in box 602, folder 18, OSS-CF; and Joint Chiefs of Staff, "Plan to Permit Friendly Japanese to Organize for Psychological Warfare against Japanese Militarism," May 16, 1945, pp. 6–7. On a study of Japanese POWs, see Ulrich Straus, *The Anguish of Surrender: Japanese POWs of World War II* (Seattle: University of Washington Press, 2003).

68. See Hubert, "The O.W.I. Saipan Operation" and "Number and Quantity of Each Leaflet and Newspaper Produced by OWI on Saipan, May 20 to August 15, 1945," in folder 2, box, RSRH-Hoover.
69. See "Leaflet Reactions of Japanese PW," New Delhi, June 5, 1945, in box 390, OWI-BOICF; "Directive for Political Warfare against the Japanese," ca. June 5, 1944, in box 228, OWI-GIDCIR; and "Preliminary Plan: Leaflet Campaign against Japan," ca. spring 1945, in ibid. On these major themes, see also Gilmore, *You Can't Fight Tanks with Bayonets*, pp. 125–45.
70. "Special Directive on Handling of Stories of Japanese Atrocities," January 1944, p. 2, in box 110, OWI-ROPC. See also "PWB Algiers," January 24, 1944, in ibid.; and Koji Ariyoshi, "Japanese Militarists' False Propaganda about American Atrocities," November 29, 1944, pp. 4–5, in box 445, OWI-FMAD.
71. See *Jisei* (June 24, 1944), with "Information Sheet on Leaflet OWI/CBI *Jisei* #17," July 29, 1944, in box 403, OWI-BOICF.
72. *Makoto* (November 24, 1944), with "Serial Number 2035," undated, in microfilm reel 37, MIP. This newspaper was prepared in Honolulu and then revised and printed in Saipan before B-29 bombers dropped over Japan. The head of OWI's Saipan outfit noted: "As was evident, the paper proved one of our best forms of propaganda. The purpose of Makoto was to infiltrate Japan with the true news of Allied victories on all fronts, thus encouraging an attitude of defeat among the Japanese people." See Hubert, "The O.W.I. Saipan Operation," p. 29.
73. See *Rakkasan Nyūsu* (June 23, 1945), p. 2, with "Newspaper '*Rakkasan Nyūsu*,' June 23, 1945," undated, in box 370 (new box number 3), OWI-BOICF. On the report of medals awarded to Nisei war heroes, see *Hawai Shūhō* (January 5, 1945), with "Serial Number 2055," undated, in microfilm reel 37, MIP. On *Rakkasan Nyūsu*, see also Gilmore, *You Can't Fight Tanks with Bayonets*, pp. 33, 110, 142, 171–72.
74. McNaughton, *Nisei Linguists*, pp. 212, 337, 382; and also see Gilmore, *You Can't Fight Tanks with Bayonets*, pp. 143–44. A joint operation with the Australian Army, the ATIS was a part of the G-2/MIS. Towards the end of the war, other sites of leaflet production included Honolulu and Saipan. On Saipan, see John L. Burns, Jr., "Monthly Narrative Report July 1945, Publication Division," ca. August 1945, in box 9, OWI-HRPWB; and Hubert, "The O.W.I. Saipan Operation." Production of Japanese-language propaganda radio programs was also carried out in Honolulu as well as OWI-OB's Japan division headquarters in San Francisco. See "Translation Section, Monthly Narrative Report July 1945," ca. August 1945, in ibid.; Davies, "Directed to Tokyo"; and Hubert, "The O.W.I. Saipan Operation," esp. pp. 4–8.
75. *Rakkasan Nyūsu* (August 11, 1945), with "Newspaper '*Rakkasan Nyūsu*,' August 11, 1945," in box 370 (new box number 3), OWI-BOICF.
76. *Rakkasan Nyūsu* (April 7, 1945), with "Newspaper '*Rakkasan Nyūsu*,' April 7, 1945," in box 370 (new box number 3), OWI-BOICF. The attached English description of the newspaper notes: "Picture lay-out of Manzanar Relocation Center showing happy normal life of interned families of Japanese descent."
77. United Newsreel, "Build Model Towns for Interned Japs" (1942), at https://www.youtube.com/watch?v=05NxNgtRn1U (viewed on July 22, 2025).
78. *Rakkasan Nyūsu* (April 7, 1945).
79. Prints of handwritten Japanese letters, April 5, 1945, with "Serial Number 535," undated, in microfilm reel 37, MIP.
80. "Washington Weekly Coordinator Number 48," June 22, 1945, in box 9, OWI-HRPWB. It featured a handwritten letter from a young Nisei girl in Hawaiʻi. See also "A Japanese POW's Evaluation of a Group of Honolulu Leaflets," New Delhi, August 11, 1945, p. 3, in box 390, OWI-BOICF.

81. Psychological Warfare Branch, OMS GHQ, "Preliminary Plan: Leaflet Campaign against Japan," ca. June–July 1945, p. 8, in box 228, OWI-GIDCIR.
82. "Long-Range Policy Directive for Japan," ca. 1943, pp. 4, 7.
83. All quotes are from Pacatte to Mann, p. 1.
84. For example, the aforementioned OSS policy planner cited Emmerson's observations extensively. See Pacatte to Mann.
85. Statistics compiled by the author from "OSS Personal List," vols. 1–2, Textual Material Research Room, NARA II. OSS-RAB had nineteen Japanese staff. On the involvement of Japanese Americans in OSS-MB and OSS-RAB, see Hayashi, *Asian American Spies*, pp. 93–111, 135–54.
86. See Hayashi, *Asian American Spies*, pp. 11–12.
87. Pacatte to Mann, pp. 1–2.
88. See K[enneth]. D. Mann to OSS Director, "Plan to Permit Friendly Japanese to Organize for Psychological Warfare against Japanese Militarism," June 4, 1945; and H. S. Little to Mr. Simpson, "Issei-Nissei (sic) for State Department Project," July 5, 1945, both in folder 18, box 602, OSS-CF. In the first source, Emmerson is cited as being "primarily responsible for this development."
89. See "Special Directive on Handling of Stories of Japanese Atrocities," p. 2; and "Basic Military Plan for Psychological Warfare against Japan with Appendices and Minutes of the Conference on Psychological Warfare against Japan," Manila, May 7–8, 1945, p. 22, in box 5, OWI-HRPWB. The quote is from the first source.
90. "Report from Captured Personnel and Material Branch," April 23, 1945, pp. 4–5, in box 229, OWI-GIDCIR. On the planning of the special broadcast to Nisei in Japan, see also Am[erican] Embassy, Chungking, to OWI, May 14, 1945, in box 110, OWI-ROPC.
91. [John K. Emmerson], "An International Organization of Japanese," February 22, 1945, in 1192-PR-6 (microfiche), DS-RHN; "Psychological Warfare against the Japanese," New Delhi, April 20, 1944, in box 228, OWI-GIDCIR; and Mann to OSS Director, "Plan to Permit Friendly Japanese to Organize for Psychological Warfare against Japanese Militarism." Earlier in May 1942, US army propagandists contemplated the formation of "a Free Japanese Corps of Japanese subjects…within the United States." But this idea was dropped from the official "Japan Plan" of May 23. See also Fujitani, "The Reischauer Memo," pp. 388–89.
92. On an example of his widely circulated report from Assam, see John K. Emmerson, "Psychological Warfare against the Japanese," February 29, 1944, enclosed in "Outpost Report," April 20, 1944, in box 228, OWI-GIDCIR. See also John K. Emmerson, *The Japanese Thread: A Life in the US Foreign Service* (New York: Holt, Reinhart and Winston, 1978), pp. 26–240; Yoneda, *Gambatte*, pp. 153–54; and Yamagiwa, "Bei Senji Jōhōkyoku (OWI) no 'En'an hōkoku,'" pp. 10–17.
93. On the instrumentalist thinking of white Japanese hands based on the presumption of racial sameness, see Fujitani, *Race for Empire*, p. 107.
94. Emmerson, "Psychological Warfare against the Japanese," February 29, 1944. On the national character discourse produced by wartime Japan experts and academicians, see John W. Dower, *War without Mercy: Race and Power in the Pacific War* (New York: Pantheon, 1986), pp. 94–146.
95. [Emmerson], "An International Organization of Japanese," pp. 1–4. One year earlier, Emmerson had already shared this idea with the military leadership in his "long-range propaganda" plan for the postwar era. See Emmerson, "Psychological Warfare against the Japanese," p. 3. This proposal went through the process of revision and resubmission three times in the span of the next three weeks. See [John Emmerson], "Plan for the Formation of an Organization of Overseas Japanese for Political Warfare against Japan," February 28, 1945; "Plan to Permit Overseas Japanese to Organize for Political Warfare against Japan," March 8, 1945; and "Plan to Permit Overseas Japanese to Organize for Political Warfare against Japanese Militarism," March 14, 1945, all in 1192-PR-6 (microfiche), DS-RHN.
96. [Emmerson], "An International Organization of Japanese," p. 4.
97. See Joint Chiefs of Staff, "Plan to Permit Friendly Japanese to Organize for Psychological Warfare against Japanese Militarism (JSC 1351)," May 16, 1945; A. J McFarland and C. J. Moore (Joint Chiefs of Staff), "Organization of Friendly Japanese Nationals for Psychological Warfare," August 2, 1945; and "Enclosure (Draft): Memorandum for Director, Office of Strategic Services," in Joint Chiefs of Staff, "Organization of Friendly Japanese Nationals for Psychological Warfare," August 9, 1945; and also Joint Staff Planners, "Psychological Warfare against Japan," July 26, 1945, pp. 18–19, all in microfilm reel 5, RJCF-PT. Along the line of the

free Japanese movement, the OSS devised a separate project in July 1945, where Nisei and Issei agents were recruited to sneak into the Japanese home islands to broker Japanese surrender. With a view to preparing for Operation Olympic (invasion of southern Japan) scheduled for November 1, 1945, the JCS was favorably disposed to OSS's proposal, forwarding it to the army and naval commanders in the Pacific Theater with a request for their comments on August 9, 1945—the day on which the second atomic bomb was dropped on Nagasaki. On this program, see A. J. McFarland and C. J. Moore (JCS), "Establishment of Intelligent Network and Subversive Activities in Japan (JCS 1452/1)," August 9, 1945, pp. 16, 21–23, in microfilm reel 8, RJCF-PT. Donovan's letter, dated July 18, 1945, is enclosed in this report as "Appendix B" (pp. 20–22). Brian Hayashi also documents this OSS proposal in his: *Asian American Spies*, pp. 140–41.

98. Pacatte to Mann, p. 3.

Chapter 3

1. Tom S. Shiinoki to Henry and Alice Kasai, December 9, 1945, in folder 2, box 109, JARP-Kasai.
2. Joe M. Takita to Alice Kasai, January 14, 1947, in folder 3, box 109, JARP-Kasai.
3. On representative works, see James C. McNaughton, *Nisei Linguists: Japanese Americans in the Military Intelligence Service during World War II* (Washington, DC: Department of the Army, 2006); Lyn Crost, *Honor by Fire: Japanese Americans at War in Europe and the Pacific* (Novato, CA: Presidio Press, 1994); Stanley Falk and Warren Tsuneishi, eds., *MIS in the War against Japan: Personal Experiences Related at the 1993 MIS Capital Reunion* (Washington, DC: Japanese American Veterans Association, 1995); "MIS in Japan," *Nikkei Heritage* 15, no. 1 (2003): pp. 4–18; Military Intelligence Service Association of Northern California (MIS NorCal) and National Japanese American Historical Society (NJAHS), eds., *The Pacific War and Peace: Americans of Japanese Ancestry in Military Intelligence Service, 1941 to 1952* (San Francisco: MIS NorCal and NJAHS, 1991); Military Intelligence Service Veterans Club of Hawaii, ed., *Secret Valor: MIS Personnel, World War II Pacific Theater, Pre-Pearl Harbor to Sept. 8, 1951* (Honolulu: MIS Veterans Club of Hawaii, 2002); and MIS-Northwest Association, *Unsung Heroes: The Military Intelligence Service Past-Present-Future* (Seattle: MIS-Northwest Association, 1996). Three film productions on Nisei linguists share similar storylines: "Fifty Years of Silence" (1992); "Prejudice and Patriotism" (1998); and "Uncommon Courage" (2000). On earlier and other references to Nisei linguists, see Bradford Smith, *Americans from Japan* (Philadelphia: J. B. Lippincott, 1948), pp. 324–28; Joseph D. Harrington, *Yankee Samurai: The Secret Role of Nisei in America's Pacific Victory* (Detroit: Harlo Press, 1979); Tad Ichinokuchi, ed., *John Aiso and the MIS: Japanese American Soldiers in the Military Intelligence Service, World War II* (Los Angeles: Military Intelligence Service Club of Southern California, 1988); and Bruce Henderson, *Bridge to the Sun: The Secret Role of the Japanese Americans Who Fought in the Pacific in World War II* (New York: Knopf, 2022).
4. McNaughton, *Nisei Linguists*, esp. p. 462. Propagated originally by Major General Charles Willoughby, chief of intelligence for General MacArthur's Command, this idea has been reproduced by many—both Japanese Americans and others. See, for example, Harry Fukuhara, "'America's Secret Weapon': MIS and the Occupation of Japan," *Nikkei Heritage* 15, no. 1 (2003): pp. 4–5; and MIS NorCal and NJAHS, *The Pacific War and Peace*, pp. 11, 85.
5. A vicious cycle of mythologizing is one unfortunate consequence of this development. Takemae Eiji's *Inside GHQ*, a seminal work on the American military government in occupied Japan, is a case in point in terms of how even serious historical studies unwittingly inherit contrived representations. Drawing on Bradford Smith's *Americans from Japan* and MIS-Northwest Association's *Unsung Heroes*, Takemae only offers unrealistically saintly depictions of Nisei linguists, whose "compassion towards the enemy" purportedly stood "in sharp contrast to the savagery displayed by [white] Americans and Japanese troops." See Takemae Eiji, *Inside GHQ: The Allied Occupation of Japan and its Legacy*, translated by Robert Ricketts and Sebastian Swann (London: Continuum, 2002), pp. 21, 571. To date, the only scholarly works that complicate, if not humanize, the experience of Nisei occupation troops and linguists are Tamotsu Shibutani, *The Derelicts of Company K: A Sociological Study of Demoralization* (Berkeley: University of California Press, 1978); and Monica Kim, *The Interrogation Rooms of the Korean War: The Untold History* (Princeton: Princeton University Press, 2019). Although Shibutani's book has been around for more than a few decades, it has been almost completely neglected. Albeit not about Nisei in occupied Japan, the following books provide less glorified

and more nuanced accounts of Asian American military service. See Franklin Odo, *No Sword to Bury: Japanese Americans in Hawai'i during World War II* (Philadelphia: Temple University Press, 2003); K. Scott Wong, *Americans First: Chinese Americans and the Second World War* (Cambridge, MA: Harvard University Press, 2005); Brian Masaru Hayashi, *Asian American Spies: How Asian Americans Helped Win the Allied Victories* (New York: Oxford University Press, 2021); Simeon Man, *Soldiering through Empire: Race and the Making of the Decolonized Pacific* (Berkeley: University of California Press, 2018); and Takashi Fujitani, *Race for Empire: Koreans as Japanese and Japanese as Americans during World War II* (Berkeley: University of California Press, 2011).

6. General Headquarters, Far East Command (GHQ FEC), "Operations of the Allied Translator and Interpreter Section GHQ, SWPA," vol. 5, Intelligence Series, p. 36, in box 686, RAGO-OPPT. ATIS was organized in September 1942 with GHQ in Australia, which later moved to Manila and then to Tokyo.
7. See McNaughton, *Nisei Linguists*, pp. 313, 432, 434; GHQ FEC, "Operations of the Allied Translator and Interpreter Section GHQ, SWPA," pp. 36, 77, appendix 3; and John Weckerling, "Japanese Americans Play Vital Role in United States Intelligence Service in World War Two" (1946), Part 4: "Recruitment," no pagination, reprinted in 1974, in box 48, folder 4, in MMMP. On the army language school, see Masaharu Ano, "Loyal Linguists: Nisei of World War II Learned Japanese in Minnesota," *Minnesota History* 45, no. 7 (1977): pp. 273–87.
8. Civil Affairs Division, "Aliens in Japan," ca. April 1947, p. 26, in folders 20–21, box 3429, GHQ/SCAP. The GHQ estimated the presence of about four thousand Nisei strandees, who would be considered as US citizens for administrative purposes. In addition, there were some 1,300 Nisei renunciants, and the vast majority of them sought to regain US citizenship after their deportation to postwar Japan. On their legal struggle, see John Christgau, "Collins versus the World: The Fight to Restore Citizenship to Japanese American Renunciants of World War II," *Pacific Historical Review* 65, no. 1 (1985): pp. 1–31.
9. On prewar US counter-intelligence activities on Japanese Americans, see Bob Kumamoto, "The Search for Spies: American Counterintelligence and the Japanese American Community, 1931–1942," *Amerasia Journal* 6, no. 2 (1979): pp. 45–75.
10. On the recruitment of Nisei informants in prewar California and incarceration camps, see Brian Masaru Hayashi, *Democratizing the Enemy: The Japanese American Internment* (Princeton: Princeton University Press, 2004), pp. 125–29, 149–51; and Peter Irons, *Justice at War: The Story of the Japanese-American Internment Cases* (Berkeley: University of California Press, 1993), pp. 79–80. In prewar Hawai'i, Sergeant Gero Iwai was the first Nisei recruit, who was ordered by the MIS to conduct surveillance over Hawai'i's Japanese in 1933. Seven years later, a local FBI agent also assembled "loyal" Nisei leaders to work for him in FBI surveillance on Japanese immigrant society. At the same time, in late 1940, the MIS in Hawai'i recruited two bilingual Nisei, Richard Sakakida and Arthur Komori, to infiltrate Japanese settlements in the Philippines. See James I. Muir to HQ Hawaiian Department, November 3, 1933, pp. 2–3, in box 3102; and "Check on American Citizens of Japanese Extraction," February 19, 1941, in box 3105, both items from MIDC. On Sakakida, see Wayne Kiyosaki, *A Spy in Their Midst, the World War II Struggle of a Japanese-American Hero: The Story of Richard Sakakida* (Lanham, MD: Madison Books, 1995).
11. Hayashi, *Democratizing the Enemy*, pp. 9–10, 17–43.
12. Franklin D. Roosevelt to Mr. Secretary [Henry Stimson], February 1, 1943, in folder: "War Relocation Authority (WRA)," OF 4849, FDRL.
13. Bradford Smith to Alan Cranston, "Mr. Warner's plan for training Japanese-Americans," January 5, 1943, pp. 1–2, in folder 2, box 1, Entry 1, OWI-ROWI. On the question of how OWI's opposition to anti-Nisei racism affected wartime foreign policies of the United States, see Justin Hart, "Making Democracy Safe for the World: Race, Propaganda, and the Transformation of US Foreign Policy during World War II," *Pacific Historical Review* 73, no. 1 (2004): pp. 79–80.
14. Elmer Davis to Joseph C. Grew, January 6, 1943, in folder 2, box 1, Entry 1, OWI-ROWI.
15. See a copy of Grew's letter, December 21, 1942, and Smith to Cranston, pp. 1–2, in ibid.
16. Smith to Cranston, p. 2. The emphasis was in the original quote.
17. Ibid.
18. Equally understandable was the original authorship of the OEM's strongly worded counterargument. The memorandum was put together by Bradford Smith, an OWI official attached to

the OEM, who later commanded an army of Nisei leaflet writers as the director of the OWI Honolulu office and published *Americans from Japan* (1948), one of the first books that celebrated the successful assimilation and loyalty of Nisei as full-fledged US citizens. Smith had an experience of working as a professor of English at several universities in prewar Japan. Thus, he might have held his own feeling of rivalry against foreign-service personnel specializing in Japan affairs. He even characterized the BFEA's letter as resembling a "Nazi theory of race." See Alan Cranston to Arthur Sweetser, January 5, 1943; and David to Grew, in folder 2, box 1, Entry 1, OWI-ROWI.

19. H. B. Lewis to Chief of Civil Affairs Division, Office of the Chief of Staff, "Training of Loyal Japanese-Americans for Civil Affairs Duties," September 24, 1943, in folder 31, box 1717, Entry 480, ROPMG-JABGF.
20. J. H. Hilldring to the Chief of Staff, "Training of Loyal Japanese-Americans for Civil Affairs Duties," August 27, 1943, in folder 30, box 1717, Entry 480, ROPMG-JABGF; and Office of the Provost Marshal General, "World War II: A Brief History," January 1946, p. 286, in box 31, RAS-HSRR.
21. See L. R. Forney to [George Veazey] Strong, "Training of Loyal Japanese-Americans for Civil Affairs Duties," September 3, 1943, in folder 10, box 1723, in Entry 480, ROPMG-JABGF; and also J. A. Ulio to Provost Marshal General, "Transfer of Clearance of American Citizens of Japanese Ancestry from the Assistant Chief of Staff, G-2, WDGS to the Provost Marshal General," July 25, 1944, in folder B, box 1717, Entry 480, ROPMG-JABGF.
22. Arthur B. Coldwell to Alton C. Miller, "Clearance of Military Personnel of Japanese Extraction for Civil Affairs Duties," August 24, 1945, in folder B, box 1717, Entry 480, ROPMG-JABGF; and John Weckerling to Commanding General, Army Service Forces, "Clearance of Americans of Japanese Americans for Positions of Trust," in folder 11, box 1729, Entry 480, ROPMG-JABGF.
23. See, for example, *Rafu Shimpo*, May 6, 1946, June 24, 1946 (Japanese section), March 6, 1947 (Japanese section), April 1, 1947, October 28, 1948, July 12, 1949, June 14, 1950, and September 15, 1951.
24. See McNaughton, *Nisei Linguists*, pp. 421–22; *Yomiuri Shinbun*, February 10, 1946; and Brenda L. Moore, *Serving Our Country: Japanese American Women in the Military during World War II* (New Brunswick, NJ: Rutgers University Press, 2003), pp. 124–31.
25. [Kenneth D. Ringle], "Japanese in America: The Problem and the Solution," *Harper's Magazine* 185 (1942): p. 492.
26. On the cultural essentialist idea of Nisei as the model minority, see Ellen D. Wu, *The Color of Success: Asian Americans and the Origins of the Model Minority* (Princeton: Princeton University Press, 2014), pp. 152–56, 162–80.
27. *Rafu Shimpo*, September 28, 1946 (Japanese section). Out of desperation, the army brass even attempted to find qualified individuals from the roster of the 442nd RCT and other Nisei replacement troops deployed in the European theater. To the officials' dismay, only a small fraction of these Americanized Nisei soldiers had the Japanese-language command sufficient to further receive special training necessary for occupation troops. This realization led to the abandonment of the initial plan to designate "elements of the 442nd RCT...as part of the Pacific Reserve." Subsequently, it was downgraded to a lukewarm policy of "permitting individuals of [the 442nd RCT] unit to volunteer for language duty in the Pacific Areas"—hardly a solution to the army's manpower problem in occupied Japan. See James S. McClendon to O. D. Brown, "Nisei Language Screening Team," August 3, 1945, with attached lists, in folder 4, box 301, Entry 208, CROLSTF-ODI; John E. Hull, "Report on 442nd Regimental Combat Team scheduled for Redeployment direct from Italy to Japan as Occupation Troops," August 24, 1945; and Robert P. Patterson to Saburo Kido, August 24, 1945, both in folder 1, box 1196, Entry 418, GR-SCGC.
28. Marion E. Nestor to Director, Provost Division, "Clearance of Americans of Japanese Ancestry for Positions of Trust" (Fred Y. Fujita), September 6, 1946, in folder 12, box 1729, Entry 480, ROPMG-JABGF.
29. Nestor to Director, Provost Division, "Clearance of Americans of Japanese Ancestry for Positions of Trust" (Hideichi Oshiro), September 26, 1946, in ibid.
30. Nestor to Director, Provost Division, "Clearance of Americans of Japanese Ancestry for Positions of Trust" (Susumu Sam Mori), December 21, 1946, in ibid.
31. Nestor to Director, Provost Division, "Clearance of Americans of Japanese Ancestry for Positions of Trust" (Takeshi Tanaka), June 8, 1946, in ibid.

32. Nestor to Director, Provost Division, "Clearance of Americans of Japanese Ancestry for Positions of Trust" (Tameo Kawabe), December 21, 1946, in ibid.
33. Tara Shioya, "The Conflict behind the Battle Lines," *San Francisco Chronicle*, September 24, 1995.
34. See McNaughton, *Nisei Linguists*, pp. 51, 147.
35. See Paul A. Gavan to Charles Willoughby, "Students for Military Intelligence Service Language School," November 4, 1946, p. 3, enclosed in "Military Intelligence Service Language School (MISLS) Data and Recommendations," ca. late 1946, in folder 4, box 287, Entry 208, CROLSTF-ODI. In August 1946, the War Department formalized a policy by which to promote the three-year enlistees to Private First Class upon entry into the MIS Language School. After completing half of their six-to-nine month studies there, the Nisei would advance to Technician Fifth Grade (T/5), and to Technician Fourth Grade (T/4) upon graduation. In this scheme, the Nisei enlistee's skilled training was deemed equivalent to one year of college education. But Japanese American linguists were still not of officer standing. See "Plan Promotion for Nisei GI Linguists at Monterey," *Rafu Shimpo*, August 2, 1946.
36. "Letter received by Miss S., a Japanese (American) college girl from Sgt. T., stationed at Australia with the USAAF," no date, in folder 3, box 2, CRF-Adams.
37. On Asian/Japanese plantation labor in Hawai'i's racially stratified sugar economy, see Moon-Kie Jung, *Reworking Race: The Making of Hawaii's Interracial Labor Movement* (New York: Columbia University Press, 2006), ch. 2; and Eileen Tamura, *Americanization, Acculturation, and Ethnic Identity: Nisei Generation in Hawaii* (Urbana: University of Illinois Press, 1994), esp. chs. 4 and 6. On the ethnic subordination of Issei and Nisei in prewar California economy, see John Modell, *The Economics and Politics of Racial Accommodation: The Japanese of Los Angeles 1900–1942* (Urbana: University of Illinois Press, 1977), pp. 94–172.
38. *Rafu Shimpo*, May 20, 1946 (Japanese section).
39. Kojiro F. Kawaguchi, "A Nisei Story: The Story of a Japanese American during World War II and the Occupation of Japan" (December 15, 2003), pp. 173–74, in box 28, Tsukiyama-JAVC.
40. Hatsumi Yamada to Charles B. Fahs, July 10, 1945, in folder 4, box 4, OSS-RAB.
41. Herbert Passin, *Encounter with Japan* (Tokyo: Kodansha International, 1982), pp. 178, 180.
42. Tally made by the author from E. Franklin, "Estimated Personnel Requirements 30 June and 31 Dec 1950," March 4, 1950, with enclosures "Strength Status Report" and Enemy Property Branch personnel chart, in folder 20, box 3659, Entry UD 1596, GHQ/SCAP. This Nisei attorney was James Adachi. Segregated from the Nisei and white American staff, the 126 native Japanese workers were all shoved into the CPC's lowest six categories of job/pay grades, where no US citizen workers (barring three female trainees) were classified.
43. Tally is made by the author from A[djutant] G[eneral] to G-1, "General Headquarters Far East Command Check Sheet, Rotation Criteria," August 15, 1951, in box 5090, Entry UD: 1647, GHQ/SCAP.
44. Takemae, *Inside GHQ*, p. 166; and McNaughton, *Nisei Linguist*, pp. 98–99.
45. See A[djutant] G[eneral] to G-1, "General Headquarters Far East Command Check Sheet, Rotation Criteria," pp. 1, 4–5.
46. McNaughton, *Nisei Linguists*, p. 447.
47. Ibid.
48. Ibid., pp. 442–45, 448–51; Takemae, *Inside GHQ*, pp. 153–59, 168–71, esp. 156, 159; and Kayoko Takeda, *Interpreting the Tokyo War Crimes Tribunal: A Sociopolitical Analysis* (Ottawa: University of Ottawa Press, 2010), esp. 52–66. On the organization and general functions of GHQ/SCAP, see Takemae, *Inside GHQ*, pp. 137–97.
49. Takemae, *Inside GHQ*, pp. 161–68; McNaughton, *Nisei Linguist*, pp. 98–99, 437–46; A[djutant] G[eneral] to G-1, "General Headquarters Far East Command Check Sheet, Rotation Criteria," pp. 1, 4–5; and A. Carly Buxton, *Unthinking Collaboration: American Nisei in Transwar Japan* (Honolulu: University of Hawaii Press, 2022), pp. 154–55. A notable exception was Lt. Colonel John Aiso, who had served as the MIS language school technical director and first instructor in 1942 and then as a top aide to Willoughby during the early phase of allied occupation. On Lt. Taro "Tom" Tsukahara of the Government Section, another "one of the small group of accomplished Japanese Americans working for GHQ," see Takemae, *Inside GHQ*, pp. 156–57.
50. Ōno Tatsuzō, *Amerika kara kita supaitachi* (Tokyo: Shin Nihon Shuppansha, 1965), pp. 30–32.
51. Bruce A. de Bourbon-Conde to Commanding Officer, 441st CIC Det., GHQ, "Recommendation for Appointment of Sgt. Kay K. Sasaki as WOJG," September 3, 1946, in folder 2, box 1, KKS-Hoover.

52. See the list of places and dates of Sasaki's service between 1944 and 1962, in folder 1, box 1, KKS-Hoover.
53. Charles G. Dorin to Commanding Officer, CIC Area 10, "Duties of Sasaki Kay K," July 21, 1947, in folder 2, box 1, KKS-Hoover.
54. Bruce A. de Bourbon-Conde to Commanding Officer, 441st CIC Det., GHQ, "Promotion of Seargent Kay K. Sasaki," September 5, 1946, folder 2, box 1, KKS-Hoover.
55. On some examples of career Nisei counter-intelligence agents, see Pamela Rotner Sakamoto, *Midnight in Broad Daylight: A Japanese American Family Caught between Two Worlds* (New York: Harper, 2016); and Bina Cady Kiyonaga, *My Spy: Memoir of a CIA Wife* (New York: William Morrow, 2000). See also n. 112 in Chapter 4.
56. John Weckerling, "Japanese Americans Play Vital Role in United States Intelligence Service in World War Two" (1946), Part 3: "Aiso Found in Motor Pool," no pagination, reprinted in 1974, in folder 4, box 48, MMMP.
57. GHQ FEC, "Operations of Military and Civil Censorship USAFFE/SWAP/AFPAC/FEC," vol. 10, Intelligence Series, p. 201, in folder 4, box 693, RAGO-OPPT. See also Hirano Kyoko, "The Occupation and Japanese Cinema," in *The Occupation of Japan: Arts and Culture*, edited by Thomas W. Burkman (Norfolk, VA: General Douglas MacArthur Foundation, 1988), p. 148.
58. Takita to Kasai. On another example of Nisei's own admission of incompetence, see Fukuhara, "'America's Secret Weapon,'" p. 5.
59. John K. Emmerson, *The Japanese Thread: A Life in the US Foreign Service* (New York: Holt, Rinehart and Winston, 1978), p. 268.
60. Moore, *Serving Our Country*, pp. 126–27. The quote is from p. 126.
61. GHQ FEC, "Operations of Military and Civil Censorship USAFFE/SWAP/AFPAC/FEC," p. 202. On the recruitment of Japanese and strandee staff for translation work, see Grant K. Goodman, *America's Japan: The First Year 1945–1946* (New York: Fordham University Press, 2005), pp. 44–51; Kayoko Takeda, "Dual Citizen Interpreters: Consequences of Assigned Loyalties in the Aftermath of War," in *Interpreting Conflicts: A Comparative Framework*, edited by Marija Todorova and Lucia Ruiz Rosendo (Cham, Switzerland: Palgrave Macmillan, 2021), pp. 28–29; and Kawaguchi, "A Nisei Story," pp. 166, 174–75.
62. GHQ FEC, "Operations of the Civil Intelligence Section, GHQ, FEC & SCAP," vol. 9, Intelligence Series (1), pp. 103–4, in box 692, RAGO-OPPT.
63. See "Repats Ousted from Japan Jobs," *Rafu Shimpo*, July 25, 1947; and "Seek Translators," *Rafu Shimpo*, January 31, 1949. The War Department asked the State Department to compile a report on the availability of Nisei in Japan for language work in November 1945. See P. R. (Acting US Political Advisor in Tokyo), "Nisei Language Personnel Residing in Japan," November 19, 1945, pp. 1–2, in box 1, DS-CGC. On Nisei strandees and renunciants working for GHQ, see also Morita Shigeru, "Zainichi Nisei, senzen, senchū, sengo," *Rafu Shimpo*, January 1, 1953: pp. B-11, B-12 (Japanese section).
64. Tsunoda Toshio, "Kaettekita Nisei, shiminken hōkisha jō," *Rafu Shimpo*, July 29, 1946; and Tamotsu Shibutani to Dorothy Swaine Thomas, May 1, 1946, in folder W 1.33:5, box 297 (BANC MSS 67/14 c), JERS-BL. The quotes are from the second source. See also Kawaguchi, "A Nisei Story," pp. 166–67, 174–77.
65. On the experience of renunciants in postwar Japan, see Eileen H. Tamura, *In Defense of Justice: Joseph Kurihara and the Japanese American Struggle for Equality* (Urbana: University of Illinois Press, 2013), pp. 135–42, esp. 136, 139.
66. See "Yūbin ken'etsu," *Mainichi Shinbun*, March 15, 2006; and Kawaguchi, "A Nisei Story," pp. 167, 175.
67. Takemae, *Inside GHQ*, p. 387.
68. See "Nisei Linguists Play Vital Role," *Nippon Times*, January 30, 1950. In his study, James C. McNaughton tells a story of Clarke H. Kawakami, who claimed credit for the English translation of massive war records prepared by a former Japanese army general. Yet, Kawakami's command of Japanese was known to be quite deficient despite his prewar experience in Japan, calling into question his ability to have translated the records. Most likely, the Nisei linguist played the role of overseer relative to native Japanese who did the actual work. This is yet another example of Nisei's taking credit for the work done by Japanese nationals, which scholars have later uncritically incorporated into their celebratory narratives on Nisei linguists. See McNaughton, *Nisei Linguists*, pp. 455–56; and Takemae, *Inside GHQ*, pp. 166, 597 (n36).

69. On Togasaki, see Azumi Suimei, "Zatsunen no kuni," *Nippon to Amerika* 21, no. 6 (1967), pp. 7–9; and Azuma Eiichirō, "Tokyo ni okeru Zainichi hokubei Nisei no shidōsō to shakai soshiki keisei," in *Ekkyō suru "Nisei"*, edited by Yoshida Ryō (Tokyo: Gendai Shiryō Shuppan, 2016), pp. 27–28.
70. Torii Hideharu, *Kokusaku tsūshinsha "Dōmei" no kōbō* (Tokyo: Kadensha, 2014), pp. 738, 753–54, 764; and Murayama Tamotsu, *Amerika Nisei* (Tokyo: Jiji Tsūshinsha, 1964), pp. 235–36. Other non-citizen Nisei also found employment at foreign news agencies after losing/quitting positions at Dōmei. Hawai'i-born Leslie Satoru Nakashima worked for United Press while Tatsuki John Fujii and Kay Kanemitsu Tateishi were staff writers of Associated Press.
71. On the collaboration of the Japanese American community and Japanese diplomats in pro-Japan publicity campaigns during the 1930s, see Eiichiro Azuma, *Between Two Empires: Race, History, and Transnationalism in Japanese America* (New York: Oxford University Press, 2005), pp. 171–82.
72. Komiya Hitoshi, "Miki Takeo josetsu," *Momoyama hōgaku* 22 (2013): pp. 11–14, 16–17.
73. Ibid., pp. 19–22; and "Service Center Tokyo" (ca. 1947), in folder Serve Center Tokyo, box 74, JCT-Hoover.
74. "Service Center Tokyo." For the same reason, the company describes the board members as having "long associations with... 'Nisei' people" instead of identifying themselves as such.
75. Komiya, "Miki Takeo josetsu," pp. 20, 23–24; and Sano Shin'ichi, *Kyokai-den: Shōriki Matsutarō to kagemusha-tachi no isseiki* (Tokyo: Bungei Shunjūsha, 1994), pp. 220, 383–86.
76. See, for example, "Service Center Tokyo," where he is mentioned as "Takizo Matsumoto, President (Harvard University)." On his speech at the Tokyo Harvard Club, see Hubert C. Armstrong letter, ca. June 1947, pp. 1–2, in folder 3, box 5, HCA-Hoover.
77. Komiya, "Miki Takeo josetsu," p. 17; and Sano, *Kyokai-den*, pp. 373–74. Matsumoto also worked closely with leaders of the Civil Education and Information (CIE) Section in the effort to democratize his "own" people. As early as October 1945, CIE viewed Matsumoto as an "official 'go-between' with the Physical Education Section of the (Japanese) Ministry of Education" because of his prewar work in relation to college football and baseball. When CIE launched a new project of compiling a 350-page comprehensive school textbook for the "Primer of Democracy" in 1947–48, Matsumoto joined it as one of the seventeen authors. Familiar with how US democracy worked on a grassroots level, he was assigned to a chapter on "an enlightened electorate," which emphasized the "basic importance of political literacy" and the "individual's responsibility for... his political opinions." See "Stopping instructions in Aeronautics," ca. December 1945, and "The revision of physical education and the elimination of *budo*," ca. December 1945, both in folder: staff studies (1945), box 51, JCT-Hoover; Howard Bell to Chief, Education Division, "Report of Activities," May 26, 1947, and Col. Nugent to Col. Bunker, "Primer of Democracy," December 30, 1948, both in folder: primer of democracy (1947–50), box 46, JCT-Hoover; "A Primer of Democracy: Contents," undated, in folder: primer of democracy (undated), box 46, JCT-Hoover; and Howard Bell to [Mark T.] Orr, "Goals in Political Education," June 1, 1948, in folder: political education, box 46, JCT-Hoover. The quotes are from the first and fifth sources.
78. Komiya, "Miki Takeo josetsu," p. 18.
79. Justin Williams, Sr., *Japan's Political Revolution under MacArthur: A Participant's Account* (Athens: University of Georgia Press, 1979), p. 257.
80. Ibid., photo caption (no pagination), second of the four photograph pages between pp. 210–11.
81. Komiya, "Miki Takeo josetsu," p. 22.
82. See Williams, *Japan's Political Revolution under MacArthur*, p. 257.
83. After his stints as a MIS battlefield linguist (1944–45) and enlisted GHQ staffer (1945–52), Motofuji completed a master's degree in Oriental language at University of California, Berkeley, in 1957, and a Ph.D. in Japanese at Stanford University seven years later. He was then appointed as acting assistant professor at U.C. Berkeley's East Asian Studies, where he taught until his retirement.
84. "Motofuji, Francis T., Job Description," April 22, 1950, in folder 18 (also folder 39), box 5921, Entry UD: 1701, GHQ/SCAP. This draws from the job description for "Religious Advisor," an expanded and reclassified position that incorporated duties of "Field Liaison Officer." Before Motofuji, another Nisei named Theodore Ohno engaged in the translation of religion-related directives; a civilian war department employee, Ohno belonged to the CIE's press unit, not RCRD. See GHQ/CIE, "Weekly Summary," December 15–21, 1945, pp. 15–16, in folder: weekly summaries December 1–28, 1945, box 76, JCT-Hoover.

85. William K. Bunce, "Justification for Retention of Unfilled T/Q Positions," March 13, 1947, in folder 37, box 5921, GHQ/SCAP.
86. Ibid.
87. Chief, R&CR Division, to Administrative Officer, "Request for Promotion for Francis T. Motofuji," May 7, 1948, in folder 37, box 5921, GHQ/SCAP.
88. "Motofuji, Francis T., Job Description."
89. Ibid.
90. See Francis T. Motofuji, "Reports of Field Trip," September 17, 1947, October 17, 1947, November 17, 1947, December 17, 1947, March 29, 1948, May 3, 1948, July 7, 1948, and September 21, 1948, in box 5166, Entry UD: 1653, GHQ/SCAP.
91. See Takemae, *Inside GHQ*, pp. 373–81, esp. p. 375.
92. See the aforementioned reports by Motofuji, esp. "Report of Field Trip to Tohoku Region, 7–14 September 1947, to Confer with Military Government Teams on Religious Problems," September 17, 1947, in box 5166.
93. See Motofuji, "Report of Field Trip to Hokkaido, 6–13 October 1947, for Conference with Military Government Team on Religious Problems," October 17, 1947, p. 5, in box 5166.
94. Mark R. Mullins, "How Yasukuni Shrine Survived the Occupation: A Critical Examination of Popular Claims," *Monumenta Nipponica* 65, no. 1 (2010): p. 103; Kai Wasson, "The Power of Invisibility: American Empire in the Conundrum of Yasukuni Shrine," pp. 13, 25n42, available at https://www.academia.edu/8519258/The_Power_of_Invisibility_American_Empire_in_the_Conundrum_of_Yasukuni_Shrine (accessed on July 23, 2025); and Nakamura Naofumi, *Yasukuni: Shirarezaru senryōka no kōbō* (Tokyo: Nihon Hōsō Kyōkai, 2007), pp. 125, 241–43. On state Shinto and religious freedom under US occupation, see Jolyon Baraka Thomas, *Faking Liberties: Religious Freedom in American-Occupied Japan* (Chicago: University of Chicago Press, 2019), ch. 5.
95. Born in Hawai'i, Tamie Tsuchiyama was the first Japanese American woman to receive a Ph.D. in anthropology at the University of California at Berkeley in 1947. During the war, she had worked as the only full-time Nisei female researcher for the Japanese American Evacuation and Resettlement Study organized by U.C. Berkeley professor Dorothy Swaine Thomas. After completing her doctoral degree, she went to occupied Japan to assume the role of a Social Science Research Analyst at CIE's Public Opinion and Sociological Research Division (hereafter POSRD) with research assignments relating to the Japanese rural family system. After returning to the United States in 1951, Tsuchiyama pursued another bachelor's degree in library science because she could not find an academic position. She subsequently found a job as the director of the Oriental Library at University of Texas, Austin, where she worked until her retirement. On an example of Tsuchiyama's work as a CIE researcher, see [Tamie Tsuchiyama], "The Japanese Rural Family: Some Structural-Functional Aspects," undated, folder 39, box 5872, Entry UD: 1700, GHQ/SCAP. On Tsuchiyama's life, see also Lane Ryo Hirabayashi, *The Politics of Fieldwork: Research in an American Concentration Camp* (Tucson: University of Arizona Press, 2016).

    Born in San Diego, Iwao Ishino was also interned at Poston, where he was recruited by Alexander H. Leighton as a field researcher for the Bureau of Sociological Research run by the Office of Indian Affairs. (The Poston camp was set up within a Native American reservation.) Ishino learned public opinion and anthropological research methods under Leighton, who later moved to Washington, DC, to head OWI's Foreign Morale Analysis Division. In 1944, Ishino got a job as an OWI analyst and worked for Leighton again. After attending the anthropology graduate program at Harvard University in 1947–49, Ishino crossed the Pacific to join POSRD as the second Social Science Research Analyst. While Tsuchiyama was about to return to the United States, Ishino was promoted to the position of Deputy Chief in charge of sociological research. His research at POSRD was concerned with "forestry survey" and "labor boss study." After his stint in occupied Japan, Ishino was appointed assistant professor of anthropology at the Ohio State University. It is likely that Ishino used his connection to POSRD Chief John W. Bennett, who was hired as faculty at Ohio State before him. In 1963, the two anthropologists co-authored a book titled *Paternalism in the Japanese Economy: Anthropological Studies of Oyabun-Kobun Patterns*—the very topic that POSRD had studied under Bennett's command. In 1956, Ishino moved to Michigan State University, where he stayed until his retirement. On Ishino's activities at POSRD, see "Iwao Ishino, Request Employment Of," July 21, 1949; "Plan for Reduction of Personnel, Reasons for Revision Of," September 3, 1949; "Resignation of T. Tsuchiyama, Request for Postponement Of," October

30, 1950, all in folder 2, box 5870, Entry UD: 1700; and Iwao Ishino, "Personnel Assignments," March 20, 1951, in folder 3, box 5870. See also Hayashi, *Democratizing the Enemy*, p. 218.

Another noteworthy Nisei was Tacoma-born John M. Maki, who had worked at OWI's Japan Desk during the war and then joined the Government Section of GHQ, where he played a notable role in civil service reform to rid the Japanese bureaucracy of militarist influences and authoritarian tendencies. With research experience in prewar Japan, Maki had already published *Japanese Militarism: Its Cause and Cure* (New York: Alfred A. Knopf, 1945) and had been widely regarded as a subject expert. After working in occupied Japan for six months, Maki obtained a doctoral degree in political science from Harvard University. He then joined the Asian Studies faculty at University of Washington, his alma mater, and later move to University of Massachusetts at Amherst to chair the Asian studies program until his retirement in 1980. On his role at GHQ's GS, see Takemae, *Inside GHQ*, pp. 159, 305–6; and also John M. Maki, *Voyage through the Twentieth Century* (Amherst, MA: Modern Memoirs Publishing, 2004), pp. 111–38.

96. Shiinoki to Kasai.
97. Moore, *Serving Our Country*, p. 125.
98. "Memo," December 31, 1946, in folder 18, box 2, CRF-Adams.
99. "Shinchūgun Nisei ga kataru Seikatsu no demokurashī," *Fujin gahō* 41, no. 3 (1946): pp. 7–14. The media appearance of Nisei spokespersons of democracy was only possible when GHQ permitted it. See R. M. Levy, "Review of situation relative to information activities," July 16, 1947, in folder: military government, box 40, JCT-Hoover.
100. See Takemae, *Inside GHQ*, pp. 185–87, 347–50. The quote is from p. 347.
101. "Shinchūgun Nisei ga kataru Seikatsu no demokurashī," p. 12.
102. Ibid., p. 13.
103. Ibid., p. 7.
104. "Minshu Nihon kensetsu no tame Nisei yo Nihon ni ike," *Rafu Shimpo*, September 21, 1946 (Japanese section); and "Japan grateful to Nisei for loyalty to US says priest," *Rafu Shimpo*, March 14, 1947.
105. "Minshu kokka Nihon no saiken ni Nisei no kōken ga hitsuyō," *Rafu Shimpo*, August 31, 1948 (Japanese section).
106. Koiso Ryōhei, "Tehon wa 'Nikkei Beijin,'" *Mainichi Shinbun*, January 1, 1951.
107. On these arguments made by both the government and JACL sides, see Eleanor Roosevelt, "A Challenge to American Sportsmanship," *Collier's Magazine* (October 16, 1943): pp. 21, 71; Larry Tajiri, "Democracy Corrects Its Own Mistake," *Asia and the Americas* 43, no. 4 (1943): pp. 213–16; and Tajiri, "Farewell to Little Tokyo," *Common Ground* 4, no. 2 (1944): pp. 90–95.
108. Takemae, *Inside GHQ*, p. 188.
109. See PO&SR Division, "Recruitment of one (1) of the Men in the Following List as a Replacement for John C. Pelzel, P-7, PO&SR Division, in the order indicated is required," April 29, 1949, in folder 2, box 5870, GHQ/SCAP. On the list, the other five were also anthropologists, who studied non-western cultures and nations, like Africa, India, and indigenous peoples of North America; the tenth person was a political scientist. On Nisei-related books produced by the white experts on the list, see Alexander H. Leighton, *The Governing of Men: General Recommendations Based on Experience at a Japanese Relocation Camp* (Princeton: Princeton University Press, 1945); Edward H. Spicer et al., *Impounded People: Japanese-Americans in the Relocation Centers* (Tucson: University of Arizona Press, 1969); Leonard Bloom and Ruth Riemer, *Removal and Return: The Socio-Economic Effects of the War on Japanese Americans* (Berkeley: University of California Press, 1949); and Andrew W. Lind, *Hawaii's Japanese: An Experiment in Democracy* (Princeton: Princeton University Press, 1946).
110. See "The Governing of Men: General Recommendations Based on Experience at a Japanese Relocation Camp," *Journal of American Medical Association* 129, no. 2 (1945): p. 176.
111. GHQ CIE, "CIE Orientation Pamphlet," ca. January 1948, p. 5, in folder: orientation pamphlet, box 7, JCT-Hoover.
112. See Hubert C. Armstrong to Tsudoki Imoto, October 16, 1942; and Armstrong to Alexander H. Leighton, December 7, 1942, both in folder 3, box 4, HCA-Hoover. The quotes are from these sources. On the strong thrust of progressive education among white camp schoolteachers, see Thomas James, *Exile Within: The Schooling of Japanese Americans 1942–1945* (Cambridge, MA: Harvard University Press, 1987), pp. 36–41, 63–64, 67.

113. Armstrong to Shuki Hayashi, March 4, 1943, in folder 4, box 4, HCA-Hoover.
114. Armstrong to Allen C. Blainsdell, November 12, 1942, in folder 4, box 4, HCA-Hoover.
115. See "The Citizens' Public Hall," June 18, 1946, in folder: social education (1945–48), box 50, JCT-Hoover.
116. Armstrong to family, December 1, 1947; and Hubert C. Armstrong to Glenn (Armstrong), ca. 1947, both in folder 3, box 5, HCA-Hoover. The quotes are from the first source. Armstrong briefly served as advisor to South Korea's ministry of education in 1948 before heading back to the United States.
117. "Personnel: Education Division," November 22, 1947, p. 3; and Kenneth M. Harkness to Chief, Education Division, CIE, "Notice of Resignation," July 19, 1950, both in folder: personnel general, box 44, JCT-Hoover; and Thomas T. Harkness, *Caucasian Boy at a Japanese Camp* (Redlands, CA: Tulahark Press, 2004), pp. 13–14, 59–60. On the mission of the Education Division, see GHQ CIE, "CIE Orientation Pamphlet," p. 3. It was, in part, "to eliminate from the Japanese educational system all elements of militarism and ultranationalism in doctrine, practice, and training…and to insure inclusion in the courses of instruction and school curricula the proper dissemination of democratic ideas and principles."
118. On the job description of the Textbook unit, including that of textbook analyst, see "Function (Col. 2)," undated, p. 2, in folder: organization & plans, box 44, JCT-Hoover; Chief, Education Division, "Proposed Reduction of TO in Education Division," September 19, 1947, p. 2, folder: personnel general, box 44, JCT-Hoover; and Education Division to Chief, CIE Section, "Job Description for Mr. Shiroma," April 24, 1950, in folder: personnel job descriptions, box 45, JCT-Hoover.
119. After resigning from his GHQ position, Harkness moved to occupied Okinawa to serve as the chief of the education division of the United States Civil Administration of the Ryukyu Islands (USCAR) through the 1950s. He is credited as a key architect of the foundation of the University of the Ryukyus, among other reforms under US governance. See Harkness, *Caucasian Boy at a Japanese Camp*, p. 62; and Masahide Ishihara, "USCAR's Language Policy and English Education in Okinawa: Featuring High Commissioner Caraway's Policies," *Okinawan Journal of American Studies* 1 (2004): esp. pp. 20–21.
120. On idealisms that shored up education endeavors both before and after segregation in Tule Lake, see Thomas James, "The Education of Japanese Americans at Tule Lake, 1942–1946," *Pacific Historical Review* 56, no. 1 (1987): pp. 31–33, 44–47.
121. This data draws from an Education Division's personnel record of April 1948. See "Members of the Education Division of CI&E as of 1 April 1948," in folder: personnel general, box 44, JCT-Hoover.
122. "Censorship of Textbooks," ca. November 1945, p. 1, in folder: staff studies 1945, box 51, JCT-Hoover.
123. "Personnel: Education Division," November 22, 1947, p. 3, in folder: personnel general, box 44, JCT-Hoover; and Harkness, *Caucasian Boy at a Japanese Camp*, p. 59. The quote is from the second source. Although it contains much misinformation and questionable recollections, Doi's video oral history was available at the time of my research at https://www.goforbroke.org/ohmsviewer/viewer.php?cachefile=2010OH1026A_01_Doi.xml and https://www.goforbroke.org/ohmsviewer/viewer.php?cachefile=2010OH1026A_02_Doi.xml (last accessed on July 23, 2025), but these links are now defunct. Its transcript and interview information are still listed at https://ndajams.omeka.net/items/show/1053539 (accessed on January 14, 2026). In his interview, Doi characterizes Harkness as "just a typical small-town missionary who gave up on his post in Kansas." Doi noted that this clueless non-educator supposedly had to depend completely on him, because the white man "had no experience." And yet, he also acknowledged that Harkness received the highest rating as a civilian CIE staffer.
124. "Education Division," October 1948, p. 3, in ibid.
125. Underscoring their (over)qualifications for the job, all but Shiroma later pursued doctoral degrees in East Asian studies and became professors of Japanese studies in the United States. After his stint at CIE, California-born Isao James Doi attended University of Chicago to pursue a doctoral degree in Sociology. Based on his work, Doi's dissertation was about educational reform in occupied Japan. He held tenured professorships at the University of Colorado, New York University, University of Michigan, University of Rochester, and finally University of Washington, where he was appointed Dean of the School of Education between 1979 and 1988. After returning to the United States in 1952, Utah-born Dixon Yoshio Miyauchi earned

a Ph.D. in East Asian studies and taught Asian history at SUNY-Plattsburgh until his retirement in 1983. Born in Northern California, Kenneth Kenichiro Yasuda graduated from University of Washington. His graduate training took place at University of Tokyo after working for CIE. He was known as the foremost expert on *haiku* poems and *noh* drama. He taught Japanese and comparative literature at Indiana University from 1966 to 1984.

126. See Harlan D. Unrau, *Manzanar National Historic Site, California: The Evacuation and Relocation of Persons of Japanese Ancestry during World War II: A Historical Study of the Manzanar War Relocation Center*, vol. 2 (Washington, DC: US Department of the Interior, National Park Service, 1996), pp. 545–47, esp. 545.
127. See Takemae, *Inside GHQ*, p. 188; and Jacob Van Staaveren, *An American in Japan 1945–1948: A Civilian View of the Occupation* (Seattle: University of Washington Press, 1994), pp. 156, 161–62, 175–78.
128. The Tokyo metropolitan government held a special farewell party for Fox when he returned to California in late 1950. An internal document stressed the desire to "pay a tribute to the unprecedented favor and services that Mr. Fox has extended to our government." See "Kantō Minjibu kyōiku kyokuchō no kansōgeikai kaisai ni tsuite," December 22, 1950, in "Showa 25-nendo kaigi keihi" (ki 103.106.005), TMGA.
129. Monbushō Chōsa Fukyū-kyoku, *Amerika no Nihonjin oyobi Nikkei Amerikajin no kyōiku* (Tokyo: Monbushō, 1951). The quotes are from "jobun" (no pagination). For his original dissertation, see Rollin C. Fox, "The Secondary School Program at the Manzanar War Relocation Center" (Ed.D. dissertation, University of California, Los Angeles, 1946).
130. See Rorin Shī Fokkusu (Rollin C. Fox), *Gendai Nihon kyōiku yōkō* (*Essentials in Modern Japanese Education*) (Tokyo: Gakugei Tosho Shuppansha, 1950). The quotes are from pp. 4 and 19. A basis of this book, the original report compiled by Fox is available in folder 32, box 2984, Entry UD: 1541, GHQ/SCAP.
131. On these characterizations, see Roosevelt, "A Challenge to American Sportsmanship," pp. 21, 71; Tajiri, "Democracy Corrects Its Own Mistake," pp. 213–16; and Tajiri, "Farewell to Little Tokyo," pp. 90–95.
132. See Shiinoki to Kasai; and Takita to Kasai.

Chapter 4

1. Hubert Coslet Armstrong letter, ca. June 1947, p. 4, in folder 3, box 5, HCA-Hoover.
2. Joe M. Takita to Alice Kasai, January 14, 1947, in folder 3, box 109, JARP-Kasai.
3. Seiko M. Kasai to Alice Kasai, November 19, 1945, in folder 2, box 109, JARP-Kasai.
4. See Takemae Eiji, *Inside GHQ: The Allied Occupation of Japan and Its Legacy*, translated by Robert Ricketts and Sebastian Swann (London: Continuum, 2002), pp. 458–90.
5. The quotes are from Kaz Kozaki to Alice Kasai, September 2, 1945, and Kozaki to Kasai, February 4, 1946, in folders 1 and 3, box 109, respectively, JARP-Kasai.
6. Naomi Hirahara, *An American Son: The Story of George Aratani, Founder of Mikasa and Kenwood* (Los Angeles: Japanese American National Museum, 2001), pp. 162–231, 240–43.
7. See Roy Hiroshige to C. Gregory, "Application for Permission to Engage in Drycleaning and Laundry Business Activities with Occupational Forces," February 25, 1950, enclosure in C. R. Liggitt to William B. Cobb, July 12, 1950, in box 1032, Entry UD 1200, GHQ/SCAP.
8. Ibid.
9. See Roy Hiroshige to Virginia Layne, March 11, 1950, enclosure in Liggitt to Cobb.
10. Hiroshige to Gregory. On the history of Davenroy Linen Supply Company in Japan, see https://www.davenroylinensupply.co.jp/company#company_greeting (accessed on July 24, 2025).
11. "Nisei among Top Earners in Japan," *Pacific Citizen*, May 27, 1966: p. 3.
12. Kadono Kōtarō, "Akutoku baiyā zaiakushi," *Bungei shunjū* 30, no. 7 (1952): pp. 88–98, esp. 88–89. See also "Nippon Returns to Pre-war Methods," *Rafu Shimpo*, May 13, 1953.
13. "Tokuju o meguru JPA no uchimaku," *Shinsō* 73 (1954): p. 56.
14. Kadono Kōtarō, "Akutoku gaishō monogatari," *Daiamondo* 40, no. 17 (1952): pp. 49, 52. See also "Tokuju o meguru JPA no uchimaku," p. 56.
15. Kadono, "Akutoku baiyā zaiakushi," p. 98.
16. Joe M. Takita to Henry Kasai, January 14, 1947, in folder 3, box 109, JARP-Kasai. On a similar story of a Nisei linguist who extorted a large sum of money from Japanese contractors, see "PM Discloses Nisei Seized for Extortion," *Pacific Stars and Stripes*, December 8, 1946.

17. Kojiro F. Kawaguchi, "A Nisei Story: The Story of a Japanese American during World War II and the Occupation of Japan" (December 15, 2003), pp. 169–70, in box 28, Tsukiyama-JAVC.
18. Takemae, *Inside GHQ*, pp. 386–99, esp. 387, 389–93, 395, 397–98; and Hiroshi Kitamura, *Screening Enlightenment: Hollywood and the Cultural Reconstruction of Defeated Japan* (Ithaca, NY: Cornell University Press, 2010), pp. 42–61.
19. See Ozaki Hideo, ed., *Purodyūsā jinsei* (Tokyo: Tōhō Kabushiki Kaisha Shuppan Jigyōbu, 1981), pp. 184–86; Kusakabe Hisatarō, "Furyō Nisei ni furimawasareta eigakai," *Hōseki* 10, no. 2 (1982): pp. 194, 196; and WYM [Walter Yoshito Mihata], "CI&E through the Motion Picture Producers' Association of Japan Bans the Showing of Old Historical Film," March 6, 1947, and WYM, "Telephone Conversation with Lt. Konno Regards Deletions Made in Toho Picture 'Yottsu no Koi' by This Department," March 10, 1947, both in box 8579, Entry UD: 1803, GHQ/SCAP.
20. Ozaki, ed., *Purodyūsā jinsei*, pp. 186–87; and Kusakabe, "Furyō Nisei ni furimawasareta eigakai," p. 196.
21. James R. Brandon, "Stanley Kaizawa Interview," July 5, 2000, p. 1, pdf available at https://evols.library.manoa.hawaii.edu/handle/10524/57068?mode=full (accessed on July 24, 2025).
22. W. P[earce], "Memorandum for Record," October 28, 1946, in box 8579, Entry UD: 1803, GHQ/SCAP.
23. W[alter] M[ihata], "Appendix," November 6, 1946; and also F. A. B., "Conference with Lt. Col. Nugent re Potential Co-operation between Film Center and Japanese," October 7, 1946, both in box 8579, ibid.
24. WYM, "CI&E through the Motion Picture Producers' Association of Japan Bans the Showing of Old Historical Film"; and WYM, "Telephone Conversation with Lt. Konno Regards Deletions Made in Toho Picture 'Yottsu no Koi' by This Department."
25. Brandon, "Stanley Kaizawa Interview," p. 1; and Kusakabe, "Furyō Nisei ni furimawasareta eigakai," p. 196.
26. "CI&E Nisei Convicted of Accepting Bribes," *Pacific Stars and Stripes*, September 9, 1947; "US Officer Guilty in Jap 'Shakedown,'" *Pacific Stars and Stripes*, September 10, 1947; and "Officer Found Guilty of Taking Tokyo Bribes," *Pacific Citizen*, September 13, 1948: p. 2. On the murder case and Japanese response to it, see "Nisei Accused of Murder," *Nippon Times*, July 11, 1947: p. 3; "Army Tribunal Convicts Three Nisei in Tokyo," *Pacific Citizen*, January 31, 1948; "Hawaii Nisei Thank Lawyer," *Nippon Times*, August 5, 1948: p. 3; and *Rafu Shimpo*, July 12, 1947 (Japanese section).
27. Brandon, "Stanley Kaizawa Interview," p. 1.
28. "First Group of US Traders," *New York Times*, August 4, 1947.
29. GHQ to American Drug Corporation, "Rescission of Authority to Engage in Commercial Transactions Involving the Transfer of Foreign Exchange or Transfers between Convertible Accounts with Occupation Force Agencies and Personnel," July 17, 1950, p. 2, in box 1035, Entry UD: 1200, GHQ/SCAP.
30. See *Yomiuri Shinbun*, February 7, 1954; "Meriken gigoku," *Shinsō* 62 (1954): pp. 23–24; "Sonogo no Hozen gigoku o kaibōsuru," *Shinsō* 65 (1954): p. 56; "Tobaku," *Shūkan Sankei* 1, no. 42 (1952): p. 5; and "Gendaiban Tōjin Okichi no seitai," *Shinsō* 68 (1954): pp. 13–14.
31. See *Yomiuri Shinbun*, January 27, 1954, February 16, 1954, and March 1, 1954.
32. See ibid., February 16, 1954, February 28, 1954; "Oshoku daigishi enmachō," *Shinsō* 79 (1954): p. 64; and also *Shinsō* 77 (1954): p. 40. Stories of outlaw Nisei, especially pimps and swindlers, continued to circulate in Japanese print media through the 1950s, suggesting the continuous presence of such individuals after this episode. See, for example, "kono hito wa sukuwarenai: furyō Nisei to naito kurabu no hosutesu," *Shūkan Shinchō* 2, no. 50 (1957): pp. 26–31.
33. A few other high-profile cases of Nisei crimes filled the pages of Japanese dailies in 1952–54. See, for example, *Yomiuri Shinbun*, December 29, 1951, and January 21, 1952, on an attempted kidnap and robbery with guns and an army jeep; and ibid., October 3–5, 1953, on an organized fraud scheme and the prime culprit's flight to the United States.
34. "Anti-Nisei Fever Rising in Japan," *Nisei in Hawaii and the Pacific* 7, no. 4 (1953): p. 15.
35. On varied American attitudes toward fraternization, prostitution, and Japanese women, see John W. Dower, *Embracing Defeat: Japan in the Wake of World War II* (New York: W. W. Norton, 1999), pp. 122–39; Yukiko Koshiro, *Trans-Pacific Racisms and the US Occupation of Japan* (New York: Columbia University Press, 1999), pp. 58–61; Naoko Shibusawa, *America's Geisha Ally: Reimagining the Japanese Enemy* (Cambridge, MA: Harvard

University Press, 2006), pp. 28–46; and Robert Kramm, *Sanitized Sex: Regulating Prostitution, Venereal Disease, and Intimacy in Occupied Japan, 1945–1952* (Berkeley: University of California Press, 2017).

36. Regina O'Connell to Asia Desk Officer, July 12, 1955, in microfilm reel 33, DS-CSDSF. On the racial anxiety that "war brides" caused in the American public, see Caroline Chung Simpson, "'Out of an Obscene Place': Japanese War Brides and Cultural Pluralism in the 1950s," *Differences: A Journal of Feminist Cultural Studies* 10, no. 3 (1998): pp. 47–81.
37. On "anti-miscegenation" laws against Asian Americans stateside, see Peggy Pascoe, *What Comes Naturally: Miscegenation Law and the Making of Race in America* (New York: Oxford University Press, 2009); Megumi Dick Osumi, "Asians and California's Anti-Miscegenation Laws," in *Asian and Pacific American Experience: Women's Perspectives*, edited by Nobuya Tsuchiya (Minneapolis: Asian/Pacific American Learning Resources Center, University of Minnesota, 1982), pp. 1–27; and Deenesh Sohoni, "Unsuitable Suitors: Anti-Miscegenation Laws, Naturalization Laws, and the Construction of Asian Identities," *Law & Society Review* 41, no. 3 (2007): pp. 587–618.
38. See Koshiro, *Trans-Pacific Racisms*, pp. 159–200; Dower, *Embracing Defeat*, pp. 55–57, 61–64, 124, 128–29, 135–38; and Shibusawa, *America's Geisha Ally*, pp. 28–29, 36–41, 45.
39. On US policies toward Japanese spouses of GIs, see Peter Kalischer, "Madame Butterfly's Children," *Collier's: The National Weekly* 130 (1952): pp. 16–17. A public view of GI-Japanese marriages turned positive by the mid-1950s, however. On this shift, see Shibusawa, *America's Geisha Ally*, pp. 47–53; and Simpson, "Out of an Obscene Place."
40. Seiko Kasai to Alice Kasai, November 19, 1945, in folder 2, box 109, JARP-Kasai; and Tamotsu Shibutani, *The Derelicts of Company K: A Sociological Study of Demoralization* (Berkeley: University of California Press, 1978), p. 384. This quote is from the first source.
41. See Kalischer, "Madame Butterfly's Children," pp. 15–18; and Koshiro, *Trans-Pacific Racisms*, pp. 57–62, 69–70, 159–200.
42. *Rafu Shimpo*, April 4, 1946.
43. On various forms of Nisei fraternization, see Shibutani, *The Derelicts of Company K*, pp. 384–86; and Elmer Yoshino to Alice Kasai, October 21, 1945, in folder 2, box 109, JARP-Kasai.
44. See *Rafu Shimpo*, June 30, 1947 (Japanese section), and July 19, 1947.
45. Kiyoshi Miyazaki to Alice Kasai, ca. 1947, in folder 3, box 109, JARP-Kasai.
46. "AJA Interpreters," ca. July-August 1945, in folder 16, box 2, CRF-Adams.
47. Shibutani, *The Derelicts of Company K*, p. 288.
48. Ibid., p. 385.
49. "Anti-Nisei Fever Rising in Japan," p. 16.
50. "GI Marriages in Japan 'On the Rocks,'" *Rafu Shimpo*, November 6, 1947. See also Hubert Coslet Armstrong letter, ca. fall 1947, no pagination, in folder 3, box 5, HCA-Hoover.
51. See Mizuki Yōko, "Konketsuji o meguru hitobito," *Sekai* 164 (1959): p. 131; *Rafu Shimpo*, September 16, 1952; and "Chōchō fujin no kodomotachi," *Shūkan Asahi* 57, no. 44 (1952): p. 4.
52. *Yomiuri Shinbun*, February 23, 1949.
53. Both in the United States and Japan, "occupation babies" were equated to "mixed blood babies," and the two terms were used interchangeably. See Kalischer, "Madame Butterfly's Children"; and also Koshiro, *Trans-Pacific Racisms*, pp. 159–200.
54. On a racialized aspect of the problem-making, see Terese Svoboda, "US Court-Martial in Occupation Japan: Rape, Race, and Censorship," *The Asia-Pacific Journal: Japan Focus* 7, no. 1 (2009): pp. 1–10, online journal essay accessed on July 24, 2025: https://apjjf.org/-Terese-Svoboda/3148/article.html.
55. Relatedly, on the making of the Nisei model minority as a consequence of their soldiering in the US domestic context, see Ellen D. Wu, *The Color of Success: Asian Americans and the Origins of the Model Minority* (Princeton: Princeton University Press, 2014), pp. 86–91, 108–10, 218–19, 236–38; and Simeon Man, *Soldiering through Empire: Race and the Making of the Decolonized Pacific* (Berkeley: University of California Press, 2018), pp. 12–13.
56. "JACL Protests Discriminatory Treatment of Nisei Technicians in Japan by British Forces," *Pacific Citizen*, November 12, 1949; and "White Australia Policy: Ad Nauseum [sic]," *Pacific Citizen*, November 19, 1949.
57. Mike Masaoka to Norman John Oswald Makin, November 2, 1949, in 894.4016/11-249 (microfilm), DS-SDCDF. See also "JACL Protests Discriminatory Treatment of Nisei Technicians in Japan by British Forces."

58. Masaoka to Makin; Mike Masaoka to Dean Acheson, November 2, 1949; and "Official Memorandum," November 15, 1949, all in 894.4016/11-249 (microfilm), DS-SDCDF; and I. H. Gordon, "By the Side of the Hill," *Pacific Citizen*, December 10, 1949. See also *Rafu Shimpo*, September 19, 1949, November 4, 1949 (Japanese section), November 9, 1949.
59. Shibutani, *The Derelicts of Company K*, p. 389. On Japanese complaints about Nisei's abuse of power and corruption, see Hirano Kyoko, "The Occupation and Japanese Cinema," in *The Occupation of Japan: Arts and Culture*, edited by Thomas W. Burkman (Norfolk, VA: General Douglas MacArthur Foundation, 1988), p. 148.
60. Shibutani, *The Derelicts of Company K*, p. 388.
61. Seiko M. Kasai to Alice Kasai.
62. Shibutani, *The Derelicts of Company K*, p. 389.
63. Kiyoshi Miyazaki to Alice Kasai, ca. November 29, 1945, in folder 2, box 109, JARP-Kasai.
64. "Nisei Aids in Formation of Boys Club," *Rafu Shimpo*, September 18, 1948; and *Rafu Shimpo*, January 31, 1949 (Japanese section).
65. Shibutani, *The Derelicts of Company K*, pp. 378–80.
66. Miyazaki to Kasai, ca. December 5, 1945, in folder 2, box 109, JARP-Kasai.
67. Jobo Nakamura, "Report on Nisei in Japan," *Rafu Shimpo*, December 22, 1952.
68. Shibutani, *The Derelicts of Company K*, p. 389.
69. Eizo Suzuki to James A. O'Brien, April 19, 1949, and "Record of Trial of Suzuki, Eizo," August 28, 1947, Kobe Base, in folder 6, box 48, MMMP.
70. Civil Censorship Detachment, "Summary of Censorship Information," June 30, 1946, p. 14, in folder 5, box 3332, Entry UD: 1583, GHQ/SCAP.
71. Mizuno Hiroshi, ed., *Nihon no teisō* (Tokyo: Sōkisha, 1953), p. 275.
72. *Rafu Shimpo*, December 5, 1947 (Japanese section). On a similar observation by another female Nisei in Japan, see Fumie Miho, "Aru Nisei no iken," *Kaitakusha* 50, no. 1 (1955): p. 44.
73. *Rafu Shimpo*, March 27, 1947 (Japanese section). In Los Angeles, Aiso made these remarks in his Japanese-language speech for an Issei audience, which often contradicted the all-flowery celebrations of Nisei patriotism and contribution in English-language discourse. Some Japanese Americans were similarly less inhibited in sharing their more complex observations and honest views when speaking in Japanese. Not only does this underscore the strategic nature of Nisei utterances and recollections, but it also reminds researchers of the importance of consulting Japanese-language sources, either produced by Nisei linguists or Japanese nationals.
74. See Shibutani, *The Derelicts of Company K*, p. 388; Suzuki to O'Brien; Miyazaki to Kasai; and Seiko Kasai to Alice Kasai, December 16, 1945, in folder 2, box 109, JARP-Kasai.
75. See, for example, "CARE Packs Dear to Nips," *Rafu Shimpo*, December 10, 1948; "41 Nip Crewmen Saved from Sinking Vessel," *Rafu Shimpo*, January 8, 1951; "Nip State Move on Tuna Tariff," *Rafu Shimpo*, March 6, 1953.
76. Almost coinciding with the restoration of Japan's sovereignty in April 1952, the US Newspapers Guild resolved not to use the term "Jap." See *Rafu Shimpo*, July 25, 1952 (Japanese section).
77. Civil Affairs Division, "Aliens in Japan," ca. April 1947, p. 26, in folders 20–21, box 3429, Entry UD: 1583, GHQ/SCAP; and also P. R. (Acting US Political Advisor in Tokyo), "Nisei Language Personnel Residing in Japan," November 19, 1945, pp. 1–2, in box 1, DS-CGC. By early 1948, the American consulate processed and certified 3,500 wartime strandees as US citizens, but as of December 1952, there were still reportedly seven thousand Nisei (including renunciants) who were seeking recognition as US citizens. See "American Consulate Reports Processing 3500 Strandees," *Rafu Shimpo*, February 18, 1948; and "7,000 Niseis in Japan Like to Return to US," *Honolulu Times*, December 17, 1952. On highly publicized treason trials of two Japanese Americans, which exacerbated the American public image of these ostracized Nisei, see Shibusawa, *America's Geisha Ally*, pp. 140–75.
78. Takita to Henry Kasai, January 14, 1947. On some of the printed Nisei letters to the editor, see "Give the Veterans Priority" and "Nisei Speaks," *Pacific Stars and Stripes*, October 13 and 28, 1946, respectively.
79. Hubert Coslet Armstrong letter, ca. fall 1947, no pagination, in folder 3, box 5, HCA-Hoover.
80. See "Nip Draftee Gets Break," *Rafu Shimpo*, July 15, 1949; "False Statement Arrests Nip GI," *Rafu Shimpo*, July 8, 1948; and "Dominion 'Turncoat' Not Too Popular among Japanese Natives," *Rafu Shimpo*, January 30, 1951. The last report is concerned with some three thousand Canadian Nisei, but there was an editor's comment to the effect that the same contempt should hold for US Nisei strandees.

81. Tsunoda Toshio, "Kaettekita Nisei, shiminken hōkisha jō," *Rafu Shimpo*, July 29, 1946.
82. "Memorandum, Anti-Discrimination Committee" (Japanese American Citizens League), p. 2, June 22, 1947, in folder 5, box 5, MMMP. Until early 1950, when the US federal court rulings finally paved the way for the restoration of US citizenship to most renunciants as well as many Nisei draftees into the Japanese imperial forces, JACL policy, especially on the former group, was that of non-involvement. As far as the various categories of strandees are concerned (see the following note), the JACL launched a special program in June 1947 to facilitate their return to the United States in cooperation with the American Civil Liberties Union. See "JACL Policy on Renunciants," *Rafu Shimpo*, January 19, 1950; and "CL Branch Sets Program to Send Home Strandees," *Rafu Shimpo*, June 4, 1947.
83. See "JACL Policy on Renunciants"; Henry J. Tsurutani, "The Strandee Problem," *Rafu Shimpo*, December 20, 1950; and Frank A. Kasama to Mike Masaoka, "Annual Report of the Nisei Problem," December 1949, in folder 2, box 34, MMMP. There were four categories of strandees who had to seek different processes of legal recourse for restoration of their American citizenship: those who "recovered" Japanese citizenship during the war ("kaifuku" case); those who participated in the first postwar Japanese general election; those who served in the imperial Japanese forces; and those who worked as Japan's government employees, including schoolteachers. Renunciants, who "voluntarily" cancelled out their American citizenship after failing the loyalty test in the stateside incarceration camps, were in a separate category.
84. "MacArthur Too Easy on Japan Nisei, Say GIs," *Rafu Shimpo*, December 2, 1946; Shibutani, *The Derelicts of Company K*, p. 402; and Takita to Kasai. The quotes are from these sources.
85. Morita Shigeru, "Zainichi Nisei, senzen, senchū, sengo," *Rafu Shimpo*, January 1, 1953: p. B-12 (Japanese section).
86. Tsunoda Toshio, "Amerikajin ni naritagaru Nihonjin," nos. 2–3, *Rafu Shimpo*, December 3–4, 1946.
87. Mary Kimoto Tomita, *Dear Miye: Letters Home from Japan, 1939–1946*, edited by Robert G. Lee (Stanford: Stanford University Press, 1995), p. 162.
88. Ibid., p. 204.
89. Ibid., p. 214.
90. Ibid., pp. 256–57.
91. "Anti-Nisei Fever Rising in Japan," p. 15.
92. Shibusawa, *America's Geisha Ally*, p. 36.
93. Bill Hume, *Babysan's World: The Hume'n Slant on Japan* (Tokyo: Charles E. Tuttle Co., 1954), p. 49.
94. See Brenda L. Moore, *Serving Our Country: Japanese American Women in the Military during World War II* (New Brunswick, NJ: Rutgers University Press, 2003), pp. 127–28.
95. As Brian Masaru Hayashi's study shows, the Office of Strategic Services (OSS) had formalized the involvement of selected Nisei agents in wartime US subversion and counter-intelligence against the Japanese enemy, including unarmed civilians. While OSS examples were mostly limited to the level of planning during the war, CIC had its Nisei staffers act as enforcers on an everyday basis. On OSS Nisei, see Brian Masaru Hayashi, *Asian American Spies: How Asian Americans Helped Win the Allied Victories* (New York: Oxford University Press, 2021).
96. Kornel Chang unravels a similar behavior of the US military regime in occupied Korea, where Koreans who had worked for Japan's prewar colonial regime were hired to muzzle anti-American protests and leftist reforms. During the Korean War, as Monica Kim unveils, Nisei linguists joined these Korean agents in the "dirty work" of extralegal political suppression and military domination, since their command of Japanese language was deemed useful for that purpose as much as Korean agents' prewar background was. See Kornel Chang, *A Fractured Liberation: Korea under US Occupation* (Cambridge, MA: Belknap Press of Harvard University Press, 2025); and Monica Kim, *The Interrogation Rooms of the Korean War: The Untold History* (Princeton: Princeton University Press, 2019).
97. Shibutani, *The Derelicts of Company K*, p. 381. On another occasion, a Nisei linguist was compelled to accompany a group of white soldiers who visited a Japanese family and proceeded to gang rape three sisters; two of them—16 years old and 13 years old—later died of injuries and went insane, while the oldest became a prostitute. See Gotō Tsutomu, *Zoku Nihon no teisō* (Tokyo: Sōkisha, 1953), pp. 14–15.
98. Takemae, *Inside GHQ*, pp. 161–68; and James C. McNaughton, *Nisei Linguists: Japanese Americans in the Military Intelligence Service during World War II* (Washington, DC: Department of the Army, 2006), pp. 98–99, 437–46.

99. "Nip Reds Stone Two Nisei GIs," *Rafu Shimpo*, May 31, 1950; *Asahi Shinbun*, May 31, 1950, June 1, 1950; and "Two LA Soldiers Hurt in Tokyo Demonstration," *Rafu Shimpo*, July 14, 1952.
100. Despite the efforts by Japanese historians to locate a paper trail of suspected American intrigues in occupied Japan, no US archival sources or government documents have turned out smoking-gun evidence or even significant leads. Nor have Nisei intelligence operatives discussed their involvement openly. Yet, their former Japanese informants and Korean collaborators have exposed various aspects of the Nisei's clandestine activities in Japanese-language publications. See some examples of these books in n. 103.
101. Charles F. McNair, "Sensitive EM Being Sent to FEC as Linguist," July 28, 1947, in folder B, box 1717, Entry 480, ROPMG-JABGF.
102. On Kaji's role in OSS, see Hayashi, *Asian American Spies*, pp. 102–4.
103. Established in December 1947, the "Z" Unit operated under the command of Lt. Colonel Canon who belonged to the Joint Special Operations Branch of the Public Safety Division under GHQ's G-2, which also controlled CIS and its branches, CIC and CCD. See Takemae, *Inside GHQ*, p. 165. On an academic study of Kaji's kidnap case, see Erik Esselstrom, "From Wartime Friend to Cold War Fiend: The Abduction of Kaji Wataru and U.S.-Japan Relations at Occupation's End," *Journal of Cold War Studies* 17, no. 3 (2015): pp. 159–83. On Canon and his Z-Unit undercover operations, see "Kyanon kikan no zenbō," *Shūkan Yomiuri* 18, no. 45 (1959): pp. 3–11; Yamamoto Noboru, ed., *Kaji Mitsuhashi jiken* (Tokyo: Surugadai Shobō, 1953); Yamada Taijirō, *Amerika no himitsu kikan* (Tokyo: Satsuki Shobō, 1953), pp. 18–53; Han Do-bong, "Kyanon kikanin to shite no kaisō," *Shūkan Shinchō* 5, no. 27 (1960): pp. 60–68; Yong Yang, *Kyanon kikan kara no shōgen* (Tokyo: Banchō Shoten, 1973); and Hatakeyama Kiyoyuki, *Kyanon kikan* (Tokyo: Tokuma Shoten, 1971). On a rare interview with Jack Canon and his mysterious death in 1981, see "Kyanon taisa ni honshi kisha ga dokusen kaiken," *Asahi geinō*, no. 1326 (1971): pp. 12–16; and "Sengo bōryaku jiken no kuroi shukai Kyanon chūsa no kaishi," *Sandē Mainichi* 60, no. 18 (1981): pp. 16–23.
104. The GHQ/SCAP records (RG 331) at NARA contain a surprisingly low volume of materials relating to the G-2 and Civil Intelligence Section; out of the aggregate 10,129 boxes, there are about 140 for the former, and 190 for the latter. In CIS materials, nothing pertaining to CIC is included. This clearly indicates a deliberate effort to sanitize the historical sources. Since the late 1990s, the NARA has released newly declassified CIC documents as part of the War Crimes "Interagency Working Group" (IWG) records. In "Investigate Records Repository" (IRR) under the Records of the Army Staff (RG 319), there are voluminous "Personal Name Files" compiled by CIC, which include hundreds of Japanese individuals. Yet, predictably Kaji's personal files do not contain materials after 1949, nor do these files encompass much information regarding CIC Nisei personnel, its operations, or the organizational structure. For the same reason, no documentary sources have been located on the US side with regards to the existence of the Z Unit, much less its activities. There are, however, plenty of written materials and testimonies by former Japanese and Korean employees and agents of the Z Unit and other US clandestine operations, as well as exposés by leftist investigative journalists. Kaji Wataru and his rescuer also published essays and memoirs on their ordeals. Given the embedded biases and anti-US political agendas in these materials, it is important to analyze the Japanese-language sources with caution and care, but they still offer useful information. This chapter relies especially on: Kaji Wataru and Yamada Zenjirō, *Damare Nihonjin* (*Shut up, Jap!*) (Tokyo: Rironsha, 1953), esp. pp. 30–44, 72–81; Kaji Wataru, "Kokumin eno shōgen," *Chūō kōron* 68, no. 2 (1953): pp. 183–86; Yamada Zenjirō, *Ketsudan* (Tokyo: Kōyō Shuppansha, 2000), pp. 36–126; and Kaji Jiken Taisaku Sewanin-kai, ed., *Kaji jiken: Bei bōryaku kikan no hanzai* (Tokyo: Kaji Jiken Taisaku Sewanin-kai, 1962), pp. 5–51. Readers may also want to consult: Haruna Mikio, *Himitsu no fairu: CIA no tainichi kōsaku* (*The Secret File*), vol. 1 (Tokyo: Kyōdo Tsūshinsha, 2000), pp. 228–34, 321–59.
105. Kaji and Yamada, *Damare Nihonjin*, pp. 74–80; Kaji, "Kokumin eno shōgen," pp. 186–93; and Yamada, *Ketsudan*, pp. 36–98.
106. Officially, both the United States government and Jack Canon denied Kaji's accusations of kidnapping, torture, and illegal imprisonment; instead, the American embassy in Tokyo issued a statement that the Japanese leftist had voluntarily requested protective custody after confessing his role as a Communist spy. In order to refute that explanation, Kaji testified at Japan's National Diet about details of his ordeal, but before long, another Japanese—accompanied by a Nisei CIA agent—"turned himself in," claiming that he had been a Soviet

spy and that he had worked with Kaji. Many pundits suspect that this development mirrored further US intrigue to tarnish the public image of Kaji and discredit his testimony. With this Japanese "spy" receiving a nominal guilty sentence in a Japanese court, Kaji's accusations quickly faded from public discourse, except in leftist circles. See Inomata Kōzō, ed., *Senryōgun no hanzai* (Tokyo: Tosho Shuppansha, 1979); Yamamoto, ed., *Kaji Mitsuhashi jiken*; and Haruna, *Himitsu no fairu*, pp. 329–49.

107. Yang, *Kyanon kikan kara no shōgen*, pp. 72–73.
108. Kaji and Yamada, *Damare Nihonjin*, p. 150.
109. Ibid., pp. 150–51.
110. Ibid., p. 152, also 30–42, 79.
111. See ibid., pp. 152–53.
112. Moronaga Yuji, *Hōmurareta natsu* (Tokyo: Asahi Shinbunsha, 2002), p. 320. In appreciation of his dedication to duty and national security, the CIA later recruited this Nisei, along with many other Japanese Americans who had worked for CIC and OSS. See Haruna, *Himitsu no fairu*, pp. 341, 349–50; and Ono Tatsuzō, *Amerika kara kita supaitachi* (Tokyo: Shin Nihon Shuppansha, 1965), pp. 70–71.
113. Military Intelligence Service Association of Northern California (MIS NorCal) and National Japanese American Historical Society (NJAHS), eds., *The Pacific War and Peace: Americans of Japanese Ancestry in Military Intelligence Service, 1941 to 1952* (San Francisco: MIS NorCal and NJAHS, 1991), p. 78. On a similar simplistic description of a Nisei intelligence agent's accomplishments, see also Pamela Rotner Sakamoto, *Midnight in Broad Daylight: A Japanese American Family Caught between Two Worlds* (New York: Harper, 2016), p. 347.
114. On the alleged involvement of CIC Nisei in another high-profile intrigue where the President of the Japan National Railways was allegedly kidnapped and murdered, see Yada Kimio, *Bōsatsu Shimoyama jiken* (Tokyo: Kōdansha, 1985), pp. 292–310, 338–49; Shimoyama Jiken Kenkyūkai, ed., *Shiryō Shimoyama jiken* (Tokyo: Misuzu Shobō, 1969), pp. 578–600; and Shibata Tetsuhiro, *Shimoyama jiken: Saigo no shōgen* (Tokyo: Shōdensha, 2005), pp. 62–65, 191–92, 271, 245, 334–37, 391, 395–96.

    Although most of these stories are based on hearsay or unconfirmed witness accounts, a relatively well-documented example involves Kay Sugahara, a Nisei OSS/CIA operative who was allegedly engaged in covert operations involving Japan's top elites as well as a kingpin of the underground world, many of whom were unconvicted war criminals. Sugahara's close ties to these individuals, and the material wealth he accumulated through his involvement in CIA operations, allowed the Nisei to reinvent himself as an international businessman, who established Fairfield-Maxwell, a global freight carrier and shipping company, in 1957. See Howard B. Schonberger, *Japanizu konekushon: Kaiunō K. Sugahara gaiden* (*"Nisei Entrepreneur," Japanese Connections: An Unauthorized Biography of Shipping Tycoon K. Sugahara*) translated by Sodei Rinjirō (Tokyo: Bungei Shunjūsha, 1995); "C.I.A. Spent Millions to Support Japanese Right in 50's and 60's," *New York Times*, October 9, 1994; and Sano Shin'ichi, *Kyokai-den: Shōriki Matsutarō to Kagemusha-tachi no isseiki* (Tokyo: Bungei Shunjūsha, 1994), pp. 456–60.

    In addition to Nisei members of CIC/CIA in occupied Japan, some linguists who served in GHQ's G-2 intelligence division or worked as court interpreters during the Tokyo International War Crime Tribunal could forge comparable ties to Japan's political and economic leaders, since their duties placed them in regular contact with elite classes of Japanese nationals. Two such Nisei, Taro Harvey Fukuda and Shig Katayama, were befriended by one of Sugahara's collaborators in the context of their official roles as a war criminal prison interpreter and as a member of CID, respectively. These Nisei were later involved with the former war criminal in the infamous Lockheed bribery case—an international political scandal of the early 1970s that resulted in the arrest and conviction of the then Japanese Prime Minister. At that time, Fukuda and Katayama separately ran consultant firms specializing in US-Japan trade, working as behind-the-door fixers for crooked Japanese politicians and business leaders. See Richard Halloran, "5 Japanese Had Key Roles in Pushing Lockheed Bids," *New York Times*, March 1, 1976; Tachibana Takashi, *Tanaka Kakuei kenkyū: zen kiroku*, vol. 2 (Tokyo: Kōdansha, 1976), pp. 242–47; Inose Naoki, *Shishatachi no rokkīdo jiken* (Tokyo: Bungei Shunjū, 1987), pp. 106–51; and Sterling and Peggy Seagrave, *Gold Warriors: America's Secret Recovery of Yamashita's Gold* (London: Verso, 2003), pp. 114–15, 148.

115. Kaji and Yamada, *Damare Nihonjin*, pp. 148, 156.

116. Ibid., p. 155.
117. Ibid., pp. 157–58.
118. "Anti-Nisei Fever Rising in Japan," pp. 15–16.
119. See *Asahi Shinbun*, January 18, 1953, and the sources in nn. 120 and 121.
120. "Anti-Nisei Fever Rising in Japan," p. 16.
121. See *Yomiuri Shinbun*, June 20, 1948, August 9, 1950, December 29, 1951; *Asahi Shinbun*, January 21, 1959; and "Gyaba-zoku seisuiki," *Shinsō* 5, no. 15 (1950): p. 45. The quote is from the last source. See also Benjamin Uchiyama, "The 'Oh, Mistake' Incident and Juvenile Delinquency in Defeated Japan," *Journal of Contemporary History* 57, no. 1 (2021): pp. 1–21, available at https://journals.sagepub.com/doi/10.1177/00220094211018490 (accessed on July 24, 2025).
122. On this robbery case, see Henshū-bu, "jīpu no sannin: Fuji ginkō gyangu jiken," *Shūkan Asahi* 57, no. 10 (1952): pp. 4–13; Shinmura Kōsaku, "Gaijin hanzai no uraomote," *Daiyamondo* 40, no. 5 (1952): pp. 54–59; *Rafu Shimpo*, February 19 and 27, 1952, and March 3, 1952 (Japanese sections).
123. Shig Matsuda, "Letters: Japan's 'Foreigners,'" *Scene* 5, no. 13 (1954): p. 3.

Chapter 5

1. War Department, Bureau of Public Relations, "Continental Liaison Bulletin," no. 43, June 16, 1945, p. 1, in folder 5, box 1726, Entry 480, ROPMG-JABGF.
2. On the larger context of such domestic anti-racist campaigns, see Takashi Fujitani, *Race for Empire: Koreans as Japanese and Japanese as Americans during World War II* (Berkeley: University of California Press, 2011), pp. 108–17; and Ellen D. Wu, *The Color of Success: Asian Americans and the Origins of the Model Minority* (Princeton: Princeton University Press, 2013), pp. 78–86.
3. On GHQ's ban on martial arts, especially *kendō* and *judō*, in November 1945, see GHQ Civil Information and Education (CIE) Section, "Basic Education Plan: Completed Staff Studies," ca. November 1945; and GHQ/CIE, untitled, November 5, 1945, pp. 1–3, both in folder: staff studies (1945), box 51, JCT-Hoover. On GHQ's policy toward militaristic motion pictures including *samurai* genres, see Kyoko Hirano, *Mr. Smith Goes to Tokyo: Japanese Cinema under the American Occupation, 1945–1952* (Washington, DC: Smithsonian Institution Press, 1992), p. 51; Hiroshi Kitamura, *Screening Enlightenment: Hollywood and the Cultural Reconstruction of Defeated Japan* (Ithaca, NY: Cornell University Press, 2010), pp. 53, 57–58, 60–61, 67–72; and Ozaki Hideki, ed., *Purodyūsa jinsei* (Tokyo: Tōhō Kabushiki Kaisha Shuppan Jigyōshitsu, 1981), pp. 183–84.
4. Hirano, *Mr. Smith Goes to Tokyo*, pp. 44–45.
5. Ibid., p. 247.
6. Eiji Takemae, *Inside GHQ: The Allied Occupation of Japan and its Legacy*, translated by Robert Ricketts and Sebastian Swann (London: Continuum, 2002), p. 397.
7. See GHQ/CIE, "Weekly Summary: December 1–14, 1945," pp. 13–15, in folder: weekly summaries December 1–28, 1945, box 76, JCT-Hoover. The quotes are from all three pages. In the context of global news, one pictorial magazine carried a report on the commendation of Nisei soldiers by President Truman as a symbol of America's anti-racist democracy in December 1946. This is the only known example of a substantial reference on Nisei soldiers that saw the light of the day under occupation censorship between late 1946 and 1947. See "NISEI sentōtai no kikan," *Sekai gahō*, no. 7 (December 1, 1946): no pagination.
8. See Takemae, *Inside GHQ*, pp. 398–99; and Ishii Seiji, *Nihon no hōsō o tsukutta otoko* (Tokyo: Mainichi Shinbunsha, 1998), esp. ch. 1 and ch. 4. The radio program later changed its title to "Shinsō bako" ("Truth Box") and then to "Shitsumon bako" ("Question Box") during the two years of its existence.
9. Some right-leaning pundits of post-1990s Japan have criticized the program as a "war guilt information campaign/program (WGIC/P)" that conspired to brainwash the Japanese into hating their own country and traditions. See, for example, Etō Jun, *Closed Linguistic Space: Censorship by the Occupation Forces and Postwar Japan* (Tokyo: Shuppan Bunka Sangyō Shinkō Zaidan, 2020).
10. See Takemae, *Inside GHQ*, pp. 392–93.
11. Rengōkoku Saikō Shireibu Minkan Jōhō Kyōiku-kyoku, ed., *Shinsōbako* (Tokyo: Kozumo Shuppansha, 1946), pp. 265–69. The quote is from pp. 268–69.

12. WYM [Walter Yoshito Mihata], "Deletions Made by CI&E on American Film, A Medal for Benny, a Central Motion Picture Exchange Importation," April 29, 1947, in box 8579, Entry UD: 1803, GHQ/SCAP.
13. H. M. Slott, "Commentary in Tokyo News," August 28, 29, 30, 1950, in folder 13, box 5308, Entry UD: 1667, GHQ/SCAP. Censors' concerns might not have been completely groundless, however. Under the tight clutches of GHQ censorship, Japanese authors and film producers still made every effort to circumvent official control and interventions by often employing implicit references to the destructive and violent power of the American military government and abusive occupational personnel. Discussions of the "destructive" pest therefore could well be a trope for US soldiers.
14. See, for example, "Renaming Army Transport for Nisei Infantry Hero," *New York Times*, March 17, 1948; and "Home Country," *TIME Magazine* 51, no. 13 (March 29, 1948): p. 26.
15. *Rafu Shimpo*, March 13, 1948 (Japanese section).
16. Ibid., and "JACL Request for Pacific Routing of Munemori Receives Backing," *Rafu Shimpo*, April 2, 1948. The quote is from the latter.
17. See *Rafu Shimpo*, March 13, 1948 (Japanese section); and "Request to Change Route for Munemori Ship Shelved," *Rafu Shimpo*, April 19, 1948. The quote is from the latter.
18. "JACL Request for Pacific Routing of Munemori Receives Backing."
19. "Sadao Munemori Ship," *New York Times*, March 20, 1948.
20. "Request to Change Route for Munemori Ship Shelved."
21. The easing of occupation censorship started to take place in mid-1947 and climaxed in late 1949. Yet, the initiative came from Washington, not SCAP. Aside from the concern for alienating anti-communist/conservative elements of Japanese society, the rationale for relaxing occupation censorship included the fear that surveillance apparatus had "the effect of continuing the authoritarian tradition in Japan." On this development and the extension of occupation control after 1948 from "fascist cleansing to Communist chasing," see Takemae, *Inside GHQ*, pp. 391, 393; and also John W. Dower, *Embracing Defeat: Japan in the Wake of World War II* (New York: W. W. Norton, 2000), pp. 432–38.
22. Takemae, *Inside GHQ*, p. 391.
23. "Army Plans Several Nisei Films for Japan Showing," *Pacific Citizen*, November 26, 1949.
24. "Documentary Nisei Film Ready," *Rafu Shimpo*, September 25, 1948; and "Army Plans Several Nisei Films for Japan Showing."
25. "Army Plans Several Nisei Films for Japan Showing."
26. WYM [Walter Yoshito Mihata], "'Good Will' propaganda sequence in United News No. 310," July 2, 1948, in box 8579, Entry UD: 1803, GHQ/SCAP. Mihata might have been instrumental in an earlier decision to permit Japan's domestic news outlets to print a translation of an Associated Press report on the army's announcement for the burials. See *Yomiuri Shinbun*, May 31, 1948.
27. WYM, "'Good Will' Propaganda Sequence in United News No. 310."
28. Lawrence H. Sakamoto, "Permission to write and sell article for publication," August 19, 1948, in box 1026, Entry UD: 1200, GHQ/SCAP. It took the complex bureaucracy of GHQ over five months to approve the application.
29. CCD white administrators appeared to have depended greatly on this bilingual Nisei for censorship of Japanese motion pictures and newsreels since the early months of occupation.
30. See "Army to Honor Dead US-Japanese Soldier," and Larry Sakamoto, "Nisei Hero Gets Honor Funeral," *Pacific Stars and Stripes*, September 23 and 27, 1948, respectively; "Military Honors for Nisei Soldier," *Nippon Times*, September 26, 1948; "Nisei yūshi no igai kaeru," *Yomiuri Shinbun*, September 26, 1948; and "Nisei no ikotsu kaeru," *Asahi Shinbun*, September 26, 1948.
31. See "Nisei yūshi no igai kaeru"; and "Nisei no ikotsu kaeru."
32. See Sakamoto, "Nisei Hero Gets Honor Funeral." Most of Nisei-related news items in the *Pacific Stars and Stripes* were likely penned by Lawrence H. Sakamoto.
33. "442-butai o unda Zaibei Nihonjin-shi eiga-ka," *Rafu Shimpo*, June 24, 1948 (Japanese section); and "Yushutsu eiga ni '442-butai,'" *Rafu Shimpo*, January 1, 1950 (Japanese section).
34. The former US residents in the film production team included Mimura Akira, noted Hollywood-trained cinematographer, and Ōkawa Heihachirō ("Henry"), a pioneering Asian American actor. Educated at Columbia University and fluent in English, Ōkawa took charge of negotiating with CIE. Many influential figures in Japan's film industry were also involved: Takimura Kazuo (producer), Yamamoto Kajirō (director), Mori Iwao (script writer), Takamine

Hideko (actress), and Yamaguchi Yoshiko (actress also known as Shirley Yamaguchi). On the US side, renowned Issei photographer Tōyō Miyatake of Los Angeles offered constant support for the project as consultant. See "442-butai o unda Zaibei Nihonjin-shi eiga-ka" and "Yushutsu eiga ni '442-butai.'" On some of these film workers and actors in prewar Japanese America, see Kudō Miyoko, *Hariuddo kara Hiroshima e* (Tokyo: Shōbunsha, 1985); and Daisuke Miyao, *Sessue Hayakawa: Silent Cinema and Transnational Stardom* (Durham: Duke University Press, 2007).

35. "442-butai o unda Zaibei Nihonjin-shi eiga-ka."
36. See Eiichiro Azuma, *Between Two Empires: Race, History, and Transnationalism in Japanese America* (New York: Oxford University Press, 2005), pp. 89–105, 111–13, 122–34.
37. "Yushutsu eiga ni '442-butai.'"
38. On a precedent in prewar Japan where the government and society co-opted the Issei-generated historical interpretations and narratives, see Eiichiro Azuma, "Pioneers of Overseas Japanese Development: Japanese American History and the Making of Expansionist Orthodoxy in Imperial Japan," *Journal of Asian Studies* 67, no. 4 (2008): pp. 1187–1226.
39. See "Yushutsu eiga ni '442-butai" and "Eiga ni naru Zaibei dōhō," *Rafu Shimpo*, December 14, 1949 (Japanese section). The latter source discusses another film project—tentatively titled "Faraway land of my mother"—that drew on a similar narrative of Issei "perseverance" and "triumph" and its relevance to the current rise of the Japanese in America ("zaibei dōhō"). As of late 1949, the project was being organized by the Daiei Film Studio with renowned Issei actor Sesshū (Sessue) Hayakawa as consultant.
40. Yukiko Koshiro, *Trans-Pacific Racisms and the US Occupation of Japan* (New York: Columbia University Press, 1999), pp. 1–48, esp. 16. She argues that white American conquerors used race as a "punitive tool" to teach vanquished Japanese a "proper sense of relations" between the two groups during the first three years of military occupation. In the context of the "reverse course" between 1949 and 1952, race worked in such a way as to upgrade the status of defeated Japanese to that of "honorary whites" and a US junior ally, to which Japanese racist thinking easily adjusted itself.
41. Takemae, *Inside GHQ*, pp. 458–59; and also Naoko Shibusawa, *America's Geisha Ally: Reimagining the Japanese Enemy* (Cambridge, MA: Harvard University Press, 2006), pp. 181–82. On how the reverse course laid the groundwork for Japan's economic ascent in the 1950s, see Aaron Forsberg, *America and the Japanese Miracle: The Cold War Context of Japan's Postwar Economic Revisal, 1950–1960* (Chapel Hill: University of North Carolina Press, 2000); and Sayuri Shimizu, *Creating a People of Plenty: The United States and Japan's Economic Alternatives, 1950–1960* (Kent, OH: Kent State University Press, 2001).
42. Takemae, *Inside GHQ*, pp. 462–68. See also Koshiro, *Trans-Pacific Racisms and the US Occupation of Japan*, pp. 89–122.
43. In August 1949, almost three-quarters of Japanese preferred "permanent neutrality" to "collective security," with the latter getting only 16.6 percent of backing. In November 1949, one month after the Communist takeover of China, the preference for unarmed neutrality decreased to 48.4 percent, while the combined support for collective security and reliance on US military protection reached 34.5 percent. Once the Korean War broke out, public opinion quickly turned more in favor of rearmament (38.9 percent) than in opposition to it (28.4 percent). See Okada Naoyuki, "Saigunbi no seijiteki tenkai to kokumin yoron no dōkō (ge)," *Seijō bungei: Seijō University arts and literature quarterly* 44 (1966): pp. 54–61. On Japanese attitude toward militarization in this period, see also David Hunter-Chester, *Creating Japan's Ground Self-Defense Force, 1945–2015* (Lanham, MD: Lexington Books, 2016), pp. 78–80, esp. 79.
44. Takemae, *Inside GHQ*, p. 458.
45. Ibid., p. 467.
46. On MacArthur's objections, see ibid., p. 462.
47. On these political developments in the American military leadership, see ibid., pp. 457–62, 467–76, 485–90; Hunter-Chester, *Creating Japan's Ground Self-Defense Force, 1945–2015*, pp. 77–88; and Masuda Hiroshi, "Chōsen sensō izen ni okeru Amerika no Nihon saigunbi kōsō," nos. 1–2, *Hōgaku kenkyū: Journal of Law, Politics, and Sociology* 72, nos. 4–5 (1999): pp. 15–51, 37–62, respectively. On the Self-Defense Force's relations to the US army, see Aaron Herald Skebelund, *Inglorious, Illegal Bastards: Japan's Self-Defense Force during the Cold War* (Ithaca, NY: Cornell University Press, 2022), pp. 32–55.
48. On Earl Finch's wartime interactions with Nisei soldiers, see *Saturday Evening Post*, November 10, 1945; Mark Santoki, *The Earl Finch Story: One Man USO* (Honolulu: Seiji F. Naya, 2000), pp. 9–35; and John Howard, *Concentration Camps on the Home Front: Japanese Americans in the House of Jim Crow* (Chicago: University of Chicago Press, 2008), pp. 1–7.

49. On examples of press reports in Japanese, see *Yomiuri Shinbun*, February 7, 1950, March 5, 1950; *Asahi Shinbun*, February 7 and 9, 1950, March 4, 1950; and "Nisei no chichi o kakonde," *Sandē Mainichi* 29, no. 12 (1950): pp. 30–32. English news reports included Larry Sakamoto, "Nisei 'Godfather' Slated in Tokyo on Business" and "Reception Held for Nisei's Pal," *Pacific Stars and Stripes*, February 2 and 7, 1950, respectively; and Leslie Nakashima, "442nd Vets Fete Finch at Gojoen," *Nippon Times*, February 8, 1950. On JCS's visit to occupied Japan, see Omar N. Bradley and Clay Blair, *A General's Life: An Autobiography* (New York: Simon and Schuster, 1983), pp. 523–29, esp. 525. In late January 1950, Bradley, JCS Chairman, and other JCS members paid their first visit to the occupied country since the end of the war to confer with MacArthur about East Asian affairs. When Bradley discussed the JCS's "scheme for the secret rearming of the Japanese," the SCAP still resisted the idea. The JCS chairman noted that their proposal did not receive much support from the State Department, either, at that juncture. Yet, the Korean War would put an end to the intra-governmental opposition to the Pentagon's plan for Japan's rearmament.
50. "Friendship of America, Japan's Need—Yoshida," and "Finch Honored by Gov. Yasui," *Pacific Stars and Stripes*, February 16 and 18, 1950, respectively; and "Nisei butai no chichi Āru Finchi-shi ikkō kangeikai kaisai ni tsuite," February 14, 1950, in Shomu-ka, "Shōwa 24-nendo Kaigi keihi," vols. 1–3 (103.006.003), TMGA.
51. "Finch Arrives: Met by Nisei," *Pacific Stars and Stripes*, February 6, 1950. See also newspaper clippings in folder 21, box 3429, Entry UD: 1583, GHQ/SCAP.
52. Nakashima, "442nd Vets Fete Finch at Gojoen."
53. See *Asahi Shinbun*, March 4 and 5, 1950; "Big Party Held for Nisei 'Godfather': Finch Giving Candy to Japanese Children," *Mainichi*, February 8, 1950; and Howard, *Concentration Camps on the Home Front*, p. 245.
54. "Godfather of Nisei Coming to Osaka: Finch Receives Many Letters and Calls," *Mainichi*, February 18, 1950; "'Santa San' Earl Finch Is Back with Good Tidings from 442nd Combat Team," *Hawaii Times*, March 13, 1950; *Yomiuri Shinbun*, March 5, 1950; and Howard, *Concentration Camps on the Home Front*, p. 245. The quote is from the first source. Finch always called his Nisei friends "boys."
55. The Japanese press picked up this analogy almost instantly. See, for example, "Nisei no chichi o kakonde," pp. 30–32.
56. "Godfather of Nisei Coming to Osaka."
57. "Yoshida shushō to Finchi Nisei no kunkō o kataru," *Hawaii Herald*, February 28, 1950 (Japanese section); and "Nihon e mata ikuyo, Finchi-shi kaeru," *Hawaii Times*, March 13, 1950 (Japanese section).
58. "Godfather of Nisei Coming to Osaka."
59. "Record of 442nd Impresses Japanese," *Hawaii Herald*, February 16, 1950; "Finch Stresses Role of Nisei in Promoting US-Japan Accord," *Hawaii Herald*, February 7, 1950; and "Record of Nisei Combat Unit Aids Japan Democracy," *Pacific Citizen*, March 11, 1950: p. 1.
60. "To de Nisei butai shōtai," *Asahi Shinbun*, February 9, 1950; "442-butai o tatae Nichibei dai-kōkankai," *Hawaii Times*, March 3, 1950 (Japanese section). Reportedly, there were about three hundred veterans of the 442nd RCT throughout the Japanese archipelago at that time.
61. See "Fukumaden Tokyo-tochō no shūjō o abaku," *Shinsō* 24 (1948): p. 20; "Tsumamigui shirabe," *Shinsō* 5, no. 14 (1950): pp. 28–29; and "Who Is Yasui?," *Nippon Times*, July 20, 1950: p. 3. The quote is from the first source.
62. See Eiichiro Azuma, *In Search of Our Frontier: Japanese America and Settler Colonialism in the Construction of Japan's Borderless Empire* (Berkeley: University of California Press, 2019), pp. 225–28.
63. Yamashita Ichirō, "Genron shuppan kara owareru hitobito 3," *Shinsō* 8 (1947): p. 23; Uozumi Akira, "Taishū wa kami de aru" no. 78, *Gendai bijinesu* (November 17, 2019) at https://gendai.ismedia.jp/articles/-/68493 (accessed on July 25, 2025); and Nakano Yoshio et al., "Mayonaka no seizetsu," *Kaizō* 34, no. 10 (1953): pp. 173–74. The quotes are from the last source.
64. "Who Is Yasui?"
65. On Kimura's leadership in the party planning and his interest in the Nisei soldier story, see "Minshu shugi jintō ni taoreta Nisei no ikun o shōkai," *Rafu Shimpo*, August 6, 1951 (Japanese section); "Yo ni deru ko-Munemori ittōhei, denki o Kimura-shi shippitsu," *Rafu Shimpo*, August 1, 1951 (Japanese section); and "Japanese Author of 442nd Story to Write of Munemori," *Rafu Shimpo*, August 1, 1951.
66. "Yo ni deru ko-Munemori ittōhei, denki o Kimura-shi shippitsu."

67. Item no. 17, "Beigun '442-butai' no kōseki o tataeru paatei kaisai ni tsuite," January 26, 1950, in "Fugi," v. 1 (328.A05.001), TMGA.
68. Seiichiro Yasui, "General Walker, A Tribute," *Nippon Times*, December 31, 1950: p. 4.
69. See "To de Nisei butai shōtai"; 442-butai o tatae Nichibei dai-kōkankai"; "Zainichi Nisei butaiin o Tokyo-to shusai de shōtai," *Rafu Shimpo*, February 9, 1950 (Japanese section); "Tokyo Will Honor 442nd Nisei Vets," *Hawaii Herald*, February 8, 1950; and "To Fete Nisei Vets," *Nippon Times*, February 9, 1950, p. 3.
70. Leslie Nakashima, "Gen. Walker Lauds Former 442d Nisei," *Pacific Stars and Stripes*, April 17, 1950; "Veteran Nisei of 442nd Combat Team Honored at Gala Tokyo Garden Party," *Mainichi*, April 16, 1950; "Japanese Fete Nisei Veterans at Tokyo Party," *Pacific Citizen*, April 22, 1950; "To Fete Nisei Vets"; and "Nisei butai to sakura," *Yomiuri Shinbun*, April 16, 1950.
71. "Ex-Members of 442nd Nisei Combat Team to be Feted: Tokyo Parade Also Slated," *Nippon Times*, April 6, 1950; "Nagoyakana tsudoi: Nisei butai kōkan," in *Yomiuri Kokusai Nyūsu*, no. 57 (newsreel), April 18, 1950, Kawasaki City Museum, Japan; and *Yomiuri Shinbun*, July 9, 1950. The quotes are from the first source.
72. "Veteran Nisei of 442nd Combat Team Honored at Gala Tokyo Garden Party." On an example of Finch's statement on Nisei's contributions to US-Japan friendship, see Nakashima, "442nd Vets Fete Finch at Gojoen."
73. "Veteran Nisei of 442nd Combat Team Honored at Gala Tokyo Garden Party."
74. Nakashima, "Gen. Walker Lauds Former 442d Nisei."
75. Sidney Forrester Mashbir, *I Was an American Spy* (New York: Vantage Press, 1953), p. 254.
76. Ibid.
77. *Yomiuri Shinbun*, August 19, 1950; and "Rentaiki wa doko ni ikuka," *Shinsō* 50 (1950), p. 27. The quote is from the former. On Nisei's involvement in Japan's National Police Reserve, see "Korega shin kokugun no shōtaida," *Shinsō* 67 (1954): p. 6; "Hoantai-in no yattsu no kyōfu," *Maru* 6, no. 11 (1953): p. 22; Hunter-Chester, *Creating Japan's Ground Self-Defense Force, 1945–2015*, p. 101; and Skebelund, *Inglorious, Illegal Bastards*, p. 47. These sources underscore that Nisei held subordinate roles and performed rather pathetically as inept interpreters, and were certainly not model soldiers or military trainers. At the same time, Skebelund explains how Nisei linguists had "more influence than (Japanese) camp commanders on (National Police Reserve/NPR) training and camp life because of their intermediary status" with white US army officers, citing the testimonies of Japanese enlistees. They also bitterly recalled instances of abusive violent actions by Nisei linguists against Japanese NPR members.
78. Eimei Kato, "Tokyo Beat," *Mainichi*, February 8, 1950.
79. See Tadao Yasuike, "The Story of 'The 442nd,'" *Mainichi*, April 5–9, 1950.
80. "Nisei to kataru Amerika seikatsu zadankai," *Chūgakusei no tomo* 27, no. 3 (1950): pp. 74–81. The quotes are from pp. 75, 78–79, 81.
81. Ibid. The quotes are from pp. 78–79, 81.

Chapter 6

1. See Howard D. Case, "Down to Cases," *Honolulu Star-Bulletin*, April 1, 1943; Lyn Crost, "Lyn Crost: Boys Proud of Hawaii," *Honolulu Star-Bulletin*, June 6, 1945; "'Larry' Sakamoto Wounded in Action," *Honolulu Star-Bulletin*, August 9, 1944; and "Larry Sakamoto Home from War," *Honolulu Star-Bulletin*, August 25, 1945.
2. See "Larry Sakamoto Home from War"; "Hawaii Soldiers War Exploits Are Published," *Honolulu Star-Bulletin*, June 11, 1946; "Pictorial Record of AJA to Be Published Here," *Honolulu Advertiser*, July 7, 1946; "Book Depicts War Feats of Hawaii AJAs," *Honolulu Advertiser*, May 6, 1947; and "'Hawaii's Own' Is Story of Wartime Courage, Gallantry," *Honolulu Star-Bulletin*, May 13, 1947.
3. Larry [Sakamoto], copy of letter, ca. April 15, 1943, enclosed in C[harles]. W. Pence to William P. Scobey, April 22, 1943, in folder 6, box 48, Entry 180, FSCCJJM.
4. Lawrence Nakatsuka, *Hawaii's Own: Picture Story of 442nd Regiment, 100th Battalion and Interpreters* (Honolulu: L. H. Sakamoto, 1946). Some of the early English-language publications on the 442nd RCT include: Orville C. Shirey, *Americans: The Story of the 442nd Combat Team* (Washington, DC: Infantry Journal Press, 1946); John A. Rademaker, *These Are Americans: The Japanese-Americans in Hawaii in World War II* (Palo Alto, CA: Pacific Books, 1951); and Thomas D. Murphy, *Ambassadors in Arms: A History of the 100th Infantry Battalion* (Honolulu: University of Hawaii Press, 1954).

5. Lawrence Nakatsuka, credited as author of "articles" (chapter essays) for *Hawaii's Own*, was a 25-year-old reporter for the *Honolulu Star-Bulletin*. He later served as an enlisted linguist in occupied Japan. The illustrator was Soji Morisawa. The book was Sakamoto's brainchild through and through, as he took charge of collecting all photos and putting together the volume.
6. Riley H. Allen, "Foreword," in Nakatsuka, *Hawaii's Own*, no pagination.
7. See Nakatsuka, *Hawaii's Own*, p. 55. The book argued: "Japanese-American soldiers fought two enemies in the last war—the Nazis and the Nipponese on the battle front and race prejudice on the home front.... The Nazis and the Nipponese have been beaten.... But race prejudice—the home front enemy—still lives on. The brilliant war record of the Japanese-Americans has quieted the voice of the intolerant and the bigoted, but not for long." This was why Sakamoto put his money, time, and energy into the publication of *Hawaii's Own*.
8. "To de Nisei butai shōtai," *Asahi Shinbun*, February 9, 1950; and "442-butai o tatae Nichibei dai-kōkankai," *Hawaii Times*, March 3, 1950.
9. Larry Sakamoto, "File and Don't Forget," *Pacific Stars and Stripes*, October 10, 1948.
10. "Nisei War Hero Finds Mother in Japan," *Pacific Stars and Stripes*, October 22, 1948.
11. Sakamoto Kijiyu and Kimura Ki, *Amerika no Nisei shukun monogatari Dai-442 butai* (Tokyo: Ōbunsha, 1949), pp. 24–26.
12. See Larry Sakamoto, "Nisei Hero Gets Honor Funeral," *Pacific Stars and Stripes*, September 27, 1948.
13. See Lawrence H. Sakamoto to Commanding General, "Permission to write and sell article for publication," August 19, 1948, in box 1026, Entry UD: 1200, GHQ/SCAP.
14. "Memo for Record," January 14, 1949, pp. 1–2; and Toshio Katsube to Foreign Investment Board, "Application of Pvt. L. H. Sakamoto to Engage in Specific Business Activity," June 7, 1949, both in box 1026, GHQ/SCAP.
15. R. M. Levy to L. H. Sakamoto, "Permission and License for Private L. H. Sakamoto," July 12, 1949, in box 1026, GHQ/SCAP; and Sakamoto Kijiyu and Kimura Ki, "Amerika no Nisei shukun monogatari Dai-442 butai," nos. 1–2, *Seikatsu bunka* 10, nos. 6–7 (1949): pp. 64–69, 62–69, respectively.
16. Sakamoto and Kimura, "Amerika no Nisei shukun monogatari Dai-442 butai," no. 1, p. 64.
17. Ibid.
18. "Shuppanbu dayori," *Seikatsu bunka* 10, no. 8 (1949): p. 72. The advertisement for the forthcoming book had this sales pitch: "What did the Nisei regiment that shares our blood do in the past war?" See *Seikatsu bunka* 10, no. 9 (1949): p. 25.
19. On the background of their co-authorship, see Sakamoto and Kimura, *Amerika no Nisei shukun monogatari Dai-442 butai*, pp. 25–31; and *Rafu Shimpo*, August 1, 1951 (Japanese section).
20. Sakamoto and Kimura, *Amerika no Nisei shukun monogatari Dai-442 butai*, pp. 27–31, esp. 31.
21. This rhetoric was not Kimura's invention. It had existed in the Japanese intellectual world ever since the publication of *Bushido: The Soul of Japan* by Nitobe Inazō in the early twentieth century. On the imperial Japanese use of *bushidō* in asserting the likeness of white Christians and Japanese warriors, see Eiichiro Azuma, *Between Two Empires: Race, History, and Transnationalism in Japanese America* (New York: Oxford University Press, 2005), pp. 130–31; and Oleg Benesch, *Inventing the Way of Samurai: Nationalism, Internationalism, and Bushido in Modern Japan* (Oxford: Oxford University Press, 2014), pp. 90–96.
22. Sakamoto and Kimura, *Amerika no Nisei shukun monogatari Dai-442 butai*, pp. 94–97.
23. See ibid., pp. 14–16.
24. Ibid., pp. 15–16.
25. Ibid., p. 16.
26. Kimura Ki, "Dai-442 butai," *Chūgaku jidai* 1, no. 3 (1949): p. 19.
27. See Kimura Ki, "Minshu shugi no eiyū Ben Kuroki monogatari," *Kingu* 26, no. 12 (1950): pp. 178–88, esp. 179, 182, 188. On Kimura's project on Munemori, see "Japanese Author of 442nd Story to Write of Munemori"; "Yo ni deru ko-Munemori ittōhei, denki o Kimura-shi shippitsu," and "Minshu shugi jintō ni taoreta Nisei no ikun o shōkai," *Rafu Shimpo*, August 1 and 6, 1951, respectively.
28. Rōrensu Sakamoto (Lawrence Sakamoto), "Nihon no chi to Amerika no kokoro," *Bungei Shunjū* 28, no. 3 (1950): pp. 116–39.
29. See, for example, ibid., pp. 129, 132–36.
30. Ibid., pp. 132–34.

31. Ibid., p. 138. Similar arguments are found in other translated articles by former members of the 442nd RCT. One good example is Ōuchi Saburō, "Dai-442 butai no Nisei damashii," *Maru* 7, no. 12 (1954): pp. 154–55.
32. Sakamoto, "Nihon no chi to Amerika no kokoro," p. 139.
33. Nagata Shigeshi, trans., *442 Butai* ["Americans"] (Tokyo: Tokyo-dō, 1950).
34. Ibid., pp. 181–224. The quote is from p. 224.
35. See Murayama Tamotsu, "Nisei monogatari," *Nihon shūhō*, 131 (1949): pp. 27–31; Murayama, "Meriken jappu, Nisei monogatari 2," *Nihon shūhō*, 132 (1949): pp. 27–31; Murayama, "Meriken jappu, Nisei monogatari 3," *Nihon shūhō*, 133 (1949): pp. 27–31; Murayama, "Meriken jappu, Nisei monogatari 4," *Nihon shūhō*, 135 (1949): pp. 28–31; Murayama, "Nisei monogatari 5," *Nihon shūhō*, 136 (1949): pp. 28–31; Murayama, "Nisei monogatari 6," *Nihon shūhō*, 137 (1949): pp. 47–50; Murayama, "Nisei monogatari 7," *Nihon shūhō*, 140 (1950): pp. 31–34; and Murayama, "Nisei monogatari, saishūkai," *Nihon shūhō*, 142 (1950): pp. 31–34. The quote is from p. 27 of the first source.
36. See Murayama, "Nisei monogatari," pp. 27–28; Murayama, "Nisei monogatari 5," pp. 29–31; and Murayama, "Nisei monogatari, saishūkai," pp. 33–34. In May 1950, he also published a magazine article on "Tokyo Rose" from the standpoint of a fellow strandee. He was sympathetic about the plight of Iva Toguri and her treason trial, but his main criticism was directed at the monolithic representation of resident Nisei as anti-American traitors and war criminals, like the despised Tokyo Rose. See Murayama Tamotsu, "Tokyo Rōzu wa sannin ita!," *Bungei shunjū* 30, no. 7 (1950): pp. 68–79.
37. Murayama, "Nisei monogatari," p. 27. See also Murayama, "Nisei monogatari 5," pp. 30–31.
38. Murayama Tamotsu, *Shūsen no koro* (Tokyo: Jiji Tsūshinsha, 1968): pp. 312–13. The banned book was published fifteen years later as Murayama Tamotsu, *Amerika Nisei* (Tokyo: Jiji Tsūshinsha, 1964).
39. Rōrensu Sakamoto (Lawrence Sakamoto), *Nisei butai* (*Edifice to Victory*) (Tokyo: Sumiyoshi Shobō, 1950).
40. The publisher's advertisement presented the book as "a story of Nisei's love and anguish." See *Tosho shinbun*, October 4, 1950, p. 3. By February 1950, Sakamoto had abandoned the idea of simply translating *Hawaii's Own*. Kimura's earlier monograph (co-authored with Sakamoto's mother) already incorporated much of the work.
41. Sakamoto, *Nisei butai*.
42. See ibid., pp. 372–74, for the quotes.
43. Ibid., p. 373.
44. Ibid., pp. 374, 377.
45. On the cursory GHQ approval of Sakamoto's book project, see Katsube to Foreign Investment Board, "Application of Pvt. L. H. Sakamoto to Engage in Specific Business Activity."
46. Sakamoto, *Nisei butai*, pp. 199, 378–80. The quote is from p. 199.
47. "Nisei butai," *Nihon dokusho shinbun*, October 15, 1950, p. 8.
48. "Books: *Nisei Butai, Edifice to Victory!*, by Lawrence Sakamoto," *Nippon Times*, November 8, 1950: p. 8.
49. Eiji Takemae, *Inside GHQ: The Allied Occupation of Japan and Its Legacy*, translated by Robert Ricketts and Sebastian Swann (London: Continuum, 2002), p. 391.
50. On occupation censorship apparatuses, see ibid., pp. 384–99; Kyoko Hirano, *Mr. Smith Goes to Tokyo: Japanese Cinema under the American Occupation, 1945–1952* (Washington, DC: Smithsonian Institution Press, 1992), pp. 34–36, 40, 97–98; and Hiroshi Kitamura, *Screening Enlightenment: Hollywood and the Cultural Reconstruction of Defeated Japan* (Ithaca, NY: Cornell University Press, 2010), pp. 42–61. On how CIE officials used the Japanese committee as an indirect means of preproduction censorship, see Satō Tadao, *Nihon eigashi*, vol. 2 (Tokyo: Iwanami Shoten, 2006), pp. 230–31. Another extra-institutional/legal layer of continuous censorship was the practice of self-censorship among Japanese writers, publishers, and cultural workers. They had developed a good sense of the permissible "limits" under which they could engage in "freedom" of speech in the semi-colonial context of military occupation. On this, see Takemae, *Inside GHQ*, pp. 392–93.
51. "Kinuyo Tanaka Pays GI Homage," *Rafu Shimpo*, November 29, 1949; Larry Sakamoto, "Japanese Star Back from Visit in States," *Pacific Stars and Stripes*, January 20, 1950.
52. On the film project by Shōchiku Cinema, see *Mainichi* (Osaka version), February 3, 1950; *Asahi Shinbun*, February 9, 1950; and *Rafu Shimpo*, June 30, 1950 (Japanese section).

53. "Kinuyo-san dokuritsu puro sōsetsu," *Mainichi Shinbun*, February 3, 1950; "Tanaka Kinuyo-san dokuritsushi 'Hawai Nikkeihei' satsuei," *Hawaii Times*, February 3, 1950; Don Bliss, "Tanaka Will Be Star in Nisei's War Story," *Pacific Stars and Stripes*, February 6, 1950; "Hashinakumo Nichibei ga kyōsaku," *Yomiuri Shinbun*, February 9, 1950; "Film Star," *Pacific Citizen*, March 4, 1950; "Nihon e mata ikuyo, Finchi-shi kaeru," *Hawaii Times*, March 13, 1950; "'Santa san' Earl Finch Is Back with Good Tidings for 442nd Combat Team," *Hawaii Times*, March 13, 1950; and "Finch Back on Cleveland," *Hawaii Herald*, March 13, 1950. The quotes are from the February 6 issue of the *Pacific Stars and Stripes*.
54. Mr. Slott, "Screening of American Short Subjects," March 24, 1950, in folder 13, box 5308, Entry UD: 1667, GHQ/SCAP. The production team included screenwriters Noda Kōgo (first script) and Hisaita Eijirō (second and third scripts); film director Kinoshita Keisuke (also listed as co-screenwriter); producers Koide Takashi and Kuwata Ryōtarō. Tanaka Kinuyo was slated for the role of the Issei mother; and Sano Shūji as the Nisei son killed in action.
55. On the different versions of the film script, see Noda Kōgo, "Amerika rikugun dai-442 butai," ca. early February 1950; Hisaita Eijirō and Kinoshita Keisuke, "Nisei butai: Nikkei shimin no haha," ca. February 23, 1950; Hisaita Eijirō and Kinoshita Keisuke, "Nisei butai (kaitei)," ca. March 9, 1950, in box 5267, Entry UD 1666, GHQ/SCAP. On the "statement of the purpose," see the first page of the last two scripts. English translations of the scripts and a narrative version of the film are also in the same box. On the submissions of these drafts, see also CIE Motion Picture and Theatrical Branch, "Weekly Report," February 16, 1950, p. 4; ibid., February 23, 1950, p. 10; ibid., March 9, 1950, p. 5; and ibid., March 23, 1950, p. 1, all in box 5304, Entry UD: 1667, GHQ/SCAP.
56. Compare Hisaita and Kinoshita, "Nisei butai: Nikkei shimin no haha," ca. February 23, 1950, with Hisaita and Kinoshita, "Nisei butai (kaitei)," ca. March 9, 1950, both in box 5267, GHQ/SCAP.
57. See Hisaita and Kinoshita, "Nisei butai (kaitei)," ca. March 9, 1950, pp. e-41 to e-43.
58. Mr. Slott, "Production of Film on 442d Combat Team (Nisei)," March 18, 1950; and Mr. Slott, "Screening of American Short Subjects," March 24, 1950, both in folder 13, box 5308, GHQ/SCAP. The quotes are taken from both sources in the order they are listed.
59. See Mr. Slott, "Production of Film on 442d Combat Team (Nisei)"; and Mr. Slott, "Screening of American Short Subjects."
60. Kiyoshi Takamura to George Gerckie, March 2, 1950, in box 5267, GHQ/SCAP.
61. Mr. Slott, "Production of Film on 442d Combat Team (Nisei)."
62. Ibid.
63. Mr. Slott, "Screening of American Short Subjects."
64. See "Tanaka Kinuyo no 442-butai," *Rafu Shimpo*, May 1, 1950; "Tanaka Kinuyo shuen 'Nisei butai' nisha teikei seisakuka," *Rafu Shimpo*, June 30, 1950; and "Nichibei de kisou eigaka," *Rafu Shimpo*, September 22, 1950; and *Asahi Shinbun*, August 1, 1950. The October 1950 advertisement for Lawrence Sakamoto's book still mentioned Shōchiku's plan for film production based on it. See *Yomiuri Shinbun*, October 3, 1950: p. 1.
65. "442nd Epic Movie Slated," *Rafu Shimpo*, January 24, 1950; and "MGM News," August 18, 1950, in GFB-CMPS. On the Pentagon's support for the film project, see Shimura Miyoko, "Reisen shoki ni okeru Beikoku Kokubōsōshō no eiga seisaku: 'Nisei butai' (1951-nen) no seisaku kyōryoku o megutte," *Intelligence* 15 (March 2015): pp. 38–48.
66. "Masaoka Assigned Work Supervising 442nd Vehicle," *Rafu Shimpo*, January 27, 1950; Thomas F. Brady, "Hollywood Agenda," *New York Times*, January 29, 1950; "Editorial: 'Go For Broke,'" *Hawaii Herald*, February 2, 1950; and "NVA to Aid in 442nd Saga," *Rafu Shimpo*, February 15, 1950.
67. Metro-Goldwyn-Mayer, "Invitational Premier of *Go For Broke!*," May 9, 1950, in GFB-JANM.
68. See Mr. Slott, "Production of Film on 442d Combat Team (Nisei)," March 18, 1950. MGM's film director Robert Pirosh recalled how he had encountered a Japanese screenwriter in Honolulu when both had visited the island on a research trip for the competing film projects in August 1950. See "Nichibei de kisou eigaka"; and Gondō Chie, "Toransunashonaru shinema to shiteno Nihon eiga," *Ritsumeikan eizōgaku* 16 (March 2023): p. 16.
69. Iwasaki Akira, *Eigashi* (Tokyo: Tōyō Keizai Shinpōsha, 1961), p. 250. The other imported war movies that the author argued supported the cause of Japan's rearmament included *Battleground* (1949) and *The Steel Helmet* (1950). In Japan, the public releases of *Sands of Iwo Jima* (1949) and *Task Force* (1949) followed those of *Go for Broke!* and the other two. The years in the parentheses refer to the time of their original showing in the United States.

70. See *Yomiuri Shinbun*, July 11, 1952.
71. On representative works, see T[akashi] Fujitani, "*Go for Broke*, the Movie: Japanese American Soldiers in US National, Military, and Racial Discourse," in *Perilous Memories: The Asia-Pacific War(s)*, edited by T. Fujitani, Geoffrey M. White, and Lisa Yoneyama (Durham: Duke University Press, 2001), pp. 239–66; and Ellen D. Wu, *The Color of Success: Asian Americans and the Origins of the Model Minority* (Princeton: Princeton University Press, 2014), pp. 88–91. On the discussion of a geopolitical context for the film production, see Shimura, "Reisen shoki ni okeru Beikoku Kokubōsōshō no eiga seisaku."
72. See also the press kit for premier; Metro-Goldwyn-Mayer, "Invitational Premier of *Go For Broke!*" in GFB-CMPS.
73. See Fujitani, "*Go for Broke*, the Movie;" and Takashi Fujitani, *Race for Empire: Koreans as Japanese and Japanese as Americans during World War II* (Berkeley: University of California Press, 2011), pp. 223–29.
74. See, for example, a characterization of the film as "one that draws our attention because it is about the war experience of Nisei who are our blood brothers," in *Yomiuri Shinbun*, December 22, 1951.
75. See "Isasaka yūtsuni naru 'Nisei butai,'" *Shūkan Asahi* 56, no. 53 (1951): p. 46; Daikoku Tōyōshi (pseudo.), "Shishashitsu yori: Nisei butai," *Kinema junpō* 26 (November 1, 1951): p. 31; "Shinshun eiga kara," *Asahi Shinbun*, December 26, 1951; and Iwanaga Denmei, "Yattsukero," *Eiga no tomo* 19, no. 7 (1951): pp. 12–13.
76. See Shiraishi Gorō, "Nisei butai," *Nyū eiji* 4, no. 1 (1952): p. 79.
77. A number of advertisements and film reviews mentioned such terms as "*dōhō*" (racial/national compatriots) and "*chi no tsunagari*" (blood ties) when referencing Nisei soldiers. See advertisements in *Yomiuri Shinbun*, December 20, 1951; *Asahi Shinbun*, January 10, 1952; *Eiga hyōron* 9, no. 1 (1952): no pagination; and a review in *Yomiuri Shinbun*, December 22, 1951. On discussions of emotional response as Japanese viewers, see Daikoku, "Shishashitsu yori"; and "Nisei butai," *Kinema junpō* 23 (September 15, 1951): no pagination.
78. Shiraishi, "Nisei butai," p. 79.
79. Wakuda Kōsuke, "Eiga monogatari, Nisei butai," *Chūgakusei no tomo* 28, no. 11 (1952): pp. 57–58.
80. Q.Q.Q. (pseudo.), "Eigahyō," *Zaisei* 17, no. 3 (1952): p. 112.
81. "Jinshu mondai eno hansei," *Mainichi Shinbun*, November 26, 1951.
82. "Kiroku-fū no katsugeki, Nisei butai (MGM)," *Asahi Shinbun*, December 28, 1951.
83. Eito Toshio, "Nisei butai (MGM)," *Mainichi Shinbun*, December 25, 1951.
84. On Cold War origins of Asian/Japanese area studies in the United States, see John W. Dower, "E. H. Norman, Japan and the Uses of History," in *Origins of the Modern Japanese State: Selected Writings of E. H. Norman*, edited by John W. Dower (New York: Random House, 1975), pp. 3–101; Harry Harootunian, *History's Disquiet: Modernity, Cultural Practice, and the Question of Everyday Life* (New York: Columbia University Press, 2000), pp. 25–58; and Carol Gluck, "House of Mirrors: American History-Writing on Japan," in *Imagined Histories: American Historians Interpret the Past*, edited by Anthony Molho and Gordon S. Wood (Princeton: Princeton University Press, 1998), pp. 434–54.
85. On representative works on postwar Japanese American integration, see Wu, *The Color of Success*, pp. 150–80, 210–41; Lon Kurashige, *Japanese American Celebration and Conflict: A History of Ethnic Identity and Festival in Los Angeles, 1934–1990* (Berkeley: University of California Press, 2002), pp. 119–85; Scott Kurashige, *The Shifting Grounds of Race: Black and Japanese Americans in the Making of Multiethnic Los Angeles* (Princeton: Princeton University Press, 2008), pp. 158–204.
86. These themes have been examined in recent works of Simeon Man and Monica Kim, for example. See Simeon Man, *Soldiering through Empire: Race and the Making of the Decolonizing Pacific* (Berkeley: University of California Press, 2018); and Monica Kim, *The Interrogation Rooms of the Korean War: The Untold History* (Princeton: Princeton University Press, 2019).

Epilogue

1. The first post-occupation Japanese film with a Nisei theme came out in early 1953. Titled *Hawai no yoru* (*Twilight of Hawaii*), this new-year feature film narrated the triumph and eternity of Japaneseness in Nisei's identity. An original production of Shin Tōhō Cinema revived a pivotal theme in Shōchiku's failed project of *Nisei butai*, which had been overshadowed by the

US-centric narrative of *Go for Broke!* exactly one year before. *Hawai no yoru* combined bilateral war stories with captivating tales of family conflict and borderless love encompassing Hawai'i and Japan, thereby obfuscating the distinction between imperial Japanese and American-born Japanese. Tracing back to the prewar years in Honolulu, the romance of a visiting Japanese athlete and a local Nisei girl forms the central thread of the film's narrative. With a focus on human emotions and bonds between these individuals beyond national borders, this film privileges the inseparable ties between Japanese Americans and their blood kin over ideological differences between imperial Japan and the United States. Moreover, the film flattens the critical distinction between the US and Japanese armed forces by juxtaposing the military experiences of the Japanese man in the imperial forces and his lover's Nisei brother in the 442nd RCT. When the former dies of wounds as a prisoner of war in Hawai'i, white military police grace him with wildflowers and a military salute as if the Japanese man is a fallen comrade. No trace of the hateful war between the Japanese empire and the United States is detectable in the actions of the white American MP. And the grieving Nisei woman, who goes on to live as a catholic nun in the postwar years, remains committed to the love and memory of her Japanese lover. Apparently, a skeleton of this film project had existed as early as June 1950, when preparation for Shōchiku's *Nisei butai* was still in full steam. See *Yomiuri Shinbun*, June 10, 1950; and Gondō Chie, "Toransunashonaru shinema to shiteno Nihon eiga," *Ritsumeikan eizōgaku* 16 (March 2023): pp. 16–19.

2. See Robert (Bob) Nobuyuki Hongo, *Hey Pineapple!* (Tokyo: Hokuseido Press, 1958). A Japanese translation was hastily put together and published in conjunction with the release of the Shōchiku film in December 1959. See Robāto Hongō, *Painappuru butai*, translated by Inoue Isamu (Tokyo: Bungei Shunjū, 1959). The Japanese version also engages in various acts of fabrications relating to the question of white racism against Japanese/Asians. The racial epithet "gook" is mistranslated as "*dojin*" (tropical savage) with which Nisei soldiers took issue and rioted against white GIs for. The arbitrary swapping of gook with *dojin* gives the impression that Nisei resented being identified with dark-skinned indigenes more than being discriminated against as Asians. Considering that the preceding scene depicted Nisei soldiers as having no problem about being mixed up with Japanese nationals, the translated version of *Hey Pineapple!* reflected more of Japanese racial/racist views than Nisei's racial views. For this reason, the Japanese version presents the white commanders and soldiers as generally fair-minded and non-discriminatory to Nisei/Japanese. Hongo's original offers a more complex picture. See Hongo, *Hey Pineapple!*, pp. 147–48, 171; and Hongō, *Painappuru butai*, pp. 134, 152.
3. "Japan Critics Rate 'Hey Pineapple Good Entertainment' War Story," *Honolulu Star-Bulletin*, December 27, 1959.
4. See Hongo, *Hey Pineapple!*, pp. 91–144, 284–89, 326–34.
5. See a published film script of the film in Oguni Hideo, "Painappuru butai," *Kinema junpō bessatsu: Meisaku shinario-shū* (November 15, 1961): pp. 92–96, 106–7, 109–10.
6. "Nikkei Nisei butai no Tokyo nikki," *Shūkan myōjō* 2, no. 30 (1959): p. 23. Hongo argued that MGM's *Go for Broke!* was not a genuine Nisei film, because Hollywood's white scriptwriters and filmmakers produced the story by "adding their own interpretations" to Nisei's tales.
7. Oguni, "Painappuru butai," pp. 96, 103.
8. Ibid., pp. 101, 108–9.
9. See Tsurumi Shunsuke, "'Painappuru butai' yogen suruka?," *Eiga hyōron* 17, no. 2 (1960): pp. 20–23, esp. 23.
10. In 1964, the saga of the 442nd RCT was published in the form of a *manga* graphic novel under the title of "*Saizensen*" (*Frontline*), and it was reprinted in 2001 with a new title: "*Nisei butai monogatari*" (*Stories of Nisei Regiment*). A sequel to this *manga* was published in 1996. These publications came out when Japan was engulfed in a crisis of one kind or another, including the worsening military situation in Vietnam of the early 1960s and the collapse of Japan's bubble economy and the subsequent "lost decades" after 1991. See Mochizuki Mikiya, *Saizensen* (Tokyo: Shōnen Gahō-sha, 1964); Mochizuki Mikiya, *Nisei butai monogatari* (Tokyo: Hōmu-sha, 2001); and Mochizuki Mikiya, *Shin Nisei butai monogatari* (Tokyo: Nihon Shuppansha, 1996). See also Kikuzuki Toshiyuki, *Nisei butai monogatari* (Tokyo: Gurīn Arō Shuppansha, 2002).
11. Yamasaki Toyoko's novel, *Futatsu no sokoku* (*Two Homelands*: 1983, 2007), typifies this narrative scheme. See also n. 40 in Chapter 1. In 2010, a major Tokyo broadcast station also

produced a different five-episode series entitled "*Kyūjū-kyū nen no ai*" (*Love That Survived Ninety-Nine Years*) around the theme of Japanese American experience with the Pacific War as a focal point. This eight-hour drama featured one family near Seattle, which was torn up by racism, war, incarceration, and military service. Yet, in 2010—ninety-nine years after the immigrant father first set foot on American soil—both sides of the family on the Pacific (strandee-turned Japanese nationals and their Nisei siblings in Seattle) finally reunite to affirm the unbreakable bonds and undying "love" for each other. Such a sentimental and triumphant narrative valorizes the timeless value of shared blood ties and the centrality of being Japanese beyond citizenship differences. This highly regarded television drama series was rebroadcasted in late 2011, several months after the devastating earthquake and nuclear disaster in Japan. See http://www.tbs.co.jp/japanese-americans/index-j.html (accessed on July 27, 2025).

12. See Ellen D. Wu, *The Color of Success: Asian Americans and the Origins of the Model Minority* (Princeton: Princeton University Press, 2014), pp. 86–91, 108–10, 218–19, 236–38. On varied aspects of postwar Japanese American integration, see also Greg Robinson, *After Camp: Portraits in Midcentury Japanese American Life and Politics* (Berkeley: University of California Press, 2012).
13. Mitchell Takeshi Maki, Harry H. L. Kitano, and S. Megan Berthold, *Achieving the Impossible Dream: How Japanese Americans Obtained Redress* (Urbana: University of Illinois Press, 1999), p. 142.
14. Ibid., pp. 192–93.
15. See ibid., pp. 195–97; and https://www.reaganlibrary.gov/archives/speech/remarks-signing-bill-providing-restitution-wartime-internment-japanese-american (accessed on July 27, 2025).
16. See Joseph D. Harrington, *Yankee Samurai: The Secret Role of Nisei in America's Pacific Victory* (Detroit: Harlo Press, 1979); and Tad Ichinokuchi, ed., *John Aiso and the MIS: Japanese American Soldiers in the Military Intelligence Service, World War II* (Los Angeles: Military Intelligence Service Club of Southern California, 1988).
17. Military Intelligence Service Association of Northern California (MIS NorCal) and National Japanese American Historical Society (NJAHS), eds., *The Pacific War and Peace: Americans of Japanese Ancestry in Military Intelligence Service, 1941 to 1952* (San Francisco: MIS NorCal and NJAHS, 1991); and Military Intelligence Service Veterans Club of Hawaii, ed., *Secret Valor: MIS Personnel, World War II Pacific Theater, Pre-Pearl Harbor to Sept. 8, 1951* (Honolulu: MIS Veterans Club of Hawaii, 1993). See also MIS-Northwest Association, *Unsung Heroes: The Military Intelligence Service Past-Present-Future* (Seattle: MIS-Northwest Association, 1996).
18. See, for example, Stanley Falk and Warren Tsuneishi, eds., *MIS in the War against Japan: Personal Experiences Related at the 1993 MIS Capital Reunion* (Washington, DC: Japanese American Veterans Association, 1995); "MIS in Japan," *Nikkei Heritage* 15, no. 1 (2003): pp. 4–18; and Hawaii Nikkei History Editorial Board, ed., *Japanese Eyes, American Heart: Personal Reflections of Hawaii's World War II Nisei Soldiers* (Honolulu: University of Hawaii Press, 1998).
19. See http://www.javadc.org/background_of_the_presidential_u.htm (accessed on July 27, 2025).
20. James C. McNaughton, *Nisei Linguists: Japanese Americans in the Military Intelligence Service during World War II* (Washington, DC: Department of the Army, 2006), quote from p. 462.
21. *JAVA (Japanese American Veterans Association) Advocate* 16 (October 2008): p. 14.
22. On an example of Obama's celebration of minority military contributions, see https://obamawhitehouse.archives.gov/the-press-office/2015/03/07/remarks-president-50th-anniversary-selma-montgomery-marches (accessed on July 27, 2025).
23. Joe M. Takita to Alice Kasai, January 14, 1947, in folder 2, box 109, JARP-Kasai.

Note on Sources

Research for this book project was complicated due to the continuous process of what can be characterized as a "grand narrative (re)production" that reinforced a notion of Nisei military heroism in public representations and memories. A vast majority of the existing works on Japanese American linguists relies on the oral histories of veterans, mostly procured after the story of Nisei war heroism helped the ethnic community successfully fight the redress and reparations movement in the late 1980s. These oral histories offer a common storyline that simplistically presents Nisei linguists as contributing to the smooth transition of Japan from a militarist regime to a democracy and peace-loving nation, and above all to a faithful friend to the United States. For this reason, I opted not to use these standard sources. Produced before the 1970s, only a handful of interviews and life stories, which are not tainted by the nationalist politics of the redress movement, were consulted; these sources also included personal letters and unpublished memoirs scattered through various archives and libraries.

For the same reason, most scholarly and popular histories of Nisei linguists tend to present a one-dimensional, celebratory narrative that goes along with an epic story of Japanese American patriots, who supposedly helped shorten the length of the war against Japan by a few years. Thus, most works concentrate on their wartime exploits, with their occupation-related work as a postscript of sorts. Combined with the problematic nature of interviews with and oral histories of Nisei veterans, these secondary sources are not generally useful for my research or an analysis of their complex thinking and practice.

In a similar vein, readers may wonder why this book's bibliography contains a rather slim list of secondary sources, especially when the US occupation of Japan remains a major theme in the study of US-Japan relations. Even though there is a massive body of scholarship on that history, including John W. Dower's Pulitzer Prize-winning *Embracing the Defeat*, these works reveal more conundrums and enigmas than clues or directions for my research or my argument. Perhaps, due to the problem of primary sources, scholars of the US military occupation rarely look at the activities of Japanese American cultural brokers in defeated Japan—as many as ten thousand strong—as if they did not even exist. At best, there may be occasional mentions of Japanese/Nisei translators, but the focus is always on white American occupiers and their relationships to Japanese nationals, or vice versa. Even the most sophisticated and detailed works on occupied Japan, like Dower's or Takemae Eiji's 750-page *Inside GHQ*, offer no substantive treatment of Nisei linguists and civilian workers there.

As a main source of information about Nisei linguists and propaganda workers in the Pacific War and the subsequent occupation of Japan, I consulted a massive collection of US military papers at the National Archives and Records Administration (NARA). This manuscript collection includes 10,129 boxes of the Records of Allied Operational and Occupation Headquarters, World War II, SCAP (hereafter GHQ/SCAP), Record Group (RG) 331; various US Army (War Department) records, particularly its Military Intelligence Service division; and other government agencies, such as the Departments of State and the Navy, as well as the Offices of War Information and Strategic Services. These sources are massive and diverse, but they were not well organized or catalogued for the purpose of my research. The names of Nisei citizen linguists, for example, are often mixed up with those of foreign Japanese employees who worked as translators, without regards to their citizenship status. Moreover, there is no sign of an attempt to create a category or classification for Japanese Americans in terms of their involvement in the Pacific War and the subsequent occupation of Japan. This state of archival organization made it necessary for me to sift through many boxes and folders that might contain documents relating to Nisei linguists, both enlisted personnel and civilian employees, under the War Department and other US agencies. Records of the Civil Intelligence Section (CIS), including the Counter Intelligence Corps (CIC), one of the most important branches of MacArthur's GHQ that employed a large portion of Nisei linguists, are almost completely missing from the GHQ/SCAP collection, presumably because the CIC and its Japanese American staffers were involved in clandestine (oftentimes borderline illegal) operations in occupied Japan. Indeed, there are less than two hundred archival boxes of CIS-related documents in the collection of over ten thousand. Still, the US government papers at the NARA served as the most important primary sources for this book.

What I could not get from the NARA sources, namely the activities of Nisei "strandees" in wartime and post-defeat Japan, Japanese American CIC agents, the linguists' relationship to enemy Japanese, and the Japanese attitudes toward Nisei occupation troops, were supplemented with the careful reading of newspapers, both in English and Japanese, as well as books and magazines published in occupied Japan and after the end of GHQ censorship. These sources provide useful information about the nuances of social and racial relations in the semi-colonial context of US military occupation, where US postwar racism and imperialism meshed with the remnants of Japanese imperial racism and militarist aspirations. Again, few of these sources specifically speak to the subject of Japanese Americans, much less make a clear distinction of Japanese US citizens and defeated Japanese. Thus, I had to cast an extremely wide net over these materials, going over a huge number of publications and newspapers as well as archival materials in Japan and beyond. Leftist sources turned out to be most useful, for they were intent on exposing everything negative about the US military and its personnel, including Nisei linguists. Yet, as with US government sources, I took special care when I analyzed these ideologically slanted primary sources. I was also a frequent visitor to Japan's Diplomatic Archives of the Ministry of Foreign Affairs and the National Diet Library for their respective holdings, especially before many of the old paper sources were digitized and more accessible remotely. Their materials are useful for salvaging Japanese views of Nisei and experiences of Japanese American strandees, as well as Japanese nationals who worked with Nisei occupation troops in various capacities. US-based archives, especially the Hoover Institution Library & Archives and UCLA's Japanese American Research Project Collection, offered personal papers and other documents relating to Nisei occupation troops and their white bosses and administrators. These materials also proved to be indispensable sources of information.

Selected Bibiliography

Manuscript Materials

US National Archives and Record Administration II, College Park, Maryland (unless otherwise noted)

War Department

Records of the Office of the Assistant Secretary of War. RG (Record Group) 107.
Formerly Security Classified Correspondence of John J. McCloy 1941–45 (FSCCJJM).
Records of the War Department General and Special Staffs. RG 165.
Military Intelligence Division Correspondence 1917–41 (MIDC).
Correspondence and Reports relating to the Operation of Language Schools and Training Facilities 1943–49. Records of the Training Group. Office of the Director of Intelligence G-2 1906–49 (CROLSTF-ODI).
General Records. Security-Classified General Correspondence 1942–45. Office of the Director of Plans and Operations (GR-SCGC).
Records of the War Relocation Authority. RG 210. NARA I. Washington, DC (RWRA).
Records of the Foreign Broadcast Intelligence Service. RG 262.
Transcripts of Monitored Foreign Broadcast 1941–46. Federal Communication Commission (TMFB-FBIS).
Records of the Army Staff. RG 319.
Historical Studies and Related Records of G-2 Components 1918–59. Records of the Office of the Assistant Chief of Staff G-2 (RAS-HSRR).
Records of the Office of the Provost Marshal General. RG 389.
Japanese-American Branch. General File 1942–46 (ROPMG-JABGF).
Records of Adjutant General's Office. RG 407.
World War II Operations Reports 1940–48: Pacific Theater (RAGO-OPPT).

US Military Government in Tokyo

Records of the General Headquarters Supreme Commander for the Allied Powers 1945–52. RG 331 (GHQ/SCAP).
Civil Affairs Subject File 1946–51. Kinki Civil Affairs Region. Civil Affairs Section.
Decimal File (unclassified) 1945–52. Administrative Division. Civil Information and Education Section (CIE).
Decimal File 1946–52. Motion Picture Branch. CIE.
General Subject File 1945–52. Public Opinion and Sociological Research Division. CIE.
Scripts and Related Files 1945–51. Motion Picture Branch. Information Division. CIE.
Topic Files 1945–52. Administrative Division. CIE.
Central Files 1945–49. Press, Publications and Broadcast Division. Civil Intelligence Section.
Decimal File 1945–51. Library and Publication Division. Civil Historical Section.
Policy Branch. Office of Policy and Management Group. Civil Property Custodian.
Correspondence Files 1948–50. Administrative Division. Legal Section.

Office of War Information (OWI)

Records of the OWI. RG 208 (OWI-ROWI).
Records of the Overseas Branch.

Bureau of Overseas Intelligence Central Files 1941–45. Regional Analysis Division (OWI-BOICF).
Foreign Morale Analysis Division. Regional Analysis Division. Bureau of Overseas Intelligence (OWI-FMAD).
General Intelligence Division Central Intelligence Records. Bureau of Overseas Intelligence 1941–45 (OWI-GIDCIR).
Records of the Analysis and Research Bureau. Analyses of Japanese Broadcasts June 1942–October 1945 (OWI-AJB).
Records of the Historian. Historians' Records of the Psychological Warfare Branch 1941–45 (OWI-HRPWB).
Records of Natalie Davison (OWI-RND).
Records of the Office of Policy Coordination. Area Policy Files (OWI-ROPC).

Office of Strategic Services (OSS)

"OSS Personal List," vols. 1–2. NARA II Textual Material Research Room.
Records of the OSS. RG 226.
Central Files (OSS-CF).
Research and Analysis Branch. Office of Chief General Correspondence (OSS-RAB).

Department of the Navy

Records of the Office of the Chief of Naval Operations. RG 38
Japanese Activities in the Far East–Japan. Oriental Desk 1936–46. Sabotage, Espionage, and Counterespionage Section. Office of Naval Intelligence (DNONI-SECS).

Department of State

Confidential US State Department Special Files, Japan 1947–56 (Microfilm). RG 59 (DS-CSDSF).
Records of Harley A. Notter 1939–45 (1192-PR-6: Microfiche). Post-World War II Foreign Policy Planning. RG 59 (DS-RHN).
State Department Central Decimal File (Microfilm). Records of the US Department of State relating to the Internal Affairs of Japan 1945–49. RG 59 (DS-SDCDF).
Classified General Correspondence. Office of the US Political Advisor for Japan. Records of the Foreign Service Posts. RG 84 (DS-CGC).

NARA II Microfilm Collections

Military Intelligence in the Pacific 1942–46 (MIP).
Papers of the US Commission on the Wartime Relocation and Internment of Civilians.
Records of the Joint Chiefs of Staff, Part I: 1942–45. The Pacific Theater (RJCF-PT).

Hoover Institution Library and Archives, Stanford

Hubert Coslet Armstrong Papers (HCA-Hoover).
Kay K. Sasaki Papers (KKS-Hoover).
Joseph C. Trainor Papers (JCT-Hoover).
Richard S. R. Hubert Papers (RSRH-Hoover).

University of California at Los Angeles

Japanese American Research Project Collection. Department of Special Collections.
Yuji Ichioka Papers (JARP-Ichioka).
Alice Kasai Papers (JARP-Kasai).

University of Hawai'i at Manoa

Confidential Research Files. Romanzo Adams Social Research Laboratory Papers (CRF-Adams).
Ted Tsukiyama Papers. Japanese American Veterans Collection (Tsukiyama-JAVC).

Franklin D. Roosevelt Library, Hyde Park, New York (FDRL)

"War Relocation Authority" Files.

Other US Archives

Go for Broke! file. Margaret Herrick Library. Center for Motion Picture Study. Academy Foundation. Los Angeles (GFB-CMPS).

Go for Broke! collection. Japanese American National Museum. Los Angeles (GFB-JANM).

Japanese American Evacuation and Resettlement Records. Bancroft Library. University of California, Berkeley (JERS-BL).

Mike M. Masaoka Papers. J. Willard Merritt Library. University of Utah (MMMP).

Diplomatic Archives of the Ministry of Foreign Affairs (DAMFA), Tokyo, Japan

Chōsa-bu Dai-rokuka. "Boku-bei kansō hōkoku" (November 25, 1941).

Foreign Office. "We Fight through the Radio," vol. 1 (1942).

Jōhōkyoku. "Kaigai kōenshū," no. 4 (December 1942).

"Tekikoku zairyū Dōhō dainikai kōkansen kikokusha kōshū nittei-an" and "Nichibei dainiji kōkansen Teia-maru Yokohama nyūkō no sai ni okeru shochiburi ni kansuru kyōgi jikō." In *Nichibei kōkansen kankei*, vol. 6. Showa series.

National Archives of Japan, Tokyo

[Okayama-ken] Tokubetsu Kōtō-ka. "Taihō kyoka daichō" (1939–45).

"Zairyū tekikokujin no jitsujō chōsa ni kansuru ken-tō" (no date).

Tokyo Metropolitan Government Archives (TMGA), Japan

"Fugi," vol. 1 (no date).

Shomu-ka, "Shōwa 24-nendo Kaigi keihi," vols. 1–3 (1949).

"Showa 25-nendo kaigi keihi" (1950).

Newspapers and periodicals

United States

Hawaii Herald (1950).

Hawaii Times (1950, Japanese and English sections).

Honolulu Advertiser (1947).

Honolulu Star-Bulletin (1943–47, 1959).

Los Angeles Times (1942–45).

National Weekly (1952).

New York Times (1942–45, 1947–48, 1950, 1976, 1994).

Nikkei Heritage (2003).

Nippu Jiji (1937).

Nisei in Hawaii and the Pacific (1949–53).

Pacific Citizen (1948–50, 1966, 1975).

Pacific Stars and Stripes (1946–50, Pacific edition).

Rafu Shimpō (1946–53, Japanese and English sections).

San Francisco Chronicle (1995).

Scene (1950–54).

TIME Magazine (1948).

Japan

Asahi geinō (1971).

Asahi Shinbun (1937-44, 1948–53, 1959).

Beifu Jihō (1969).

Bungei shunjū (1950, 1952).

Chūgaku jidai (1949).
Chūgakusei no tomo (1950, 1952).
Chūgoku Shinbun (2000).
Chūō kōron (1953).
Daiamondo (1952).
Eiga hyōron (1960).
Eiga no tomo (1951).
Fujin gahō (1946).
Gendai bijinesu (2019).
Hōseki (1982).
Japan Times (1941–42).
Kaitakusha (1955).
Kaizō (1953).
Kinema junpō (1951, 1961).
Kingu (1950).
Mainichi (1950, English).
Mainichi Shinbun (1950–51, 2006, 2011, Japanese).
Maru (1953–54).
Nihon dokusho Shinbun (1950).
Nihon shūhō (1949–50).
Nippon Times (1943–52).
Nippon to Amerika (1967).
Nyū eiji (1952).
Reimei (1943).
Sandē Mainichi (1950, 1981).
Seikatsu bunka (1949).
Sekai (1959).
Shinsō (1947–48, 1950, 1954).
Shūkan Asahi (1951–52).
Shūkan myōjō (1959).
Shūkan Sankei (1952).
Shūkan Shinchō (1957, 1960).
Shūkan Yomiuri (1959).
Yomiuri Shinbun (1943, 1946–54).
Zaisei (1952).

Films

"Build Model Towns for Interned Japs." United Newsreel (1942).
Go For Broke! Metro-Goldwyn-Mayer Pictures (1951).
Hawai no yoru (*Twilight of Hawaii*). Shin Tōhō (1953).
"Japanese Relocation." Office of War Information (with War Relocation Authority) (1942).
"Little Tokyo USA." Twentieth-Century Fox (1942). In Motion Picture Collection, UCLA Film and Television Archive.
"Nagoyakana tsudoi: Nisei butai kōkan." In *Yomiuri Kokusai Nyūsu*, no. 57 (newsreel) (April 18, 1950). Kawasaki City Museum, Japan.
"Pres. Truman Honors Nisei Combat Group." Universal Newsreel (1946).

Selected Primary Sources

Aoki Hisa. *Teia-Maru no hōkoku* (Tokyo: Maeda Shobō, 1944).
Bradley, Omar N., and Clay Blair. *A General's Life: An Autobiography* (New York: Simon and Schuster, 1983).

Dodo Masao. "Beikokumin no zangyakusei." *Shin wakōdo* 4, no. 1 (1943): pp. 112–16.
Ebina Kazuo. *Kariforunia to Nihonjin* (Tokyo: Rōkkō Shuppanbu, 1943).
Emmerson, John K. *The Japanese Thread: A Life in the US Foreign Service* (New York: Holt, Reinhart and Winston, 1978).
Fokkusu, Rorin Shī (Rollin C. Fox). *Gendai Nihon kyōiku yōkō* (*Essentials in Modern Japanese education*) (Tokyo: Gakugei Tosho Shuppansha, 1950).
Fox, Rollin C. "The Secondary School Program at the Manzanar War Relocation Center" (Ed.D. dissertation, University of California, Los Angeles, 1946).
Fujii Tatsuki. *Shōnan sōseiki* (Tokyo: Takubundō, 1943).
Fujii, Tatsuki. *Singapore Assignment* (Tokyo: Nippon Times, 1943).
Gotō Tsutomu. *Zoku Nihon no teisō* (Tokyo: Sōkisha, 1953).
Hongo, Robert (Bob) Nobuyuki. *Hey Pineapple!* (Tokyo: Hokuseidō Press, 1958).
Hongō, Robāto. *Painappuru butai*, trans. Inoue Isamu (Tokyo: Bungei Shunjū, 1959).
Hume, Bill. *Babysan's World: Hume's Slant on Japan* (Tokyo: Charles E. Tuttle Co., 1954).
Iwasaki Akira. *Eigashi* (Tokyo: Tōyō Keizai Shinpōsha, 1961).
Kaji Jiken Taisaku Sewanin-kai, ed. *Kaji jiken: Bei bōryaku kikan no hanzai* (Tokyo: Kaji Jiken Taisaku Sewanin-kai, 1962).
Kaji Wataru, and Yamada Zenjirō. *Damare Nihonjin* ("Shut up, Jap!") (Tokyo: Rironsha, 1953).
Kawamura Masahei. *Taiheiyō no senkusha* (Tokyo: Tōzaisha, 1943).
Kimura Ki. "Dai-442 butai." *Chūgaku jidai* 1, no. 3 (1949): pp. 16–19.
Kimura Ki. "Minshu shugi no eiyū Ben Kuroki monogatari." *Kingu* 26, no. 12 (1950): pp. 178–88.
Kitō Itsuko. *Hawai-shi monogatari* (Tokyo: Tōtō Shoseki, 1943).
Mashbir, Sidney Forrester. *I Was an American Spy* (New York: Vantage Press, 1953).
Matsumoto, Takizo. *The American Ventures in East Asia* (Tokyo: Meiji University Press, 1943).
Matsumoto Takizō. "Beikoku oyobi Beikokujin." *Han-kōtsu* 44, no. 8 (1943): pp. 15–27.
Matsumoto Takizō. "Daitōa Sensō to Amerika umare Dai-Nisei no dōkō." *Zaisei* 7, no. 12 (1942): pp. 58–60.
Matsumoto Takizō. "Kokusai senden no saikentō." *Senden* 8725 (1942): pp. 11–14.
Matsumoto Takizō. "Nisei no tachiba yori mitaru tekikoku Amerika." *Bunmei Kyōkai nyūsu* 200 (1943): pp. 1–26.
Matsumoto Takizō. "Nisei yori mitaru teki Beikoku no jitsujō." *Nihon kōen* 676 (1943): pp. 2–30.
Miike Noboru, with Takahara Shirō. *Watashi no umareta Hawai* (Tokyo: Seitoku Shoin, 1942).
Mizuno Hiroshi, ed. *Nihon no teisō* (Tokyo: Sōkisha, 1953).
Monbushō Chōsa Fukyū-kyoku. *Amerika no Nihonjin oyobi Nikkei Amerikajin no kyōiku* (Tokyo: Monbushō, 1951).
Murayama Tamotsu. *Amerika Nisei* (Tokyo: Jiji Tsūshinsha, 1964).
Murayama Tamotsu. *Shūsen no koro* (Tokyo: Jiji Shuppansha, 1968).
Murphy, Thomas D. *Ambassadors in Arms: A History of the 100th Infantry Battalion* (Honolulu: University of Hawaii Press, 1954).
Nagata Shigeshi (translation). *442 Butai* (*Americans*) (Tokyo: Tokyo-dō, 1950).
Nakatsuka, Lawrence. *Hawaii's Own: Picture Story of 442nd Regiment, 100th Battalion and Interpreters* (Honolulu: Lawrence H. Sakamoto, 1946).
Nakazawa Ken. *Amerika no gokuchū yori Dōhō ni tsugu* (Tokyo: Masu Shobō, 1943).
Rademaker, John A. *These Are Americans: The Japanese-Americans in Hawaii in World War II* (Palo Alto, CA: Pacific Books, 1951).
Rengōkoku Saikō Shireibu Minkan Jōhō Kyōiku-kyoku, ed. *Shinsōbako* (Tokyo: Kozumo Shuppansha, 1946).
[Ringle, Kenneth D.]. "Japanese in America: The Problem and the Solution." *Harper's Magazine* 185 (1942): pp. 489–97.
Roosevelt, Eleanor. "A Challenge to American Sportsmanship." *Collier's Magazine* 112 (October 16, 1943): pp. 21, 71.

Sakamoto Kijiyu, and Kimura Ki. *Amerika no Nisei shukun monogatari Dai-442 butai* (Tokyo: Ōbunsha, 1949).
Sakamoto Kijiyu, and Kimura Ki. "Amerika no Nisei shukun monogatari Dai-442 butai," no. 1. *Seikatsu bunka* 10, no. 6 (1949): pp. 64–69.
Sakamoto Kijiyu, and Kimura Ki. "Amerika no Nisei shukun monogatari Dai-442 butai," no. 2. *Seikatsu bunka* 10, no. 7 (1949): pp. 62–69.
Sakamoto, Rōrensu (Lawrence Sakamoto). "Nihon no chi to Amerika no kokoro." *Bungei Shunjū* 28, no. 3 (1950): pp. 116–39.
Sakamoto, Rōrensu (Lawrence Sakamoto). *Nisei Butai* ("Edifice to Victory") (Tokyo: Sumiyoshi Shobō, 1950).
Sawada Miki. *Kuroi hada to shiroi kokoro* (Tokyo: Nihon Keizai Shinbunsha, 1963).
Shirey, Orville C. *Americans: The Story of the 442nd Combat Team* (Washington, DC: Infantry Journal Press, 1946).
Smith, Bradford. *Americans from Japan* (Philadelphia: J. B. Lippincott, 1948).
Tajiri, Larry Tajiri. "Democracy Corrects Its Own Mistake." *Asia and the Americas* 43, no. 4 (1943): pp. 213–16.
Tajiri, Larry. "Farewell to Little Tokyo." *Common Ground* 4, no. 2 (1944): pp. 90–95.
Uno, Kazumaro. *Corregidor, Isle of Delusion* (Shanghai: Mercury Press, 1942).
Uno Kazumaro. *Korehidoru saigo no hi*, translated by Shibata Kenjirō and Mochizuki Motoo (Tokyo: Seitoku Shoin, 1944).
War Department. *Final Report: Japanese Relocation from the West Coast, 1942* (Washington, DC: GPO, 1943).
War Relocation Authority. *WRA: A Story of Human Conservation* (Washington, DC: GPO, 1946).
Yamada Taijirō. *Amerika no himitsu kikan* (Tokyo: Satsuki Shobō, 1953).
Yamada Zenjirō. *Ketsudan* (Tokyo: Kōyō Shuppansha, 2000).
Yamamoto Noboru, ed. *Kaji Mitsuhashi jiken* (Tokyo: Surugadai Shobō, 1953).
Yang, Yong. *Kyanon kikan kara no shōgen* (Tokyo: Banchō Shoten, 1973).

Online Sources

Brandon, James R. "Stanley Kaizawa Interview." July 5, 2000. University of Hawai'i Library. https://evols.library.manoa.hawaii.edu/handle/10524/57068?mode=full (accessed on July 27, 2025).
Doi, Isao J. "Oral history." October 26, 2010. Go For Broke Foundation. https://www.goforbroke.org/ohmsviewer/viewer.php?cachefile=2010OH1026A_01_Doi.xml, and https://www.goforbroke.org/ohmsviewer/viewer.php?cachefile=2010OH1026A_02_Doi.xml (last accessed on July 27, 2025, but defunct as of January 14, 2026). See also https://ndajams.omeka.net/items/show/1053539 (accessed on January 14, 2026).
Obama, Barack. "Remarks by the President at the 50th Anniversary of the Selma to Montgomery Marches." March 7, 2005. The White House: President Barack Obama. https://obamawhitehouse.archives.gov/the-press-office/2015/03/07/remarks-president-50th-anniversary-selma-montgomery-marches (accessed on July 27, 2025).
Reagan, Ronald. "Remarks on Signing the Bill Providing Restitution for the Wartime Internment of Japanese-American Civilians." August 10, 1988. Ronald Reagan Presidential Library and Museum. https://www.reaganlibrary.gov/archives/speech/remarks-signing-bill-providing-restitution-wartime-internment-japanese-american (accessed on July 27, 2025).

Selected Secondary Sources

Adams, Clarence. *An American Dream: The Life of an African American Soldier and POW Who Spent Twelve Years in Communist China* (Amherst: University of Massachusetts Press, 2007).
Ano, Masaharu. "Loyal Linguists: Nisei of World War II Learned Japanese in Minnesota." *Minnesota History* 45, no. 7 (1977): pp. 273–87.
Asahina, Robert. *Just Americans: How Japanese Americans Won a War at Home and Abroad* (New York: Gotham, 2006).

Azuma, Eiichiro. *Between Two Empires: Race, History, and Transnationalism in Japanese America* (New York: Oxford University Press, 2005).
Azuma, Eiichiro. *In Search of Our Frontier: Japanese America and Settler Colonialism in the Construction of Japan's Borderless Empire* (Berkeley: University of California Press, 2019).
Azuma, Eiichiro. "Pioneers of Overseas Japanese Development: Japanese American History and the Making of Expansionist Orthodoxy in Imperial Japan." *Journal of Asian Studies* 67, no. 4 (2008): pp. 1187–1226.
Azuma Eiichirō. "Tokyo ni okeru Zainichi Hokubei Nisei no shidōsō to shakai soshiki keisei," in *Ekkyō suru "Nisei"*, edited by Yoshida Ryō (Tokyo: Gendai Shiryō Shuppan, 2016), pp. 21–51.
Buxton, A[nne]. Carly. "The Enemies among Us: Race, Trust, and Allied Internment in World War II Japan," in *Defamiliarizing Japan's Asia-Pacific War*, edited by W. Puck Brecher and Michael W. Myers (Honolulu: University of Hawai'i Press, 2019), pp. 194–95, 198–203.
Buxton, A[nne]. Carly. *Unthinking Collaboration: American Nisei in Transwar Japan* (Honolulu: University of Hawai'i Press, 2022).
Carruthers, Susan L. *The Good Occupation: American Soldiers and the Hazards of Peace* (Cambridge, MA: Harvard University Press, 2016).
Chang, Kornel. *A Fractured Liberation: Korea under US Occupation* (Cambridge, MA: Belknap Press of Harvard University Press, 2025).
Christgau, John. "Collins versus the World: The Fight to Restore Citizenship to Japanese American Renunciants of World War II." *Pacific Historical Review* 65, no. 1 (1985): pp. 1–31.
Coffman, Tom. *The Island Edge of America: A Political History of Hawai'i* (Honolulu: University of Hawai'i Press, 2003).
Commission on the Wartime Relocation and Internment of Civilians. *Personal Justice Denied: The Report of the Commission on the Wartime Relocation and Internment of Civilians* (Seattle: University of Washington Press, 1997).
Crost, Lyn. *Honor by Fire: Japanese Americans at War in Europe and the Pacific* (Novato, CA: Presidio Press, 1994).
Daniels, Roger, ed. *American Concentration Camps*, vol. 2 (New York: Garland, 1989).
Dingman, Roger. *Deciphering the Rising Sun: Navy and Marine Corps Codebreakers, Translators, and Interpreters in the Pacific War* (Annapolis, MD: Naval Institute Press, 2009).
Dower, John W. *Embracing Defeat: Japan in the Wake of World War II* (New York: W. W. Norton, 1999).
Dower. John W. *War without Mercy: Race and Power in the Pacific War* (New York: Pantheon, 1986).
Drinnon, Richard. *Keeper of the Concentration Camps: Dillon S. Myer and American Racism* (Berkeley: University of California Press, 1989).
Dudziak, Mary. *Cold War Civil Rights: Race and the Image of American Democracy* (Princeton: Princeton University Press, 2011).
Duus, Masayo. *Tokyo Rose: Orphan of the Pacific*, translated by Peter Duus (New York: Kodansha USA, 1979).
Duus, Masayo Umezawa Duus. *Unlikely Liberators: The Men of the 100th and 442nd*, translated by Peter Duus (Honolulu: University of Hawaii Press, 1987).
Etō Jun. *Closed Linguistic Space: Censorship by the Occupation Forces and Postwar Japan* (Tokyo: Shuppan Bunka Sangyō Shinkō Zaidan, 2020).
Falk, Stanley and Warren Tsuneishi, eds. *MIS in the War against Japan: Personal Experiences Related at the 1993 MIS Capital Reunion* (Washington, DC: Japanese American Veterans Association, 1995).
Feinman, Ilene Rose. *Citizenship Rites: Feminist Soldiers and Feminist Antimilitarists* (New York: New York University Press, 2000).
Fredman, Zach. *The Tormented Alliance: American Servicemen and the Occupation of China, 1941–1949* (Durham: University of North Carolina Press, 2022).

Fujitani, Takashi. "*Go for Broke*, the Movie: Japanese American Soldiers in US National, Military, and Racial Discourses," in *Perilous Memories: The Asia-Pacific War(s)*, edited by T. Fujitani, Geoffrey M. White, and Lisa Yoneyama (Durham: Duke University Press, 2001), pp. 239–66.

Fujitani, Takashi. *Race for Empire: Koreans as Japanese and Japanese as Americans during World War II* (Berkeley: University of California Press, 2011).

Fujitani, Takashi. "The Reischauer Memo: Mr. Moto, Hirohito, and Japanese American Soldiers." *Critical Asian Studies* 33, no. 3 (2001): pp. 379–402.

Gallicchio, Marc. *The African American Encounter with Japan and China: Black Internationalism in Asia, 1895–1945* (Chapel Hill: University of North Carolina Press, 2000).

Gilmore, Allison B. *You Can't Fight Tanks with Bayonets: Psychological Warfare against the Japanese Army in the Southwest Pacific* (Lincoln: University of Nebraska Press, 1998).

Goodman, Grant K. *America's Japan: The First Year 1945–1946* (New York: Fordham University Press, 2005).

Green, Michael Cullen. *Black Yanks in the Pacific: Race in the Making of the American Military Empire after World War II* (Ithaca, NY: Cornell University Press, 2010).

Guglielmo, Thomas A. *Divisions: A New History of Racism and Resistance in America's World War II Military* (New York: Oxford University Press, 2021).

Harkness, Thomas T. *Caucasian Boy at a Japanese Camp* (Redlands, CA: Tulahark Press, 2004).

Harrington, Joseph D. *Yankee Samurai: The Secret Role of Nisei in America's Pacific Victory* (Detroit: Harlo Press, 1979).

Hart, Justin. "Making Democracy Safe for the World: Race, Propaganda, and the Transformation of US Foreign Policy during World War II," *Pacific Historical Review* 73, no. 1 (2004): pp. 49–84.

Haruna Mikio. *Himitsu no fairu: CIA no tainichi kōsaku* (*The Secret File*), vol. 1 (Tokyo: Kyōdo Tsūshinsha, 2000).

Hatakeyama Kiyoyuki. *Kyanon kikan* (Tokyo: Tokuma Shoten, 1971).

Hawaii Nikkei History Editorial Board, ed. *Japanese Eyes, American Heart: Personal Reflections of Hawaii's World War II Nisei Soldiers* (Honolulu: University of Hawaii Press, 1998).

Hayashi, Brian Masaru. *Asian American Spies: How Asian Americans Helped Win the Allied Victory* (New York: Oxford University Press, 2021).

Hayashi, Brian Masaru. *Democratizing the Enemy: The Japanese American Internment* (Princeton: Princeton University Press, 2004).

Henderson, Bruce. *Bridge to the Sun: The Secret Role of the Japanese Americans Who Fought in the Pacific in World War II* (New York: Knopf, 2022).

Hirabayashi, Lane Ryo. *The Politics of Fieldwork: Research in an American Concentration Camp* (Tucson: University of Arizona Press, 2016).

Hirahara, Naomi. *An American Son: The Story of George Aratani, Founder of Mikasa and Kenwood* (Los Angeles: Japanese American National Museum, 2001).

Hirano, Kyoko. *Mr. Smith Goes to Tokyo: Japanese Cinema under the American Occupation, 1945–1952* (Washington, DC: Smithsonian Institution Press, 1992).

Hirano, Kyoko. "The Occupation and Japanese Cinema," in *The Occupation of Japan: Arts and Culture*, edited by Thomas W. Burkman (Norfolk, VA: General Douglas MacArthur Foundation, 1988), pp. 140–53.

Hosokawa, Bill. *Out of the Frying Pan* (Boulder: University Press of Colorado, 1998).

Howard, John. *Concentration Camps on the Home Front: Japanese Americans in the House of Jim Crow* (Chicago: University of Chicago Press, 2008).

Hunter-Chester, David. *Creating Japan's Ground Self-Defense Force, 1945–2015* (Lanham, MD: Lexington Books, 2016).

Ichinokuchi, Tad, ed. *John Aiso and the MIS: Japanese American Soldiers in the Military Intelligence Service, World War II* (Los Angeles: Military Intelligence Service Club of Southern California, 1988).

Ichioka, Yuji. *Before Internment: Essays in Prewar Japanese American History*, edited by Gordon H. Chang and Eiichiro Azuma (Stanford: Stanford University Press, 2006).

Inomata Kōzō, ed. *Senryōgun no hanzai* (Tokyo: Tosho Shuppansha, 1979).

Irons, Peter. *Justice at War: The Story of the Japanese-American Internment Cases* (Berkeley: University of California Press, 1983).

Ishihara, Masahide. "USCAR's Language Policy and English Education in Okinawa: Featuring High Commissioner Caraway's Policies." *Okinawan Journal of American Studies* 1 (2004): pp. 19–27.

Ishii Seiji. *Nihon no hōsō o tsukutta otoko* (Tokyo: Mainichi Shinbunsha, 1998).

James, Thomas. "The Education of Japanese Americans at Tule Lake, 1942–1946." *Pacific Historical Review* 56, no. 1 (1987): pp. 25–58.

James, Thomas. *Exile Within: The Schooling of Japanese Americans 1942–1945* (Cambridge, MA: Harvard University Press, 1987).

Jin, Michael R. *Citizens, Immigrants, and the Stateless: A Japanese American Diaspora in the Pacific* (Stanford: Stanford University Press, 2022).

Jung, Moon-Kie. *Reworking Race: The Making of Hawaii's Interracial Labor Movement* (New York: Columbia University Press, 2006).

Kim, Monica. *The Interrogation Rooms of the Korean War: The Untold History* (Princeton: Princeton University Press, 2019).

Kitamura, Hiroshi. *Screening Enlightenment: Hollywood and the Cultural Reconstruction of Defeated Japan* (Ithaca, NY: Cornell University Press, 2010).

Kiyosaki, Wayne. *A Spy in Their Midst, the World War II Struggle of a Japanese-American Hero: The Story of Richard Sakakida* (Lanham, MD: Madison Books, 1995).

Komiya Hitoshi. "Miki Takeo josetsu," *Momoyama hōgaku* 22 (2013): pp. 1–42.

Koppes, Clayton R., and Gregory D. Black. *Hollywood Goes to War: How Politics, Profits, and Propaganda Shaped World War II Movies* (New York: Free Press, 1987).

Koshiro, Yukiko. *Trans-Pacific Racisms and the US Occupation of Japan* (New York: Columbia University Press, 1999).

Kramer, Paul A. *The Blood of Government: Race, Empire, the United States, and the Philippines* (Chapel Hill: University of North Carolina Press, 2006).

Kramm, Robert. *Sanitized Sex: Regulating Prostitution, Venereal Disease, and Intimacy in Occupied Japan, 1945–1952* (Berkeley: University of California Press, 2017).

Kudō Miyoko. *Hariuddo kara Hiroshima e* (Tokyo: Shōbunsha, 1985).

Kumamoto, Bob. "The Search for Spies: American Counterintelligence and the Japanese American Community, 1931–1942." *Amerasia Journal* 6, no. 2 (1979): pp. 45–75.

Kushner, Barak. *The Thought War: Japanese Imperial Propaganda* (Honolulu: University of Hawai'i Press, 2005).

Leighton, Alexander H. *The Governing of Men: General Recommendations Based on Experience at a Japanese Relocation Camp* (Princeton: Princeton University Press, 1945).

Lind, Andrew W. *Hawaii's Japanese: An Experiment in Democracy* (Princeton: Princeton University Press, 1946).

Maki, John M. *Voyage through the Twentieth Century* (Amherst, MA: Modern Memoirs Publishing, 2004).

Maki, Mitchell T., Harry H. L. Kitano, and S. Megan Berthold. *Achieving the Impossible Dream: How Japanese Americans Obtained Redress* (Urbana: University of Illinois Press, 1999).

Man, Simeon. *Soldiering through Empire: Race and the Making of the Decolonizing Pacific* (Berkeley: University of California Press, 2018).

Masaoka, Mike, with Bill Hosokawa. *They Call Me Moses Masaoka: An American Saga* (New York: William Morrow, 1987).

Masuda Hiroshi. "Chōsen sensō izen ni okeru Amerika no Nihon saigunbi kōsō," no. 1. *Hōgaku kenkyū: Journal of Law, Politics, and Sociology* 72, no. 4 (1999): pp. 15–51.

Masuda Hiroshi. "Chōsen sensō izen ni okeru Amerika no Nihon saigunbi kōsō," no. 2. *Hōgaku kenkyū: Journal of Law, Politics, and Sociology* 72, no. 5 (1999): pp. 37–62.

McNaughton, James C. *Nisei Linguists: Japanese Americans in the Military Intelligence Service during World War II* (Washington, DC: Department of the Army, 2006).

Military Intelligence Service Association of Northern California (MIS NorCal) and National Japanese American Historical Society (NJAHS), eds. *The Pacific War and Peace: Americans of Japanese Ancestry in Military Intelligence Service, 1941 to 1952* (San Francisco: MIS NorCal and NJAHS, 1991).

Military Intelligence Service Veterans Club of Hawaii, ed. *Secret Valor: MIS Personnel, World War II Pacific Theater, Pre-Pearl Harbor to Sept. 8, 1951* (Honolulu: MIS Veterans Club of Hawaii, 1993).

MIS-Northwest Association. *Unsung Heroes: The Military Intelligence Service Past-Present-Future* (Seattle: MIS-Northwest Association, 1996).

Miyao, Daisuke. *Sessue Hayakawa: Silent Cinema and Transnational Stardom* (Durham: Duke University Press, 2007).

Mizuno, Takeya. "A Disturbing and Ominous Voice from a Different Shore: Japanese Radio Propaganda and Its Impact on the US Government's Treatment of Japanese Americans during World War II." *Japanese Journal of American Studies* 24 (2013): pp. 105–24.

Moore, Brenda L. *Serving Our Country: Japanese American Women in the Military during World War II* (New Brunswick, NJ: Rutgers University Press, 2003).

Moronaga Yūji. *Hōmurareta natsu* (Tokyo: Asahi Shinbunsha, 2002).

Moye, J. Todd. *Freedom Flyers: The Tuskegee Airmen of World War II* (New York: Oxford University Press, 2010).

Muller, Eric L. *Free to Die for Their Country: The Story of the Japanese American Draft Resisters in World War II* (Chicago: University of Chicago Press, 2001).

Mullins, Mark R. "How Yasukuni Shrine Survived the Occupation: A Critical Examination of Popular Claims." *Monumenta Nipponica* 65, no. 1 (2010): pp. 89–136.

Nackenoff, Carol, and Julie Novkov. *American by Birth: Wong Kim Ark and the Battle for Citizenship* (Lawrence: University Press of Kansas, 2022).

Nakamura Naofumi. *Yasukuni: Shirarezaru senryōka no kōbō* (Tokyo: Nihon Hōsō Kyōkai, 2007).

Ngai, Mae. *The Lucky Ones: One Family and the Extraordinary Invention of Chinese America* (New York: Houghton Mifflin Harcourt, 2010).

Odo, Franklin. *No Sword to Bury: Japanese Americans in Hawai'i during the Pacific War* (Philadelphia: Temple University Press, 2004).

Okihiro, Gary Y. *Storied Lives: Japanese American Students and World War II* (Seattle: University of Washington Press, 1999).

Ōno Tatsuzō. *Amerika kara kita supaitachi* (Tokyo: Shin Nihon Shuppansha, 1965).

Ozaki Hideo, ed. *Purodyūsā jinsei* (Tokyo: Tōhō Kabushiki Kaisha Shuppan Jigyōbu, 1981).

Paik, A. Naomi. *Rightlessness: Testimony and Redress in US Prison Camps since World War II* (Chapel Hill: University of North Carolina Press, 2016).

Parker, Christopher S. *Fighting for Democracy: Black Veterans and the Struggle against White Supremacy in the Postwar South* (Princeton: Princeton University Press, 2009).

Passin, Herbert. *Encounter with Japan* (Tokyo: Kodansha International, 1982).

Peiss, Kathy. *Information Hunters: When Librarians, Soldiers, and Spies Banded Together in World War II Europe* (New York: Oxford University Press, 2020).

Robinson, Greg. *After Camp: Portraits in Midcentury Japanese American Life and Politics* (Berkeley: University of California Press, 2012).

Robinson, Greg. *The Great Unknown: Japanese American Sketches* (Boulder: University Press of Colorado, 2016).

Robinson, Greg. *The Unsung Great: Stories of Extraordinary Japanese Americans* (Seattle: University of Washington Press, 2020).

Sakamoto, Pamela Rotner. *Midnight in Broad Daylight: A Japanese American Family Caught between Two Worlds* (New York: Harper, 2016).

Sano Shin'ichi. *Kyokai-den: Shōriki Matsutarō to kagemusha-tachi no isseiki* (Tokyo: Bungei Shunjūsha, 1994).

Santoki, Mark. *The Earl Finch Story: One Man USO* (Honolulu: Seiji F. Naya, 2000).

Satō Tadao. *Nihon eigashi*, vol. 2 (Tokyo: Iwanami Shoten, 2006).

Schonberger, Howard B. *Japanizu konekushon: Kaiunō K. Sugahara gaiden* (*"Nisei Entrepreneur," Japanese Connections: An Unauthorized Biography of Shipping Tycoon K. Sugahara*), translated by Sodei Rinjirō (Tokyo: Bungei Shunjūsha, 1995).

Shibata Tetsuhiro. *Shimoyama jiken: Saigo no shōgen* (Tokyo: Shōdensha, 2005).

Shibusawa, Naoko. *America's Geisha Ally: Reimagining the Japanese Enemy* (Cambridge, MA: Harvard University Press, 2006).

Shibutani, Tamotsu. *The Derelicts of Company K: A Sociological Study of Demoralization* (Berkeley: University of California Press, 1978).

Shimizu, Sayuri. *Creating a People of Plenty: The United States and Japan's Economic Alternatives, 1950–1960* (Kent, OH: Kent State University Press, 2001).

Shimizu, Sayuri Guthrie. *Transpacific Field of Dreams: How Baseball Linked the United States and Japan in Peace and War* (Chapel Hill: University of North Carolina Press, 2012).

Shimoyama Jiken Kenkyūkai, ed. *Shiryō Shimoyama jiken* (Tokyo: Misuzu Shobō, 1969).

Shimura Miyoko. "Reisen shoki ni okeru Beikoku Kokubōsōshō no eiga seisaku: 'Nisei butai' (1951-nen) no seisaku kyōryoku o megutte." *Intelligence* 15 (March 2015): pp. 38–48.

Simpson, Caroline Chung. "'Out of an Obscene Place': Japanese War Brides and Cultural Pluralism in the 1950s." *Differences: A Journal of Feminist Cultural Studies* 10, no. 3 (1998): pp. 47–81.

Skebelund, Aaron Herald. *Inglorious, Illegal Bastards: Japan's Self-Defense Force during the Cold War* (Ithaca, NY: Cornell University Press, 2022).

Sohoni, Deenesh. "Unsuitable Suitors: Anti-Miscegenation Laws, Naturalization Laws, and the Construction of Asian Identities." *Law & Society Review* 41, no. 3 (2007): pp. 587–618.

Stephan, John J. *Hawaii under the Rising Sun: Japan's Plans for Conquest after Pearl Harbor* (Honolulu: University of Hawaii Press, 1984).

Straus, Ulrich. *The Anguish of Surrender: Japanese POWs of World War II* (Seattle: University of Washington Press, 2003).

Svoboda, Terese. "US Court-Martial in Occupation Japan: Rape, Race, and Censorship." *Asia-Pacific Journal: Japan Focus* 7, no. 1 (2009): pp. 1–10.

Swift, Jr., David W. *First Class: Nisei Linguists in World War II* (San Francisco: National Japanese American Historical Society, 2008).

Takeda, Kayoko. "Dual Citizen Interpreters: Consequences of Assigned Loyalties in the Aftermath of War," in *Interpreting Conflicts: A Comparative Framework*, edited by Marija Todorova and Lucia Ruiz Rosendo (Cham, Switzerland: Palgrave Macmillan, 2021), pp. 17–35.

Takeda, Kayoko. *Interpreting the Tokyo War Crimes Tribunal: A Sociopolitical Analysis* (Ottawa: University of Ottawa Press, 2010).

Takemae Eiji. *Inside GHQ: The Allied Occupation of Japan and Its Legacy*, translated by Robert Ricketts and Sebastian Swann (London: Continuum, 2002).

Tamura, Eileen. *Americanization, Acculturation, and Ethnic Identity: Nisei Generation in Hawaii* (Urbana: University of Illinois Press, 1994).

Tamura, Eileen H. *In Defense of Justice: Joseph Kurihara and the Japanese American Struggle for Equality* (Urbana: University of Illinois Press, 2013).

Thomas, Jolyon Baraka. *Faking Liberties: Religious Freedom in American-Occupied Japan* (Chicago: University of Chicago Press, 2019).

Tomita, Mary Kimoto. *Dear Miye: Letters Home from Japan, 1939–1946*, edited by Robert G. Lee (Stanford: Stanford University Press, 1995).

Torii Hideharu. *Kokusaku tsūshinsha "Dōmei" no kōbō* (Tokyo: Kadensha, 2014).

Uchiyama, Benjamin. "The 'Oh, Mistake' Incident and Juvenile Delinquency in Defeated Japan." *Journal of Contemporary History* 57, no. 1 (2021): pp. 1–21.

Van Staaveren, Jacob. *An American in Japan 1945–1948: A Civilian View of the Occupation* (Seattle: University of Washington Press, 1994).

Wake, Naoko. *American Survivors: Trans-Pacific Memories of Hiroshima and Nagasaki* (Cambridge: Cambridge University Press, 2021).

Watanabe Takashi. *Puropaganda rajio* (Tokyo: Chikuma Shobō, 2014).

Weglyn, Michi Nishiura. *Years of Infamy: The Untold Story of America's Concentration Camps* (New York: William Morrow, 1976).

Williams, Sr., Justin. *Japan's Political Revolution under MacArthur: A Participant's Account* (Athens: University of Georgia Press, 1979).

Wong, K. Scott. *Americans First: Chinese Americans and the Second World War* (Philadelphia: Temple University Press, 2008).

Wu, Ellen D. *The Color of Success: Asian Americans and the Origins of the Model Minority* (Princeton: Princeton University Press, 2014).

Yada Kimio. *Bōsatsu Shimoyama jiken* (Tokyo: Kōdansha, 1985).

Yamagiwa Akira. "Bei Senji Jōhōkyoku (OWI) no 'En'an hōkoku': Yenan Reports by the Office of War Information (OWI), USA." *Nishōgakusha Daigaku kokusai seikei ronshū* 8 (2000): pp. 1–19.

Yoneda, Karl G. *Gambatte: Sixty-Year Struggle of a Kibei Worker* (Los Angeles: UCLA Asian American Studies Center, 1983).

Index

Note: Tables and figures are indicated by an italic "*t*" or "*f*" following the page number.

For the benefit of digital users, indexed terms that span two pages (e.g., 52–53) may, on occasion, appear on only one of those pages.